Restoring the Ancient Church:

Joseph Smith and Early Christianity

Second Edition

by Barry Robert Bickmore

Cover Art: The Restoration of the Melchizedek Priesthood by
Kenneth Riley
Christ Ordaining the Twelve Apostles by Harry Anderson
© By Intellectual Reserve, Inc. Used by permission.

ISBN: 978-1-893036-16-1

FairMormon
PO Box 491677
Redding, CA 96049
www.fairmormon.org

About FairMormon

FairMormon was formed in late 1997 by a group of LDS defenders of the faith who frequented the America Online Mormonism message boards. In defending the Church against detractors, this small alliance realized that they had no way of sharing their information with each other, much less the rest of the Church. As a result, FairMormon was born.

On December 1997, this fledgling organization was incorporated as a non-profit organization in the state of New York as the Foundation for Apologetic Information and Research, or FAIR. The word "apologetics" comes from the Greek *apologia* which means to defend one's position. In March, 1998, FAIR launched its first website and it soon became an international, all-volunteer organization. Then, in 2013, the group became known as FairMormon.

FairMormon, is staffed by devout Latter-day Saint students and scholars with an enthusiastic or academic fervor for the scriptures, ancient languages, early Christian history, science, early LDS history, and LDS doctrine and apologetics. Most FairMormon members have been involved in online services and Internet-based LDS apologetics for many years. Many of our members are authors of currently-available publications.

Table of Contents

Preface

"I wrote books I should have liked to read. That's always been my reason for writing. People won't write the books I want, so I have to do it for myself: no rot about 'self-expression.'"
- *C.S. Lewis*[1]

I have endeavored to make this book exactly the kind of book I would like to have read when I first became interested in comparing Mormonism to early Christianity. As I read the few books available on this subject, I noted various aspects of their differing approaches and styles of presentation and found that none of them fit my needs. Some were excessively difficult for a beginner like myself to fully appreciate, being written for a readership more familiar with the subject. Others were intended only as short surveys, and tended to put forth rather simplistic arguments that robbed the reader of a solid understanding of the various issues involved as well as of the dynamics of the apostasy. These often quoted essentially from other LDS authors rather than from non-Mormon or even early Christian sources.[2] On the other hand, works by non-Mormon authors tended to gloss over the issues that are of interest to Latter-day Saints.

In order to fill the gap I perceive in the LDS literature, I have included the following elements in the text to help a broad spectrum of readers come away with a better understanding of the subject and greater confidence in the truthfulness of the Restored gospel. 1) An appendix has been included which introduces the most often quoted early Christian writers and documents. Thus, I believe anyone can follow and evaluate the arguments presented in this study in their proper historical context. 2) I have tried to include enough background information to allow the average reader to understand the information presented in context. 3) My documentation is taken almost exclusively from non-Mormon, English-language sources. I concentrated on non-Mormon sources because, generally, they cannot be accused of being biased toward the LDS position, and I have used English language sources so that readers can more readily verify the information cited in the text. In a few instances when non-Mormon English sources were not available, I have included translations of non-English passages from scholarly works found in reputable Mormon publications. In all cases, however, I have made sure that my arguments do not stand or fall on the strength of these citations, since I was not capable of checking them myself. 4) Finally, I have tried to avoid oversimplification. Sometimes complex subjects require simplification due to limitations in space or the technical expertise of the intended audience, but simplification in the context of a book like this should never result in giving the reader the impression that the case for the Restoration of the gospel has been entirely proven. I don't believe that spiritual things can be proven by human wisdom. After all, Paul explained that God had "made foolish the wisdom of this world. For after that in the wisdom of God the world by wisdom knew not God, it pleased God by the foolishness of preaching to save them that believe." (1 Corinthians 1:20-21) And he exhorted the Corinthians that their "faith should not stand in the wisdom of men, but in the power of God." (1 Corinthians 2:5) Accordingly, Latter-day Saints proclaim that anyone can empirically test the truthfulness of the gospel by studying it out, and then praying to God in faith to obtain an answer respecting its truthfulness. Millions have put Mormonism to the test in this manner, and the same method should be employed when considering the ideas presented in this book.

Since proof of religious matters is not to be expected, it has been necessary to approach this subject from the point of view of faith, to a certain extent.[3] Given the incomplete nature of the historical record, as well as the fact that Joseph Smith claimed to reveal some doctrines that had never before been revealed, it would be fruitless to search the extant early Christian literature for data to "falsify" LDS claims. Instead, we must for the moment assume these claims are legitimate, and then honestly and carefully explore the extent to which these claims are supported by the available evidence. Readers must decide for themselves how compelling the assembled evidence is. Similarly, I accept as a given that Jesus was and is the Son of God, that the New Testament record is for the most part accurate, and that it was actually written by Jesus' Apostles and their associates. Those who reject these assumptions will no doubt find the arguments presented here less compelling, but even so I believe these arguments demonstrate conclusively that Mormonism is very similar in many respects to some very early forms of Christianity.

About the author: Barry Robert Bickmore was born in Redwood City, California, and grew up in various places in California and Utah. Raised a Latter-day Saint, he fulfilled a two-year mission to Iowa. He graduated magna cum laude with a major in geology and minors in chemistry and philosophy from Brigham Young University in 1994. While attending BYU, he married the former Keiko Ann Guay, with whom he now has three children. Having received a National Science Foundation Graduate Fellowship, Barry then obtained a Ph.D. in geochemistry at Virginia Polytechnic Institute and State University. Barry has fulfilled various callings in the Church, including elders quorum president, counsellor, and teacher, seminary teacher, stake missionary, and ward clerk. He is now a professor in the department of geological sciences at Brigham Young University (BYU). He is also the author of several articles that have been published in the *FARMS Review*.

Acknowledgments: I wish to thank the many people who made the production of this book possible. First and foremost, my wife Keiko put up with an obsession for several years, occasionally gently reminding me to keep my priorities straight. My children, Elijah and Amaya, cut into my writing time considerably, but in the process made life worth living. My parents and siblings have continually encouraged my work, and have inspired me with their excitement about it. Rob Page, Ph.D., Richard Bird, Ph.D., Robert Rees, Ph.D., Clark Goble, and Russell Anderson provided helpful reviews of the text at various stages of the writing process. The people at FAIR believed in the project and made it happen. Finally, I wish to thank the many people who challenged and encouraged me to continue to refine my thoughts on the links between Mormonism and early Christianity

Note on conventions: Bracketing of words and phrases within quotations indicates summarization or commentary by the author, except where noted in the endnotes. In cases where quoted material uses Greek words spelled in the Greek alphabet, I have chosen to transliterate them.

Chapter 1: Introduction

"Either this man was, and is, the Son of God: or else a madman or something worse. You can shut him up for a fool, you can spit at him and kill him as a demon; or you can fall at his feet and call Him Lord and God. Let us not come up with any patronizing nonsense about his being a great human teacher. He did not leave that open to us. He did not intend to."
- C.S. Lewis[4]

A Restoration Church

The Church of Jesus Christ of Latter-day Saints (Mormon) is a radical religion by the standards of most modern religions -- and it was considered even more strange in the time and place it originated. Perhaps no other major religious movement in American history has given rise to so much controversy, curiosity, admiration, and animosity. The Church has been variously described as a non-Christian "revival of primitive paganism in a modified form"[5], a "cult,"[6] and, by a much more sympathetic observer, a completely new Christian religious tradition.[7] But what does it claim for itself?

Mormonism emphatically claims to be Christian -- but considers itself neither Protestant nor Catholic. Rather, it differs from both in that it claims to be the restored Church of Jesus Christ. That is, the Church claims that all other Christian traditions have come down to us as incomplete remnants of the original Church which Jesus organized, which necessitated God restoring the true body of Christ to the earth through a prophet -- Joseph Smith, Jr. Thus, the Latter-day Saints claim their church is an actual restoration of primitive Christianity, as it existed under the Apostles in the first century A.D.

Joseph Smith -- The Prophet of the Restoration

Before we go on, however, we must set the stage by summarizing how the LDS Church claims this restoration took place, and why it was needed. Therefore, we must begin with the story of the Prophet of the Restoration. Joseph Smith, Jr. (1805-1844) grew up as a farm boy in frontier Vermont and upstate New York. When Smith, who had little formal education, was fourteen years old, a series of religious revivals swept through his part of the country, exciting intense religious feelings as well as sharp divisions between those belonging to different religious sects. Confused by this "strife of words and . . . contest about opinions" (Joseph Smith History 1:6), young Joseph visited the various religious camps trying to decide which one to attend. He leaned toward the Methodists, but was unsure.

Upon reading a passage in the book of James, Joseph thought he had found a way to resolve his difficulties. He read: "If any of you lack wisdom, let him ask of God, that giveth to all men liberally, and upbraideth not; and it shall be given him." (James 1:5) Joseph recounted:

> Never did any passage of scripture come with more power to the heart of man than this did at this time to mine. It seemed to enter with great force into every feeling of my heart. I reflected on it again and again, knowing that if any person needed wisdom from God, I did; for how to act I did not know, and unless I could get more wisdom than I then had, I would never know; for the teachers of religion of the different sects understood the same passages of scripture so differently as to destroy all confidence in settling the question by an appeal to the Bible. (Joseph Smith History 1:12)

After reading this scripture, young Joseph retired to a grove of trees near his house to pray for an answer as to which church he should join. On a spring day in 1820, he did just that. While he was praying in the grove, two personages "whose glory def[ied] all description" descended in a pillar of light. One of them pointed to the other and said, "This is My Beloved Son. Hear Him!" (Joseph Smith History 1:16-17) When Joseph asked which church to join, the Savior replied that he "must join none of them, for they were all wrong . . . they teach for doctrines the commandments of men, having a form of godliness, but they deny the power thereof." (Joseph Smith History 1:18-19) Nearly four years later, Smith received another visionary experience. An angel identifying himself as an ancient American prophet appeared in Joseph's bedroom and informed him that he would be entrusted with the translation of a certain prophetic record. This record told of an ancient American people, now extinct, who had migrated to this hemisphere from Jerusalem about 600 B.C. He was informed that God had a work for him to do and that his "name should be had for good and evil among all nations, kindreds, and tongues, or that it should be both good and evil spoken of among all people." (Joseph Smith History 1:33) After being shown where the metal plates upon which this record was inscribed were hidden, Joseph was commanded to meet with the angel at that place for instruction each year. These meetings took place each year until September 22, 1827, when Joseph was given the plates, and the spiritual discernment to translate them. This record, known as the *Book of Mormon*, was finally published early in 1830, although when historians consider Joseph's other activities during this period, they conclude he must have produced the book in about two months. After the translation was finished the angel took back the plates, since they contained prophecies and other information that the world was not yet prepared to receive. However, included in each edition of the *Book of Mormon* are the testimonies of eleven other men who claimed to have seen the record Joseph translated.

In 1829, while in the business of translating, Joseph and Oliver Cowdery (Smith's scribe who was also one of the witnesses of the plates) were visited by the angel of John the Baptist, who ordained them to the priesthood of Aaron. Later the two were visited by the Apostles Peter, James, and John who ordained them to the higher priesthood, that of Melchizedek, and to the Apostleship. (For more information on these two priesthoods, see Hebrews 7 and D&C 107.)

Shortly after the *Book of Mormon* had been published, Joseph was commanded by revelation to organize the Church of Jesus Christ on April 6, 1830. Through the rest of his life, Joseph Smith received revelation upon revelation restoring what he claimed were doctrines and practices related to the ancient gospel, which Christianity had lost over time after the first century A.D. Finally, in 1844, Joseph Smith was martyred at the hands of a mob.

A Bold Claim and an Exacting Test

These assertions of angels appearing with metal books to translate, visions of God Himself, and a restoration of the ancient Church were outrageous to the society in which Joseph Smith was reared.

What is more, Joseph claimed to have restored various doctrines and practices that properly belonged to antiquity, especially ancient Christianity. But the scientific, historical study of early Christianity was barely in its infancy at the time. Many new documents from that period have been discovered since then, and what documents had been discovered (other than the New Testament) were for the most part not available to Joseph Smith. Were the beliefs and practices he "restored" truly early Christian? The purpose of this book is to explore that question.

Methods

The purpose of this study is not to create a portrait of ancient Christianity and then compare Mormonism to it. Although it will be possible to identify some of the characteristics of the primitive Church with reasonable certainty, such a methodology would, I believe, be inappropriate if too broadly applied. Since scholars agree that "conditions [in the early centuries of Christianity] were favorable to the coexistence of a wide variety of opinions even on issues of prime importance,"[8] it is difficult to say with absolute certainty that the doctrines and organization Joseph Smith restored were identical to those revealed by Jesus. The question as to what the original Church taught and practiced is the subject of serious and sometimes heated debate.

But what if we find that the doctrines Joseph Smith restored were, indeed, legitimate early Christian beliefs and practices from the first two or three centuries after Christ? If Joseph Smith taught doctrines that are in harmony with those of the early church but which were essentially unknown in his time, the skeptic must provide an explanation for the phenomenon. We shall see that the Prophet did restore legitimate early Christian doctrines, many of which can be shown to have preceded the present doctrines of the mainline Christian denominations -- and he did so in the absence of much of the primary data available today. How could this have happened? If Joseph Smith's explanation does not suffice, some other explanation must be put forth.

Chapter 2: Apostasy and Restoration

"Mormonism has no claim to be a viable religion in the present unless it has been a viable religion in the past."
- Truman Madsen[9]

The simple fact is that had there been no "apostasy," or "falling away," from Christ's original Church, there would have been no need for God to restore the Church through Joseph Smith. In this chapter we will establish the fact that there was, indeed, such an apostasy and describe its history and some of its effects.[10] Finally, we will present evidence that a restoration of the gospel was also predicted in the early Church.

The Apostasy -- A History

The Apostasy Foretold

When faced with the LDS belief in a "great" apostasy, many people ask, "If God is omnipotent, how could He let His Church fail and fall away?" We will address this question directly later on, but for now it should be enough to point out that not only did God let it happen -- He even predicted it through His prophets and Apostles.

Paul spoke of this apostasy ("falling away") when he told the elders at Ephesus that "after my departing shall grievous wolves enter in among you, not sparing the flock. Also of your own selves shall men arise, speaking perverse things, to draw away disciples after them." (Acts 20:29-30) Thus the Church would be under attack both from without (persecution) and from within (heresy). Indeed, Paul had serious concerns about the Church's stability when he wrote to Timothy that the saints would turn away from sound doctrine:

> Preach the word; be instant in season, out of season; reprove, rebuke, exhort with all longsuffering and doctrine. For the time will come when they will not endure sound doctrine; but after their own lusts shall they heap to themselves teachers, having itching ears; and they shall turn away their ears from the truth, and shall be turned unto fables. But watch thou in all things, do the work of an evangelist, make full proof of thy ministry. (2 Timothy 4:3-5)

17

Notice how Paul entreated Timothy to do *his* duty as an evangelist, but indicated that the Church in general would forsake the faith. In the same letter Paul intimated that "all they which are in Asia be turned away from me" (2 Timothy 1:15) -- and Asia Minor was exactly where most of the Christian converts lived.[11]

Peter also warned the saints that "there shall be false teachers among you, who privily shall bring in damnable heresies, even denying the Lord that bought them, and bring upon themselves swift destruction. And many shall follow their pernicious ways; by reason of whom the way of truth shall be evil spoken of." (2 Peter 2:1-2)

The Apostasy -- Rebellion in the Church

What exactly was this "apostasy," and when was it supposed to happen? According to LDS scholar Kent Jackson, the word *apostasy* is derived from the Greek word "*apostasia*," which means "'rebellion,' 'mutiny,' 'revolt,' or 'revolution,' and is used in ancient contexts with reference to uprisings against established authority."[12] Thus, the apostasy was to be a rebellion against God's established authority on earth.

Latter-day Saints believe that the apostasy was underway even while the Apostles were alive, and that it inevitably completed its course after the last Apostles were gone. While the New Testament does not give many specifics about the timetable of the rebellion in its predictions, it contains a number of clues pointing to the fact that a massive rebellion was taking place in the Church, and that there was not much time left.

The apostasy was to happen before the second coming of Christ. Paul told the Thessalonians not to worry about Christ coming back anytime soon saying, "Let no man deceive you by any means: for that day shall not come, except there come a falling away [Greek *apostasia*] first, and that man of sin be revealed, the son of perdition." (2 Thessalonians 2:3) This apostasy was already underway. "For already the secret power of wickedness is at work, secret only for the present until the Restrainer disappears from the scene." (2 Thessalonians 2:7 NEB) Who was the "Restrainer" Paul spoke of? When we remember that Paul told the elders at Ephesus that persecutions would rage and heretics would arise from within the Church after he departed (Acts 20:29-30), it becomes clear that this was a reference to the Apostles themselves.

Such references to an apostasy already underway are to be found throughout the New Testament. For instance, Paul rebuked the Galatians for turning to a perverted form of the gospel:

> I marvel that ye are so soon removed from the grace of
> Christ unto another gospel: which is not another, but there

be some that trouble you, and would pervert the gospel of Christ. But though we, or an angel from heaven, preach any other gospel unto you than that which we have preached unto you, let him be accursed. (Galatians 1:6-8)

Paul also warned the Corinthians against "false Apostles" (2 Corinthians 11:13) who preached "another Jesus, whom we have not preached." (2 Corinthians 11:4) Remember also that Paul told the elders at Ephesus that as soon as he was gone, false teachers would arise out of their ranks and deceive many.

Paul and Peter wrote in the 50's and 60's, and evidently they were witness to serious troubles within the Church. However, when we turn to later writings, such as Jude (ca. 80 A. D.) and John (late 90's), clearly the situation had become critical.

Jude, the brother of Jesus, wrote a general epistle to combat the many false teachers who had crept into the Church:

It was needful for me to . . . exhort you that ye should earnestly contend for the faith which was once delivered unto the saints. For there are certain men crept in unawares, who were before of old ordained to this condemnation, ungodly men, turning the grace of our God into lasciviousness, and denying the only Lord God, and our Lord Jesus Christ. (Jude 1:3-4)

The Jerusalem Bible is more specific about the identity of these false teachers. "Certain people have infiltrated among you, and they are the ones you had a warning about, in writing, long ago." Who warned the saints "in writing" about the infiltration of false teachers? Jude goes on to explain that this warning came from the Apostles, so it stands to reason that this was the apostasy foretold in the earlier New Testament writings. "But, beloved, remember ye the words which were spoken before of the Apostles of our Lord Jesus Christ; How that they told you there should be mockers in the last time, who should walk after their own ungodly lusts." (Jude 1:17-18)

"The Last Time" -- The Totality of the Predicted Apostasy

Many mainstream Christians will admit that the predicted rebellion did occur at this time. However, they reason that the rebellion did not completely overrun Christ's Church, and eventually true Christianity triumphed over heresy.[13] The passage last quoted from Jude's epistle brings up an important question with respect to this reasoning. That is, why did Jude refer to his day as "the last time?" John wrote, "Little children, it is the last time: and as ye have heard that antichrist shall come, even now are there many antichrists; whereby we know that it is the last time." (1 John 2:18) Did Jude and John believe it was "the last time" because Christ was about to come back, or because the Church was filled with antichrists, and would not long survive?

The Apostles were apparently indifferent to the specific time of Christ's return, as we saw with Paul's comment to the Thessalonians.[14] Peter even told the Church not to worry about the Lord fulfilling his promise to return because, "one day is with the Lord as a thousand years, and a thousand years as one day." (2 Peter 3:8) Therefore, it was not the "last time" because the Lord was about to return (a fact that should be obvious by this time), but because the Antichrist had come and the Church was about to be taken from the earth.

In the last few years before John, the last Apostle, was taken from the Church, he recorded more indications of the rebellion that was about to find its fulfillment. John complained that a certain local leader in the Church, Diotrephes, would not receive John's letters and turned out "the brethren" from the Church as well as those who would receive them:

> I wrote unto the church: but Diotrephes, who loveth to have the preeminence among them, receiveth us not. Wherefore, if I come, I will remember his deeds which he doeth, prating against us with malicious words: and not content therewith, neither doth he himself receive the brethren, and forbiddeth them that would, and casteth [them] out of the church. (3 John 9-10)

Finally, John recorded "letters" from the Lord to seven churches in Asia in Revelation 2-3. These churches were obviously meant to represent the Church as a whole.[15] The messages in the letters ranged from praise to rebuke, but it is instructive to look at the consequences the Lord promised for the actions of the Church members. In the cases where praise was given, the Lord said, "be thou faithful unto death, and I will give thee a crown of life." (Revelation 2:10) Where rebuke was given the Lord commanded them to "repent . . . or else I will . . . remove thy candlestick out of his place . . . ." (Revelation 2:5) Earlier the Lord had stipulated that "the seven candlesticks which thou sawest are the seven churches." (Revelation 1:20) Therefore, the faithful were promised a crown of life after their martyrdom, and the unfaithful were threatened with the expulsion of their entire churches. Certainly this was a time of crisis for the Church, and it is clear why the Apostles called it the "last time."[16]

Several of the Biblical prophecies of the apostasy support the conclusion that God's authority was to be completely removed from the earth. Amos prophesied that there would be a famine of hearing the word of God:

> The time is coming, says the Lord God, when I will send famine on the land, not hunger for bread or thirst for water,

but for hearing the word of the Lord. Men shall stagger
from north to south, they shall range from east to west,
seeking the word of the Lord, but they shall not find it . . . .
(Amos 8:11-12 NEB)

It might be countered that Amos referred to the time of apostasy in
Israel between the Old and New Testaments, when we have no further record
of any prophets adding their witness to the Bible. However, the New
Testament clearly demonstrates that Israel had not undergone a *total* apostasy,
which is clearly what was predicted in this passage. For example, the case of
Zacharias shows that the Aaronic priesthood was still operative (see Luke 1),
and Jesus' statement to the Samaritan woman that "salvation is of the Jews"
(John 4:22) indicates that their laws and ordinances retained some efficacy.
Indeed, Luke referred to Anna as a "prophetess" (Luke 2:36), so clearly the
word of the Lord *could be found* during the intertestamental period, even
though it was not generally accepted. Latter-day Saints do not argue that there
was absolutely no inspiration or revelation during the period between the
apostasy and Restoration, but post-Apostolic Christianity in general does not
claim to have had any prophets who could speak the word of the Lord with
authority.

Similarly, John saw in vision that a beast, representing an agent of
Satan, was allowed to "make war with the saints, and to overcome them: and
power was given him over all kindreds, and tongues, and nations." (Revelation
13:7)

The most specific reference to the totality of the apostasy, however, is
in Paul's second letter to the Thessalonians. Here Paul noted not only that an
apostasy was inevitable, but that the "son of perdition" would sit "as God . . .
in the temple of God, shewing himself that he is God." (2 Thessalonians 2:1-4)
It is difficult to imagine how this prophecy was to be fulfilled if the Church
was to remain.

The Loss of Apostolic Authority in the Church

As a consequence of the apostasy, the Apostolic authority was taken
from the Church. That is, the Church was in rebellion so God took away the
Apostles from the earth, and with them, the Apostolic authority. Although
Catholics since the second century have been fond of calling their church
"Apostolic," by virtue of having descended from the churches established by
the Apostles, we shall see that living Apostles are meant to be part of the true
Church of Christ, and a Church cannot be "Apostolic" without Apostles.

Some have espoused the idea that the Apostles were just twelve men
whom Christ ordained for a specific mission -- and were thus no longer needed
after the Church was established in the world. However, it is admitted by
some prominent Christian scholars that the Apostles "did not live to see the

Church fully organized and at work,"[17] and the New Testament record is quite clear that when vacancies occurred in the Twelve they were promptly filled. Matthias was chosen to take the place of Judas, who betrayed Jesus (Acts 1:23-26), and Paul said he had been "called to be an Apostle." (1 Corinthians 1:1) Barnabas was called an Apostle along with Paul by the writer of Acts (probably Luke), (Acts 14:14) and apparently Jesus' brother James had become an Apostle, for Paul reported to the Galatians that on a trip to Jerusalem, "other Apostles [besides Peter] saw I none, save James the Lord's brother." (Galatians 1:19)[18] Polycrates, bishop of Ephesus near the end of the second century, reported the tradition that Philip had become "one of the twelve Apostles."[19]

Furthermore, Paul insisted that the organization set up by Christ, headed by Apostles and prophets, should remain essentially unchanged:

> And he gave some, Apostles; and some, prophets; and some, evangelists; and some, pastors and teachers; for the perfecting of the saints, for the work of the ministry, for the edifying of the body of Christ: till we all come in the unity of the faith, and of the knowledge of the Son of God, unto a perfect man, unto the measure of the stature of the fulness of Christ: that we henceforth be no more children, tossed to and fro, and carried about with every wind of doctrine, by the sleight of men, and cunning craftiness, whereby they lie in wait to deceive. (Ephesians 4:11-14)

Has there ever been a time when Christianity or the world in general has been "in the unity of the faith?" Has the Church been perfected? Are not the sects of Christendom "tossed to and fro, and carried about by every wind of doctrine"? Latter-day Saints answer that none of Paul's conditions have ever been satisfied, and so the Church still needs Apostles and prophets. For "surely the Lord God will do nothing, but he revealeth his secret unto his servants the prophets." (Amos 3:7) Paul also revealed that the Church is "built upon the foundation of the Apostles and prophets, Jesus Christ himself being the chief corner stone." (Ephesians 2:20) So what happened to the Church when it lost its foundation?

The Rebellion Continues

The New Testament clearly indicates the need for Apostles to continue in the Church, but certainly there were still those with legitimate authority still around even after the Apostles all left the scene. After all, John's last recorded communications all contain pleas for the faithful to endure to the end. Those hailing from Catholic traditions claim the Apostolic authority continued with the episcopate, or the brotherhood of bishops whom the Apostles ordained. Some cite the following passage from Clement of Rome's letter to the Corinthians (ca. A.D. 96) as evidence:

> Our Apostles also knew, through our Lord Jesus Christ, that there would be strife on account of the office of the episcopate . . . . For this reason, therefore, inasmuch as they had obtained a perfect fore-knowledge of this, they appointed those [ministers] already mentioned, and afterwards gave instructions, that when these should fall asleep, other approved men should succeed them in their ministry.[20]

In fact, the Apostles may have approved certain men to succeed the bishops they personally ordained. However, just as the Church turned away from the Apostles, why would they not also rebel against those the Apostles appointed to the ministry? For example, in the passage cited above Clement was actually giving the Corinthians a stern rebuke for rejecting those ministers who had been approved by the Apostles. He continued:

> We are of opinion, therefore, that those appointed by them, or afterwards by other eminent men, with the consent of the whole Church, and who have blamelessly served the flock of Christ in a humble, peaceable, and disinterested spirit, and have for a long time possessed the good opinion of all, cannot be justly dismissed from the ministry. For our sin will not be small, if we eject from the episcopate those who have blamelessly and holily fulfilled its duties.[21]

In another passage Clement asked, "Why are there strifes and tumults, and divisions, and schisms, and wars among you?"[22] To prove the point that rejection of approved authority was widespread, a few more examples will be provided.

Ignatius of Antioch chastised some of the Magnesian Christians for rebelling against their bishop in the first decade of the second century: "It is fitting, then, not only to be called Christians, but to be so in reality: as some indeed give one the title of bishop, but do all things without him . . . ."[23] And there seems to have been some general problem in this area at the time, since Ignatius included exhortations to submit to the authority of the bishops in all but one of his six epistles to various churches.[24] Apparently there had been some serious schism even in Ignatius' own church at Antioch, for he requested that the Smyrnaeans send a delegate to Antioch to "congratulate them that they are [now] at peace, and are restored to their proper greatness, and that their proper constitution has been re-established among them."[25] Indeed, W.H. Wagner notes that Ignatius willingly gave himself up to be martyred as a sacrifice for problems within the whole church. "He prayed not for pagans to stop hounding Christians, but for Christians to stop fighting one another and for them to recover unity and harmony."[26]

In one passage Ignatius wrote, "Remember in your prayers the Church in Syria [i.e. his own church at Antioch], which now has God for its shepherd, instead of me. Jesus Christ alone will oversee it . . . ."[27] This fits very nicely with the LDS theory that the Church was in the process of shutting down at the time, and the true "succession" was about to end, especially when one remembers that Ignatius insisted that "Apart from [the bishops, deacons, and presbyters], there is no Church."[28] These statements take on even greater significance in light the familiar warning he gave the Ephesians, "The last times are come upon us."[29]

The angel in Hermas's vision invited the Church to heal its schisms, but gave a stern warning if they would not:

> Lay aside, therefore, the recollection of your offences and bitternesses, and you will be formed in one spirit. And heal and take away from you those wicked schisms, that if the Lord of the flocks come, He may rejoice concerning you. And He will rejoice, if He find all things sound, and none of you shall perish. But if He find any one of these sheep strayed, woe to the shepherds! And if the shepherds themselves have strayed, what answer will they give Him for their flocks?[30]

Around the turn of the third century Hippolytus wrote his *Apostolic Tradition* "because of that apostasy or error which was recently invented out of ignorance."[31] Who were these apostates? Hippolytus asserted that the "many heresies increased because those who were at the head would not learn the purpose of the Apostles but according to their own pleasure do what they choose and not what is fitting."[32] Whether one accepts Hippolytus's version of the "Apostolic tradition" or not, it is clear that heresy and schism reached even the highest levels of the Church during this early period.

Hermas and the Final Curtain Call

The final call to repentance was given in the early second century by one of the "Apostolic Fathers."[33] The *Pastor of Hermas* records a series of revelations, probably given over a period of a few decades in the first half of the second century, to Hermas, brother of Pius, bishop of Rome.[34] For centuries it was considered inspired scripture by many Christians, although it did not end up being canonized.[35] One aspect of the *Pastor* that has excited a great deal of heated controversy is the repeated insistence that there would be but one opportunity for repentance of post-baptismal sins.[36] Why would Hermas have preached such a harsh doctrine?

24

The key to interpreting Hermas's purpose is contained in the first section of his work, the Visions. Here the Church was represented as a tower being built of stone, the stones representing individual Christians. Hermas related:

"And I began to ask her about the times, if the end were yet. But she cried out with a loud voice saying, "Foolish man, do you not see the tower still being built? Whenever therefore the building of the tower has been finished, the end comes. But it will quickly be built up; ask me nothing more. "[37]

The impending completion of the tower was given as the reason for the urgent call to one more chance for repentance. When asked what was represented by some stones which had been cast away by the builders but left on the ground near the tower, the angel explained that these were Christians who had sinned, but could still become part of the tower if they repented immediately. "For if the building be finished, there will not be more room for any one, but he will be rejected. This privilege, however, will belong only to him who has now been placed near the tower."[38]

Here we must ask the same question we asked in relation to the New Testament references to "the last time." Did Hermas mistakenly believe that Christ was about to return, or that the Church was about to be taken from the earth? Just as with Jude, John, and Ignatius, Hermas gave no indication that the completion of the tower (or Church) coincided with the end of the world. Quite the opposite! "Filled up are the days of repentance to all the saints; but to the heathen, repentance will be possible even to the last day."[39] "Ye, therefore, who are high in position, seek out the hungry as long as the tower is not yet finished; for after the tower is finished, you will wish to do good, but will find no opportunity."[40]

Obviously the wicked world was to continue, but not the Church. What was to take the place of the Church? Of those who delayed their repentance, the angel said:

"Repentance . . . is yet possible, but in this tower they cannot find a suitable place. But in another and much inferior place they will be laid, and that, too, only when they have been tortured and completed the days of their sins. And on this account will they be transferred, because they have partaken of the righteous Word. "[41]

The tower was built and the Church of that age completed. Another "and much inferior" institution took its place. This was the final curtain call.

Politics and Christianity

It is unclear exactly when all priesthood authority was lost, but the evidence from Hermas suggests sometime in the early to mid-second century. However, some may not have been convinced by the foregoing discussion that the apostasy was to be complete, so what of the claim that the episcopal authority weathered the apostasy and continued in the Church? It can be conclusively shown that even if we grant that Priesthood authority continued beyond the second century, Christianity cut itself off from that authority after it became embroiled in the politics of the Empire in the fourth century.

The Emperor Constantine allied the Roman Empire with Christianity in the early fourth century, and immediately began asserting control over the affairs of the Church. It was he who called the council at Nicea, although he was never a baptized Christian until he was on his deathbed. As evidence for his meddling, consider the Emperor's relationship with Eusebius, the great Church historian of the fourth century and bishop of Caesarea:

> Constantine had called on him to deliver the opening address at Nicea, and six years later, declaring that he was fitted to become bishop of the whole world, he had desired to translate him from Caesarea to the much more important see of Antioch, an offer which Eusebius was humble enough to decline.[42]

How could the emperor of Rome, who was not even a Christian, have the authority to appoint bishops? Apparently he assumed he had that authority, but obviously it was not authority from God by revelation.

Indeed, after the Council of Nicea in 325 A.D., J.N.D. Kelly notes that the "success or failure of a doctrine might hinge upon the favour of the reigning emperor . . . ."[43] Thus secular authority intruded into all the central aspects of the Church.

Once the Church had become so inextricably tied to the government of Rome, politics was the driving force in the administration of the Church. Former Anglican Bishop of London, J.W.C. Wand, admits that by the fifth century there was "a much closer association between the Church and the State than is sometimes recognized." He illustrates his point by showing that a large number of public officials were given the office of bishop, and if a conqueror wanted to remove his rival from contention, he would compel him to become a priest.[44] He goes on to state that "the new Christian church was frankly national. The people were converted *en bloc*; the temples were turned into churches and the pagan priests were ordained into the Christian ministry."[45]

Consider the seriousness of the charge -- bishops, popes, patriarchs, etc. were at one time or another appointed by worldly rulers in nearly all the catholic and orthodox branches of Christianity. The *Apostolic Constitutions*, a fourth century collection of Catholic canon law (some of which dates from the first and second centuries) states the following: "If any bishop makes use of the rulers of this world, and by their means obtains to be a bishop of a church, let him be deprived and suspended, and all that communicate with him."[46] *Therefore, by the standard of the canon law of early Christianity, the authority of nearly the Catholic and Orthodox branches of Christianity is in question. Every bishop, pope, or patriarch who was appointed by political machinations, as well as all those who submitted to his authority in any way, have cut themselves off from the Church.*[47]

Floundering in the Dark

When discussing this loss of authority, it is instructive to compare the way doctrinal disputes were settled before and after the loss of the apostolate. Consider, for instance, the mandate to carry the gospel to the gentiles. The tenth and eleventh chapters of Acts record that Peter, the senior Apostle, had a vision in which God made it clear that gentiles were to be accepted in the Church and not avoided as "unclean." When Peter returned to Jerusalem "they that were of the circumcision [Jewish Christians] contended with him, saying, Thou wentest in to men uncircumcised, and did eat with them." (Acts 11:2-3) But then Peter rehearsed his vision to them and the matter was settled. "When they heard these things, they held their peace, and glorified God, saying, Then hath God also to the Gentiles granted repentance unto life." (Acts 11:18)

Clearly the Apostolic Church had well-defined methods for solving doctrinal disputes and other matters. On the other hand, when the Apostles were lost to the Church, Christianity split into a multitude of factions all of which accused each other of being apostate. The Marcionites, Gnostics, Montanists, Arians, etc., all accused each other and the main church of having rebelled against the Apostolic faith.[48] Jean Cardinal Daniélou admits that in the late second century, "the situation, so far as ideas about tradition were concerned, was . . . extremely confused. The word . . . was fashionable enough; but it meant something different to almost everyone who used it."[49]

The Catholic Church took to solving its disputes through councils of bishops, but conditions were such that it took decades and sometimes centuries to decide even the most fundamental issues. For instance, it took fourteen ecumenical councils between the years 325 and 381 A.D. to settle the controversy about the doctrine of the Trinity[50], and there seems to have been no generally accepted solution to this problem for centuries before.[51] Even Athanasius, a leading figure at many of these councils, had grave doubts about the way in which the theological controversies of his age were solved. He asked:

> What defect of teaching was there for religious truth in the Catholic Church, that they should enquire concerning faith now, and should prefix this year's Consulate to their

27

profession of faith? . . . Next, this too was on the mind of myself and my true brethren here, and made us anxious, the impropriety of this great gathering which we saw in progress; for what pressed so much, that the whole world was to be put in confusion, and those who at the time bore the profession of clergy, should run about far and near, seeking how best to learn to believe in our Lord Jesus Christ? Certainly if they were believers already, they would not have been seeking, as though they were not. And to the catechumens [investigators], this was no small scandal; but to the heathen, it was something more than common, and even furnished broad merriment, that Christians, as if waking out of sleep at this time of day, should be enquiring how they were to believe concerning Christ; while their professed clergy, though claiming deference from their flocks, as teachers, were unbelievers on their own shewing, in that they were seeking what they had not.[52]

Cyril of Jerusalem, who also lived during this period, claimed outright that this state of affairs was the beginnings of the apostasy predicted by Paul:

Thus wrote Paul, and now is the falling away. For men have fallen away from the right faith; and some preach the identity of the Son with the Father, and others dare to say that Christ was brought into being out of nothing. And formerly the heretics were manifest; but now the Church is filled with heretics in disguise. For men have fallen away from the truth, and have itching ears. Is it a plausible discourse? all listen to it gladly. Is it a word of correction? all turn away from it. Most have departed from right words, and rather choose the evil, than desire the good. This therefore is the falling away, and the enemy is soon to be looked for . . . .[53]

This state of affairs had prevailed since the second century, which is commonly known as the "age of heresy." "Well into the second century, . . ." as R.M. Grant observes, "there was within Christianity no sharp dividing line between what was orthodox and what was heretical."[54] With the Apostles gone and the papacy not yet established, who was to draw the line between orthodoxy and heresy? No wonder the second century Christian writer Hegesippus could theorize that "the Church remained a 'pure virgin' in the Apostles' day (until the reign of Trajan [A.D. 98-117]) and was then corrupted by heresies."[55]

It is perhaps easy to see why the controversies about the nature of God in the fourth century were so troubling to Christianity. However, the atmosphere in the Church of the second century was such that even minor disputes were the cause of great upheavals. For example, in the middle of the century there was a dispute about the day Easter was to be celebrated. R.M. Grant comments on the situation:

> To us to-day such questions [as the date Easter is to be celebrated] may not seem important. But to early Christians, especially Asiatics, anything involving the rites which the Lord instituted was an essential matter. Irenaeus has to plead with Victor of Rome not to try to excommunicate whole churches.[56]

Without the light of revelation, or even any semblance of a central authority[57], Christianity floundered in the dark, grasping for any bits of information left from the days of the Apostles. And yet we shall see that in their anxiousness to put these bits together, the early Christians persistently adopted many pagan philosophical ideas in place of older doctrines, and reinterpreted the Christian message in light of them. How different the post-Apostolic period would have been if revelation had not ceased, and there had been even one person who "taught them as one having authority, and not as the scribes." (Matthew 7:29)

Directions of Apostasy

Up to this point we have concentrated on what happened to the tradition of Christianity, namely the *Catholic* tradition, which has *survived* till the present. However, we have seen that in the first centuries after the Apostles Christianity was extraordinarily fragmented, and indeed, the Catholic tradition was only one branch of a larger movement. For the purposes of this study, we will briefly describe three main branches of apostate Christendom -- Jewish Christianity, Gnostic Christianity, and Catholic Christianity.

Jewish Christianity

The first forms of the Christian faith can be described as "Jewish Christianity" because, as has often been recognized, their theology "was taking shape in predominantly Judaistic moulds."[58] Also, the Jews of the diaspora "provided the initial basis for church growth during the first and early second centuries [and] continued as a significant source of Christian converts until at least as late as the fourth century . . . ."[59]

In fact, Mormonism has significant ties to this first form of Christianity. W.D. Davies of Duke University observed that "Mormonism is the Jewish-Christian tradition in an American key . . . . What it did was to re-Judaize a Christianity that had been too much Hellenized."[60] So what happened to Jewish Christianity when it was set adrift through apostasy?

The New Testament gives evidence that certain factions within Jewish Christianity rebelled against the authority of the Apostles, and refused to accept the fact that Christ had fulfilled the Law of Moses. As the missionary efforts of the Church moved beyond Palestine, the question came up as to whether Gentile converts should be circumcised and be subject to the Law of Moses. Acts 15 describes a council in Jerusalem where the "Apostles and elders" considered the matter and decided that the converts *did not* have to keep the ritual requirements of the Law. However, many of those who had originally insisted on the continuity of the Law would not accept this decision, and went around preaching their views to the churches. For instance, Paul complained the Galatians had turned to "another Gospel" (Galatians 1:6), and specifically censured those who desired "to be under the law." (Galatians 4:21) He further explained, "For all the law is fulfilled in one word, even in this; Thou shalt love thy neighbor as thyself." (Galatians 5:14) Paul also dealt with this issue in other letters, such as that to the Romans.

Cardinal Daniélou[61] describes a host of Jewish Christian heretical sects, including the Ebionites, Elkesaites, and others. These ranged from strictly Jewish groups who merely believed in Jesus as the greatest of the prophets, to Gnostic speculations that drew heavily on the apocalyptic tradition of Israel for their beliefs. Apart from these were more moderate strains of Jewish Christianity known to us from their apocryphal literature, as well as such writings as *Barnabas*, the *Pastor of Hermas*, and miscellaneous traditions scattered throughout the writings of more Hellenized Christians. Gradually, these groups lost their vitality and were melded into the Hellenized congregations.[62]

Gnostic Christianity

It is well known that for a few centuries there existed alongside the Catholic Christian tradition various heretical groups categorized as "Gnostic."[63] This name comes from *gnosis*, the Greek word for "knowledge." Hans Jonas explains that Gnostics believed they were saved by knowledge, specifically the knowledge of God, or that knowledge was the form of salvation itself. They believed in a radically transcendent God, however, so this knowledge was not something innate, but something that had to be divinely bestowed on the gnostic.[64]

While it may be tempting to equate this sentiment to Jesus' statement: "Ye shall know the truth, and the truth shall make you free" (John 8:32) or to Joseph Smith's that "a man is saved no faster than he gets knowledge,"[65] upon further reflection it becomes obvious that the gnostic belief was very different from the original Christian teaching. Knowledge itself cannot save without the atonement of Jesus Christ. On the other hand, in Gnostic circles Christ's incarnation and atonement were thought to have been illusory, since Gnosticism radicalized the common notion that matter is a lesser reality into the doctrine that matter is evil. (If matter is evil, how could a divine being associate himself with it?) And while true Christians viewed the physical body as necessary, the Gnostics thought of it as a prison into which the pre-existent spirit had fallen and from which it must escape.[66] A Manichean Gnostic prayer poignantly made this point: "As I have been born in this terrible, phantasmic house, this castle of death, this poisonous form, the body made of bone . . . ."[67]

The birth of the Gnostic Christian movement took place during the Apostolic period, but Gnostics probably never became terribly prevalent at that time because the Apostles actively combated this heresy, calling it the "science [*gnosis*] falsely so called." (1 Timothy 6:20)[68] John condemned these "docetists" (from the Greek *dokein* = "to seem") who claimed Jesus only "seemed" to come in the flesh as antichrists. "And every spirit that confesseth not that Jesus Christ is come in the flesh is not of God: and this is that spirit of antichrist . . . ." (1 John 4:3) But according to Eusebius, Gnostic teachers came out of the woodwork in great profusion after the Apostles were all gone:

> But when the sacred college of Apostles had suffered death in various forms, and the generation of those that had been deemed worthy to hear the inspired wisdom with their own ears had passed away, then the league of godless error took its rise as a result of the folly of heretical teachers, who, because none of the Apostles was still living, attempted henceforth, with a bold face, to proclaim, in opposition to the preaching of the truth, the "knowledge [*gnosis*]which is falsely so-called."[69]

Why did the Gnostic teachers become so popular? We shall see in a later discussion of early Christian esoteric rites and doctrines that it is clear the original Church had a true "*gnosis*," in contrast to the "knowledge falsely so called." Perhaps a good portion of the true *gnosis* was lost when the Apostles left the scene, however, and many in the Church were so hungry for what had been lost that they were willing to accept the hodgepodge of "oriental mythologies, astrological doctrines, Iranian theology, elements of Jewish tradition, . . . Christian salvation-eschatology, [and] Platonic terms and concepts,"[70] that the Gnostics had to offer in its place.

That said, there are some significant parallels between Gnostic Christianity and Latter-day Saint beliefs and practices, and since the latter considers Gnosticism just another branch of apostate Christianity, it is legitimate for us to point out some of these as we explore the relationship of the LDS faith with early Christianity. However, we should be careful to note from the outset that in our view *none* of the various branches of post-Apostolic

31

Christianity had "the fulness of the gospel." Therefore, it might be misleading to note only the similarities and ignore the differences.

Catholic Christianity

Catholic Christianity grew out of the original Jewish Christianity as the faith moved more and more into a Gentile world saturated by Greek, or "Hellenistic" culture. As Adolf von Harnack observed, this move catalyzed "the greatest transformation which the new religion ever experienced . . . ."[71]

Christianity in the Greek World

Although the Jews of the diaspora were probably the major source of converts for Christianity well into the second century, especially after the destruction of Jerusalem in 70 A.D., these Jews had already accommodated Hellenistic culture and thought-forms to a large extent. As Rodney Stark puts it, "the Jews outside Palestine read, wrote, spoke, thought, and worshipped in Greek . . . . Moreover, many Hellenized Jews had embraced some elements of pagan religious thought."[72]

However, these "elements of pagan religious thought" were not what one might think. Every age and culture has a set of ideas used to explain the world that practically everyone just assumes to be true, and these ideas may be called the "science" or "common wisdom" of the day. While the Hellenized Jews certainly would not have adopted the pantheons of pagan mythology, which were not taken seriously by the Greek intellectual community either, they did adapt their religion to the "science" of the day, which was an amalgamation of the thought of various Greek philosophical schools, especially the Middle Platonists and the Stoics. Therefore, when Hellenized Jews and Gentiles converted to Christianity, they naturally sought to make sense of their new faith in terms of their cultural assumptions.

At first, Christian thought was quite foreign to Greek philosophy. As Harnack notes, "Yet we cannot say that the earliest Christian writings, let alone the gospel, show, to any considerable extent, the presence of a Greek element."[73] For instance, Paul warned, "Beware lest any man spoil you through philosophy and vain deceit, after the tradition of men, after the rudiments of the world, and not after Christ." (Colossians 2:8) James Shiel of the University of Sussex agrees that "Saint Paul's letters [contain] a severe warning against Greek philosophy as a dangerous deception"[74] Cardinal Daniélou writes that "If we now examine the forms of thought and philosophical systems current at the time when Christianity first made its appearance in the world, it is clear that they were by no means ready to assimilate this Christian conception: on the contrary, they were wholly antagonistic thereto."[75] However, Shiel notes that a few generations after the Apostles, one "comes upon a reversed situation. The religious message is now framed in philosopher's language, reminiscent at every turn of Heraclitus or

Plato or Aristotle or Cleanthes or Epictetus. Indeed, the Christian religion is now occasionally called a philosophy and its founder described as a philosopher."[76]

An example of this clash of cultures can be seen in Paul's attempt to preach to a group of intellectuals at Mars Hill in Athens. (Acts 17:22-32) Although Paul made a serious attempt to create common ground from which he could preach Christ, "when they heard of the resurrection of the dead, some mocked . . . ." As will be shown in the next chapter, the very idea that God would come to earth and live as a human being, and then that he would actually want the body back after he was done with it was patently ridiculous to the Greek mind. Therefore, pagan intellectualism was viewed with suspicion by the earliest Christians,[77] and it is no coincidence that Paul chastised the Corinthians for doubting the reality of the resurrection in the same letter where he intimated that the gospel was "unto the Greeks foolishness," and contrasted the wisdom of God with the "wisdom of the world." (1 Corinthians 15; 1-2.)

The Influx of Greek Philosophy

And yet, it was not possible for the Church to stay completely sheltered from the sphere of Greek culture and thought, for if the gospel was to be preached in the Hellenistic world, it had to be done on Hellenistic terms. Thus, even the Apostles sometimes used Greek terms (e.g. John's *logos*) to get across their message, and it was recognized that the "wisdom of the world" contained some kernels of truth.[78] By the middle of the second century, however, the situation had changed.[79] A class of Christian writers came on the scene which later historians have termed the "Apologists." These included Aristides, Justin, Tatian, Athenagoras, and others. Intellectuals themselves, they sought to express their faith in intellectually respectable terms, but the net result of their labors was not just to translate Christian ideas into a Hellenistic idiom. Rather, they imported philosophical ideas into their thought that had been anathema to the original Christians.[80] One can certainly understand the temptation to make such accommodations, since the Greeks normally saw the Christians as intellectually feeble barbarians, but in the end "the efforts of the apologists succeeded in enabling Christianity to be labeled a third-rate philosophy rather than a first-rate superstition."[81]

The position of the Apologists and later second and third-century Catholic writers was an unenviable one. While on the one hand they were trying to convince the pagan world that they had not accepted some unreasonable superstition, on the other, they found it necessary to assuage the fears of more conservative Christians, to whom pagan philosophy was still anathema.[82] Edwin Hatch of Oxford University summarizes how these writers presented themselves to the pagans:

> "We teach the same as the Greeks," says Justin Martyr,
> "though we alone are hated for what we teach." "Some of

our number," says Tertullian, "who are versed in ancient literature, have composed books by means of which it may be clearly seen that we have embraced nothing new or monstrous, nothing in which we have not the support of common and public literature . . . ." "The teachings of Plato," says Justin Martyr, "are not alien to those of Christ, though not in all respects similar . . . .For all the writers (of antiquity) were able to have a dim vision of realities by means of the indwelling seed of the implanted Word . . . ."[83]

Hatch also points out the patent hypocrisy of this class of writers:

> For Tatian, though he ridicules Greek philosophy and professes to have abandoned it, yet [he] builds up theories of the Logos, of free-will, and of the nature of spirit, out of the elements of current philosophical conceptions. Tertullian, though he asks, "What resemblance is there between a philosopher and a Christian, between a disciple of Greece and a disciple of heaven?" expresses Christian truths in philosophical terms, and argues against his opponents -- for example, against Marcion -- by methods which might serve as typical examples of the current methods of controversy between philosophical schools. And Hippolytus, though he reproves another Christian writer for listening to Gentile teaching, and so disobeying the injunction, "Go not into the way of the Gentiles," is himself saturated with philosophical conceptions and philosophical literature.[84]

Indeed, Harnack calls the influx of Greek thoughtforms into Christianity "the greatest fact in the history of the Church in the second century,"[85] and, once it was thus established, the trend continued through the centuries. Hatch summarizes his study with the following observation:

> A large part of what are sometimes called Christian doctrines, and many usages which have prevailed and continue to prevail in the Christian Church, are in reality Greek theories and Greek usages changed in form and colour by the influence of primitive Christianity, but in their essence Greek still.[86]

In fairness it should be noted that these Christian theologians who imported Greek ideas into their faith were generally not the wolves among the sheep of whom Paul spoke. They were the inheritors rather than the perpetrators of apostasy, and by their time the light of revelation had essentially been extinguished. Indeed, the early Christian Fathers made honest attempts to make sense of their religion in light of the cultural assumptions they had inherited, and in point of fact they did reject many of the doctrines of philosophy as incompatible with the Christian revelation.[87] But in the absence of direct divine guidance it was only natural for there to have been some drift from the pure faith.

Philosophy vs. Revelation

The "chronic Hellenization" of Christianity[88] culminated with the greatest theologian in Christian history -- St. Augustine (b. 354 A.D.) Etienne Gilson, perhaps the greatest twentieth century authority on the middle ages, reports that Augustine was the greatest of a long line of Christian fathers who had "built up theological doctrines in which the fundamental agreement of natural and revealed knowledge was everywhere either stated or pre-supposed." Augustine was thoroughly converted to the philosophy of Plato as it was reinterpreted by the Neoplatonists. "Consequently, . . . the whole philosophical activity of Saint Augustine had to be a rational interpretation of the Christian Revelation, in terms of platonic philosophy."[89] Even now Augustine's theology forms the bulk of Catholic doctrine.

Augustine, however, realized that philosophy could only go so far. In one passage he recounted how his mother and he longed to hear the voice of the living God, even if just for a brief moment:

> If this could be sustained, and other visions of a far different kind be withdrawn, and this one ravish, and absorb, and envelope its beholder amid these inward joys, so that his life might be eternally like that one moment of knowledge which we now sighed after, were not this "Enter thou into the joy of Thy Lord"? And when shall that be ?[90]

What a poor substitute for revelation philosophy is. Augustine and the earliest Christians knew it. Unfortunately, the new generation of Christians decided they could throw off the "ignorance" of their forbears -- and substitute intellect for spiritual inspiration. Consider the example of Justin Martyr, who continued to wear his philosopher's cloak even after he became a Christian.[91] Sadly, he didn't listen to the old Christian man who was responsible for his conversion: "'How then,' he said, 'should the philosophers judge correctly about God, or speak any truth, when they have no knowledge of Him, having neither seen Him at any time, nor heard Him?'"[92]

The Effect of the Apostasy

We have seen the *causes* of the apostasy -- rebellion against God's appointed ministers and accommodation of false doctrines. The *effect* of the apostasy, on the other hand, was the loss of certain distinguishing marks of the true Church of Christ -- namely, the gifts of the Spirit and continuing revelation.

The Loss of Spiritual Gifts

The Necessity of Spiritual Gifts

Mark recorded that the resurrected Christ promised certain gifts and powers to his disciples:

> And these signs shall follow them that believe; In my name shall they cast out devils; they shall speak with new tongues; they shall take up serpents; and if they drink any deadly thing, it shall not hurt them: they shall lay hands on the sick, and they shall recover. (Mark 16:17-18)

Paul gave a more complete list of these spiritual gifts to the Corinthians:

> But the manifestation of the Spirit is given to every man to profit withal. For to one is given by the Spirit the word of wisdom; to another the word of knowledge by the same Spirit; to another faith by the same Spirit; to another gifts of healing by the same Spirit; to another the working of miracles; to another prophecy; to another discerning of spirits; to another divers kinds of tongues; to another the interpretation of tongues . . . . (1 Corinthians 12:7-10)

Admittedly, Paul indicated that these gifts would one day pass away, but only when they were not needed because "that which is perfect" had come:

> But whether there be prophecies, they shall fail; whether there be tongues, they shall cease; whether there be knowledge, it shall vanish away. For we know in part, and we prophesy in part. But when that which is perfect is come, then that which is in part shall be done away. (1 Corinthians 13:8-10)

Have we received perfect knowledge? Have all things been prophesied? Certainly the world still needs prophecy, since the angel indicated to John that "the testimony of Jesus is the spirit of prophecy." (Revelation 19:10) Indeed, the *Book of Mormon* insists that "it is by faith that miracles are wrought; . . . wherefore, if these things have ceased wo be unto the children of men, for it is because of unbelief, and all is vain." (Moroni 7:37)

Grasping At Straws

But what happened to the gifts? Few Christians today, besides some Pentecostals and charismatic Evangelicals, as well as the Mormons, claim to have all the gifts of the Spirit. The ancient American prophet Nephi predicted the cry of latter-day religionists when they were presented with the *Book of Mormon*: "A Bible! A Bible! We have got a Bible, and there cannot be any more Bible." (2 Nephi 29:3) And, true to this prediction, the most damning charge they brought against Joseph Smith was that he had the temerity to claim a new revelation.

We shall see, on the other hand, that the earliest Christians did not see the gifts of the Spirit as dispensable, even though they could see them being gradually lost. Although Hennecke and Schneemelcher report, "By the end of the 1st century prophecy has lost its original significance . . .," and show that this gift was considered heretical after the middle of the second century [93], the Christian fathers of the second and early third centuries consistently used the presence of *a remnant of* the gifts of the spirit in the Church to argue for the Catholic faith against various heretical sects and the Jews. For example, Justin Martyr, in the mid-second century, cited the presence of the prophetic gifts in the Church and their absence in Judaism to argue that the Lord's favor had been transferred.

> For the prophetical gifts remain with us, even to the present time. And hence you ought to understand that [the gifts] formerly among your nation have been transferred to us. And just as there were false prophets contemporaneous with your holy prophets, so are there now many false teachers amongst us, of whom our Lord forewarned us to beware . . . [94].

In the fourth century Eusebius recorded that Irenaeus of Lyons (late second century) also appealed to the presence of the gifts in the Catholic church against the claims of the heretics. "'As also we hear that many brethren in the Church possess prophetic gifts . . . .'" And Eusebius, in turn, used this evidence to show that even though the church of his day had none of these gifts, at least the succession could be shown to have lasted until nearly the end of the second century.[95] Thus, Eusebius wanted to claim spiritual authority for the Catholic Church on the basis of spiritual gifts that had been completely lost for more than a century.[96]

On the contrary, Irenaeus had earlier claimed that "where the Church is, there is the Spirit of God; and where the Spirit of God is, there is the Church, and every kind of grace . . . ."[97] (It should also be noted that Irenaeus had only *heard of* the gifts, but said nothing of actually *seeing* them, although he was bishop of Lyons.)

Origen, in the early third century, used the same argument against the Jews of his time, but could only point to *traces* of the gifts:

> Therefore we may see, that after the advent of Jesus the Jews were altogether abandoned, and possess now none of what were considered their ancient glories, so that there is no indication of any Divinity abiding amongst them. For they have no longer prophets nor miracles, traces of which to a considerable extent are still found among Christians . . . .[98]

Commenting on this passage, Roberts and Donaldson reveal that "The Fathers, while they refer to extraordinary divine agency going on in their own day, also with one consent represent miracles as having ceased since the Apostolic era."[99] Thus, it appears that after the passing of the Apostles, the Church gradually lost the gifts of the Spirit, until in the late second and early third centuries, only traces and hints of the Church's former glory remained.

The Montanist Crisis

Shortly before Origen's time, the Church faced a crisis of sorts related to the loss of the gifts of the Spirit. In Syria there arose a sect that was strictly orthodox in belief, but claimed to have received the lost gifts of the Spirit. These Christians were led by a man named Montanus and his two female consorts, Priscilla and Maximilla. Apparently these charismatics would go into some sort of trance, uttering various prophecies. According to Apolinarius of Hierapolis, the guiding lights of the Church were quite distressed about this development:

> There first, they say, when Gratus was proconsul of Asia, a recent convert, Montanus by name, through his unquenchable desire for leadership, gave the adversary opportunity against him. And he became beside himself, and being suddenly in a sort of frenzy and ecstasy, he raved, and began to babble and utter strange things, prophesying in a manner contrary to the constant custom of the Church handed down by tradition from the beginning. Some of those who heard his spurious utterances at that time were indignant, and they rebuked him as one that was possessed, and that was under the control of a demon, and was led by a deceitful spirit, and was distracting the multitude; and they forbade him to talk, remembering the distinction drawn by the Lord and his warning to guard watchfully against the coming of false prophets? But others imagining themselves possessed of the Holy Spirit and of a prophetic gift, were elated and not a little puffed up; and forgetting the distinction of the Lord, they challenged the mad and insidious and seducing spirit, and were cheated and deceived by him.[100]

Note that the churchmen had no genuine gifts to offer in contrast to whatever it was the Montanists had, but they had received instructions from their forebears about how to tell true from false prophecy. Apolinarius wrote that it had been passed down in the Church "that a prophet ought not to speak in ecstasy . . . ."[101] Perhaps this statement referred to Paul's pronouncement that "the spirits of the prophets are subject to the prophets." (1 Corinthians 14:32)

But in the next passage Apolinarius unintentionally condemned his Church, as well. Here he lambasted the Montanists because, although they claimed Montanus and his colleagues had received the gifts as part of a prophetic succession from the Apostles, after these "prophets" died they could point to no others of their sect who were thus gifted. But, insisted Apolinarius, the prophetic gifts must continue in the church until the end of the world:

> They cannot show that one of the old [Testament] or one of the new [Testament] prophets was thus carried away in spirit. Neither can they boast of Agabus, or Judas, or Silas, or the daughters of Philip, or Ammia in Philadelphia, or Quadratus, or any others not belonging to them . . . . For if after Quadratus and Ammia in Philadelphia, as they assert, the women with Montanus received the prophetic gift, let them show who among them received it from Montanus and the women. For the Apostle thought it necessary that the prophetic gift should continue in all the Church until the final coming. But they cannot show it, though this is the fourteenth year since the death of Maximilla.[102]

Notice also that the last *bona fide* example of a prophet he gave was that of Quadratus, who wrote an apology for the Christians during the reign of Hadrian (117-138 A.D.)[103]

But if the "Apostle thought it necessary" that the "prophetic gift must continue in the whole Church until the final coming," how does this affect mainline Christian claims to spiritual authority? Tertullian, an important early Christian writer who defected to the Montanist camp, rebuked Catholic officials for claiming Apostolic authority to forgive sins, while having no gifts to back up their claims: "Exhibit therefore even now to me, Apostolic sir, prophetic evidences [or, "Apostolic and prophetic evidences"], that I may recognize your divine virtue, and vindicate to yourself the power of remitting such sins!"[104]

What was the Church to do? The leaders realized that they *should* have the prophetic gifts, and those of the Montanists were clearly counter to the rule of the Church, but they had nothing to exhibit in their place.[105] It should be noted here that instead of resolving the conflict through revelation, as the Apostolic Church did, the Catholics were forced to hold *councils* to put down this heresy. Indeed, J.G. Davies reports that the first councils or synods known in Christian history were the result of the Montanist controversy.[106]

By the fourth century, as we saw with the example of Eusebius, the churchmen still realized that the gifts were essential for any claim to spiritual authority, but contented themselves with tracing the gifts as far as they could in the Catholic tradition and then announcing that they were no longer needed.[107]

The Closing of the Canon of Scripture

As a result of the Montanist controversy, the Church was forced to face the fact that the gifts were essentially gone. And in order to deal with that fact they were compelled to do an about-face on the issue of the canon of scripture.

As was mentioned above, modern Christians are adamant that they have a Bible and there can be no more Bible. But was this always the case? Bishop Wand discloses that the canon was not closed by divine decree, but out of the necessity to combat the Montanist heresy. "The best defence set up by the Church against such conversions [as Tertullian's] was to close the canon of scripture, and by so doing to deny any authority to the Montanist prophecies." In this way "the possibility of a new revelation was excluded . . . ."[108]

But it never occurred to anyone to close the canon until nearly the third century! Historian Willem Van Unnik notes that until that time the Christians would have had no objection whatever to "someone . . . add[ing] something to the word of the Gospel."[109] The very existence of a document such as the *Shepherd of Hermas* shows that the possibility of a new word of revelation was nothing to be wondered at. The *Shepherd*, which purports to be a series of revelations given to *one other than* the Apostles or their associates in the first half of the second century, hovered on the edge of the canon for centuries.[110] Indeed, included in the *Shepherd* is a series of mandates which Hermas was commanded to write for the benefit of all who might read them.[111]

Andrie B. du Toit, Professor of New Testament at the University of Pretoria, South Africa, explains that before the middle of the second century the "oral tradition was used alongside and even preferred to the Gospels."[112] Even in the latter half of the second century, Clement of Alexandria could report that "the first elders . . . preferred to speak the truth rather than write it down."[113] Therefore, while there was always a set of authoritative texts, the idea that the canon was forever fixed, or that the prophetic word was only to be found in a certain set of written works, was foreign to the first Christians.

Mainstream Christians, especially Protestants, often counter Mormon arguments on this point by citing a statement near the end of John's Revelation:

> For I testify unto every man that heareth the words of the prophecy of this book, If any man shall add unto these things, God shall add unto him the plagues that are written in this book: And if any man shall take away from the words of the book of this prophecy, God shall take away his part out of the book of life, and out of the holy city, and from the things which are written in this book. (Revelation 22:18-19)

Since Revelation is placed last in the New Testament, many assume that this is an official proclamation that the canon was to be closed. However, apart from the fact that Revelation may not have been the last New Testament book written by John, it should be pointed out that the New Testament canon was not even established at that time. It would be centuries before a final list of canonical books was agreed upon. Another fact that must be taken into account is that the Lord made an identical proclamation through Moses: "Ye shall not add unto the word which I command you, neither shall ye diminish ought from it, that ye may keep the commandments of the LORD your God which I command you." (Deuteronomy 4:2) Were all the prophetic books written after the Law of Moses false? Jesus took away certain commandments of the Law, so was he just another false prophet? The answer, of course is that Jesus was God, and God can add or take away whatever He wants from His word. True prophets and Apostles speak for God, so their writings can be added to God's word, as well.

Why did God include these warnings about tampering with His scriptures and commandments? Evidently the Jews of Jesus' time had added many of their own commandments to the Law of Moses, and in the next section we shall see that God had ample reason for including a warning not to tamper with His holy scriptures, for such tampering was almost standard procedure in ancient times.

Missing Scripture?

Which Scripture?

Not only did the Church close the door on any further revelation when they closed the canon, but they excluded certain writings that earlier generations of Christians had considered inspired -- e.g. certain "apocryphal" writings. For instance, J.N.D. Kelly notes that during the first two centuries Christianity treated the apocrypha now contained in Catholic Bibles as scripture without question.[114]

And even when it was agreed upon that the canon *should be* fixed, there was great disagreement over which books should be included or excluded. Kelly calls the final fixation of the canon a very gradual process, and notes that even when its broad outline was agreed upon in the second century, churches in different localities still maintained different canonical traditions. In addition, some localities were less inclined to a fixed set of books than others. [115] The final list of canonical books was not agreed upon until the fourth century[116], and even today the various Christian traditions have some differences in their canons. [117]

Editing the Scriptures

Aside from the differences of opinion about which books should be canonical, it appears that certain parts of the canonical books have been *removed* by Jews and Christians alike! Justin Martyr accused the Jews of having removed certain passages from the Old Testament related to the Christian message:

> Here Trypho [the Jew] remarked, "We ask you first of all to tell us some of the Scriptures which you allege have been completely cancelled." [Justin quotes some passages which the Jews evidently removed from Esdras and Jeremiah.] "And again, from the sayings of the same Jeremiah these have been cut out: 'The Lord God remembered His dead people of Israel who lay in the graves; and He descended to preach to them His own salvation.'"[118]

We will deal with this doctrine of Christ's preaching to the dead in a later chapter, but for now it is sufficient to note that Justin claimed some of the Biblical manuscripts in his time still had these verses in them. But where are they now?

Henri Daniel-Rops quotes Origen saying that even the New Testament texts of his time (early third century) had been corrupted extensively: "Today the fact is evident, that there are many differences in the manuscripts, either through the negligence of certain copyists, or the perverse audacity of some in correcting the text."[119] Harnack reminds us that the question of the canon was complicated by the fact that "there were often different recensions of one and the same writing."[120]

Sadly, this habit of "correcting the text" seems to have been quite common in antiquity. For instance, commenting on a passage by Clement of Alexandria preserved in the writings of a later church father, Cassiodorus, Roberts and Donaldson reveal that "Cassiodorus says that he had in his translation corrected what he considered erroneous in the original."[121] And Bishop Dionysius of Corinth (110-180 A.D.) complained that "the devil's Apostles" had not only tampered with the scriptures, but his own writings: "It is, therefore, not to be wondered at if some have attempted to adulterate the Lord's writings also, since they have formed designs even against writings which are of less accounts."[122]

In a recent study of the New Testament variants, Bart Ehrman of the University of North Carolina shows that many of them were created by scribes in the second and third centuries *for theological reasons*. That is, these scribes lived in an age when the proto-Catholic Church had not even achieved an absolute majority within Christianity, and its ideas of how various passages in the New Testament writings should be interpreted were challenged on all sides. Therefore, scribes often rewrote passages of the scriptures to make them conform more easily to their interpretations, and exclude those of the "heretics." This was not necessarily done in bad faith -- the scribes merely rewrote passages according to what they already "knew" they meant. [123] Under these conditions, it was inevitable that significant corruptions would creep into the text.

Interpretation of Prophecy Without Prophets?

Clearly the loss of the prophetic gifts was the source of great upheaval in the Church -- and just picking a set of books as scripture and relying on them did not solve the problem, for the earliest Christians insisted that one cannot interpret the words of the prophets without the aid of prophecy itself. Peter warned the Church that "no prophecy of the scripture is of any private interpretation." (2 Peter 1:20) But who *is* to interpret it? One modern Roman Catholic author, Marie Joseph Le Guillou, admits that the post-Apostolic Church did not have the gift of inspiration, but still had the gift to correctly interpret scripture: "The Church of the Fathers did not have the charism of inspiration, but it did have the charism of interpretation of Christ's mind . . . ."[124]

On the other hand, according to the earliest Christians there were many truths hidden in the text of the scriptures that could not be removed without the aid of a prophet or the gift of prophecy. In the *Clementine Recognitions* Peter told Clement of Rome: "For otherwise it is impossible to get knowledge of divine and eternal things, unless one learns of that true Prophet . . . ."[125] In a later passage Peter went on to say that a seeker should not only examine the credentials of a prophet and seek truth by the exercise of reason, "but that they should ask it, not from themselves, but from Him who has hidden it, and should pray that access and the way of knowledge might be given to them . . . ." [126] As Jesus told Peter, "flesh and blood hath not revealed [that I am the Christ] to thee, but my Father which is in heaven." (Matthew 16:17)

Indeed, Ignatius of Antioch rebuked those who naively assumed that if any truth was to be had they could just read it out of the scriptures:

> For I have heard some saying, 'If I do not find the Gospel in the archives [i.e. the Old Testament], I will not believe it.' To such persons I say that my archives are Jesus Christ, to disobey whom is manifest destruction. My authentic archives are His cross, and death, and resurrection, and the faith which bears on these things, by which I desire, through

your prayers, to be justified. He who disbelieves the Gospel disbelieves everything along with it. For the archives ought not to be preferred to the Spirit.[127]

And Papias, who heard John preach, said he tried to gather together all the *oral* teachings of the inspired men because they could not be found in books:

> If, then, anyone who had attended on the elders came, I asked minutely after their sayings, -- what Andrew or Peter said, or what was said by Philip, or by Thomas, or by James, or by John, or by Matthew, or by any other of the Lord's disciples: which things Aristion and the presbyter John, the disciples of the Lord, say. For I imagined that what was to be got from books was not so profitable to me as what came from the living and abiding voice.[128]

Irenaeus, living at a time when there were few, if any, prophets still around, insisted that one could not interpret the Scriptures correctly without the aid of the elders who had passed down the unwritten tradition from the Apostles: "And then shall every word also seem consistent to him, if he . . . diligently read the Scriptures in company with those who are presbyters in the Church, among whom is the Apostolic doctrine . . . ."[129]

So we see that prophets and prophecy are indispensable -- and yet both were dispensed with. As Justin Martyr told Trypho the Jew:

> For neither by nature nor by human conception is it possible for men to know things so great and divine, but by the gift which then descended from above upon the holy men, who had no need of rhetorical art, nor of uttering anything in a contentious or quarrelsome manner . . . .[130]

But as we have seen, even as Justin spoke those words the Church was changing in such a way that men were indeed left to try to know divine things through "human conception."

The Necessity of a Restoration

Unless one considers the substitution of Greek philosophical methods for revelation a good thing -- and some people do[131] -- it must be admitted that an apostasy did, indeed, take place just as early Christian leaders had warned it would. After all, Paul did say that the gospel as it was originally preached was "unto the Greeks foolishness." (1 Corinthians 1:23) Over time, as sacred principles became mingled with the "foolishness" of Greek philosophy, pure, unadulterated gospel truth was lost. And, as a result, a restoration of the gospel was necessary -- a restoration that could have only taken place through the agency of prophets. We shall explore several avenues of evidence for this fact.

The Restitution of "All Things"

While speaking to the crowd on the day of Pentecost, Peter predicted that the heavens must receive Jesus "until the times of restitution of all things." (Acts 3:20-21) Was this merely a reference to the Millennial reign of Christ, or was it an oblique reference to the fact that the gospel would have to be restored in preparation for that reign? Peter gives us a clue in his first general letter where he announced that "the end of all things is at hand" (1 Peter 4:7); later he warned the saints of the "fiery trial" which was coming to them, for "judgment must begin at the house of God." (1 Peter 4:12, 17) "All things" was here a reference to the pure gospel teaching. "According to his divine power hath given unto us *all things* that pertain unto life and godliness, through the knowledge of God, and of Jesus our Lord." (2 Peter 1:3, italics mine) Therefore, unless Peter was greatly mistaken about the timing of the Lord's second advent -- and Peter's second letter makes it clear that he had no such starry-eyed expectations (see 2 Peter 3:8) -- what was the "end of all things" but the loss of the pure gospel message through apostasy? And what could a "restitution of all things" be but the restoration of the gospel?

Elias and the "Restoration of All Things"

This point is supported by the Latter-day Saint and early Christian doctrine of *Elias*. "Elias" is the Greek form of the Hebrew name "Elijah." In the last verses of the Old Testament the promise is made: "Behold, I will send you Elijah the prophet before the coming of the great and dreadful day of the Lord . . . ." (Malachi 4:5) After Elijah himself appeared before Jesus, Peter, James, and John on the Mount of Transfiguration, Jesus told his disciples to tell no one of the vision until after His resurrection from the dead. But then the Apostles asked:

> Why then say the scribes that Elias must first come? And Jesus answered and said unto them, Elias truly shall first come, and restore all things. But I say unto you, That Elias is come already, and they knew him not, but have done unto him whatsoever they listed. Likewise shall also the Son of man suffer of them. Then the disciples understood that he spake unto them of John the Baptist." (Matthew 17:3-13)

45

What did Jesus mean when He said that John the Baptist was Elias, even though Elijah and Moses had just appeared? The angel Gabriel told John's father that he would "go before him [Christ] *in the spirit and power of Elias . . . .*" (Luke 1:17) Therefore, it must be that certain people who are called of God to be forerunners of the Kingdom, as John was, act in the "spirit and power of Elias."

This principle must apply to other prophets as well as John, for Jesus not only said that "Elias has come already," but also that "Elias truly *shall* first come, and restore all things." Thus, a restoration would still be needed in the future, just as Latter-day Saints have proclaimed. Noting the many persons the revelations of Joseph Smith identify as "Elias," modern Apostle Bruce R. McConkie summarized the LDS doctrine: "Elias is a composite personage. The expression must be understood to be a name and a title for those whose mission it was to commit keys and powers to men in this final dispensation."[132] And as with the Lord's first advent, Latter-day Saints believe that Elijah himself was one of the heavenly visitors who appeared to Joseph Smith (as well as Oliver Cowdery) to restore the original "keys and powers." (See D&C 110)

Although one might argue that Joseph Smith could have extracted this doctrine from the Bible, but the fact that no other group has developed a similar dogma would seem not to support such a conclusion. Here again, Joseph struck upon a prominent doctrine of the early Church that had been lost. For example, Hippolytus (ca. 200 A.D.) indicated that various forerunners would appear to prepare the way for the second advent of the Savior:

> [The Savior] is to be manifested again at the end of the world as Judge. It is a matter of course that His forerunners must appear first, as He says by Malachi and the angel, [Malachi 4:5-6]. These, then, shall come and proclaim the manifestation of Christ that is to be from heaven; and they shall also perform signs and wonders, in order that men may be put to shame and turned to repentance for their surpassing wickedness and impiety. [133]

Justin Martyr explained the doctrine of Elias in similar terms to Trypho the Jew, asking, "shall we not suppose that the word of God has proclaimed that Elijah shall be the precursor of the great and terrible day, that is, of His second advent? . . ." [134] According to John Chrysostom, John was to be the forerunner of Christ's First Advent, and Elias would be the forerunner of the Second: "John is Elias, and Elias John. For both of them received one ministry, and both of them became forerunners."[135] Similarly, Victorinus, Methodius, Cyprian, Lactantius, Jerome, Augustine, and Theophylact all expressed the belief that Elijah would come to "restore all things" before the Second Coming of the Lord.[136]

Therefore, it is safe to say that the early Christians had a certain belief that the way would be paved for the Lord's Second Advent through the agency of various prophetic forerunners, including Elijah the prophet, who the Savior said would come and "restore all things." And it is also safe to say that Joseph Smith preached a very similar doctrine. What is more important, this belief of the early Church, combined with the evidence for the apostasy, underscores the fact that *a restoration of the gospel was necessary and expected.*

The Angel of the Restoration

Of what was the restoration to consist? Joseph Smith promised not only to restore all the knowledge and powers of past dispensations, but also "things that have not been before revealed."[137] A striking confirmation of this interpretation comes from an early Christian exegesis of Revelation 14:6. In this verse John spoke of an angel who was to appear before the second coming of Christ, "having the everlasting Gospel to preach unto them that dwell on the earth, and to every nation, and kindred, and tongue, and people." Traditionally, Latter-day Saints have interpreted this as a reference to the restoration of the gospel, which was accomplished through the agency of various angels. Similarly, the third-century theologian, Origen, interpreted the verse as a reference to the preaching of a gospel that was even greater than the one had by the Christianity of his day. More than a century after Origen wrote, Jerome gave this summary of Origen's teaching, which was condemned by the Church of his time:

> [Origen says] that according to the apocalypse of John "the everlasting gospel" which shall be revealed in heaven as much surpasses our gospel as Christ's preaching does the sacraments of the ancient law . . . .[138]

Referring to the same passage, Origen remarked that the gospel would be preached to the world for *those who had fallen away.* "For at the end an exalted and flying angel, having the Gospel, will preach it to every nation, for the good Father has not entirely deserted those who have fallen away from Him."[139] Origen did not make clear whether he was referring to a total apostasy from Christ's Church. The restoration of the gospel was not only *necessary* and *expected,* but Joseph Smith correctly promised an *expansion* of the principles formerly revealed.

Chapter Notes

Note 1: Upon This Rock . . .

The Gates of Hades

Unwilling to accept the possibility that a total apostasy occurred, mainline Christians often counter that Christ told Peter "upon this rock I will build my church; and the gates of hell shall not prevail against it." (Matthew 16:18) To interpret this passage we must first define terms.

What is "the Church" (Greek *ekklesia* = "assembly") that Jesus spoke of? The mainline interpretation suggests it was "the Church" in its manifestation as an earthly organization. However, in a broader sense, "the Church" is much more inclusive. Two of the earliest post-New Testament Christian writings, *The Pastor of Hermas* and *2 Clement* (both early second century) claimed that God created the Church even before he created the world. "She was created first of all . . . and for her sake was the world made."[140] "Moreover, the books and the Apostles declare that the Church belongs not to the present, but existed from the beginning."[141] Paul wrote, "He hath chosen us in him before the foundation of the world." (Ephesians 1:3) The author of the Epistle to the Hebrews went on: "But we are come unto mount Sion, and unto the city of the living God, the heavenly Jerusalem, and in an innumerable company of angels. To the general assembly and church of the firstborn, which are written in heaven, and to God the Judge of all, and to the spirits of just men made perfect." (Hebrews 12:22-23) The message here is clear. "The Church" is not just an earthly organization -- it existed before the foundation of the world, and it exists with the saints of all ages, both those who are on the earth and those who have passed on. Therefore, even if the Church as an earthly organization disappears and reappears periodically, the Church will always survive!

But is there any reason to believe Jesus was speaking primarily of the earthly Church? On the contrary, the text says that "the gates of hell [Greek *hades* = "the world of the dead"] shall not prevail against it." What are "the gates of   "? Hades is not hell -- it is the underworld, and in early Christian and Jewish thought it was believed to be a place of waiting where the spirits of the dead, both the just and unjust, remained until the resurrection. (If Jesus had been speaking in Roman Catholic terms he might have said, "the gates of Purgatory shall not prevail against it.") Thus Tertullian (ca. 200 A.D.): "All souls, therefore; are shut up within Hades: do you admit this? (It is true, whether) you say yes or no . . . ."[142] The "gates of hades," then, represent the "powers of death"[143], and "the sting of death is sin." (1 Corinthians 15:56) Thus the text seems to be a promise of protection from the powers of death and sin for Christ's assembly (*ekklesia*) of believers. For this reason Michael M. Winter, former lecturer in Fundamental Theology at St. John's Seminary (Roman Catholic), in his excellent scholarly defense of the papacy, admits that "although some writers have applied the idea of immortality to the survival of the church, it seems preferable to see it as a promise of triumph over evil."[144]

Furthermore, there are numerous allusions in the early Christian literature to Christ, when he died and went to hades, breaking down the gates of Hades and leading out the faithful to glorious resurrection. For instance, Athanasius related the following tradition: "He burst open the gates of brass, He broke through the bolts of iron, and He took the souls which were in Amente [the Coptic equivalent of Hades] and carried them to His Father . . . . Now the souls He brought out of Amente, but the bodies He raised up on the earth . . . ."[145] Therefore it is clear what Jesus was talking about when he said "the gates of hades" would not prevail against the Church, and to apply this statement to the perpetuation of the earthly Church would make no sense.[146]

Further Objections

There are a few other passages in the New Testament which some interpret to mean that there could never be a total apostasy. For example, some Bible translations have Jude referring to "the faith which God entrusted to his people once and for all." (Jude 1:3 NEB) "Once and for all" certainly has a ring of finality about it, but a quick look in the lexicon reveals that the Greek word translated as "once and for all," *hapax*, can also be rendered as "once," and other translations such as the KJV speak only of the "faith which was once delivered unto the saints." Indeed, two verses later Jude wrote, "I will therefore put you in remembrance, though ye once (*hapax*) knew this . . . ." (Jude 1:5) Clearly it is preferable to translate *hapax* as "once" in this case, and thus it is also clear that Jude was warning the saints to cling desperately to the faith that had once been delivered to them, but which was already being forgotten. Also, we will see in a later discussion of the doctrine of dispensations that the idea of the faith being delivered "once for all" would have made absolutely no sense in the context of early Christian salvation history.

Another passage marshaled in defense of mainline Christian claims is Galatians 1:8: "But though we, or an angel from heaven, preach any other Gospel unto you than that which we have preached unto you, let him be accursed." Did this mean that no more revelations of truth were to be expected, or does it just mean that "revelations" which *contradicted* the fundamentals the Apostles had laid out were to be rejected as spurious? Our discussion of the closing of the canon in this chapter should make clear that the second option is much more plausible.

A Witness to the Wickedness of the World

Why did God allow his Church to be subverted by "another Gospel" (that of the Greek philosophers)? Certainly it cannot be denied that God allows humans free will. Thus, when Christians chose to "turn away from the truth, and be turned to fables," God allowed them to reject His Church.

Why did Christ set up a Church in the first place if its light was to be so quickly extinguished? Christ said repeatedly of Himself that he would suffer and be killed, not only to save repentant sinners, but to condemn the wicked generation into which He was born. "But first must he suffer many things, and be rejected of this generation." (Luke 17:25) And his disciples were not to be immune:

> I send unto you prophets, and wise men, and scribes: and some of them ye shall kill and crucify; and some of them shall ye scourge in your synagogues, and persecute them from city to city: That upon you may come all the righteous blood shed upon the earth, from the blood of righteous Abel unto the blood of Zacharias son of Barachias, whom ye slew between the temple and the altar. (Matthew 23:34-35)

> It is enough for the disciple that he be as his master, and the servant as his lord. If they have called the master of the house Beelzebub, how much more shall they call them of his household? (Matthew 10:25)

> And ye shall be hated of all men for my name's sake: but he that shall endure unto the end, the same shall be saved. (Mark 13:13)

> If the world hate you, ye know that it hated me before it hated you. If ye were of the world, the world would love his own: but because ye are not of the world, but I have chosen you out of the world, therefore the world hateth you . . . . If they have persecuted me, they will also persecute you . . . . (John 15:18-20)

> They shall put you out of the synagogues: yea, the time cometh, that whosoever killeth you will think that he doeth God service. (John 16:2)

What a dismal picture! The disciples were not only sent out into the world to preach the Kingdom of God, but to give themselves up as martyrs for the faith. The word *martyr*, of course, comes from the Greek word for "witness" -- and that is exactly what Jesus' disciples were. They were martyred as witnesses to the truthfulness of the message and the wickedness of the world.

Note 2: Monasticism -- Replacing the Spiritual Gifts

What replaced the spiritual gifts? We have seen that, in large part, the light of revelation was replaced by the philosophies of men. However, another movement, known as "monasticism" was born out of the effort to reclaim the lost gifts. In Eastern Orthodoxy and Roman Catholicism today, there are thousands of ascetic monks and nuns who separate themselves from the world to live apart, seeking union with God. This lifestyle is held out as the ideal of human life, and many devout seekers are attracted to the movement.[147]

How did this ascetic movement get started? No mention of such a thing is made in the New Testament[148], although the roots of Christian monasticism can be traced back to the second century, when Christianity was rapidly incorporating pagan culture and belief.[149] It never really took hold in the Church[150], however, until the persecutions had ended and Christianity was adopted as the official religion of the state in the fourth century.[151] In this atmosphere, a great number of "lukewarm" Christians were attracted to the Church, and many were disturbed at the course the Church was taking.[152] As J.G. Davies says, "The desert fathers indeed fled not so much from the world as from the Church."[153]

What were these desert fathers seeking? It was not just seclusion from worldliness they sought, but the development of techniques that would produce the lost gifts. Even today in the Eastern Orthodox Church, monks and nuns "are often called the prophets of the New Covenant and the forerunners of the Kingdom to come."[154] One modern champion of the monastic way, Robin Amis, compares this discipline with Zen or Raja Yoga and explains that the gifts of the spirit are produced by following certain psycho-spiritual techniques:

> The inner tradition is a Christian equivalent of Zen or Raja Yoga . . . . In its full form, the psychological method to which I refer represents what was known in the early church as the Royal Road. This name was once given to certain therapeutic psychological and psycho-spiritual techniques developed by Christians who followed Christ's narrow way. The Royal Road was a science based on the gospel teaching about the cure of the soul -- by curing the *nous* [Greek "mind"], sometimes known as the eye of the soul. This leads to what was then known as the illumination of the nous, and so develops the hidden potential or talents of the individual, once described by Saint Paul as the Gifts of the Spirit.[155]

In contrast, the *Didache* warned that a true prophet will not teach others to prophesy, etc., by following any "psycho-spiritual technique" -- it is a gift of God! "And every prophet, proved true, working unto the mystery of the Church in the world, yet not teaching others to do what he himself doeth, shall not be judged among you, for with God he hath his judgment; for so did also the ancient prophets."[156] In addition, the author of *Barnabas* warned the Church not to go live apart from the world: "Do not, by retiring apart, live a solitary life, as if you were already [fully] justified; but coming together in one place, make common inquiry concerning what tends to your general welfare."[157] Indeed, the acceptance of monasticism by the Church in general was a very gradual process, and even as late as ca. A.D. 360 a converted pagan is reported to have asked: "Explain to me now what is the congregation or sect of monks, and why it is an object of aversion, even amongst our own people?"[158] Robert Markus calls the ascetic takeover of the Church "the end of ancient Christianity."[159]

Chapter 3: The Doctrine of God and the Nature of Man

"Could you gaze into heaven five minutes, you would know more than you would by reading all that ever was written on the subject."
- Joseph Smith[160]

Perhaps the most fundamental questions a religion must answer are those relating to the nature of God and man's relationship to Him. Jesus said, "This is life eternal, that they might know thee the only true God, and Jesus Christ, whom thou hast sent." (John 17:3) In order to "know God" fully, one must also know *about* Him. As our Lord told the Samaritan woman, "Ye worship ye know not what: we know what we worship . . . ." (John 4:22)

The Prophet Joseph Smith claimed to have restored vital truths about God and man that had been lost for many centuries. However, some of these doctrines are controversial to the rest of the Christian world, and so this is exactly the area where Latter-day Saints are most often criticized by their Christian neighbors. For example, Evangelical leader E. Calvin Beisner, in the introduction to his defense of the mainline Trinity doctrine, brushes aside the Latter-day Saint doctrine of God as "polytheism."[161]   And Anti-Mormon activists Ed Decker and Dave Hunt go further, insisting that Mormons "have a completely different God from what the Bible presents," and that the Mormon idea that men have the potential to become like God "is basically derived from ancient pagan traditions."[162]

Where exactly do the doctrines Joseph Smith restored relating to these issues fit in with the corresponding mainline teachings, and how do each of these systems compare to the earliest Christian beliefs? In this chapter it will be shown that Joseph Smith restored early Christian doctrines about God and man that were gradually replaced in a complex struggle between the original Church, Greek philosophy, and Gnosticism.

The LDS Godhead vs. the Mainstream Trinity

As has been discussed, the purpose of this book is to examine the thesis that the Church of Jesus Christ of Latter-day Saints is a restoration of ancient Christianity. Given this, one would expect to see a trend in the history of Christian doctrine starting from something very similar to the LDS position and ending with current mainstream teachings. Therefore, before we examine this hypothesis with respect to the doctrine of God, it will be necessary to define exactly what the LDS and mainstream belief systems include.

The LDS Concept of the Godhead

"We believe in God, the Eternal Father, and in His Son, Jesus Christ, and in the Holy Ghost." (Article of Faith 1) While this statement of faith may seem perfectly mainstream, there are many significant differences between the LDS doctrine of God and that of the bulk of the Christian world. Moreover the differences between any two doctrines of the Godhead in Christianity can usually be understood by comparing the ways in which a number of scriptural propositions are combined and interpreted.

The Godhead of the Bible

The Bible contains four propositions about God that every Christian denomination must reckon with in its theology. (1) First, is that the Bible contains several strongly monotheistic statements. When Moses says, "Hear, O Israel: The LORD our God is one LORD" (Deuteronomy 6:4), he means, as the Muslims say, "There is no God but God." This view also finds support in God's statement to Isaiah that, "I am he: before me there was no God formed, neither shall there be after me." (Isaiah 43:10) This tradition is continued in the New Testament as, for example, when Jesus prayed to the Father he said, "And this is life eternal: that they might know thee the only true God, and Jesus Christ, whom thou hast sent." (John 17:3)

(2) Second, there is a person called the Father, who is identified as God. The example of Christ's "high-priestly prayer," quoted in part above, should be ample evidence of this fact.

(3) Third, there is a person called the Son in the New Testament, namely Jesus Christ, who is called God. Clearly identifying Jesus as "the Word," John wrote, "In the beginning was the Word, and the Word was with God, and the Word was God." (John 1:1)[163] Here Jesus is presented as God, but also as distinct from the Father, hence the phrase, "and the Word was with God." There are numerous other examples of this throughout the New Testament. For instance, when confronted by the resurrected Christ, Thomas exclaimed, "My Lord and my God." (John 20:28) Paul preached to the Church that they should, "Take heed . . . to feed Church of God, which he hath purchased with his own blood." (Acts 20:28) Finally, Jesus Christ unequivocally identified himself as Jehovah, the God of the Old Testament when he said, "Before Abraham was, I am." (John 8:58)

(4) Fourth, there is a person called the Holy Spirit who is identified as God. That the Holy Spirit is God is shown by Peter's accusation of Ananias, "Why hath Satan filled thine heart to lie to the Holy Ghost? . . . Thou hast not

lied unto men, but unto God." (Acts 5:3-4) The New Testament also teaches that the Holy Spirit is a person, distinct from the Father and Son: "But the Comforter, which is the Holy Ghost, whom the Father will send in my name, he shall teach you all things, and bring all things to your remembrance, whatsoever I have said unto you." (John 14:26; see also Acts 13:2)

One God or Three?

Naturally, these propositions present a problem. Are there three Gods or one? For Latter-day Saints, it is acceptable to say both that there is one God, and that there is a plurality of Gods, depending on the context. For example, in one sense the Father is "the only true God." "Paul says there are Gods many and Lords many . . . ; but to us there is but one God -- that is *pertaining to us*; and he is in all and through all."[164] That is, even if there are other Gods, the one with ultimate power and authority pertaining to us is the Father. In another sense there is a plurality of Gods. Again, quoting Joseph Smith, "I have always declared [that] . . . these three constitute three distinct personages and three Gods."[165]

And in yet another sense, the Father, Son, and Holy Spirit can be spoken of as "one God." The *Book of Mormon* prophet Nephi preached the way to salvation, which he called "the doctrine of Christ, and the only and true doctrine of the Father, and of the Son, and of the Holy Ghost, which is one God, without end." (2 Nephi 31:21) What is the nature of this "oneness"? In Jesus' great Intercessory Prayer (see John 17)[166], He asked that His disciples would be made one in Him as He was one in the Father. Joseph Smith explained:

> Many men say there is one God; the Father, the Son and the Holy Ghost are only one God. I say that is a strange God anyhow -- three in one, and one in three! It is a curious organization. "Father, I pray not for the world, but I pray for them which thou hast given me." "Holy Father, keep through Thine own name those whom thou has given me, that they may be one as we are." All are to be crammed into one God, according to sectarianism. It would make the biggest God in all the world. He would be a wonderfully big God -- he would be a giant or a monster. I want to read the text to you myself -- "I am agreed with the Father and the Father is agreed with me, and we are agreed as one." The Greek shows that it should be agreed. "Father, I pray for them which Thou has given me out of the world, and not for those alone, but for them also which shall believe on me through their word, that they all may be agreed, as Thou, Father, are with me, and I with Thee, that they also may be agreed with us," and all come to dwell in unity, and in all the glory and everlasting burnings of the Gods; and then we

shall see as we are seen, and be as our God and He as His Father.[167]

Therefore, the Godhead consists of truly separate beings -- even separate Gods -- who are one in the sense of their total unity of will and love. The Prophet correctly noted that this type of oneness is consistent with Jesus' expectation that his disciples would be "one" as He and the Father are "one." (John 17:11, 21-24)

Consistent with the idea that the Father is the "only true God," the Prophet also preached "subordinationism," the idea that the Son and Spirit are subordinate in power, rank, and glory to the Father. "Any person that had seen the heavens opened knows that there are three personages in the heavens who hold the keys of power, and one [the Father] presides over all."[168]

What Kind of Being is God?

The Prophet also taught a startling doctrine about the *physical* nature of God. He preached that "if you were to see [God] today, you would see him like a man in form,"[169] and that "the Father has a body of flesh and bones as tangible as man's; the Son also; but the Holy Ghost has not a body of flesh and bones, but is a personage of Spirit." (D&C 130:22) Indeed, the Spirit of God and the spirit of man are both *material* substance. (D&C 131:7-8) Consistent with all of this, Joseph Smith taught that man is of the same race as God. The spirit of man existed before this mortal life, and man is capable of becoming like his Father in Heaven.[170]

The Mainstream Trinity

The Nicene Creed

When mainline Christians see the basic propositions about God discussed above, along with statements that "[Christ] and the Father are one" (John 10:30), they conclude that the doctrine of the Trinity as expressed in the Nicene Creed of 325 A.D. is the only logical explanation:

> We believe in one God, the Father Almighty, maker of all things visible and invisible; and in one Lord Jesus Christ, the Son of God, the only-begotten of his Father, of the substance of the Father, God of God, Light of Light, very God of very God, begotten, not made, being of one substance with the Father. By whom all things were made, both which be in heaven and in earth. Who for us men and for our salvation came down [from heaven] and was incarnate and was made man. He suffered and the third day he rose again, and ascended into heaven. And he shall come again to judge

both the quick and the dead. And [we believe] in the Holy Ghost. And whosoever shall say that there was a time when the Son of God was not, or that before he was begotten he was not, or that he was made of things that were not, or that he is of a different substance or essence [from the Father] or that he is a creature, or subject to change or conversion -- all that so say, the Catholic and Apostolic Church anathematizes them.[171]

That is, there is only one God, but that God is composed of three distinct persons who share in the same *substance* or *essence*.[172]

"Of One Substance"

Was this the original interpretation of the scriptural passages in question? Modern scholars agree that the Nicene view introduced new elements into the standard interpretations that had not been accepted by the earliest Church. For example, Maurice Wiles concludes that, "The emergence of the full trinitarian doctrine was not possible without significant modification of previously accepted ideas."[173]

Specifically, the phrase, "of one substance or essence," expresses a concept that was adopted and adapted from contemporary Greek philosophy, but was foreign to the thought of the original Christianity. This concept may seem strange to the modern reader because Greek philosophy is no longer the predominant system of thought, although it has remained the basis of many aspects of mainstream Christian theology even to the present time. At the time the Nicene Creed was adopted, the predominant philosophy was a hodgepodge of ideas, mostly based on Neoplatonism and a few other schools of thought. These schools, in turn, largely based their ideas on the thought of a few earlier philosophers, notably Plato, Empedocles and Xenophanes. A quick summary of how these philosophers viewed God should make the language of the Nicene Creed clear to the reader. (Although the Christians modified the terminology of the philosophers to fit their purposes, one still cannot make sense of their language without reference to these Hellenistic ideas.)[174]

Plato, realizing the material world was ever changing, speculated that it was impossible to obtain true knowledge by observing the natural world. But he had faith that true knowledge was possible, so he posited an unchanging, perfect world that was a higher reality than the material. He called this region or dimension the world of "Ideas" or "Forms." These "Ideas" were considered the perfect essences of various objects or attributes. For example, a waterfall and a person can both be said to be "beautiful" although they seem to have nothing material in common. Plato suggested that there must be an "Idea" or essence in the world of Forms -- perfect and unchanging -- called "The Beautiful," in which both the person and the waterfall participate.[175] Similarly, Plato's idea of God was a perfect, unchanging, indivisible essence known as "The Divine," or "The One."[176]

Xenophanes and Empedocles expressed similar ideas of what God must be like. Xenophanes (570-475 B.C.) conceived of "God as thought, as presence, as all powerful efficacy." He is one God -- incorporeal, "unborn, eternal, infinite, . . . not moving at all, [and] beyond human imagination."[177] And Empedocles (ca. 444 B.C.) claimed that God "does not possess a head and limbs similar to those of humans . . . . A spirit, a holy and inexpressible one . . . ."[178]

Therefore, in the Greek world it was more acceptable for the Christians to say that there are three, distinct persons who are a single "Divine essence or substance" -- or as Plato would say, "The Divine." But these three persons cannot be said to be three Gods, because the divine essence must be indivisible and simple. Many Christians envision the Trinity as three "centers of consciousness" within the one God, but even this is inadequate to express the ineffable reality of God.

More on the "Being" of God

Consistent with this conception of the "Divine Substance," God cannot be said to be a material being, for matter is a lower reality than a pure "Idea." Thus, the ancient Greek philosophers and modern mainstream Christians would agree that God is incorporeal, without a material body or human emotions, immovable, indivisible, and therefore ultimately incomprehensible to humanity.

This theory of the nature of God began to be adopted into Christian thought in the late second century. Christopher Stead writes that the early Christian writers Irenaeus (A.D. 130-200), Clement of Alexandria (A.D. 150-215) and Novatian (ca. 250) believed in a God who is "simple and not compounded, uniform and wholly alike in himself, being wholly mind and wholly spirit . . . wholly hearing, wholly sight, wholly light, and wholly the source of all good things." This, Stead points out, is almost identical to Xenophanes' assertion that "All of him sees, all thinks and all hears." And "since Clement elsewhere quotes Xenophanes verbatim, we have good grounds for thinking that Clement's description, and indeed the theory as a whole, derives from Xenophanes."[179]

Thus, we see that to interpret what is meant by the mainstream Christian creeds, we must appeal to the ideas of the Greek philosophers. We also see that the concepts of deity derived from these sources are contrary to the doctrines and teachings presented in the New Testament.

From "the One True God" to "the One"

As stated in the beginning, the purpose of this study is to examine the relationship between the system of thought Joseph Smith restored and original Christian doctrine. To do this effectively, we will both provide evidence that the Prophet restored the original Christian doctrine of God and discuss how this doctrine was lost during the first few centuries after Christ. We have seen that there are commonalities between the LDS and mainstream doctrines, but in some of the most important areas there are significant differences between them. Accordingly, the journey from "point A" to "point B" did not happen overnight, but the first fatal step was taken early on, when the framers of early Christian thought substituted the New Testament concept of the one true God for "the One" of the philosophers.

The God of Israel and the God of the Philosophers

At first, Christianity did not appeal to Greek philosophy to explain its doctrines. Edwin Hatch points out that the earliest Christians eschewed philosophical speculations in favor of *revealed* truths.[180] This ceased more and more to be the case, however, as Christianity foundered in the spiritual darkness left by the loss of the prophetic gifts.

Although we have established that the mainline doctrine of God was based on Greek philosophical tenets[181], it still remains to be shown how these concepts infiltrated the Church to such an extent that they became the official doctrine of Christianity. We shall see that after adopting this Greek conception of God, it took many years of struggle to work out the logical conclusions of such a doctrine. And in this struggle, the old doctrines about God were consistently and steadily compromised.

As mentioned above, the Greek conception of God began to creep into mainstream Christianity around the middle of the second century. Christian apologists such as Justin, Athenagoras, and others who wished to rebut pagan criticisms of their doctrine, defended their faith by claiming that they worshipped the same God as the pagan philosophers. In doing so they were following the lead of earlier Hellenized Jews such as Philo of Alexandria, who had spiritualized the biblical account of the God of Israel in order to identify Him with the God of the philosophers. While, as Hatch indicates, there was no significant evidence of Greek influence in the Primitive Church, consider the similarity between the conceptions of God taught by the Middle Platonists Plutarch and Numenius, and various late second-century Christian intellectuals. First the philosophers:

> Socrates and Plato held that (God is) the One, the single self-existent nature, the monadic, the real Being, the good: and all this variety of names points immediately to mind. God therefore is mind, a separate species, that is to say what is purely immaterial and unconnected with anything passible.[182]

But let no one laugh, if I affirm that the name of the incorporeal is "essence" and "being." And the cause of the name "being" is that it has not been generated nor will be destroyed, nor is it subject to any other motion at all, nor any change for better or for worse; but is simple and unchangeable, and in the same idea, and neither willingly departs from its sameness, nor is compelled by any other to depart.[183]

Now the teachings of early Christian thinkers -- Athenagoras, Clement of Alexandria, and Irenaeus, respectively:

That we are not atheists, therefore, seeing that we acknowledge one God, uncreated, eternal, invisible, impassible, incomprehensible, illimitable, who is apprehended by the understanding only and the reason, who is encompassed by light, and beauty, and spirit, and power ineffable, by whom the universe has been created through His Logos, and set in order, and is kept in being -- I have sufficiently demonstrated.[184]

No one can rightly express Him wholly. For on account of His greatness He is ranked as the All, and is the Father of the universe. Nor are any parts to be predicated of Him. For the One is indivisible; wherefore also it is infinite, not considered with reference to inscrutability, but with reference to its being without dimensions, and not having a limit. And therefore it is without form and name. And if we name it, we do not do so properly, terming it either the One, or the Good, or Mind, or Absolute Being, or Father, or God, or Creator or Lord.[185]

For the Father of all is at a vast distance from those affections and passions which operate among men. He is a simple, uncompounded Being, without diverse members, and altogether like, and equal to himself, since He is wholly understanding, and wholly spirit, and wholly thought, and wholly intelligence, and wholly reason, and wholly hearing, and wholly seeing, and wholly light, and the whole source of all that is good -- even as the religious and pious are wont to speak concerning God.[186]

And as if it weren't enough that Clement called the Father "the One" and "Mind," witness Tertullian's identification of the Father as "the God of the philosophers" around the turn of the third century:

> Whatever attributes therefore you require as worthy of God, must be found in the Father, who is invisible and unapproachable, and placid, and (so to speak) the God of the philosophers; whereas those qualities which you censure as unworthy must be supposed to be in the Son . . . .[187]

Therefore, by the end of the second century the Father was evidently identified with "the One" of the philosophers.

The Abandonment of Anthropomorphism

If Christianity was to accept the God of the philosophers, however, it had to shed certain "primitive" beliefs that characterized the God of Israel. Chief among these beliefs was the idea that God is a material being whose physical form is that of a man. This type of "anthropomorphism"[188] was unacceptable, since as Grace Jantzen observes, "According to a Platonic system of thought, it would be utterly inconceivable that God should have a material body."[189]

The Anthropomorphic God of the Bible

On the other hand, in the Bible God often appeared as a man. For instance, Moses, Aaron, Nadab, and Abihu, and seventy of the elders of Israel "saw the God of Israel: and there was under his feet as it were a paved work of sapphire stone." (Exodus 24:9-11) And in another appearance, God told Moses that he could not see His face at that time, but said he would "cover thee with my hand while I pass by: And I will take away mine hand, and thou shalt see my back parts." (Exodus 33:22-23) Ezekiel recounted yet another example: "Above the vault over their heads there appeared, as it were, a sapphire in the shape of a throne, and high above all, upon the throne, a form in human likeness." (Ezekiel 1:26 NEB) Edmond LaB. Cherbonnier of Trinity College summarizes these ideas as follows: "In short, to use the forbidden word, the biblical God is clearly anthropomorphic -- not apologetically so, but proudly, even militantly."[190] Christopher Stead of the Cambridge Divinity School agrees that, "The Hebrews . . . pictured the God whom they worshipped as having a body and mind like our own, though transcending humanity in the splendour of his appearance, in his power, his wisdom, and the constancy of his care for his creatures."[191]

Anthropomorphism in Early Christianity

Evidently the earliest Christians believed in the anthropomorphic God of the Old Testament. For example, Stephen saw in vision "the Son of Man standing at God's right hand." (Acts 7:56 NEB) And according the early reports of the rabbis about the "Two Powers" heresies, which included Christianity, all of these sects "picture God Himself as a man or posit a principal angel, with the shape of a man, who aids God in the governance of the world."[192] The *Clementine Homilies*, a Jewish Christian document based on a second-century source, also expressed the early anthropomorphic belief:

> And Simon said: "I should like to know, Peter, if you really believe that the shape of man has been moulded after the shape of God." And Peter said: "I am really quite certain, Simon, that this is the case . . . . It is the shape of the just God."[193]

> For He has shape, and He has every limb primarily and solely for beauty's sake, and not for use. For He has not eyes that He may see with them; for He sees on every side, since He is incomparably more brilliant in His body than the visual spirit which is in us, and He is more splendid than everything, so that in comparison with Him the light of the sun may be reckoned as darkness. Nor has He ears that He may hear; for He hears, perceives, moves, energizes, acts on every side. But He has the most beautiful shape on account of man, that the pure in heart, may be able to see Him, that they may rejoice because they suffered. For He moulded man in His own shape as in the grandest seal, in order that he may be the ruler and lord of all, and that all may be subject to him.[194]

A third century document, the apocryphal *Gospel of Bartholomew*, was also very specific about the physical nature of God. In this account the Father made an appearance to Mary in human form and ate and drank with her:

> When I abode in the temple of God and received my food from an angel, on a certain day there appeared unto me one in the likeness of an angel, but his face was incomprehensible . . . . I was not able to endure the sight of him . . . . And said unto me: Hail, thou that art highly favoured, the chosen vessel, grace inexhaustible. And he smote his garment upon the right hand and there came a very great loaf, and he set it upon the altar of the temple and did eat of it first himself, and gave unto me also. And again he smote his garment upon the left hand and there came a very great cup full of wine: and he set it upon the altar of the temple and did drink of it first himself, and gave also unto me . . . . And he said unto me: Yet three years, and I will

send my word unto thee and thou shalt conceive my . . . son, and through him shall the whole creation be saved.[195]

In the fourth century, certain monks of the Thebaid in Egypt "were of strongly anthropomorphic views."[196] One of the monks, Serapion, disagreed with the teaching of God's incorporeality, calling it a "novelty." After being reluctantly convinced on intellectual grounds that he was wrong, he burst into tears and exclaimed, "They have taken away my God from me, and now I don't have anything to lay hold of; I don't know whom to worship, whom to call upon."[197] Similarly, group called the Audians , who founded monasteries in Gothic territory in the fourth century, also refused change their belief that God was in form like a man. "Had not God said 'Let us make man in our image'? then what form could He bear other than that of man? they asked."[198]

Naturally, since a different view finally prevailed, many of the early sources that explicitly taught anthropomorphism have been lost. However, several Christian writers from the second through the fifth centuries gave witness to the fact that even though they themselves rejected the old doctrine, there were many contemporary Christians who still accepted it. For example, Jean Daniélou reports that Clement of Alexandria testified to the existence of early Christian belief in God's material body in human form, even though such an idea flatly contradicted Clement's own thought.[199]

Clement's successor, Origen, presents another interesting case. Against the second-century pagan critic Celsus, who scoffed at this early Christian belief, Origen actually *denied that such a belief even existed within Christianity!*

> After this Celsus relates at length opinions which he ascribes to us, but which we do not hold, regarding the Divine Being, to the effect that "he is corporeal in his nature, and possesses a body like a man." As he undertakes to refute opinions which are none of ours, it would be needless to give either the opinions themselves or their refutation. Indeed, if we did hold those views of God which he ascribes to us, and which he opposes, we would be bound to quote his words, to adduce our own arguments, and to refute his. But if he brings forward opinions which he has either heard from no one, or if it be assumed that he has heard them, it must have been from those who are very simple and ignorant of the meaning of Scripture, then we need not undertake so superfluous a task as that of refuting them.[200]

And yet, in another work Origen named Melito, bishop of Sardis in the late second century, as one of the Christians who believed God to have a material body in human form.[201] Similarly, in yet another work, he confessed that the issue of God's corporeality was still an open question in Christian teaching:

We shall inquire, however, whether the thing which Greek philosophers call *asomaton*, or "incorporeal," is found in holy Scripture under another name. For it is also to be a subject of investigation how God himself is to be understood, -- whether as corporeal, and formed according to some shape, or of a different nature from bodies, -- a point which is not clearly indicated in our teaching.[202]

Origen rejected anthropomorphism, not because the scriptures or unanimous Christian tradition specifically rejected it, but because *the philosophers* "despised" it: "The Jews indeed, but also some of our people, supposed that God should be understood as a man, that is, adorned with human members and human appearance. But the philosophers despise these stories as fabulous and formed in the likeness of poetic fictions."[203]

Evidently Augustine tried the same tactic in the fifth century. Augustine, who grew up as a well-educated pagan, but had a Christian mother, rejected the Church at first because he thought all the Christians believed in an anthropomorphic God, which to him was philosophically absurd:

I was hopeless of finding the truth, from which in Thy Church, O Lord of heaven and earth, Creator of all things visible and invisible, [the Manichaeans] had turned me aside, -- and it seemed to me most unbecoming to believe Thee to have the form of human flesh, and to be bounded by the bodily lineaments of our members. And because, when I desired to meditate on my God, I knew not what to think of but a mass of bodies (for what was not such did not seem to me to be), this was the greatest and almost sole cause of my inevitable error.[204]

But when he heard Ambrose of Milan speak, claiming that all those passages in the Bible which suggested anthropomorphism were to be interpreted figuratively, Augustine was intrigued and was eventually converted.

For first, these things also had begun to appear to me to be defensible; and the Catholic faith, for which I had fancied nothing could be said against the attacks of the Manichaeans, I now conceived might be maintained without presumption; especially after I had heard one or two parts of the Old Testament explained, and often allegorically -- which when I accepted literally, I was "killed" spiritually . . . . But so soon as I understood, withal, that man made "after the image of Him that created him" was not so understood by Thy spiritual sons . . . as though they believed and imagined Thee to be bounded by human form, -- although what was the nature of a spiritual substance I had not the faintest or dimmest suspicion, -- yet rejoicing, I blushed that for so many years I had barked, not against the Catholic faith, but against the fables of carnal imaginations.[205]

It is perfectly obvious that if Augustine, who grew up with a Christian mother and even went to Christian catechism, believed all his life that Christians believed in an anthropomorphic God, there must have been a fair number of Christians who *actually did* retain that belief. Indeed, in another place Augustine complained of the "carnal and weak of our faith, who . . . picture God to themselves in human form."[206] But like Origen, we find him later denying that such a belief existed at all.

The Son Becomes the Anthropomorphic God

When the Father became "the One" of the philosophers, it was not acceptable to ascribe any type of anthropomorphism to Him, so various strategies were employed to sidestep the language of the Bible. For example, we have seen that later theologians such as Augustine took the relevant passages figuratively. But in the second century, when the God of the Philosophers was first being adopted, this was not necessarily the case. Some of these Christian thinkers *accepted* Biblical anthropomorphism, but ascribed it all to the Son. For instance, consider the following passages from Justin Martyr and Irenaeus which state, respectively, that 1) God the Father does not have a human form; 2) nevertheless, the body of man is created in the *physical image* of God; and 3) the Son was the God who appeared to the prophets in human form. First Justin:

These and other such sayings are recorded by the lawgiver and by the prophets; and I suppose that I have stated sufficiently, that wherever God says, "God went up from Abraham," or, "The Lord spake to Moses," and "The Lord came down to behold the tower which the sons of men had built," or when "God shut Noah into the ark," you must not imagine that the unbegotten God Himself came down or went up from any place. For the ineffable Father and Lord of all neither has come to any place, nor walks, nor sleeps, nor rises up, but remains in His own place, wherever that is, quick to behold and quick to hear, having neither eyes nor ears, but being of indescribable might; and He sees all things, and knows all things, and none of us escapes His observation; and He is not moved or confined to a spot in the whole world, for He existed before the world was made.[207]

For does not the word say, "Let Us make man in our image, and after our likeness?" What kind of man? Manifestly He means fleshly man. For the word says, "And God took dust of the earth, and made man." It is evident, therefore, that man made in the image of God was of flesh.[208]

For I have proved that it was Jesus who appeared to and conversed with Moses, and Abraham, and all the other patriarchs without exception, ministering to the will of the Father; who also, I say, came to be born man by the Virgin Mary, and lives for ever.[209]

Next Irenaeus:

Again, as to their malignantly asserting that if heaven is indeed the throne of God, and earth His footstool, and if it is declared that the heaven and earth shall pass away, then when these pass away the God who sitteth above must also pass away, and therefore He cannot be the God who is over all; in the first place, they are ignorant what the expression means, that heaven is [His] throne and earth [His] footstool. For [the Valentinian Gnostics] do not know what God is, but they imagine that He sits after the fashion of a man, and is contained within bounds, but does not contain.[210]

But man He fashioned with His own hands, taking of the purest and finest of earth, in measured wise mingling with the earth His own power; for He gave his frame the outline of His own form, that the visible appearance too should be godlike -- for it was an image of God that man was fashioned and set on earth . . . .[211]

For not alone upon Abraham's account did He say these things, but also that he might point out how all who have known God from the beginning, and have foretold the advent of Christ, have received the revelation from the Son Himself . . . . He is therefore one and the same God, who called Abraham and gave him the promise . . . . Therefore have the Jews departed from God, in not receiving His Word, but imagining that they could know the Father [apart] by Himself, without the Word, that is, without the Son; they being ignorant of that God who spake in human shape to Abraham, and again to Moses . . . .[212]

66

"God is a Spirit" -- That is, Corporeal

In response to the LDS doctrine that God has a material body, mainline Christians often point to Jesus' teaching that "God is a Spirit" (John 4:24) and conclude that God has no physical form, but is "everywhere present." However, it is not a contradiction to say that "God is a spirit" and that He also has a body. For example, Paul wrote that "he that is joined unto the Lord is one spirit." (1 Corinthians 6:17) Be that as it may, since there is no indefinite article in ancient Greek, John 4:24 could just as easily be translated, "God is Spirit." Certainly this statement must be interpreted in the same sense that John also said, "God is light" (1 John 1:5) and "God is love" (1 John 4:8). Indeed, many modern translations[213] do translate it thus.[214] These do not characterize God's "being," but rather His actions and relationship with men. "God is light" because "in him there is no darkness at all," and "if we walk in the light as he himself is in the light, then we share together a common life . . . ." (1 John 1:5-7 NEB) "God is love" because of "the love he showed to us in sending his Son . . . ." (1 John 4:8-10 NEB) "God is Spirit" because He enlightens men through His Holy Spirit, and "those who worship him must worship in spirit and in truth." (John 4:24 NEB) With respect to the ancient Hebrew concept of God, Christopher Stead notes:

> By saying that God is spiritual, we do not mean that he has no body . . . but rather that he is the source of a mysterious life-giving power and energy that animates the human body, and himself possesses this energy in the fullest measure.[215]

Furthermore, even those of the earliest Christians who rejected the notion of God having a body in human shape, and believed in a God who is "a spirit," nevertheless taught that this "spirit" was itself material.[216] Adolf von Harnack summarizes:

> God was naturally conceived and represented as corporeal by uncultured Christians, though not by these alone, as the later controversies prove . . . . In the case of the cultured, the idea of a corporeality of God may be traced back to Stoic influences; in the case of the uncultured popular ideas co-operated with the sayings of the old Testament literally understood, and the impression of the Apocalyptic images.[217]

Specifically, the "cultured" Christians who were influenced by Stoicism believed that there is nothing that is "immaterial." For instance, even though Tertullian did not believe that God has a human form[218], he argued strenuously that He must be material. "For who will deny that God is a body, although 'God is a Spirit?' For Spirit has a bodily substance of its own kind, in its own form."[219] Later, Origen argued for the *incorporeality* of God, but felt he had to defend his thesis against those who would point to John 4:24 as proof of God's *corporeality*.

> I know that some will attempt to say that, even according to the declarations of our own Scriptures, God is a body, because in the writings of Moses they find it said, that "our God is a consuming fire;" and in the Gospel according to John, that "God is a Spirit, and they who worship Him must worship Him in spirit and in truth." Fire and spirit, according to them, are to be regarded as nothing else than a body.[220]

Compare the aforementioned with Joseph Smith's teaching that there is no fundamental dichotomy between matter and "spirit":

> There is no such thing as immaterial matter. All spirit is matter, but it is more fine or pure, and can only be discerned by purer eyes. We cannot see it; but when our bodies are purified we shall see that it is all matter. (D&C 131:7-8)

Thus, when Latter-day Saints speak of God as a "spirit" or of the "spirit" in man they do not visualize something essentially different from any other matter--just a finer and purer substance.

Allegorical Interpretation

As was mentioned above, all traces of anthropomorphism were later suppressed through the allegorical interpretation of the scriptures. But consider the danger in this type of arbitrary exegesis. In practice, one can throw out any doctrines that are inconvenient or out of date and replace them with whatever philosophies are in vogue. In fact, Augustine took it as his rule to do just that. "Whatever there is in the word of God that cannot, when taken literally, be referred either to purity of life or soundness of doctrine, you may set down as figurative."[221] Who is to judge whether a doctrine is "sound"? For Augustine, that which was philosophically absurd could not be taken literally.

Some argue that scripture often speaks of God having "wings" (e.g. Ruth 2:12; Psalm 17:8; 36:7; 57:1; 63:7; 91:4; Malachi 4:2), etc., so why should we not take the biblical references to God's human members figuratively, as well? In all cases where God is said to have wings, the context indicates a clear metaphor. For instance, when the Psalmist wrote, "in the shadow of thy wings will I make my refuge" (Psalm 57:1), he alluded to the image of a mother hen gathering her chicks under her wings (cf. Matthew 23:37). On the other hand, when Ezekiel wrote that he saw God with "a form in human likeness" (Ezekiel 1:26 NEB), he stated it as a fact, not as a poetic metaphor for some abstract principle.

Christianity adopted the practice of allegorical interpretation from the Greek philosophical schools. The exploits of the Greek gods and goddesses are well known, of course, but it is less well known that no educated Greek would have taken these myths seriously. However, these legends, as recorded in the tales of Homer and others, were an integral part of the religious heritage of the Greeks, so they couldn't just throw them out when belief in a pantheon of gods went out of fashion. Therefore, the myths were interpreted allegorically. Edwin Hatch writes that this method of interpretation became standard procedure in the Hellenistic world.[222]

This was unquestionably *not* the case for the first Christians.[223] For example, Aristides, the earliest apologist, roundly rebuked the Greeks for allegorically interpreting their legends. "For if the stories about them be mythical, the gods are nothing more than mere names; . . . and if the stories be allegorical, they are myths and nothing more."[224] How sad that Christianity adopted this thoroughly Greek practice wholesale, at least with respect to passages dealing with God's physical form.[225] Cherbonnier comments on the fundamental incompatibility of the anthropomorphic God of the Bible and the God of the philosophers:

> Such authoritative utterances, expressing the consensus of most religious philosophers, have persuaded theologians that no thinking person could subscribe to the idea of God as Person. In the name of reason, therefore, they long ago made a fateful decision. They decided to tone down this conception and to reach an accommodation with the philosophical conception of "the divine." With the wisdom of hindsight, it is not difficult to see that their enterprise was doomed to fail. For while making overtures to philosophy, they could not, as Christians, abandon completely the anthropomorphic God of their own liturgies, hymns, and creeds. They were thus caught in a logical dilemma. For when they ascribe to the biblical God the attributes of "the divine" as conceived by philosophy, they tacitly contradict themselves. Though they aspired to rationality, they were trying to combine two ideas of God that are mutually exclusive, and were therefore bound to end in self-contradiction.[226]

The Transcendent God

The problem of anthropomorphism in the early Church illustrates the nature of the struggle between the God of Israel and the God of the philosophers. That is, the God of Israel is a being who is in some senses not far distant from His human offspring. The God of the philosophers, however, is "transcendent" in the sense of being utterly remote from humankind, and indeed the material world as a whole. "One of the most important themes of late Hellenistic intellectualism is that of the transcendency of the supreme God, who is regarded as utterly remote from this universe and as completely incomprehensible to the mind of man."[227] After all, if the Divine Substance is a pure, Platonic form, how can God be any part of the material world, which is a lesser reality? And as material beings we must necessarily find the reality of God inexpressible, or "ineffable" -- and ultimately beyond our comprehension.

Augustine epitomized this belief when he said that "the super-eminence [or 'transcendence'[228]] of the Godhead surpasses the power of customary speech."[229] And in contrast to Jesus, who taught that "this is life eternal, that they might know thee the only true God, and Jesus Christ, whom thou hast sent" (John 17:3),[230] Gregory of Nyssa taught that the highest knowledge of God is to "comprehend that he cannot be comprehended."[231]

But according to Edwin Hatch, the earliest Christians had no concept of "transcendence." Indeed, they thought of themselves very literally as the children of God:

> From the earliest Christian teaching, indeed, the conception
> of the transcendence of God is absent. God is near to men
> and speaks to them: He is angry with them and punishes
> them: He is merciful to them and pardons them. He does all
> this through His angels and prophets, and last of all through
> His Son . . . . The conception which underlies the earliest
> expression of the belief of a Christian community is the
> simple conception of children . . . .[232]

These "simple conceptions" were soon lost, however, with the importation of Greek philosophy into the Church. "The conception . . . of the one God whose kingdom was a universal kingdom and endured throughout all ages, blended with, and passed into, the philosophical conception of a Being who was beyond time and space."[233] Thus, for Christian philosophers like Origen, "the divine nature is remote from all affection of passion and change, remaining ever unmoved and untroubled in its own summit of bliss."[234]

However, it can easily be seen that this aspect of the God of the philosophers creates numerous problems for the interpretation of the Bible. As Eric Osborn observes, "How a changeless God may be involved in history is a persistent problem in Christian thought."[235] Again, the Christian thinkers could allegorize the relevant Bible passages to some extent, but in the final analysis, it must be admitted that a God who "so loved the world that he sent his only Begotten Son" (John 3:16) is fundamentally incompatible with a God who "is remote from all affection of passion and change, remaining ever unmoved and untroubled in its own summit of bliss."

Creation "Ex Nihilo"

The Adoption of a New Doctrine

This transcendence from matter did not just mean that God is "a most pure spirit, invisible, without body, parts, or passions . . . ."[236] In addition, the post-Apostolic Christians came to believe that God created the entire material universe out of absolutely nothing (i.e. *creatio ex nihilo*), rather than out of pre-existent, chaotic matter. Perhaps in a misguided attempt to give more glory to God, Christian philosophers of the late second century discarded the early Christian and Jewish idea of creation from chaos in favor of the theory of *creatio ex nihilo*, as formulated by the Gnostic philosopher Basilides. According to Hatch, this theory penetrated the Christian community through Tatian in the second half of the second century:

> With Basilides [a second century Gnostic philosopher], the conception of matter was raised to a higher plane. The distinction of subject and object was preserved, so that the action of the Transcendent God was still that of creation and not of evolution; but it was "out of that which was not" that He made things to be . . . . The basis of the theory was Platonic, though some of the terms were borrowed from both Aristotle and the Stoics. It became itself the basis for the theory which ultimately prevailed in the Church. The transition appears in Tatian [ca. 170 A.D.][237]

Others also agree that Basilides was the ultimate author of this doctrine, and in fact Peter Hayman indicates that there is only one recognized scholar who has recently worked on the problem of its origin -- Jonathan Goldstein, who still maintains that the doctrine originated within Judaism.[238] Frances Young of the University of Birmingham gives Basilides credit for coming up with the idea of creation out of nothing and then explains that Basilides' theory was a radicalizing of the Greek idea of the transcendence of God:

> The driving force of Basilides' logic is his notion of radical transcendence . . . [is] his critique of human analogies--the ultimate God is not an anthropomorphic world-builder . . . . His idea of creation out of nothing . . . is not so much a confrontation with Greek conceptions as a radicalising of them . . .[239]

The Earliest Christians and Creation

The earliest Christians, as Hatch intimates, believed the Jewish doctrine[240] of creation from chaos. For instance, Justin Martyr wrote, "And we have been taught that He in the beginning did of His goodness, for man's sake, create all things out of unformed matter . . . ."[241] Peter himself echoed the picture presented in Genesis 1:1-2 of a watery chaos from which the world was created. The *New English Bible* translates these passages in the following way: "In the beginning of creation . . . the earth was without form and void, with darkness over the face of the abyss, and a mighty wind that swept over the surface of the waters." (Genesis 1:1-2 NEB) "There were heavens and earth long ago, created by God's word out of water and with water . . . ." (2 Peter 3:5 NEB)

Young also lists Athenagoras, Hermogenes, and Clement of Alexandria among the early Christian writers who explicitly taught creation from chaos. For example, in his *Hymn to the Paedagogus,* Clement rhapsodized: "Out of a confused heap who didst create this ordered sphere, and from the shapeless mass of matter didst the universe adorn . . . ."[242] Indeed, in the third century Origen complained that he could not understand how so many learned people could have held this opinion: "And I cannot understand how so many distinguished men have been of [the] opinion that this matter . . . was uncreated, i.e., not formed by God Himself, who is the Creator of all things, but that its nature and power were the result of chance."[243]

Reasons for the Change

If Christianity had become so enamored with Greek philosophy, why did the Church take hold of this strange doctrine of creation out of nothing when Plato himself believed in the eternity of matter? Young postulates that Christians may have accepted creation *ex nihilo* as a reaction to the rapid influx of secular philosophy. That is, they were trying to separate themselves from the mainstream of Greek philosophy, which they realized had made inroads into the Church. If so, we can see that without the guide of revelation Christians were apt to accept philosophical ideas in place of revelation and reject other revelation where it coincided with philosophy.

Perhaps it is more realistic to postulate that these second century Christian thinkers were merely eager to express their belief in God in terms the Greek world could accept, therefore they had to incorporate a radically transcendent view of deity. For example, Theophilus of Antioch was eager for chance to show that the Christian God was even more transcendent than other gods because he created everything out of nothing!

> And what great thing is it if God made the world out of existent materials? For even a human artist, when he gets material from some one, makes of it what he pleases. But the power of God is manifested in this, that out of things that are not He makes whatever He pleases . . . .[244]

Another view, adopted by David Winston, is that Christian thinkers readily adopted creation *ex nihilo* because it provided a good argument against the extreme Gnostic position that matter is not just a lower reality, but actually *evil*.[245] If this is the case, it is ironic that the doctrine apparently originated with a Gnostic teacher.

A New Terminology

In any case, the transition to this mode of thought happened nearly instantaneously. "The adoption of the view that the world was created out of nothing was almost universal in Christian circles very quickly."[246] This transition was most likely aided by the fact that seemingly contradictory language was used in the scriptures and by earlier Christian and Jewish writers. For instance, the creation account in Genesis indicates creation from a watery chaos, and the Wisdom of Solomon taught that God "created the world out of formless matter"[247], but 2 Maccabees asserted that "God made [the sky and the earth] out of nothing, and . . . man comes into being in the same way."[248] Paul seemed to imply creation out of nothing: "God . . . summons things that are not yet in existence as if they already were" (Romans 4:17 NEB), and yet we saw that Peter's language recalled the Genesis account of creation from a watery chaos. Indeed, in the very same verse Paul wrote that God "fashioned" (Greek *katertisthai* = "adjusted, put in order again, restored, repaired") the universe, but in such a way that "the visible came forth from the invisible." (Hebrews 11:3 NEB) The second-century *Pastor of Hermas* asserted that God "made out of nothing the things that exist,"[249] but in another passage clearly presupposed creation from a watery chaos: "By His strong word [He] has fixed the heavens and laid the foundations of the earth upon the waters . . . ."[250] Similarly, Frances Young writes that Philo the Jew, who was a near contemporary of Christ, spoke of things being "created from nothing" in some passages in his writings, but clearly took for granted the concept of creation from chaos in others.[251] To these ancient writers "existence" meant organized existence, and "non-existence" meant chaos.

This difficulty in expression is illustrated by the way Basilides had to pound home his idea that there was really *nothing* in the beginning: "There was nothing, no matter, no substance, nothing insubstantial, nothing simple, nothing composite, nothing non-composite, nothing imperceptible . . . ."[252] If the expression, "creation from nothing," would have had the same meaning to everyone in his audience, audience, he would not have had to take such great pains to explain himself.[253]

Theological Implications of Creation Ex Nihilo

Frances Young concludes that "underlying the most crucial episode in the emergence of the Christian doctrine of God, namely the reply to Arianism [culminating in the Nicene Council], was affirmation of creation out of nothing."[254] That is, we shall see that the argument at Nicea was all about whether Jesus Christ was part of the "Divine Substance" or a created being who could have no part in this eternal, indivisible, unchangeable Platonic "essence." For, if there are two classes of beings -- those created out of nothing and those united in the uncreated Divine Substance -- it had to be decided whether Jesus was "truly God," a part of the Divine Substance, or merely a created being. Therefore, if creation from nothing was not the original doctrine, the whole discussion at the Nicene Council was irrelevant to the earliest form of the Christian Church!

Joseph Smith on the Creation

On the other hand, Joseph Smith is again in company with the earliest Christians, and Latter-day Saints reject the notion of creation *ex nihilo*.[255] In one of the LDS creation accounts Christ says, "We will take of these materials, and we will make an earth whereon these may dwell." (Abraham 3:24) Joseph Smith spoke of this principle when he said:

> Now, the word create came from the word *baurau* which does not mean to create out of nothing; it means to organize; the same as a man would organize materials and build a ship. Hence, we infer that God had materials to organize the world out of chaos--chaotic matter, which is element . . . . Element had an existence from the time he had. The pure principles of element are principles which can never be destroyed; they may be organized and re-organized, but not destroyed. They had no beginning, and can have no end.[256]

From Godhead to Trinity

The Father had become "the One" of the philosophers. But where did that leave the Son and the Holy Spirit? The adoption of the idea of a transcendent God created a dichotomy between God and everything else, for if He created everything else out of nothing, that which is self-existent or "uncreated" is God, while "the world was made from nothing; wherefore it is not God."[257] Were the Son and Spirit "God" or part of "the world"? If they were part of the world, then they might be called "gods" in some subsidiary sense, but in reality they could never *really* be "God." And if they were really "God," then this seems to go against the axiom that the "Divine Substance" must be simple, uncompounded, eternally unchanging, etc. One can readily see that, philosophically, this was no easy problem to solve, and it took centuries for theologians to finally iron it out. In this section we will examine how this debate transformed the Christian concept of the Godhead from something quite similar to the LDS doctrine into the nebulous "Trinity" of the creeds.

The Problem of "Monotheism"

Kelly reminds us that for all the early Fathers, the "monotheistic idea, grounded in the religion of Israel, loomed large in [their] minds . . . ."[258] But what exactly was Israel's monotheistic idea, and how did Christians over the centuries adapt it to their faith? We have already seen that both Latter-day Saints and mainstream Christians can justly be called "monotheists," but in different senses. So what exactly was the tradition that "loomed large" in the minds of the early Christian fathers?

Yahweh -- Prince of Angels, Second God

A growing number of Old Testament scholars are beginning to realize that "Israel's oldest religion was not monotheistic."[259] Much of the evidence for the foregoing assertion by Margaret Barker lies with the use of the names of God in the Hebrew Bible. Four names or titles are commonly used to connote God in the Old Testament. First, the Hebrew or Canaanite word "El" simply means "God." The plural form of this word, "Elohim," literally means "Gods," but is often used to connote a single god whose supremacy and omnipotence make him "the God of gods." (Psalm 136:2; Daniel 11:36)[260] Another such designation is "Elyon" or "Most High."   "Jehovah," the anglicized version of the Hebrew "Yahweh" or "Jahveh," is the name of the God of Israel, who identified Himself as the great "I AM" (Exodus 3:14) to Moses. With few exceptions the KJV translates "Jehovah" as "LORD" in all capitals. Most mainline Christians see all these designations as referring to one divine being. However, Latter-day Saints believe that Jesus Christ, in his pre-existent state, was named "Yahweh," the God of Israel, and the Father is given the title "Elohim."

According to Margaret Barker and others, Elohim or El and Yahweh were originally considered separate deities by the ancient Israelites. El was the high God, while Yahweh was the chief among the "sons of El" -- the second God and chief archangel.[261] But according to Otto Eissfeldt, "El was never conceived of as a rival of Yahweh. He was rather considered as a figure to acknowledge whose authority meant an enhancement rather than a restriction of the authority of Yahweh."[262] Consider the following passage from Deuteronomy:

> When the Most High parceled out the nations, when he dispersed all mankind, he laid down the boundaries of every people according to the number of the sons of God; but the LORD's [Yahweh's] share was his own people, Jacob was his allotted portion. (Deuteronomy 32:8-9 NEB)

This passage seems to indicate that Yahweh was seen as the chief son of El, and was given special charge over the nation of Israel. Several other passages point to the same interpretation. For instance, according to Barker "the text of Ps. 91.9 does actually say: 'You, O Yahweh, are my refuge, You have made Elyon your dwelling place.'"[263] To show that Yahweh was originally thought of as both God and an angel, Barker demonstrates that an ancient Old Testament figure known as "the Angel of Yahweh" was equated with Yahweh himself. There is considerable evidence that the Angel of Yahweh was so interpreted, including the following:

> Gideon saw the Angel of Yahweh, and this storyteller too identified Yahweh and the Angel of Yahweh. The Angel of Yahweh appeared to Gideon (Judg. 6:11-12), and introduced himself as Yahweh (Judg. 6.12). It is then as Yahweh that he speaks to Gideon (Judg. 6.14, 16). The Angel of Yahweh disappears, and Gideon realizes whom he has seen. He fears because he has seen the Angel of Yahweh face to face (Judg. 6.22) but Yahweh reassures him that he will not die (cf. Exod. 33.20, where Yahweh said 'You cannot see my face; for man shall not see me and live')."[264]

Other passages underscore the presence of a class of beings called "the gods." For example, "God [Elohim] takes his stand in the court of heaven to deliver judgment among the gods [elohim] themselves." (Psalm 82:1 NEB) Similarly, a passage from the Dead Sea Scrolls says that God "will raise up the kingdom of Michael in the midst of the gods . . . ."[265]

After the exile, reformers promulgated the idea that there was only one God, and consequently, El and Yahweh were fused into the one God, Yahweh.[266] Although this faction never completely erased the original belief, they did succeed in inserting their view into several passages of scripture. For example, the passages from Deuteronomy quoted above are from the NEB, which has followed the text of the Greek Septuagint or the Dead Sea Scrolls. However, an examination of the King James Version shows that the Masoretic texts upon which it is based were changed to remove all reference to the gods.[267] Similarly, in Barker's view some texts like the following from Isaiah attest to the fact that the Israelites were being thus propagandized:

> I myself have made it known in full, and declared it, I and no alien god amongst you, and you are my witnesses, says the LORD [Yahweh]. I am God [El]; from this very day I am He. (Isaiah 43:12-13 NEB)

> Was it not I the LORD [Yahweh]? There is no god [El] but me; there is no god [El] other than I, victorious and able to save. Look to me and be saved, you peoples from all corners of the earth; for I am God [El] and beside me there is no other. (Isaiah 45:21-22 NEB)

Latter-day Saints can interpret these passages in two ways. First it would be acceptable to suppose, with Margaret Barker and others, that scribes succeeded in changing the texts of many of the aforementioned passages into more strongly monotheistic statements. It is perhaps more acceptable to suppose that the prophets, such as Isaiah, did write these monotheistic passages to emphasize the "oneness" of the council of the gods under the monarchy of Elohim. (E.g. witness Nephi's designation of the Godhead as "one God" in 2 Nephi 31:21.) Later on the scribes could have misinterpreted these statements and fused the two principal deities.

In any case, in later texts where Yahweh was equated with El, various angels, including Michael, were shifted to fill Yahweh's former roles.[268] It is noteworthy that in a number of these texts there were actually *two Yahwehs!* Both the High God and principal angel were so designated.[269]

However, the original belief seems to have survived among certain groups of Jews at least until the time of Christ. During the first Christian centuries the rabbis engaged in furious debate with *minim* (i.e. cultists or heretics) whom they referred to as "Two Powers" heresies. These sects, which included Christianity, all seem to have claimed that there was a second God, in many cases identifying him with Yahweh.[270]

> [One of the crucial issues in the "two powers" debate was] a tradition about a principal angel, based on Ex. 20f, said to be Metatron in the amoraic traditions but whose real significance is that he is YHWH or the bearer of the divine name (using Ex. 23:21 f.). These passages may have little in common with their origin. But they all picture God Himself as a man or posit a principal angel, with the shape of a man, who aids God in the governance of the world.[271]

Philo of Alexandria, who lived in the first century A.D., is a well-known example of a Jew who inherited such a tradition. Philo called the second God the "Word" (Greek *logos*) and indicated that He was also the chief angel. "For nothing mortal can be made in the likeness of the most high One and Father of the universe but (only) in that of the second God, who is His Logos."[272] "But if there be any as yet unfit to be called a Son of God, let him press to take his place under God's First-born, the Word, who holds the eldership among the angels, their ruler as it were."[273]

That Philo identified the second God with Yahweh can be seen in the following text: "Why does (Scripture) say that when Abraham was ninety-nine years old, 'the Lord God appeared to him and said, I am the Lord [Yahweh] thy God [Elohim]'? It gives the two appellations of the two highest powers . . ."[274]

Finally, how did Philo preserve Jewish "monotheism," such as it was? It is evident that he did so by asserting the absolute monarchy of the High God: "Not that there is any other not Most High -- for God being One 'is in heaven above and on earth beneath and there is none beside Him.' (Deut. 4:39)"[275]

Philo was a thoroughly Hellenized Jew, and some have concluded that his peculiar brand of polytheism was due to the influence of the philosophical systems. However, Barker points out that this is highly unlikely, since Philo often disagreed with the philosophers while at the same time expressing his views in their language. Also, Philo was a leader of his Jewish community, and if his theology was a significant departure from the tradition they inherited, he certainly would not have been tolerated in that capacity.[276] Therefore, "it seems more likely that Philo drew his ideas of the mediator from his people's most ancient beliefs, and only *adapted* them to Greek ways of thinking."[277]

After the first century, rabbinical Judaism moved even further away from the old doctrine. Larry Hurtado of the University of Manitoba summarizes:

> The reactions against the known "heresies" the rabbis had in mind, Jewish Christianity and Gnostic groups, may well have produced a hardening of rabbinic monotheism in the direction away from the more inclusive and monarchial monotheism and toward a more monistic or unitarian character in some rabbinic circles, as Dunn has suggested.[278]

Jesus as Yahweh -- Prince of Angels, Second God

A comparison of passages from the Old and New Testaments makes clear that Jesus was thought by the earliest Christians to be identical with Yahweh.[279] For example, Isaiah saw Yahweh in vision and John claimed that this vision was of Jesus Christ. (Isaiah 6; John 12:40-41) Isaiah identified Yahweh as the "Holy One," while in the Gospel of Matthew Jesus is called the "Holy One." (Isaiah 54:5; Matthew 11:27) Yahweh told Isaiah that beside him "there [was] no saviour"; Jesus was obviously identified as the Savior in the New Testament. (Isaiah 43:11; Luke 2:11) Just as Moses called Yahweh "the Rock," Paul insisted that "the Rock" who led the children of Israel through the wilderness was Christ. (Deuteronomy 32:3-4; 1 Corinthians 10:1-4) And, employing the same language he used in Exodus 3:14, Jesus unequivocally announced that "Before Abraham was, I am." (John 8:58)

The identification of Jesus with Yahweh was made by many early Christians after the Apostolic age. For example, Justin Martyr recorded a conversation with his Jewish friend, Trypho:

> And I said, "As you wish, Trypho, I shall come to these proofs which you seek in the fitting place; but now you will permit me first to recount the prophecies, which I wish to do in order to prove that Christ is called both God and Lord [Yahweh] of hosts . . . . The Psalm of David is this: 'The

earth is the Lord's, and the fulness thereof; the world, and all that dwell therein . . . . Who is this King of glory? The Lord [Yahweh] of Hosts, He is the King of glory.' (Ps. 24)[280]

In harmony with the LDS practice of calling the Father by the title "Elohim," which is the Hebrew plural of "God," Justin claimed that the Father has no name, only titles.

> But to the Father of all, who is unbegotten, there is no name given. For by whatever name He be called, He has as His elder the person who gives Him the name. But these words, Father, and God, and Creator, and Lord, and Master, are not names, but appellations derived from His good deeds and functions.[281]

Not only did many Christian writers identify Jesus with Yahweh, until the fifth century it was quite common to call Jesus either a "second god," the chief angel, or both.[282] (Similarly, it was made clear that the Holy Spirit occupies the third place.) For example, during the second century Justin Martyr wrote that the "first-begotten," the Logos, is the "first force after the Father:" he is "a second God, second numerically but not in will," doing only the Father's pleasure.[283] And he designated the Son as "this power which the prophetic word calls God . . . and Angel . . . ."[284] He also maintained that the Son is "in the second place, and the prophetic Spirit in the third . . . ."[285] In the same vein Hermas spoke of "the angel of the prophetic Spirit"[286] and Jesus as the "'glorious . . . angel' or 'most venerable . . . angel' . . . ."[287] The *Ascension of Isaiah* referred to both Jesus and the Spirit as angels, as well: "And I saw how my Lord worshipped, and the angel of the Holy Spirit, and how both together praised God."[288] Finally[289], Clement of Alexandria referred to Jesus as the "Second Cause"[290], and Peter in the *Clementine Recognitions* not only called Jesus both "God" and "angel," but also identified Him with Yahweh, the prince of the Sons of God mentioned in Deuteronomy 32:7-8:

> For the Most High God, who alone holds the power of all things, has divided all the nations of the earth into seventy-two parts, and over these He hath appointed angels as princes. But to the one among the archangels who is greatest, was committed the government of those who, before all others, received the worship and knowledge of the Most High God . . . . Thus the princes of the several nations are called gods. But Christ is God of princes, who is Judge of all.[291]

Around the turn of the third century, Hippolytus called Jesus "the Angel of [God's] counsel"[292], and Tertullian spoke of Christ as "second" to the Father:

> This is the perfect nativity of the Word, when He proceeds forth from God--formed by Him first to devise and think out all things under the name of Wisdom -- "The Lord created or formed me as the beginning of His ways;" . . . while I recognize the Son, I assert His distinction as second to the Father.[293]

However, he stopped short of saying there was a "second God," because he considered the Father to be the "only true God" and Jesus to be a secondary being, dependent upon the Father:

> God forbid, (is my reply) . . . . That there are, however, two Gods or two Lords, is a statement which at no time proceeds out of our mouth: not as if it were untrue that the Father is God, and the Son is God, and the Holy Ghost is God, and each is God; but because in earlier times Two were actually spoken of as God, and two as Lord, that when Christ should come He might be both acknowledged as God and designated as Lord, being the Son of Him who is both God and Lord.[294]

Well into the third century, Origen could speak of Jesus as a "second God"[295], but he added a qualification: "We are not afraid to speak, in one sense of two Gods, in another sense of one God."[296] In what sense are they "one"? "And these, while they are two, considered as persons or subsistences, are one in unity of thought, in harmony and in identity of will."[297] In another passage he identified the Son and Spirit with the seraphim in Isaiah 6:

> My Hebrew master also used to say that those two seraphim in Isaiah, which are described as having each six wings, and calling to one another, and saying, "Holy, holy, holy, is the Lord God of hosts," were to be understood of the only-begotten Son of God and of the Holy Spirit.[298]

Similarly, the presbyter Novatian maintained that Christ was both angel and God: "He has constantly received on the faith of the heavenly Scriptures, which continually say that He is both Angel and God."[299] And he equated this God/angel with the Lord (Yahweh) of Hosts:

> For, behold, Hosea the prophet says in the person of the Father: "I will not now save them by bow, nor by horses,

nor by horsemen; but I will save them by the Lord [Yahweh] their God." If God says that He saves by God, still God does not save except by Christ.[300]

He also made clear that the Spirit is subject to the Son: "But the Paraclete being less than Christ, moreover, by this very fact proves Christ to be God, from whom He has received what He declares . . . ."[301] Indeed, the unity of the Godhead is not some mysterious metaphysical "oneness," but a unity of will:

> And since He said "one" thing, let the heretics understand that He did not say "one" person. For one placed in the neuter, intimates the social concord, not the personal unity . . . . Moreover, that He says one, has reference to the agreement, and to the identity of judgment, and to the loving association itself, as reasonably the Father and Son are one in agreement, in love, and in affection; and because He is of the Father, whatsoever He is, He is the Son; the distinction however remaining, that He is not the Father who is the Son, because He is not the Son who is the Father . . . . For when two persons have one judgment, one truth, one faith, one and the same religion, one fear of God also, they are one even although they are two persons: they are the same, in that they have the same mind.[302]

Novatian didn't hesitate to name other angels "gods" as well: "[If] even the angels themselves . . . as many as are subjected to Christ, are called gods, rightly also Christ is God."[303] And yet in another sense Novatian hesitated to say there is more than one God, because all gods are subject to the Father: "Thus making Himself obedient to His Father in all things, although He also is God, yet He shows the one God the Father by His obedience, from whom also He drew His beginning. And thus He could not make two Gods . . . ."[304]

Lactantius approvingly quoted a Hermetic text which spoke of a "second God"[305], and another third-century text called *The Threefold Fruit of the Christian Life* described Jesus as the angel, Yahweh of Hosts: "When the Lord created the angels from the fire he decided to make one of them his son, he whom Isaiah called the Lord [Yahweh] of Hosts."[306]

In the fourth century, Methodius of Olympus could say that Christ was filled with the "pure and perfect Godhead," but also designated Him as first among the Archangels:

> And this was Christ, a man filled with the pure and perfect Godhead, and God received into man. For it was most suitable that the oldest of the Aeons and the first of the

81

Archangels, when about to hold communion with men, should dwell in the oldest and the first of men, even Adam.[307]

Eusebius of Caesarea likewise called Jesus a "secondary being" who is both angel and God:

Remember how Moses calls the Being, Who appeared to the patriarchs, and often delivered to them the oracles afterwards written down in Scripture sometimes God and Lord, and sometimes the Angel of the Lord. He clearly implies that this was not the Omnipotent God, but a secondary Being, rightly called the God and Lord of holy men, but the Angel of the Most High His Father.[308]

Again, Eusebius equated Jesus with Yahweh, prince of the sons of El, spoken of in Deuteronomy 32:7-8:

In these words [Deut. 32:8] surely he names first the Most High God, the Supreme God of the Universe, and then as Lord His Word, Whom we call Lord in the second degree after the God of the Universe. And their import is that all the nations and the sons of men, here called sons of Adam, were distributed among the invisible guardians of the nations, that is the angels, by the decision of the Most High God, and His secret counsel unknown to us. Whereas to One beyond comparison with them, the Head and King of the Universe, I mean to Christ Himself, as being the Only-begotten Son, was handed over that part of humanity denominated Jacob and Israel, that is to say, the whole division which has vision and piety.[309]

In another interesting passage, Eusebius compared the hierarchy of being to the sun, moon, and stars spoken of in 1 Corinthians 15:40-42:

"For there is one glory of the sun, and another glory of the moon, and another glory of the stars," says the divine Apostle; "for one star differeth from another star in glory." In this way, therefore, we must think of the order in incorporeal and intelligent Beings also, the unutterable and infinite power of the God of the universe embracing all of them together; and the second place, next to the Father, being held by the power of the Divine Word . . . . And next after this second Being there is set, as in place of a moon, a third Being, the Holy Spirit, whom also they enroll in the first and royal dignity and honour of the primal cause of the universe . . . . But this Spirit, holding a third rank, supplies those beneath out of the superior powers in Himself, notwithstanding that He also receives from another, that is from the higher and stronger, who, as we said, is second to the most high and unbegotten nature of God the King of all . . . [310]

However, in the aftermath of the Council of Nicea in 325 A.D., such language became unpopular, and some theologians tried to sweep its former popularity under the rug. For example, in the late fourth century Basil of Caesarea feigned that such a thing as a "second God" was unheard of in the "orthodox" faith:

For we do not count by way of addition, gradually making increase from unity to multitude, and saying one, two, and three, -- nor yet first, second, and third. For "I," God, "am the first, and I am the last." And hitherto we have never, even at the present time, heard of a second God.[311]

The Subordination of the Son and Spirit

Within "orthodox" circles of the pre-Nicene Church, even where terms like "second God" and "angel" were rejected, it was always made clear that the Son and Holy Spirit are subjected to the Father, who is "greater than" them. The various forms of this doctrine are known as "subordinationism," and Bettenson admits that "'subordinationism' . . . was pre-Nicene orthodoxy."[312] After all, Jesus said that "My Father is greater than I" (John 14:28), and He asserted that the He does not know the hour of His Second Coming -- only the Father knows. (Matthew 24:36) Paul wrote that the Father is "the God and Father of our Lord Jesus Christ" (Romans 15:6, NEB), and revealed that *after* the resurrection Jesus will "be subject unto him [the Father] that put all things under him, that God may be all in all." (1 Corinthians 15:24-28)

In the post-Apostolic era, Hippolytus wrote that the Father is "the Lord and God and Ruler of all, and even of Christ Himself . . . ."[313] And Irenaeus insisted that the Father surpasses the Son in knowledge:

For if any one should inquire the reason why the Father, who has fellowship with the Son in all things, has been declared by the Lord alone to know the hour and the day [of judgment], he will find at present no more suitable, or becoming, or safe reason than this (since, indeed, the Lord is the only true Master), that we may learn through Him that the Father is above all things. For "the Father," says He, "is greater than I."[314]

Clement of Alexandria taught that while the Father cannot be known, the Son is the object of knowledge:

> God, then, being not a subject for demonstration, cannot be the object of science. But the Son is wisdom, and knowledge, and truth, and all else that has affinity thereto. He is also susceptible of demonstration and of description.[315]

The Fathers maintained a form of "monotheism," however, by asserting the absolute monarchy of the Father as the "only true God." For instance, Irenaeus states:

> This, therefore, having been clearly demonstrated here (and it shall yet be so still more clearly), that neither the prophets, nor the Apostles, nor the Lord Christ in His own person, did acknowledge any other Lord or God, but the God and Lord supreme: the prophets and the Apostles confessing the Father and the Son; but naming no other as God, and confessing no other as Lord: and the Lord Himself handing down to His disciples, that He, the Father, is the only God and Lord, who alone is God and ruler of all; -- it is incumbent on us to follow, if we are their disciples indeed, their testimonies to this effect.[316]

Because of the monarchy and harmony within the Godhead, in a sense the diversity of power, rank, and glory was not thought to particularly matter in practice. As Origen put it:

> Moreover, nothing in the Trinity can be called greater or less, since the fountain of divinity alone contains all things by His word and reason, and by the Spirit of His mouth sanctifies all things which are worthy of sanctification . . . [317]

Likewise, Athenagoras spoke of the "diversity in rank"[318] within the Godhead, but qualified this by saying, "The son is in the father and the father is in the son by a powerful unity of spirit . . . ."[319]

Problems With Subordinationism

As we have seen, subordinationism was perpetuated within Christianity for centuries, even after the almost universal adoption of the God of the philosophers. In itself this was not a problem, because many of the philosophers, such as Plato and Numenius, believed in a second God or "demiurge" who created the material world.[320] On the other hand, these same philosophers strongly contrasted the transcendent "One" with all other beings. For example, Plotinus:

> The One is infinite, the others finite, the One is creator, the others creatures, the One is entirely itself, entirely infinite, the others are both finite and infinite . . . the One has no otherness, the others are other than the One.[321]

Adoption of such philosophies led some Christian theologians to contrast the Father too strongly with the other members of the Godhead. For instance, Origen noted: "We say that the Son and the Holy Spirit excel all created beings to a degree which admits of no comparison, and are themselves excelled by the Father to the same or even greater degree."[322] Therefore, Christ and the Holy Spirit could never be "God" in the fullest sense. But since the earliest times Christians had inherited the tradition that Jesus *was fully God*. He was Christ Jesus, "Who, being in the form of God, thought it not robbery to be equal with God . . . ." (Philippians 2:6)

In short, both subordinationism and the idea that the Son and Spirit are fully God were passed down from the earliest Christian traditions. However, both of these propositions could not be harmonized with the God of the philosophers, and so for centuries the Christian Church struggled with the question of which proposition to drop. In the end, Christianity chose to reject subordinationism and meld the Son and Spirit into "the One."

The "Word" Becomes the "Logos"

The first step in the absorption of the Son and Spirit into "the One" was the transformation of the "Word" of John into the "Logos" of the philosophers. Actually, the Greek word *logos* can be translated "Word," and John employed this language at the beginning of his Gospel: "In the beginning was the Word [Greek *logos*], and the Word was with God, and the Word was God." (John 1:1)

Jesus Becomes an Abstraction

Why did John call Christ the Logos, or Word? In Jewish documents such as the *Wisdom of Solomon*, the "almighty Word" (Wisdom 18:15 NEB) appears as a great angel, which is not surprising considering the foregoing discussion. Also, in Greek thought the Logos could represent "a divine principle that ordered existence and made knowledge possible"[323], or alternatively the "Reason" of God.[324] And while this was perhaps more abstract than the Jewish equivalent, it was certainly an apt analogy for the role of Jesus Christ. However, as Adolf von Harnack notes, the Christian Apologists of the second century completely transformed the "Word" of John into the abstract "Logos" of the philosophers:

The most important step that was ever taken in the domain of Christian doctrine was when the Christian apologists at the beginning of the second century drew the equation: the Logos = Jesus Christ. Ancient teachers before them had also called Christ "the Logos" among the many predicates which they ascribed to him; nay, one of them, John, had already formulated the proposition: "The Logos is Jesus Christ." But with John this proposition had not become the basis of every speculative idea about Christ; with him, too, "the Logos" was only a predicate. But now teachers came forward who previous to their conversion had been adherents of the platonico-stoical philosophy, and with whom the conception "Logos" formed an inalienable part of a general philosophy of the world.[325]

A Portion of the "Divine Substance"

The solution the Apologists and some later theologians came up with was to theorize that in the beginning God was alone, but when the time came to create the universe, He generated Jesus, or the Logos, from His own eternally existent Reason.[326] The important thing to note, however, that the Logos was thought to have been generated *at a certain point in time.* The Logos did not always exist as a separate entity. Tertullian explained:

> For before all things God was alone -- being in Himself and for Himself universe, and space, and all things. Moreover, He was alone, because there was nothing external to Him but Himself. Yet even not then was He alone; for He had with Him that which He possessed in Himself, that is to say, His own Reason . . . . Now, as soon as it pleased God to put forth into their respective substances and forms the things which He had planned and ordered within Himself, in conjunction with His Wisdom's Reason and Word, He first put forth the Word Himself, having within Him His own inseparable Reason and Wisdom . . . .[327]

Again, Tertullian insisted that "There was, however, a time when neither sin existed with Him, nor the Son . . . ."[328] In contrast, Origen and later theologians realized that the generation of the Logos was problematic. Didn't that imply a change in "the One"? Therefore, they postulated the "eternal generation" of the Logos. That is, the Logos was generated outside of time, and there was never a time when He was not.[329]

In any case, the view of these early theologians seems to have been that the Father is the entire "Divine Substance," while Son and Spirit are *portions*, or at least *generated from* portions of the substance. "For the Father is the entire substance, but the Son is a derivation and portion of the whole, as He Himself acknowledges: 'My Father is greater than I,'" explained Tertullian. "The Paraclete [is] distinct from Himself, even as we say that the Son is also distinct from the Father; so that He showed a third degree in the Paraclete . . . ."[330] This is significant, for on the one hand it allowed the Son and Spirit to *really* be God, since they are derived from God's own "substance" rather than from "nothing." On the other hand, the Son and Spirit could not be *fully* God, because they were not considered to comprehend the fullness of the "Divine Substance." In contrast, Paul taught that in Jesus "dwelleth all the fullness of the Godhead bodily." (Colossians 2:9)

The Impassible Logos

When the Logos became a portion of "the One," however, it had to take on the characteristics of the Divine Substance. This meant, of course, that the Logos had to have been "without body, parts, or passions," etc. This was, philosophically speaking, a problem, because the Christian doctrine had always been that the Logos *actually became a man*. Christopher Stead asserts that "In a Palestinian milieu it was still possible to picture the heavenly Father in human form and to see the contrast between heaven and earth as one of light and glory against relative darkness and indignity,"[331] and hence the Incarnation represented a condescension, but not a fundamental change. However, to the Greek mind the implied change was very nearly absolute, and such a change in God would necessarily have been a change for the worse.[332] As Eusebius put it, "For if it is unreasonable to suppose that the unbegotten and immutable essence of the almighty God was changed into the form of man . . . ."[333] In response to this problem, Christians such as Origen taught that the Logos became man, but doing so implied no change. The Logos animated a truly human nature, but remained itself in heaven, suffering none of the things the human part of Him did:

> But if the immortal God -- the Word -- by assuming a mortal body and a human soul, appears to Celsus to undergo a change and transformation, let him learn that the Word, still remaining essentially the Word, suffers none of those things which are suffered by the body or the soul . . . .[334]

The traditional type of christology seems to have been what Kelly calls a "Spirit Christology," where the Logos, a divine spirit, took on a body of flesh. In short, "the Word became flesh" (John 1:14), or the "Logos we know to have received a body from a virgin."[335] Granted the Word was not "merely human," but if the Logos was totally different from the human soul, how could it *really* become human?

Some theologians from Origen on taught that Jesus took on both a human body and soul. "For the soul and body of Jesus formed . . . one being with the Logos of God."[336] Therefore, it could be maintained that Jesus was fully human and fully God, and all the frailties of human nature could be ascribed to something other than the Logos.

But the Logos was supposed to be intimately united with Jesus' humanity, so how could Jesus really suffer and do all that he did for humanity? John Chrysostom reasoned that "sometimes he leaves the flesh deprived and stripped of his own activity, so that, by showing its weakness, he may help men to believe in the reality of his physical nature . . . ."[337] Ambrose of Milan taught that Jesus' hunger was "a holy deception," perpetrated to trick the Devil.[338] Augustine believed that Jesus was ignorant of the day and hour of His Second Coming only in that he was keeping His *disciples* ignorant.[339] And Hilary of Poitiers concluded that Jesus really wept, ate, etc., but not because He was really sad or hungry. "He conformed to the habits of the body to prove the reality of His own body, to satisfy the custom of human bodies by doing as our nature does."[340]

This "Word-man" Christology never really became dominant, however, until late in the fourth century.[341] In the final Christological settlements of the fifth through seventh centuries, it was agreed that Christ must have had two natures -- one human, and one divine -- including Logos, body, and human soul.

This was not the end of the story, however. In the third council of Constantinople (680 A.D.) it was resolved that Christ must have had "two wills" as well as "two natures."[342] For, if Christ had a will separate from the Father's ("nevertheless not what I will, but what thou wilt" -- Mark 14:36) that will must not have been connected with the Word, which is part of the indivisible "Divine Substance." But having two wills by no means made Christ a schizophrenic. John of Damascus explained that Christ's human will "wills of its own free will those things which the divine will willeth it to will."[343]

Such were the demands of the God of the philosophers. But did all this philosophizing really solve the problem? The reader will remember that the early Gnostics and their predecessors were "docetists,"[344] who believed that Christ only "seemed" to take on a material nature. The later Catholic theologians granted that Jesus had a material nature, but denied that it affected His divine nature in any real sense. And indeed, they postulated, His divine nature prevented His human nature from being truly human. As Cyril of Alexandria lamented:

> Hence they speak with undue precision of him suffering in the nature of the humanity, as if they separate it from the Word and set it apart by itself, so that they mean two and not one . . . .[345]

Consider also the criticism of Adolf von Harnack:

Even though the Christological formula were the theologically right one -- what a departure from the Gospel is involved in maintaining that a man can have no relationship with Jesus Christ, nay, that he is sinning against him and will be cast out, unless he first of all acknowledges that Christ was *one* person with two natures and two powers of will, one of them divine and one human. Such is the demand into which intellectualism has developed.[346]

The "Only Begotten" Son

The identification of Jesus with the Logos of the philosophers created yet another problem. That is, in what sense is Jesus the "Only Begotten" of the Father? Kelly observes that the majority of Christian writers before Origen seem to have dated Jesus' "sonship" to His *incarnation*.[347] Likewise, Latter-day Saints designate Jesus as the Only Begotten Son *in the flesh.* The LDS belief in a premortal existence allows for any number of sons of God in the spirit, but if there were no such premortal existence, the phrase "Only Begotten" takes on a different meaning. We have already seen that it came to be believed that the Logos was "begotten" out of the very divine substance, putting him in the "God" category, rather than in that of the created "world."

This is where the problems started. First, what did it mean to be "begotten" out of an essence that is supposedly unchangeable and indivisible? The theologians decided that "begetting" in this sense must be some process totally unlike anything within human experience, thus maintaining the divine unity:

> If any one, therefore, says to us, "How then was the Son produced by the Father?" we reply to him, that no man understands that production, or generation, or calling, or revelation, or by whatever name one may describe His generation, which is in fact altogether indescribable.[348]

Second, what does that make the Holy Spirit? Some early witnesses, like the *Pastor of Hermas*, called the Spirit a "son of God," as well.[349] But if Jesus is the Only Begotten Son, then the Spirit must be something different. Gregory of Nazianzus explained the dilemma:

> But of the wise men amongst ourselves, some have conceived of him [the Holy Spirit] as an Activity, some as a Creature, some as God; and some have been uncertain which to call Him, out of reverence for Scripture, they say, as though it did not make the matter clear either way.[350]

The answer? Appealing to the language of John 15:26, the later Fathers reasoned that the Spirit "proceeds" from the Father, which is something altogether different than being "begotten."[351] What is the difference between "proceeding" and being "begotten"? Well, we have already seen that they had no idea what being "begotten" meant, and it was no different with the issue of "procession." Gregory of Nazianzus explained:

> The Holy Ghost, which proceedeth from the Father; . . . . inasmuch as He proceedeth from That Source, is no Creature; and inasmuch as He is not Begotten is no Son; and inasmuch as He is between the Unbegotten and the Begotten is God. And thus escaping the toils of your syllogisms, He has manifested himself as God, stronger than your divisions. What then is Procession? Do you tell me what is the Unbegottenness of the Father, and I will explain to you the physiology of the Generation of the Son and the Procession of the Spirit, and we shall both of us be frenzy-stricken for prying into the mystery of God.[352]

And that was that. The Word had become the Logos, who was eternally "begotten" from the "Divine Substance" in some inexplicable way, and the Spirit had become who knows what that "proceeds" from the "Divine Substance" of the Father in some equally inexplicable way. Of course, "procession" and "begetting" are two completely different things, but we just do not know how or why they are different.

The Monarchian Crisis

As was mentioned above, the idea that the Son and Spirit were generated from a portion of the Divine Substance was not entirely satisfying for some. A "portion" seemed to imply that the Divine Substance was not "simple" or "uncompounded," and "generation" seemed to imply some sort of change in the Divine Substance. Also, even though the monarchy of the Father was unequivocally proclaimed, there were still those who felt it smacked of polytheism. Consequently, in the closing decades of the second century, factions arose within Christianity that tried to preserve the *monarchia*, or divine unity of "the One."[353] These "heretics" have been dubbed "monarchians."

There were two types of monarchians, Dynamic monarchians, and Modalistic monarchians. The Dynamic monarchians, or "adoptionists," were essentially intellectuals who denied the divinity of Jesus Christ. To them, Jesus was a "mere man" upon whom the Spirit of God had descended. Some allowed that He had been deified after his resurrection, but their main concern was to keep Him separate from "the One," and eliminate the crass concept of an incarnate deity.[354]

The Modalistic monarchians, on the other hand, were concerned both to preserve the divine unity and to preserve the *full* divinity of Christ. Therefore, they claimed that the Father, Son, and Holy Spirit were not separate persons, but different "modes" of presentation of the same Divine person.[355]

It was recognized that the monarchians were clearly wrong.[356] The Dynamic monarchians denied the full divinity of Christ, which had clearly been taught from the beginning -- "the Word was God." (John 1:1) The Modalists, on the other hand, destroyed the distinction between the Father and Son. But both the distinction of the Son from the Father, and His subordination to the Father had also been clearly taught since the beginning.

We shall see that, in a sense, the monarchian crisis defined the later Trinitarian controversies. That is, if "God" is defined as "the One" -- an indivisible, simple, uncompounded, eternally unchanging "essence" that is fundamentally different than the rest of the universe, created out of "nothing" -- how can the full divinity of the Son and Spirit be preserved without erasing their distinction from the Father? Furthermore, we have already seen that the full *humanity* of Christ had to be preserved, as well.

"Of One Substance"

In response to the monarchians, the "orthodox" merely pointed to the tradition of the Church, which had always taught the full divinity of Christ and his distinction from and subordination to the Father. They pressed home the idea that the Son and Spirit had been generated from the Divine Substance rather than *ex nihilo*, but that this generation implied no division or compounding of the Divine Substance.

This controversy led two "orthodox" writers, Tertullian and Hippolytus, to utilize a particular phrase that later proved quite important. The phrase was "of one substance," the Greek word *homoousios* or its Latin equivalent *una substantia*. That is, the Son and Spirit are "of one substance" with the Father. According to Tertullian:

> Thus the connection of the Father in the Son, and of the Son in the Paraclete, produces three coherent Persons, who are yet distinct One from Another. These Three are one essence, not one Person, as it is said, "I and my Father are One," in respect of unity of substance, not singularity of number.[357]

Eric Osborn summarizes the meaning of Tertullian's language:

> Substance for Tertullian means 'stuff' or 'material'. One substance was one physical thing. The soul, as well as God, logos and holy spirit were all corporeal realities . . . . He

thought of one substance divided into three parts which remained together . . . ; each part was the embodiment of one of the three members of the trinity . . . . A quick reading of *Against Praxeas* suggests that Tertullian has not avoided a division of the divine substance, and a closer reading indicates that he may not have given the son and the spirit a totality of divine substance.[358]

Hippolytus taught essentially the same thing at about the same time: "The Logos alone of this God is from God himself; wherefore also the Logos is God, being the substance of God. Now the world was made from nothing, wherefore it is not God . . . ."[359] But Hippolytus stressed the subordination of the Son, as well, and spoke of the Father as "the Lord and God and Ruler of all, and even of Christ Himself . . . ."[360]

Tertullian and Hippolytus seem to have borrowed the term "of one substance" from the Gnostics, who used it to denote a "generic" unity. That is, the same *kinds* of things are "of one substance" with each other; for instance, one horse would be "of one substance" with another horse. Kelly writes that "in both its secular and its theological usage prior to Nicea it always conveyed, primarily at any rate, the 'generic' sense."[361] That is, the Father, Son, and Spirit are the same kind of being, or "made of the same kind of stuff."[362] But we have already seen that "'subordinationism' . . . was pre-Nicene orthodoxy,"[363] and indeed many still referred to Jesus as a "second God" or an "Angel." This naturally precluded the sort of deep metaphysical unity that was meant by *"homoousios"* after the Council of Nicea. Thus, even in the fourth century Eusebius could say, "But the Word of God is other than this: It has its own substance in Itself altogether divine and spiritual, It exists in Itself . . . ."[364]

Given this background, it can readily be seen that the assertion of "one substance" did not really answer the objections of the monarchians. As Osborn pointed out, a division of the Divine Substance, a philosophical impossibility, was still implied by this teaching.

The Arian Crisis

Accordingly, the same issue popped up again in the early fourth century when a man named Arius and his followers came forward with a teaching somewhat similar to that of the Dynamic monarchians. The Arians not only rejected the idea of identity of substance in the Godhead, they also preached that the Son was merely a created being and that the Holy Spirit was God's impersonal force.[365] While they recognized that scripture used titles such as "Logos" for Jesus, they asserted that Jesus merely "participated" in God's Logos.[366] Jesus was a "god" to the Arians, but not in the sense of being any part of "the One."

The Arians appealed to a great number of scriptural passages that seemed to indicate the subordination of the Son. Luke 2:52 said that Jesus grew in wisdom and stature. Hebrews 5:8-9 reported that He learned obedience. In John 14:28 He said "the Father is greater than I." In Matthew 26:39, Christ said He would submit his will to his Father's. In Mark 13:32, he said he did not know when He would return, but that the Father did. In Hebrews 1:4, Paul said He had "inherited" a name superior to the angels. In Colossians 1:15, Paul called Him the "firstborn" of all creation. And the same Apostle, in 1 Corinthians 15:28, told the saints that Jesus would, in the end, be subjected under God.

According to Kelly, Arius's fault was to carry the traditional subordinationism to radical lengths, reducing the Son to the status of a created being. However, by doing this he was following "a path inevitably traced for him by the Middle Platonist preconceptions he had inherited."[367] It bears repeating that Arius's logic was "inevitable" because of his Platonist assumptions about God. In short "the One" could not become incarnate and suffer pain and death. Richard Hanson explains:

> There was one important aspect of the witness of the New Testament to the nature and activity of God which Arianism (and, I believe, Arius) grasped fully and courageously: this collection of documents witnessed to a suffering God. Arianism was carefully designed to enable Christians to believe just this.[368]

In any case, Arius's success pressed the Christian world into resolving the question that had plagued the Church ever since the second century. That is, "How divine is Jesus Christ?"

The Council of Nicea and its Aftermath

Arius was suspended from the office of Elder in Alexandria by his bishop, but he had friends in high places, and soon gained a substantial following. This caused great uneasiness in the Eastern Church, but it wasn't until the Emperor Constantine turned his attention to the affair that a resolution was reached.[369] Constantine, though not yet a Christian himself, had effected a reconciliation between the Christian faith and the Roman state, and Christianity became the *official* religion. Thus the unity of the Church was of prime importance to him[370], so the Emperor called together a council of bishops at Nicea in the year 325 to resolve the issue.

However, such a resolution was no simple proposition, because at that time there really was no single "orthodox" position on the nature of the Trinity. As Richard Hanson states:

In the first place, on the central subject of the dispute, how divine is Jesus Christ, there was in the year 318 no universally recognized orthodox answer. This is one reason why the controversy lasted so long. It was a controversy which resulted in the determination of orthodoxy, not one consisting solely or even mainly in the defence of orthodoxy . . . . There were indeed certain extreme views which virtually everybody repudiated: that Jesus was a 'mere man' and nothing more . . . , that there were no distinctions within the Godhead but only one God in three different aspects . . . ; that the doctrine of the Trinity meant that God was cut up, divided or diminished. But within these very broad limits no doctrine could properly be said to be heretical. Even Arius's views when they were first propounded could have been regarded (as Eusebius of Caesarea regarded them) as no more than a radical version of an acceptable tradition of theology.[371]

Three major parties were represented at the Council of Nicea and in subsequent controversies.[372] First were the Arians; second and most numerous were those that Kelly calls "the great conservative 'middle party'";[373] third was a group later called the "Nicene" party, led by Athanasius and others.[374]

The "middle party," of which Eusebius of Caesarea was a representative, taught that there were three divine persons, "separate in rank and glory but united in harmony of will."[375] This, as we have seen, had been the doctrine of the Church from the beginning, but there were a variety of interpretations which fell under this heading. As Hanson pointed out above, the Arian doctrine was not far removed from that of some factions of the middle party. After all, Arius taught that Jesus was the "prince of angels"[376] and a "second god" subordinate to the Father, just as Eusebius himself did. Thus, the only truly radical component of Arian Christology was the belief that Jesus had been created out of nothing rather than out of the Divine Substance.[377]

Athanasius and the Nicenes, on the other hand, started with the assumption that the Son must be *fully God*. This naturally precluded the Arian position, but also that of the "middle party," because an indivisible, uncompounded, and simple "One" cannot admit of the division, or at least the compound nature, implied by traditional subordinationism. Athanasius reasoned that the Trinity must be "one being," but not so as to destroy the distinction between the three "persons." How can this be? Athanasius balked at explaining *how* this could be, because, after all, the subject of any such explanation is infinite, eternal, and ultimately beyond the grasp of the human mind. Therefore, he merely affirmed as fact that the Father, Son, and Holy Spirit are "one being" with respect to the "Divine Substance," with no divisions as implied by differences in rank and glory, and yet in some very real sense, "three persons."[378]

In keeping with their philosophy, the Nicenes proposed the use of the word "*homoousios*" or "of one substance" in the Nicene Creed, but gave to it a meaning that it had not had before within Christian circles. According to J.N.D. Kelly, the root word *ousia* or "substance" could signify either the "essence" common to a class, in the sense that earlier Christians had used it, or alternatively an individual thing. He writes that "there can be no doubt" that as applied to an immaterial and indivisible Godhead, the term *"homoousios"* requires the latter meaning.[379] And indeed, this is the manner in which modern mainstream Christian theologians interpret the wording of the Nicene Creed. Although it is apparent that Athanasius and his followers applied this meaning to the word, they were in the minority. The "middle party," on the other hand, constituted the majority, and they applied the word *"homoousios"* in the traditional sense, implying only that the Father, Son, and Holy Spirit are the same *kind* of being, differing in rank and glory.[380] Therefore, when the Nicene Council affirmed that the Trinity is "of one substance," they were not attempting to create any sort of precise definition of the oneness of the Godhead. Rather, they were affirming the deity of the Son in terms that could attract broad agreement so they could formally discredit the Arians.[381]

This was not the end of the controversy, however. Many who aligned themselves with the middle party were uneasy with the language of the Nicene Creed. They felt that Athanasius's interpretation of it was nothing more than thinly veiled modalism.[382] Therefore, some of them suggested substituting the word *"homoiousios"* or "of *like* substance" into the creed. Over the next 50 years the battle raged back and forth, and some 14 councils produced competing creeds ranging from Nicene to Arian positions.[383]

Eventually, the Nicene position won out, and from the time of the Council of Constantinople (381) on, subordinationism was officially rejected. Davies summarizes:

> This meant the end of subordinationism. The Son and the Spirit are equal to the Father as touching their divinity because each is a presentation of an identical divine being. The only priority of the Father is a logical, not a temporal, one since the Son and the Spirit derive from him as their source; but this priority involves no superiority.[384]

Likewise, there was no more talk of a "second god." As Basil of Caesarea explained, this was considered no better than heathen polytheism:

> They on the other hand who support their sub-numeration by talking of first and second and third ought to be informed that into the undefiled theology of Christians they are importing the polytheism of heathen error. No other result

can be achieved by the fell device of sub-numeration than the confession of a first, a second, and a third God. For us is sufficient the order prescribed by the Lord. He who confuses this order will be no less guilty of transgressing the law than are the impious heathen.[385]

Certainly this represented a break from tradition. However, it is clear that given the concept of God as "the One," either the full deity of the Son had to be rejected (as in the case of the Arians), or subordinationism had to be rejected.

The Mystery of the Trinity

With the rejection of subordinationism, Christianity finally had resolved the issue of how the three persons of the Godhead could all be fully God, and the Son and Spirit had been melded into "the One." But consider the irony of the situation. The Church had gotten itself into this mess by adopting "the One" as their God in the first place in order to make Christianity philosophically acceptable. But since the God of the philosophers was in many ways antithetical to the God of Israel, the Church ended up having to adopt a solution that was "beyond human reason" to maintain the full deity of Christ. Consequently, as Grace Jantzen observes, "The perplexity of the Arians is still with us . . . ."[386]

Again, what we have is the concept of combining "three persons" into "one God" in a way that is wholly incomprehensible to the human mind. As Augustine put it: "What three? human language labors altogether under great poverty of speech. The answer, however, is given, three 'persons,' not that it might be [completely] spoken, but that it might not be left [wholly] unspoken."[387] In other words, Augustine had to say *something* about the nature of the Trinity, but he didn't really understand *just what it was he was saying*. After pointing out the logical inconsistencies in the Trinity doctrine, philosopher Richard Cartwright critiqued this sort of mysticism:

> At this point I need to anticipate an objection. It will be said that a philosopher is trespassing on the territory of the theologian: the doctrine of the Trinity is a mystery, beyond the capacities of human reason, and hence the tools of logic are irrelevant to it. The objection is based on a misunderstanding. The doctrine of the Trinity is indeed supposed to be a mystery. That simply means, however, that assurance of its truth cannot be provided by human reason but only by divine revelation. It is to be believed "not because of the natural light of reason, but because of the authority of God who reveals it." But a mystery is not

supposed to be refutable by human reason, as if a truth of reason could somehow contradict a revealed truth; on the contrary, putative refutations are supposed themselves to be refutable. Nor is a mystery supposed to be unintelligible, in the sense that the words in which it is expressed simply cannot be understood. After all, we are asked to believe the propositions expressed by the words, not simply that the words express some true propositions or other, we know not which.[388]

Mainstream Christianity has been placed in the unenviable position of requiring belief in a doctrine that no one can understand. Thus, in the midst of the Trinitarian controversies, Cyril of Jerusalem gave the following advice to new converts:

For there is one Salvation, one Power, one Faith; One God, the Father; One Lord, His only-begotten Son; One Holy Ghost, the Comforter. And it is enough for us to know these things; but inquire not curiously into His nature or substance: for had it been written, we would have spoken of it; what is not written, let us not venture on; it is sufficient for our salvation to know, that there is Father, and Son, and Holy Ghost.[389]

It is no wonder that, in my experience, most Christians are either modalists, tritheists (in the same sense as the Latter-day Saints), or they do not bother with any sort of rational explanations of the godhead at all.

The Origin and Destiny of Man

As we saw in our discussion of anthropomorphism, one cannot describe any concept of the nature of God without reference to the nature of man. Walter H. Wagner writes, "A community's anthropology influences its understanding of God, and vice versa. To ask whether theology or anthropology came first is to pose the old chicken-or-egg conundrum."[390] This is at least as true for the Latter-day Saints as for anyone else because of our belief that humans are eternal beings who can become like God. In this section we will discuss this belief in the context of the LDS doctrines of premortal existence and deification.

The Premortal Existence

The Latter-day Saint Doctrine

Related to the doctrine of creation *ex nihilo* is the belief that the soul of man is also created out of nothing, along with the rest of the material world. Most Christian denominations today other than the Latter-day Saints accept this doctrine as fact. God did not "create" the spirit of man out of nothing, however. According to Joseph Smith:

> I am dwelling on the immortality of the spirit of man. Is it logical to say that the intelligence of spirits is immortal, and yet that it had a beginning? The intelligence of spirits had no beginning, neither will it have an end. That is good logic. That which has a beginning may have an end. There never was a time when there were not spirits; for they are [co-eternal] with our Father in heaven.[391]

Therefore, Mormons believe the entire human family was formed from eternal intelligence which became, through a process that has not been clearly revealed, the literal spirit children of our Father in heaven.

The purpose of human life on earth, according to Mormonism, is to be tested, to grow, and to make covenants with God, so that at some point in the eternity after mortal life humans can be exalted to become like their Father. The Father devised a plan whereby this process could take place, and presented it in a great council in heaven. Abraham saw part of this council in a vision:

> Now the Lord had shown unto me, Abraham, the intelligences that were organized before the world was; and among all these there were many of the noble and great ones; And God saw these souls that they were good, and he stood in the midst of them, and he said: These I will make my rulers; for he stood among those that were spirits, and he saw that they were good; and he said unto me: Abraham, thou art one of them; thou wast chosen before thou wast born. And there stood one among them that was like unto God [the pre-existent Christ], and he said unto those who were with him: We will go down, for there is space there, and we will take of these materials, and we will make an earth whereon these may dwell; And we will prove them herewith, to see if they will do all things whatsoever the Lord their God shall command them; And they who keep their first estate shall be added upon; and they who keep not their first estate shall not have glory in the same kingdom with those who keep their first estate; and they who keep

their second estate shall have glory added upon their heads
for ever and ever. (Abraham 3:22-26)

As part of the plan, a savior was needed to save mankind from sin and
death. The Father presented Jesus as his chosen one, but another of the spirits,
named Lucifer (Satan), offered a plan which would have taken away free will
and therefore forced everyone to be saved, while he would have kept the glory
and allegiance of the spirits for himself. (See Moses 4:1-3) In the cosmic
conflict which followed, Lucifer was cast out of heaven along with one-third
of the spirits. These became the Devil and his angels. (Abraham 3:22-28)

For the mainline Christian, the only pre-existent soul was that of
Christ. However, we shall see that Joseph Smith restored another legitimate
early Christian and Jewish doctrine with his assertion that the souls of all men
were also pre-existent. We hope to show conclusively that this was *the
original* Christian dogma.

The Pre-Existence of Christ

The New Testament states specifically and clearly that Christ's soul
existed from before the creation of the earth, and on this point there is almost
universal agreement. Remember John's declaration that, "In the beginning was
the Word, and the Word was with God . . . ." (John 1:1) Peter wrote of this
fact when he said: "But with the precious blood of Christ, as of a lamb
without blemish and without spot: Who verily was foreordained before the
foundation of the world, but was manifest in these last times for you." (1 Peter
1:19-20) Paul wrote that Jesus was the "firstborn of every creature":

> The Father . . . who hath delivered us from the power of
> darkness, and hath translated us into the kingdom of his dear
> Son: In whom we have redemption through his blood, even
> the forgiveness of sins: Who is the image of the invisible
> God, the firstborn of every creature. (Colossians 1:12-15)

While mainline Christians believe that Christ existed eternally as part
of the "Divine Substance," Latter-day Saints hold that all of the human family
had a pre-existence.[392]

The Pre-Existence in Early Christianity

Early on in post-Apostolic Christianity there was great confusion
about the origin of the soul. There were three basic beliefs current at least as
early as the second century: 1) the belief in the pre-existence of the soul,
which we have already discussed; 2) creationism, or the view that each soul is
newly created by God together with the body; and 3) traducianism, the idea
that the soul is produced by the souls of the parents through psychic
copulation.[393] Origen stated that by his time there was no clear teaching in the
Church on this matter:

> But with respect to the soul, whether it is derived from the seed by a process of traducianism, so that the reason or substance of it may be considered as placed in the seminal particles of the body themselves, or whether it has any other beginning; and this beginning, itself, whether it be by birth or not, or whether bestowed upon the body from without or no, is not distinguished with sufficient clearness in the teaching of the Church.[394]

However, the doctrine of the pre-existence of the soul was quite common in the early centuries of Christianity. This was quite natural since Christianity was in many respects a continuation of apocalyptic Judaism, in which various forms of the pre-existence doctrine were fundamental.[395] The most well-known proponent of the pre-existence doctrine was Origen himself, who wrote during the early third century. Origen believed that God created a certain number of souls, all of them alike, and gave them free-will. These could, by their own choice, advance in glory and status by imitating God or rebel against Him, and except for Christ's pre-existent soul, everyone opted to rebel to one extent or another. All those who rebelled experienced a "pre-cosmic fall," and this gave rise to the various gradations of spiritual beings in the world.[396]

> He created all whom He made equal and alike, because there was in Himself no reason for producing variety and diversity. But since those rational creatures themselves, as we have frequently shown, and will yet show in the proper place, were endowed with the power of free-will, this freedom of will incited each one either to progress by imitation of God, or reduced him to failure through negligence. And this, as we have already stated, is the cause of the diversity among rational creatures, deriving its origin not from the will or judgment of the Creator, but from the freedom of the individual will.[397]

This is very similar to Mormon doctrine. However, Origen is famous for his philosophic speculations (he was a thoroughgoing Platonist), so if he were the only (or first) proponent of this theory one might suspect it as his own invention. However, the doctrine does go back much earlier than Origen. For example, according to Peter in a second-century Christian document, the *Clementine Recognitions,* "after all these things He made man, on whose account He had prepared all things, whose internal species is older, and for whose sake all things that are were made . . . ."[398] Regarding the "internal species" of man mentioned here, the Presbyterian translators of this passage

100

declare in the footnote: "That is, his soul, according to the doctrine of the pre-existence of souls."

Origen's teacher, Clement of Alexandria, may have believed in some sort of pre-existence, as well. Commenting on Jeremiah 1:5 he wrote:

> But the Lord hath also said in Jeremiah: "Say not that I am a youth: before I formed thee in the belly I knew thee, and before I brought thee out of the womb I sanctified thee." Such allusions prophecy can make to us, destined in the eye of God to faith before the foundation of the world; but now babes, through the recent fulfillment of the will of God, according to which we are born now to calling and salvation.[399]

It must be cautioned, however, that "if [Clement] accepts the pre-existence of souls, he does not allow uncreatedness."[400] But Clement's idea of the origin of the soul may have been completely compatible with the LDS view, given the fact that he rejected creation *ex nihilo*, because Mormons believe that God affected a "spiritual creation" for humankind (and everything else) before the creation of the world[401], even though the "intelligence" or bare essence of each soul has existed throughout eternity.

Justin Martyr must have held a similar view. While he taught that the world was made "for man's sake"[402], he also believed that souls must have been begotten at one time, even though they were begotten apart from (and presumably before) the body:

> If the world is begotten, souls also are necessarily begotten; and perhaps at one time they were not in existence, for they were made on account of men and other living creatures, if you will say that they have been begotten wholly apart, and not along with their respective bodies.[403]

Similarly, the very early epistle of Mathetes to Diognetus insisted that the soul does not have its origin in the body, and that Christians think of themselves as strangers on the earth:

> They [Christians] live on earth, but their citizenship is in Heaven . . . . As the soul lives in the body, yet does not have its origin in the body, so the Christians live in the world yet are not of the world . . . . Immortal, the soul lives in a mortal house; so too the Christians live in corruptible existence as strangers and look forward to incorruptible life in Heaven.[404]

The Codex Sinaiticus version of the *Epistle of Barnabas* may contain a reference to our participation in the premortal councils of God: "But we said above, 'Let them increase, and rule over the fishes' . . . . If, therefore, this does not exist at present, yet still He has promised it to us. When? When we ourselves also have been made perfect [so as] to become heirs of the covenant of the Lord."[405]

Two of the earliest post-New Testament Christian writings, *The Pastor of Hermas* and *2 Clement* claim that God created the Church even before he created the world. "She was created first of all . . . and for her sake was the world made."[406] "Moreover, the books and the Apostles declare that the Church belongs not to the present, but existed from the beginning."[407]

This concept is traced by R.G. Hammerton-Kelly, professor of New Testament at McCormick Theological Seminary, in his illuminating study of the idea of pre-existence in the New Testament. Hammerton-Kelly shows that not only is the pre-existence of Christ explicitly taught therein, but also the pre-existence of the Church is implied in many passages, including in Paul's writings. "The main pre-existent entity, however, as far as Paul is concerned, is the Church. It is the heavenly city or heavenly temple, to be revealed at the end but pre-existent now in heaven."[408] Hammerton-Kelly also finds this concept taught explicitly in John's Revelation, and implicitly in the Synoptic Gospels and the Gospel of John.[409]

But the Church was not just some abstract idea that existed in the mind of God before the foundation of the world -- individual Christians also were pre-existent as part of the Church. Commenting on Paul's doctrine of foreordination as expounded in Romans 8:28-30, Hammerton-Kelly explains that the Greek verb for "foreknow" used in the passage means "'to take note of', 'to fix regard upon' something, preliminary to selecting it for some special purpose." But when did this selection occur? "Most commentators believe that it took place in the eternal counsels of God, before the creation of the world."[410] While the doctrine of the pre-existence of souls is never made explicit in the New Testament, there is no question but that it was part of the mindset of early Christians. As Hammerton-Kelly says about Paul:

> One is impressed by the ease with which the idea of pre-existence is assumed as the background for certain aspects of Paul's theology, especially for his doctrines of Christ and the Church . . . . Although Paul would never have used the term 'pre-existence', the concept which it describes is constitutive of his whole soteriological scheme.[411]

Albert Schweitzer agrees that "the Pauline mysticism is therefore nothing else than the doctrine of the making manifest in consequence of the death and resurrection of Jesus, of the pre-existent Church (the community of God)."[412]

The doctrine of the pre-existence is also found in a wide variety of Christian apocryphal literature. For instance in the *Gospel of Thomas*, which many believe to contain sayings of Jesus which are closer to His original statements than those found in the Gospels, Jesus said, "Blessed are the solitary and elect, for you shall find the Kingdom; because you come from it, (and) you shall go there again."[413] And the *Christian Sibyllines* state that "The world is my origin, but soul have I drawn from the stars."[414]

Various of these texts also anticipate the Latter-day Saint doctrine that Jesus, the Holy Ghost, and Satan were members of the pre-existent family of God. Hennecke and Schneemelcher report that the writer of *The Questions of Bartholomew*, as well as a gnostic group called the Bogomils, taught that "Christus is the elder son of God, Satan . . . is the younger."[415] And in the Gnostic *Pistis Sophia*, Mary tells Jesus that the Holy Spirit appeared to her and said, "Where is Jesus, my brother, that I may meet him?"[416]

Indeed, even the undeniably orthodox Lactantius implied that Jesus and Satan were brothers.[417]

The Loss of the Doctrine of Pre-Existence

The doctrine of pre-existence was never formally condemned until 543 A.D. when Origen's "errors" were listed and pronounced heretical at a council of bishops.[418] So why did Christianity finally reject this doctrine? We can identify three possible reasons, which may have worked together against its acceptance. First, the doctrine may have come into disrepute in the second century, since it was a staple of the various gnostic systems.[419]

Second, the doctrine of pre-existence may have been part of the early Christian secret tradition. We shall discuss this secret tradition in a later chapter, but suffice it to say that the earliest Christians had certain doctrines and rites which they did not publicly speak about, and so in the event of an apostasy these would likely have been some of the first things to be lost. We can point to two clues that might indicate this was the case. We have seen that the New Testament writers often referred obliquely to the pre-existence, assuming the readers knew about it, but never teaching it in full detail. Also, a clue is given by the author of the *Clementine Recognitions*. It has already been shown that in this account Peter taught Clement the doctrine of pre-existence, but when the arch-heretic Simon Magus confronted Peter with the question of the origin of souls, Peter said:

> You seem to me not to know what a father and a God is: but I could tell you both whence souls are, and when and how they were made; but it is not permitted to me now to disclose these things to you, who are in such error in respect of the knowledge of God.[420]

Third, the second century was the scene of an intense debate about the origin of souls and of the universe itself that affected the entire Hellenistic world, cutting across religious boundaries. The debate revolved around the interpretation of two statements by Plato. In the *Timaeus*, Plato described the creation of the soul, while in the *Phaedrus*, he argued that the soul was uncreated.[421] Since Plato's writings were considered to be a systematic whole, the argument centered on which statement to take literally, and which to take figuratively.   This was not just some dry scholarly debate carried out by academics. Rather, this issue struck at the heart of the hopes and fears of the common man.   An example of this can be seen in the *Clementine Recognitions*, where Clement of Rome described his teenage angst over this question:

> I Clement, who was born in the city of Rome, was from my earliest age a lover of chastity; while the bent of my mind held me bound as with chains of anxiety and sorrow. For a thought that was in me -- whence originating, I cannot tell -- constantly led me to think of my condition of mortality, and to discuss such questions as these: Whether there be for me any life after death, or whether I am to be wholly annihilated: whether I did not exist before I was born, and whether there shall be no remembrance of this life after death, and so the boundlessness of time shall consign all things to oblivion and silence; so that not only we shall cease to be, but there shall be no remembrance that we have ever been. This also I revolved in my mind: when the world was made, or what was before it was made, or whether it has existed from eternity. For it seemed certain, that if it had been made, it must be doomed to dissolution; and if it be dissolved, what is to be afterwards? -- unless, perhaps, all things shall be buried in oblivion and silence, or something shall be, which the mind of man cannot now conceive.[422]

Given that revelation had ceased and the possibility that the doctrine of pre-existence was part of the secret tradition, it is not at all surprising that a state of confusion existed in the second-century Church on this issue. As the intellectuals of the Church rapidly brought Greek philosophical methods and ideas into their theological discourse, they naturally became entangled in the same debate that affected the rest of the Hellenistic world. In the confusion they may have decided to reject the idea of pre-existence in reaction to its acceptance by the heretical gnostic schools.

Although we cannot be sure about the exact dynamics of the loss of the doctrine of pre-existence, the example of Augustine is perhaps illustrative of the process. Initially, Augustine favored a theory similar to Origen's where the soul fell down into matter as a result of pre-cosmic sin.[423] (Origen was a Platonist who believed matter to be a crass, lesser reality, so the descent of man into matter could not have been God's fault!) However, Augustine still considered four hypotheses to be possible: "creationism, traducianism, and two variants on the soul as pre-existent: either it was divinely 'sent' or it sinfully 'fell' into the body."[424]

As he struggled to choose between these theories he came up with a list of "certainties" about the soul to work from. First, he maintained that:

> [The] soul cannot be 'turned into' a body, an irrational soul, or God; nor can any of these be 'turned into' a soul. Secondly, the soul cannot be anything else than a creature of God, Who cannot have made it out of a body, an irrational soul, or His own substance. He must, therefore, have made it either from nothing or from some reasonable, spiritual creature.[425]

So we see that the stage was set for Augustine's abandonment of the pre-existence doctrine by his acceptance of the doctrines of God as a Platonic "essence or substance," and creation *ex nihilo*, neither of which were present in the original Church.

Eventually, Augustine leaned toward a version of the traducianist theory, since it harmonized best with his view of original sin. (If all human souls were generated from Adam's then all men would be guilty of Adam's transgression.) However, he remained open to various forms of creationism and, despite his bias toward traducianism, near the end of his life Augustine confessed that he still did not have any idea how the soul came into being.[426]

By the fifth century, the issue had become polarized between pagans and Christians, with the pagans embracing creation from chaos and the eternal nature of the soul and the Christians asserting the creation of both from nothing. John Whittaker, of the Memorial University of Newfoundland, remarks on this situation: "Thus, the second century was a period of doubt and uncertainty preceding a period of dogmatic assurance. It is above all this uncertainty and hesitancy which give to the second century its peculiar quality."[427]

Deification

If one accepts the idea of a pre-existent creation of humanity, that in some way we are the offspring of Deity (Acts 17:28), and if one adds to this Jesus' commandment that we be perfect as the Father is perfect (Matthew 5:48), then one might argue that we have the potential to become like our creator, at least in some ways and to some degree. In a revelation given to Joseph Smith, the promise is made that those who are faithful will be given all things which the Father has (D&C 84:38), including, one may presume, all his knowledge, power and glory. This then is basis for the radical but truly glorious Latter-day Saint belief that God's highest aspiration is for his creatures to become like Him, and that His greatest glory is in sharing His glory with us, His sons and daughters. This is what it means in Latter-day Saint doctrine to become gods. Joseph Smith taught that those who fully keep God's law will "be gods, because they have no end; therefore shall they be from everlasting to everlasting, because they continue; then shall they be above all, because all things are subject unto them." (D&C 132:20) Perhaps nothing in Mormon doctrine has so shocked and dismayed the Christian world, even though the Latter-day Saints believe that we will always be the sons and daughters of God, subordinate and dependent upon Him.[428]

Deification in the Bible

Latter-day Saints find a great deal of support for their belief about exaltation to godhood within the pages of the Bible itself. While not explicitly stating the doctrine, many scriptures point toward it. For example, John wrote, "Beloved, now are we the sons of God, and it doth not yet appear what we shall be: but we know that, when he shall appear, we shall be like him; for we shall see him as he is." (1 John 3:2.) And Jesus Christ told John that, "To him that overcometh will I grant to sit with me in my throne, even as I also overcame, and am set down with my Father in his throne." (Revelation 3:21) Also, "He that overcometh shall inherit all things; and I will be his God, and he shall be my son." (Revelation 21:7) Paul wrote to the Romans, "The Spirit itself beareth witness with our spirit, that we are the children of God: And if children, then heirs; heirs of God, and joint-heirs with Christ . . ." (Romans 8:16-17)[429]

Deification in Early Christianity

Can these verses be interpreted to mean that men can become beings like God Himself? A host of early Christian writers testify that this is exactly what the early Christian Church believed. Indeed, Kelly explains that the doctrine that the final Christian hope was deification and "participation in the divine nature" permeated the early theology of Christianity.[430]

Perhaps this important belief is best summed up by Irenaeus, who wrote in the latter half of the second century that "we have not been made gods from the beginning, but at first merely men, then at length gods . . . ."[431] He also wrote, "our Lord Jesus Christ, who did, through His transcendent love, become what we are, that He might bring us to be even what He is Himself."[432] Justin Martyr, in the middle of the second century, said that "all men are deemed worthy of becoming 'gods,' and of having power to become sons of the Highest . . . ."[433] Jerome, who translated the Bible into Latin, wrote that God, "made man for that purpose, that from men they may become gods."[434] Clement of Alexandria explained that true knowledge of the divine leads to godhood:

> Whence at last . . . it is that knowledge is committed to those
> fit and selected for it. It leads us to the endless and perfect
> end, teaching us beforehand the future life that we shall lead,

according to God, and with gods; after we are freed from all punishment and penalty which we undergo, in consequence of our sins, for salutary discipline. After which redemption the reward and the honours are assigned to those who have become perfect; when they have got done with purification, and ceased from all service, though it be holy service, and among saints. Then become pure in heart, and near to the Lord, there awaits them restoration to everlasting contemplation; and they are called by the appellation of gods, being destined to sit on thrones with the other gods that have been first put in their places by the Saviour.[435]

Although mainline Christians often scoff at the Latter-day Saints for interpreting 1 Corinthians 8:5-6 to mean that there are actually beings "in heaven" who "are called gods" other than the One God we worship, Origen agreed that the passage does not have reference only to false gods:

Now it is possible that some may dislike what we have said representing the Father as the one true God, but admitting other beings besides the true God, who have become gods by having a share of God. They may fear that the glory of Him who surpasses all creation may be lowered to the level of those other beings called gods. We drew this distinction between Him and them that we showed God the Word to be to all the other gods the minister of their divinity . . . . As, then, there are many gods, but to us there is but one God the Father, and many Lords, but to us there is one Lord, Jesus Christ . . . .[436]

Statements such as these led Christian scholar G.L. Prestige to conclude that the ancient Christians "taught that the destiny of man was to become like God, and even to become deified."[437]

Objections to the LDS Doctrine

Unfortunately, the doctrine of deification was gradually diluted. Some critics of the LDS Church have appropriated the statements of later theologians, claiming that although the Church Fathers certainly used unorthodox language to express their views on the subject, deification to them meant nothing more than "endowing [Christians] in the resurrection with immortality and God's perfect moral character."[438] As Robert M. Bowman, Jr. argues, "Thus, the meaning of deification in Mormonism is radically different than that of the church fathers who used similar terms, despite Mormon arguments to the contrary."[439]

Objections Answered

To bolster his argument, Bowman cites only Augustine and Athanasius, both of whom were steeped in Nicene Trinitarianism. Given the fact that these theologians believed in the indivisible, eternal, unchanging "Divine Substance" theory of the Trinity, and rejected the pre-existence of humankind, it is obvious why they would conclude that the final deity of man must be fundamentally different than that of the Godhead. According to Davies, Athanasius drew a distinction between the deity of men, who can only be divine by *participation* in the "Divine Substance," and that of the Godhead, who *are* the "Divine Substance."[440] "Thus He is Son of God by nature, and we by grace."[441] The same belief is held in the Eastern Orthodox tradition today, but the doctrine of deification was *completely* lost in the West because they saw it as a negation of God's essential unity and simplicity.[442]

But what about the earlier theologians -- the ones who did not accept the doctrine of the Trinity in its full sense, and perhaps even rejected creation *ex nihilo*? How did they interpret the language of deification? In many cases it is clear that they were more emphatic in their deification language than the later Fathers, but in most cases they were not very precise about what they meant. However, in the fourth century Gregory of Nazianzus gave us a key by which we may interpret how any particular early Christian felt about this issue: "I too might be made God so far as He is made Man."[443]

To what extent *did* Jesus become man? In our discussion of the Logos doctrine we saw that for later thinkers at least part of Jesus (i.e., the Logos) was never really touched or changed by Jesus' human nature, so for them evidently men could never become God in as full a sense as Jesus was. On the other hand, we must remember that these same churchmen believed that Jesus' human nature was deified at Christ's resurrection. For instance, Athanasius taught:

> For as Christ died and was exalted as man, so, as man, is He said to take what, as God, He ever had, that even such a grant of grace might reach to us. For the Word was not impaired in receiving a body, that He should seek to receive a grace, but rather He deified that which He put on, and more than that, 'gave' it graciously to the race of man.[444]

So what happened to Christ's human nature according to the later theology? It was deified in some very real sense, and human beings can become deified *in exactly the same sense.* Certainly this is not the same as the LDS doctrine, but neither is it the same as saying that human beings can only reach the status of angels.

When we go back further in history, we encounter those, like Eusebius and Origen, who taught that Christ Himself was infinitely surpassed by the Father. For them, the Father was "the One," while the Son was only an image of the Father. How did they view human deification? Eusebius taught that "the saints also can enjoy precisely the same kind of fellowship with the Father" as Jesus Christ.[445]

Origen believed that Jesus was one of a multitude of spiritual beings (including humans) created by God. Jesus had a human body and a human soul, and he was "God" by virtue of having perfectly attached Himself to the Logos of the Father. Thus Origen could teach that "with respect to His mortal body, and the human soul which it contained, we assert that not by their communion merely with Him, but by their unity and intermixture, they received the highest powers, and after participating in His divinity, were changed into God."[446] Therefore, although Origen recognized that Jesus would remain higher in rank than those who followed after Him, he taught that humans could become Gods in exactly the same sense as Jesus did -- an image of the prototype:

> And thus the first-born of all creation, who is the first to be with God, and to attract to Himself divinity, is a being of more exalted rank than the other gods beside Him, of whom God is the God, as it is written, "The God of gods, the Lord, hath spoken and called the earth." It was by the offices of the first-born that they became gods, for He drew from God in generous measure that they should be made gods, and He communicated it to them according to His own bounty. The true God, then, is "The God," and those who are formed after Him are gods, images, as it were, of Him the prototype.[447]

Furthermore, Origen claimed that God

> will be 'all' in each individual in this way: when all which any rational understanding, cleansed from the dregs of every sort of vice, and with every cloud of wickedness completely swept away, can either feel, or understand, or think, will be wholly God . . . .[448]

And he dismissed the distinction Athanasius made between deity in itself and deity by participation: "Every one who participates in anything, is unquestionably of one essence and nature with him who is partaker of the same thing."[449]

Earlier in this chapter we saw that for Justin Martyr the Father was "the One," while Jesus was a "second God" with anthropomorphic characteristics. With that in mind, consider the following statement by Justin: "We reverence and worship Him and the Son who came forth from Him and taught us these things, and the host of other good angels who are about Him and are made quite like Him, and the Prophetic Spirit."[450] Father William Jurgens insists that this is the correct translation of Justin's statement, and admits that here Justin "apparently [made] insufficient distinction between Christ and the created Angels." Father Jurgens continues, "There are theological difficulties in the above passage, no doubt. But we wonder if those who make a great deal of these difficulties do not demand of Justin a theological sophistication which a man of his time and background could not rightly be expected to have."[451] If Justin, with his lack of "theological sophistication," could blur the fundamental distinction between Christ, the Spirit, and the angels, it is certain that when he said, "all men are deemed worthy of becoming 'gods,'"[452] he meant that humans can be "made quite like" Jesus Christ.

Clearly then, thinkers such as Eusebius, Origen, and Justin would have repudiated any notion of the saints becoming part of "the One," but they did teach that men may participate in deity and become "God" in the *same sense that Christ is God.*[453]

Similarly, Peter in the *Clementine Homilies* taught that all humans are of the same substance of God, so it is no more improper to call Christ "God" than it is to call any other human a "god":

> Learn this also: The bodies of men have immortal souls, which have been clothed with the breath of God; and having come forth from God, they are of the same substance, but they are not gods. But if they are gods, then in this way the souls of all men, both those who have died, and those who are alive, and those who shall come into being, are gods. But if in a spirit of controversy you maintain that these also are gods, what great matter is it, then, for Christ to be called God? for He has only what all have.[454]

This reference to the Jewish-Christian *Homilies* brings us back to the era when many Christians had an extremely anthropomorphic concept of God. To what extent did Jesus become a man? "He has only what all have." To what extent are men related to God? Although they are not gods at this point, "they are of the same substance." Obviously, any concept of deification with them would have been much closer to the LDS belief, because for them there was no great chasm between human nature and divine nature.

In any case, the early Fathers were often much more emphatic in their deification language than the later churchmen. For instance, Irenaeus taught that the saints would pass "beyond the angels, and be made after the image and likeness of God"[455], and that they would attain "even unto God."[456] Lactantius taught that the chaste man will become "identical in all respects with God (*consimilis Deo*)."[457] And Clement of Alexandria preached the following:

> It is then, as appears, the greatest of all lessons to know one's self. For if one knows himself, he will know God; and knowing God, he will be made like God . . . . But that man

with whom the Word dwells does not alter himself, does not get himself up: he has the form which is of the Word; he is made like to God; he is beautiful; he does not ornament himself: his is beauty, the true beauty, for it is God; and that man becomes God, since God so wills. Heraclitus, then, rightly said, "Men are gods, and gods are men."[458]

Finally, Peter himself told the saints that they would "come to share in the very being of God." (2 Peter 1:4 NEB) Therefore, according to many early Christian writers, we will *not*, in the end, be fundamentally different than God, or at least than Christ.

We have seen that there were a variety of interpretations of the doctrine of deification in ancient Christianity. And although the earliest Christians undoubtedly had a concept of divinization that was very close to the LDS belief, even the doctrine of some of the later church Fathers was emphatically *not* limited to the modern dogma that men can only become angels. Thus, non-Mormon scholar Ernst Benz can say of Joseph Smith's doctrine:

> One can think what one wants of this doctrine of progressive deification, but one thing is certain: with this anthropology Joseph Smith is closer to the view of man held by the Ancient Church than the precursors of the Augustinian doctrine of original sin were, who considered the thought of such a substantial connection between God and man as *the* heresy, par excellence.[459]

The Deification of God

One final point should be brought out about Joseph Smith's teachings concerning deification. While it is true that the final doctrine revealed to the Prophet about God -- that "God himself was once as we are now, and is an exalted man, and sits enthroned in yonder heavens!"[460] -- is not advocated by any of the early Christian Fathers, it is fair to say that every other doctrine leading up to this conclusion *was* present in early Christianity, and perhaps this further knowledge was lost with the Apostles. In any case, Joseph Smith preached that "things that have not been before revealed" would be known in this dispensation,[461] so the fact that the one doctrine at the pinnacle of his teaching on this subject is missing in early Christian literature is perfectly consistent with his claims.[462]

Does this doctrine contradict the scriptures? Even the *Book of Mormon* states, "I know that God is not a partial God, neither a changeable being; but he is unchangeable from all eternity to all eternity . . . ." (Moroni 8:18) In order to understand the LDS view, our readers will have to step into an ancient Hebrew mindset for a moment. The ancient Greeks were absolutely enamored with metaphysics -- with "being," "essence," "eternity," etc. The

Greek philosophers pondered incessantly about how the material world relates to the true reality, whereas for the Hebrews the material world *was* reality. When they wrote about God, they didn't obsess about his "being" or "essence," but rather focused on His relationship to men and the world. Likewise, when they spoke of God's nature and eternity, they used *relative* terms -- relative, that is, *to them*. For example, many of the Biblical passages which speak of God's immutability do so in terms of His honesty, justice, mercy, and constancy. (See Titus 1:2; Numbers 23:19; 1 Samuel 15:29; Hebrews 6:18; Genesis 18:25; Ezekiel 18:14-32; Isaiah 46:10-11; Mark 13:31; Matt. 24:35; Luke 1:20; James 1:17; Daniel 6:26: Hebrews 6:18-19) Christopher Stead explains, "The Old Testament writers sometimes speak of God as unchanging . . . . In Christian writers influenced by Greek philosophy this doctrine is developed in an absolute metaphysical sense. Hebrew writers are more concrete, and their thinking includes two main points: (1) God has the dignity appropriate to old age, but without its disabilities . . . ; and (2) God is faithful to his covenant promises, even though men break theirs . . . ."[463] (Cf. Isaiah 40:28; Exodus 34:9-10) When God is described as "From everlasting to everlasting" (Psalm 41:13 NEB), the word translated as "everlasting" is the Hebrew *olam*, which means "(practically) eternity" or "time out of mind."[464] Another Psalm (104:5 New American Standard Bible) says that God "established the earth upon its foundations, so that it will not totter forever and ever." And yet Isaiah (24:20 NEB) saw a future time when "the earth reels to and fro like a drunken man . . . ." To the Hebrew mind these passages were not contradictory, because terms like "everlasting" and "forever" were relative terms, and they had no conception of "eternity" and "infinity" as modern people see them.

So it is with the Latter-day Saints. We see such scriptural statements about the "everlasting" and "unchanging" God as an indication of God's perfect and unchanging moral character, as well as God's eternity *relative* to men. God is spoken of as the "only true God," because *in relation to us* this is perfectly true. Given this Hebrew mindset, it is easy to see how Latter-day Saints can accept the biblical statements about God and also believe that God was once a man, having a Father Himself. And as it turns out, some early Christians may have believed the same type of doctrine. Consider the reasoning of Irenaeus of Lyons (ca. 180 A.D.) while arguing against the Gnostic belief that the Creator was only a secondary God.[465] Irenaeus pounded home the fact that the true God *is* the Creator, but what about the possibility that there is a God above God? And what was God doing before the creation of the world? Irenaeus cited Matthew 24:36, where Christ indicates that only the Father knows the time of the Second Advent, and asserted that since even Jesus doesn't know everything, we ought to leave such unrevealed questions to God.

> "If, for instance, any one asks, 'What was God doing before
> He made the world?' we reply that the answer to such a

question lies with God Himself. For that this world was formed perfect by God, receiving a beginning in time, the Scriptures teach us; but no Scripture reveals to us what God was employed about before this event . . . . The Father, therefore, has been declared by our Lord to excel with respect to knowledge; for this reason, that we, too, as long as we are connected with the scheme of things in this world, should leave perfect knowledge, and such questions [as have been mentioned], to God, and should not by any chance, while we seek to investigate the sublime nature of the Father, fall into the danger of starting the question whether there is another God above God."[466]

Certainly Irenaeus believed no such thing, though he came as close as possible to this view, given his own Greek conception of God (which he quoted almost verbatim from the philosopher Xenophanes).[467] Irenaeus taught that though at first we are "merely men," we can become "at length gods . . . ."[468] He also wrote, "our Lord Jesus Christ, who did . . . become what we are, that He might bring us to be even what He is Himself."[469] However, for him God was the "uncreated One" of the philosophers, and everything else was created from nothing, so "inasmuch as they are not uncreated, for this very reason do they come short of the perfect." Men who become gods will "receive a faculty of the Uncreated," and God "shall overcome the substance of created nature" by bestowing eternal life. Progress toward godhood will result in "approximating to the uncreated One" and bring one "nigh unto God," but in the final analysis men will still be contingent beings.[470] Irenaeus was not shy at all about labeling the Gnostic heresies as damnable and ridiculous falsehoods, yet in this case his language was strangely subdued. It is not clear whether this particular doctrine had been revealed to the early Christians, but certainly the Hebrew conception of God had not died out in all quarters of the Church, and in this mindset these "speculations" could be seen as a distinct possibility. There were some Christians -- "orthodox" Christians -- who were "speculating" about these things, or Irenaeus would have said things differently.

Conclusion: The True Nature of the Universe

What is the nature of God? What is the nature of humankind? What relationship does the material universe have to the things of the spirit? All of these questions lead back to the question of what the nature of the Universe itself is. The answers one chooses cannot be verified experimentally -- they are just assumed, and these assumptions dictate how one interprets the various passages of scripture. Protestant theologian Elmer Towns of Liberty University explains that a system of doctrine may be completely consistent with itself, but still be inconsistent with "natural revelation," or the nature of the Universe: "A system of theology may be a consistent doctrinal system, but when the second test is applied, its theory does not correspond with truth found in natural revelation."[471]

It has been shown that the Universe revealed through Joseph Smith is closer to the earliest Christian cosmology than the Universe of mainstream Christian thought. But isn't it conceivable that God just allowed the Church to believe in fantasies about material Gods and creation out of chaos until it was ready to accept the truth, which God brought into the Church through Greek philosophy? Indeed, many historians of early Christianity accept the fact that Greek philosophical tenets were adopted into the Church, but believe it was actually a good thing! Finally the Church was grounded on a solid foundation of Reason, they say.

However, Joseph Smith presents us with a dilemma. If he was not inspired by God to restore the original doctrines, which represent the true nature of the Universe, where did he get them? At a time when not much information was available about the early Church, Joseph Smith came up with exactly the type of doctrines that were believed by these primitive saints. Was Joseph inspired by God? By Satan? Did he just get lucky? The reader must answer these questions for himself.

Chapter Notes

Note 1: The "Angel of God's Presence" in Abraham 1:15-16

One of the most striking extra-biblical accounts in the *Book of Abraham* is the story of Abraham's harrowing escape from the idolatrous priests who were about to sacrifice him.

> And as they lifted up their hands upon me, that they might offer me up and take away my life, behold, I lifted up my voice unto the Lord my God and the Lord hearkened and heard, and he filled me with the vision of the Almighty, and the angel of his presence stood by me, and immediately unloosed my bands; And his voice was unto me: Abraham, Abraham, behold, my name is Jehovah, and I have heard thee, and have come down to deliver thee, and to take thee away from thy father's house, and from all thy kinsfolk, into a strange land which thou knowest not of . . . . (Abraham 1:15-16)

Certainly the passage seems innocuous enough at first glance, but upon reflection certain phrases in this passage become troubling. The angel figure who came to save Abraham is identified as the "angel of [God's] presence," a rather unusual phrase, but on the other hand the angel identifies himself as Jehovah! Was the "angel of the presence" merely a messenger, speaking as if he were Jehovah, or was this actually the manifestation of the God of Abraham, Isaac, and Jacob? The answer is given away when Jehovah says, "I have heard thee, and *have come down to deliver thee* . . . ." And so we can be reasonably sure that Jehovah himself was the "angel of God's presence."

Within LDS theology, this designation is certainly not commonplace, but it would be an acceptable one for Jehovah (or Yahweh), who was the preincarnate Jesus Christ. Thus, Jehovah is the Word, the messenger (Greek *angellos*) of salvation, the Son of God who is one in Godhead with His Father (Elohim or El Elyon = "God Most High"), but in another sense a "second God," the greatest of the sons of God. In other words, for Latter-day Saints it would not be a contradiction to designate Jehovah as both an "angel" and "God."

No doubt this is blatant heresy for both modern Judaism and mainstream Christianity, which make no distinction between Elohim and Yahweh, but recently many (non-Mormon) scholars have begun to recognize that not only were the Most High God and Yahweh conceived of as distinct beings in the oldest stratum of Israelite and early Christian thought, but *Yahweh (and later Jesus) were given the designation "Angel of the Presence."* We will now examine some of the evidence for this interpretation.

The "Angel(s) of the Presence"

We have seen in this chapter that Yahweh was originally thought of as both God and angel, but what of this strange title, "Angel of the Presence"? Barker intimates that this was once one of Yahweh's titles as well, which was later given to the archangels.[472] Segal explains that whoever was designated as the chief angel in the Israelite literature was also given the title "Angel of the Presence," and was regarded as superior to the others. [473]

Accordingly, Luke and the apocryphal book of Tobit refer to angels who stand in the presence of God. "And the angel answering said unto him, I am Gabriel, that stand in the presence of God . . . ." (Luke 1:19, KJV) "I am Raphael, one of the seven angels who stand in attendance on the Lord and enter his glorious presence." (Tobit 12:15, NEB) However, Isaiah is the only Biblical writer to use the phrase "angel of his presence." Speaking of the goodness of Yahweh toward the house of Israel, the Hebrew text of Isaiah 63:8-9 (followed by the KJV) reads: "For he [Yahweh] said, Surely they are my people, children that will not lie: so he was their Saviour. In all their affliction he was afflicted, and the angel of his presence saved them . . . ." It is clear from the text that Yahweh saved his people by the "angel of his presence," but it is not at all evident that Yahweh was *equated with* this angel, although this is most certainly the case. The ancient translators of the Greek Old Testament (Septuagint or LXX, translated in the second and third centuries B.C.) knew of this tradition, and therefore made no reference to the "angel of his presence," but translated the verse in question as, "It was no envoy, no angel, but he himself that delivered them." (Isaiah 63:9, NEB) Clearly, Yahweh *was* the "angel of his presence."

Jesus as Yahweh and the "Angel of the Presence"

The belief in Yahweh as Israel's second God, the chief angel, was the basis of early Christian Christology. But even more to the point is Jean Daniélou's claim that in certain early Jewish Christian traditions both Jesus and the Holy Spirit were believed to be the two "Angels of the Presence transcending all others."[474]

Conclusion

We have established that Abraham's identification of Yahweh with "the angel of his presence" was consistent with the earliest Israelite traditions, and with the earliest Christian traditions. But if we assume, as the critics of the *Book of Abraham* do, that Joseph Smith created this remarkable document by applying his fertile imagination to the sources he had at hand, how did he come up with this strange designation for Yahweh? The only Biblical source for the phrase would have been Isaiah 63:9, but we have seen that this verse gives no hint that Yahweh *was equated with* "the angel of his presence." This conclusion can only be drawn when the Greek text is compared with the Hebrew. However, it seems unlikely that Joseph Smith had access to a translation of the Septuagint, so again we are at a loss to find a source for the Prophet's teaching. Consider also that we have not been able to find even a single case where Joseph Smith used this title to refer to Yahweh, apart from this solitary passage in the *Book of Abraham,* or even to the Septuagint. Therefore, we are forced to conclude that Joseph Smith was inconceivably lucky in his choice of words, or *the Patriarch Abraham* actually chose these words to describe his God.

Note 2: The Pre-Existence in Judaism

Hammerton-Kelly reports that "the idea that certain things pre-exist in the mind of God or in heaven has a long history in the Biblical and early Jewish traditions."[475] For instance, "in Job 15:8 the primal man is pictured in the council of the gods before the world was made . . . ."[476] Also, the translation of Jeremiah 23:18 in the *New English Bible* has the Lord rebuking the false prophets, because they were not foreordained in the pre-mortal council: "But which of them has stood in the council of the LORD, seen him and heard his word?" E. Theodore Mullen explains: "The divine council formed the background for prophecy . . . . This is the true prophet's claim to authority. From the pronouncement of the council he receives the decree that he is to deliver. Those prophets who have not participated in the council are unable to proclaim the divine decree."[477]

An intriguing account of the great council occurs in the apocryphal *Apocalypse of Abraham*, which had its origin in Judaism but in its present form has been modified by Jewish Christian groups. (Note the similarities between this ancient account of Abraham's vision of the council and that translated by Joseph Smith in Abraham 3, quoted above.)

> And everything I had planned to be came into being: it was already pre-figured in this, for all the things and all the people you have seen stood before me before they were created. And I said, Mighty and Eternal Ruler, who then are the people in this picture on this side and on that? And he said to me, Those on the left side are the many peoples which have existed in the past, and after you are appointed, some for judgment and restoration, some for vengeance and perdition, until the end of the age. And those on the right side of the picture, they are the people set apart for me from the people with Azazil [Satan]. These are the people who are going to spring from you and will be called my people.[478]

Additionally, David Winston reports that the *Bereshith Rabba* and *Ruth Rabba* tell of God consulting the souls of the righteous before deciding to create the world.[479] *The Wisdom of Solomon*, in the Apocrypha, states: "As a child I was born to excellence, and a noble soul fell to my lot; or rather, I myself was noble; and I entered into an unblemished body."[480] The *Midrash Kee Tov* states that all the souls of the righteous, including Adam, Noah, Abraham, Moses, etc. "were with God before the creation of the world."[481] And an important Jewish theologian at about the time of Christ, Philo, taught that "the heavenly man is God's offspring . . . while the earthly man is merely the work of an artificer."[482]

Origen quoted a Jewish apocryphal document called the *Prayer of Joseph*, which asserted that Jacob was one of the archangels in his premortal existence:

> Thus Jacob says: "I, Jacob, who speak to you, arid Israel, I am an angel of God, a ruling spirit, and Abraham and Isaac were created before every work of God; and I am Jacob, called Jacob by men, but my name is Israel, called Israel by God, a man seeing God, because I am the first-born of every creature which God caused to live."[483]

The Enoch texts also contain the common element of the pre-existence. (This is significant, since the early Christians apparently took at least one of these documents very seriously. Indeed, Jude referred to one of them in his general epistle. (See Jude 1:14) 2 *Enoch* states that, "all souls are prepared to eternity, before the formation of the world,"[484] and cites Adam as the prime example:

> And I placed on the earth, a second angel, honorable, great and glorious, and I appointed him as ruler to rule on earth and to have my wisdom, and there was none like him of earth of all my existing creatures . . . . I called his name Adam.[485]

Also, *1 Enoch* relates that before God created the world he held a consultation with the souls of the righteous.[486]

These passages from the Enoch literature are also important because they are some of the stock texts of the Jewish Apocalyptic genre, and many scholars see "Jewish apocalyptic as the dominant conceptual framework of earliest Christianity."[487] Indeed, the Revelation of John is more properly titled the "Apocalypse of John." Therefore, the source from which the earliest Christians got their doctrine of the pre-existence seems obvious, but some may be surprised to learn that the belief that men, angels and gods are of the same race may have been *the original* Jewish belief, as well. This, of course, is the essence of the Latter-day Saint doctrine. According to The *Universal Jewish Encyclopedia* the heavenly beings, including Jehovah, who appeared to Abraham in Genesis 18 and 19 were originally referred to simply as "men."

> They appear in the guise of human beings and, probably for want of a better term, the story speaks of them as "men." In the continuation of the narrative they are twice called "angels" (Gen. 19:1, 15), but the very fact that the story continues to speak of them also and more frequently as "men" (Gen. 19:5, 8, 10, 12 and 16) indicates that the term "angel" was undoubtedly substituted by a later age for the original term "men."[488]

Chapter 4: Salvation History and Requirements

"The great plan of salvation is a theme which ought to occupy our strict attention, and be regarded as one of heaven's best gifts to mankind. No consideration whatever ought to deter us from showing ourselves approved in the sight of God, according to His divine requirement. Men not unfrequently forget that they are dependent upon heaven for every blessing which they are permitted to enjoy, and that for every opportunity granted them they are to give an account."

- Joseph Smith[489]

In the previous chapter we discussed the fact that Christianity was cast in the mold of Jewish Apocalyptic thought. And according to Hennecke and Schneemelcher:

> The outstanding characteristic of the apocalyptic thought-world is determinism. God has fore-ordained everything: all that happens happens precisely according to the fixed plan of God, which human plans and actions can neither advance nor hinder.[490]

It is not surprising, therefore, that early Christian documents such as the *Epistle of the Apostles* speak of "the plan of the Father."[491] We have already seen that early Christianity, as well as the Prophet Joseph Smith, preached that this plan was formulated in the great councils in heaven before the creation of the world, and that the final purpose of the plan is the deification of God's children.

But it is not sufficient to know *that there exists* such a plan and *what the end result of it will be*. Of more immediate concern to those of us working out our salvation are the specifics of the plan. That is, we must know what will happen to us between birth and our final state, as well as how to make sure our final state is that which God intended for us. Therefore, the purpose of this chapter will be to map the way to salvation, as taught by Christ, as believed by the early Christians, and as restored by Joseph Smith.

Adam and the Fall

Adam and Eve -- the First Members of the Human Family

Salvation history must necessarily begin with Adam, the first man, and Eve, his wife. And as it turns out, Joseph Smith restored two points[492] of doctrine concerning the first man that are supported by early Christian evidence, but which are completely at odds with the interpretations of modern mainstream Christianity.

Adam and Michael

First, according to Joseph Smith, Adam was Michael the Archangel in the premortal existence.[493] Even now Adam retains his authority: "The keys have to be brought from heaven whenever the gospel is sent. When they are revealed from heaven, it is by Adam's authority."[494] Consider the similarity of the preceding statement with that about Michael in an ancient Coptic Christian document:

> And I answered and said unto the Cherubim, "How doth it come to pass that the name of Michael is written upon their garments? And wherefore do they cry out?" And the Cherubim answered and said unto me, "No angel is allowed to come upon the earth unless the name of Michael is written upon his garments, for otherwise the Devil would lead them astray."[495]

Joseph Smith also taught that Adam, as Michael, helped the Father and Son in the creation. Similarly, Alan Segal reports that the ancient rabbis wrote polemics against various "Two Powers" heresies, which included Christianity, which taught that Adam had been a helper in the creation.[496] Thus the Gnostic Christian *Apocalypse of Adam* taught that Adam "helps in creation and is higher in rank than the god who created him and Eve . . . ."[497] And interestingly enough, some of these "heretics" believed that "Michael and Gabriel were associates of God in creation."[498] Therefore, while I have found no direct evidence that Adam was equated with Michael, there are some tantalizing clues that indicate this might once have been the case. At any rate, certain aspects of Joseph Smith's teaching on the matter *are* confirmed in the ancient literature.

The Necessity of the Fall

Second, Adam and Eve are important figures in all of Jewish, Muslim, and Christian theology because not only were they the parents of the entire human race, but it was their sin which caused the Fall of all humankind into this sinful world of pain and sorrow. This made necessary the atonement of Jesus Christ, to bring mankind back from this sinful condition into the blessedness, immortality, and peace our first parents enjoyed before the Fall in the Garden of Eden.

But Joseph Smith took a different view of the Fall from the rest of the Christian world. Consider his doctrine of deification, for example. Certainly Adam was no "god" when he lived in innocence. It was only *after* the Fall that God said, "Behold, the man is become as one of us, to know good and evil . . . ." (Genesis 3:22) Joseph Smith looked on the Fall as a necessary step in the process of salvation, and Adam and Eve's act of disobedience as a "transgression" of the law of the Garden rather than a "sin." Thus, the prophet Lehi in *The Book of Mormon* explained:

> And now, Behold, if Adam had not transgressed he would not have fallen, but he would have remained in the garden of Eden. And all things which were created must have remained in the same state in which they were after they were created; and they must have remained forever, and had no end. And they would have had no children; wherefore they would have remained in a state of innocence, having no joy, for they knew no misery; doing no good, for they knew no sin. But behold, all things have been done in the wisdom of him who knoweth all things. Adam fell that men might be; and men are, that they might have joy. (2 Nephi 2:22-25)

The writings of several early Christian writers agree with the Prophet that the Fall was "fortunate." Clement of Alexandria exclaimed: "O mystic wonder! The Lord was laid low, and man rose up; and he that fell from Paradise receives as the reward of obedience something greater [than Paradise]--namely, heaven itself."[499] Referring to the Fall, Irenaeus wrote:

> "Thine own apostasy shall heal thee;" God thus determining all things beforehand for the bringing of man to perfection, for his edification, and for the revelation of His dispensations, that goodness may both be made apparent, and righteousness perfected, and that the Church may be fashioned after the image of His Son, and that man may finally be brought to maturity at some future time, becoming ripe through such privileges to see and comprehend God.[500]

Certain Jewish Christian documents, especially the *Clementine Homilies*,[501] went even further. In the *Homilies*, Peter stated that Adam "was ignorant of nothing,"[502] "neither was Adam a transgressor."[503]

But while Willis Barnstone pegs this as a major theme of Gnostic Christianity, and we have shown it to have been present in early Catholic and Jewish Christianity, later Christian mystics such as Pseudo-Dionysius (sixth century) claimed that since partaking of the tree of knowledge was what got Adam and Eve into trouble in the first place, the true Christian should actually strive for ignorance![504]

Original Sin and Original Guilt

The Mainstream Doctrine of Original Sin

Since mainstream Christians have essentially lost the doctrine of deification, they consider the Fall a wholly unfortunate event. Likewise, the loss of the doctrine of pre-existence has allowed many of them to adopt the view that even infants, newborn into the sinful world, are guilty of Adam's sin, and may be excluded from the Kingdom of God if steps (completely beyond the infants' control) are not taken to protect them.

The mainstream doctrine of "original sin" thus includes the following elements. 1) Adam's Transgression had the effect of passing along a "sinful nature" to his posterity. 2) The "nature" spoken of includes both body and soul, so that an infant comes into the world not only with a body that is beset by animal passions, but a spirit that has a disposition to commit sin. 3) Not only is everyone *affected* by Adam's transgression, but they are *guilty* of it since they were present "in Adam" when he sinned. 4) Some churches, notably those with a Calvinist background, actually believe that the fall of human nature has been so complete that humans are incapable of truly righteous actions without the aid of the grace of Jesus Christ.

Latter-day Saints and Original Sin

Latter-day Saints, on the other hand, reject this doctrine of "original sin" as it is taught by the churches and proclaim that the atonement of Christ automatically pays for those effects of the Fall that are beyond our individual control. "We believe that men will be punished for their own sins, and not for Adam's transgression." (Articles of Faith 2)[505] However, the Fall *did* have an effect. Mankind *has* inherited a "fallen nature," but that is not to imply the "total depravity" of the Calvinists because while the human body is subject to animal passions, the immortal soul comes from God pure and righteous. Thus, all people are innocent from birth, and (except for those with diminished intellectual and moral capacity) are equipped with the moral agency for choosing between good and evil.

The New Testament and Original Sin

Paul spoke of the effects of the Fall in three closely related passages in Romans 5. "Wherefore, as by one man sin entered into the world, and death by sin; and so death passed upon all men, for that all have sinned." (Romans 5:12) "Nevertheless, death reigned from Adam to Moses, even over them that had not sinned after the similitude of Adam's transgression . . . ." (Romans

5:14) "For as by one man's disobedience many were made sinners, so by the obedience of one shall many be made righteous." (Romans 5:19) It is clear from these passages that Paul believed that somehow Adam brought sin and death into the world, but it is not clear exactly what he believed was passed from Adam to his descendants. Elsewhere Paul explained, "Now if I do that I would not, it is no more I that do it, but sin that dwelleth in me." (Romans 7:20) Therefore, it seems obvious that Adam was not just the first *example* of a transgressor, but his transgression actually had the effect of passing a *fallen nature* to his descendants. We shall see that the New Testament gives some clues about what exactly fallen nature is, but it must be admitted that it is not really explicit about the matter. In spite of this, it can easily be shown that the LDS view of original sin was in harmony with the earliest known Christian teachings.

The Sinful Nature

What exactly is the sinful nature of mankind? For Latter-day Saints it is closely linked to the mortal body. Thus the prophet Nephi lamented, "And why should I yield to sin, because of my flesh?" (2 Nephi 4:27) The immortal soul is basically good[506] and mortal life is a constant struggle between the desires of the flesh and spirit. However, the spirit can be marred and transformed as the desires of the flesh prevail, and indeed, all human souls except that of Jesus have sustained the damage of personal sin. In addition, the very environment of the fallen world and the temptations of the Devil and his angels combine with the flesh in its war against the soul. Bible-believing Christians have always believed in the fallen nature of the world and the reality of the devil, but they do not agree with the Latter-day Saints about the initial purity of the souls that come from God.

But Paul at least hinted that he held a view similar to that of the Latter-day Saints. For instance, in several passages he spoke of the war between the flesh and the soul. "For the flesh lusteth against the Spirit, and the Spirit against the flesh: and these are contrary the one to the other: so that ye cannot do the things that ye would." (Galatians 5:17; cf. Romans 8:1-4) "Wretched man that I am, who shall deliver me from this body of death?" (Romans 7:24) Peter spoke of "fleshly lusts, which war against the soul." (1 Peter 2:11)[507] And little children were certainly considered innocent by Jesus, who told his disciples to let the children come to him, for "of such is the kingdom of heaven." (Matthew 19:14) Many of the early Fathers were even more explicit in their beliefs.

For example, the *Epistle to Diognetus* asserted that "The flesh hates the soul, and wars against it . . . ."[508] Clement of Alexandria elaborated:

> This is the true athlete -- he who in the great stadium, the fair world, is crowned for the true victory over all the passions. For He who prescribes the contest is the Almighty God, and He who awards the prize is the only-begotten: Son

of God. Angels and gods are spectators; and the contest, embracing all the varied exercises, is "not against flesh and blood," but against the spiritual powers of inordinate passions that work through the flesh.[509]

And the *Clementine Recognitions* preached the same doctrine:

> For it is his duty to examine with just judgment the things which we say, and to understand that we speak the words of truth, that, knowing how things are, and directing his life in good actions, he may be found a partaker of the kingdom of heaven, subjecting to himself the desires of the flesh, and becoming lord of them, that so at length he himself also may become the pleasant possession of the Ruler of all.[510]

Barnabas preached that the new birth heals the spirit so that it can become as it was in childhood: "He hath made us after another pattern, [it is His purpose] that we should possess the soul of children, inasmuch as He has created us anew by His Spirit."[511] Papias wrote that the early Christians "called those who practised a godly guilelessness, children . . . ."[512] Finally, the undeniably orthodox *Pastor of Hermas* taught that it is impossible for evil to originate in the heart of an infant:

> And they who believed from the twelfth mountain, which was white, are the following: they are as infant children, in whose hearts no evil originates; nor did they know what wickedness is, but always remained as children. Such accordingly, without doubt, dwell in the kingdom of God, because they defiled in nothing the commandments of God; but they remained like children all the days of their life in the same mind. All of you, then, who shall remain stedfast, and be as children, without doing evil, will be more honoured than all who have been previously mentioned; for all infants are honourable before God, and are the first persons with Him.[513]

From these early witnesses we can infer that Christianity originally did not believe that the soul came from God already tainted by "original sin." However, as the second century drew to a close, and the doctrine of the pre-existence of souls began to be lost, the situation changed. The great theologian, Tertullian, was the major player in this shift.

Tertullian believed a theory of the soul's origin known as "traducianism," which teaches that both the bodies and souls of all humans were contained in embryo within Adam, and new souls are created by the "psychic copulation" of the souls of the parents. Thus, when Adam's soul was tainted with sin, so were ours, and so no human soul comes into the world in purity.[514] Tertullian dismissed the passages in the New Testament that speak of the war between the flesh and spirit by saying that the flesh is merely an instrument that does the bidding of the soul:

> Every soul, then, by reason of its birth, has its nature in Adam until it is born again in Christ; moreover, it is unclean all the while that it remains without this regeneration; and because unclean, it is actively sinful, and suffuses even the flesh (by reason of their conjunction) with its own shame. Now although the flesh is sinful, and we are forbidden to walk in accordance with it, and its works are condemned as lusting against the spirit, and men on its account are censured as carnal, yet the flesh has not such ignominy on its own account. For it is not of itself that it thinks anything or feels anything for the purpose of advising or commanding sin. How should it, indeed? It is only a ministering thing, and its ministration is not like that of a servant or familiar friend -- animated and human beings; but rather that of a vessel, or something of that kind: it is body, not soul.[515]

Tertullian also explained the end result of the contamination of the soul:

> All these endowments of the soul which are bestowed on it at birth are still obscured and depraved by the malignant being who, in the beginning, regarded them with envious eye, so that they are never seen in their spontaneous action, nor are they administered as they ought to be.[516]

It is interesting to note that even though Origen believed in the pre-existence of the soul, he still accepted the doctrine that the soul is tainted at birth.[517] Origen was a Platonist who believed that immortal souls would not have voluntarily associated themselves with matter, so he reasoned that they must have had a "pre-cosmic Fall" where, because of various degrees of rebellion, they were thrust down into the material world.[518]

Throughout the various arguments associated with this doctrine, it was recognized by all that the question of original sin was intimately tied to the question of the soul's origin.[519] As was discussed above, this question was not a settled matter even as late as the fifth century, and Augustine himself was baffled by it to the end of his life. Augustine wrote in a letter to Jerome that the chief reason he could not decide between the various theories of the soul's origin was that none of them really explained the transmission of "original sin":

Some years ago, when I wrote certain books concerning Free Will, which have gone forth into the hands of many, and are now in the possession of very many readers, after referring to these four opinions as to the manner of the soul's incarnation, -- (1) that all other souls are derived from the one which was given to the first man [i.e. traducianism]; (2) that for each individual a new soul is made; (3) that souls already in existence somewhere are sent by divine act into the bodies; or (4) glide into them of their own accord . . . . Leaving, therefore, out of the question this heretical error, I desire to know which of the other four opinions we ought to choose. For whichever of them may justly claim our preference, far be it from us to assail this article of faith, about which we have no uncertainty, that every soul, even the soul of an infant, requires to be delivered from the binding guilt of sin, and that there is no deliverance except through Jesus Christ and Him crucified.[520]

Note that by this time Augustine could call the doctrine of the tainted nature of the soul an "article of faith." Eventually, Augustine leaned toward traducianism, but he was still uncomfortable with this solution since it implied Tertullian's belief in the corporeality of the soul.[521]

"Total Depravity" and Predestination

Whether they believed in the effect of original sin on the soul or not, Christians since the earliest times have maintained that human nature has elements of both good and evil, and hence people are capable of choosing either path. However, some theologians, notably the Reformer John Calvin and his followers, adopted the doctrine of "total depravity." That is, the fallen nature is such that humans are not even capable of choosing good. John Calvin admitted that his doctrine was not preached by the Fathers, but he still claimed support from the Bible:

For under the *second* head, where [the early Fathers] treat of Original Sin, they declare that free-will, though impaired in its powers and biased, is not however extinguished. I will not dispute about a name, but since they contend that liberty has by no means been extinguished, they certainly understand that the human will has still some power left to choose good . . . . Therefore, if we believe them, Original Sin has weakened us, so that the defect of our will is not pravity but weakness. For if the will were wholly depraved, its health would not only be impaired but lost until it were renewed. The latter, however, is uniformly the doctrine of Scripture. To omit innumerable passages where Paul

126

discourses on the nature of the human race, he does not charge free-will with weakness, but declares all men to be useless, alienated from God, and enslaved to the tyranny of sin; so much so, that he says they are unfit to think a good thought. (Rom. 3:12; 2 Cor. 3:5)[522]

But Calvin mischaracterized Paul's teachings. Note the following passage: "For when the Gentiles, which have not the law, do by nature the things contained in the law, these having not the law, are a law unto themselves: Which shew the work of the law written in their hearts . . . ." (Romans 2:14-15) Now, if men can obey the law of God "by nature," then it seems certain that their "nature" is not entirely depraved.

Since Calvin himself admitted that the writings of the early Fathers did not support his arguments, the matter is not in dispute, but we will examine a portion of this evidence, anyway. In the second century we have the testimony of the *Epistle to Diognetus*, Justin Martyr, Irenaeus, Clement of Alexandria, and the *Clementine Recognitions*, (presented below, respectively) among others:

He sent Him; as to men He sent Him; as a Saviour He sent Him, and as seeking to persuade, not to compel us; for violence has no place in the character of God.[523]

But lest some suppose, from what has been said by us, that we say that whatever happens, happens by a fatal necessity, because it is foretold as known beforehand, this too we explain. We have learned from the prophets, and we hold it to be true, that punishments, and chastisements, and good rewards, are rendered according to the merit of each man's actions. Since if it be not so, but all things happen by fate, neither is anything at all in our own power. For if it be fated that this man, e.g., be good, and this other evil, neither is the former meritorious nor the latter to be blamed. And again, unless the human race have the power of avoiding evil and choosing good by free choice, they are not accountable for their actions, of whatever kind they be.[524]

For there is no coercion with God, but a good will [towards us] is present with Him continually. And therefore does He give good counsel to all. And in man, as well as in angels, He has placed the power of choice (for angels are rational beings), so that those who had yielded obedience might justly possess what is good, given indeed by God, but preserved by themselves . . . . But if some had been made by nature bad, and others good, these latter would not be deserving of praise for being good, for such were they created; nor would the former be reprehensible, for thus they were made [originally].[525]

For believing and obeying are in our own power.[526]

Whether any one, truly hearing the word of the true Prophet; is willing or unwilling to receive it, and to embrace His burden, that is, the precepts of life, he has either in his power, for we are free in will. For if it were so, that those who hear had it not in their power to do otherwise than they had heard, there were some power of nature in virtue of which it were not free to him to pass over to another opinion. Or if, again, no one of the hearers could at all receive it, this also were a power of nature which should compel the doing of some one thing, and should leave no place for the other course. But now, since it is free for the mind to turn its judgment to which side it pleases, and to choose the way which it approves, it is clearly manifest that there is in men a liberty of choice.[527]

The following statement by Lactantius is representative of the attitude of the third-century theologians:

He devised an unspeakable work, in what manner He might create an infinite multitude of souls, which being at first united with frail and feeble bodies, He might place in the midst between good and evil, that He might set virtue before them composed as they were of both natures; that they might not attain to immortality by a delicate and easy course of life, but might arrive at that unspeakable reward of eternal life with the utmost difficulty and great labours.[528]

In the fourth century, Gregory of Nazianzus and Cyril of Jerusalem made the following comments:

For there are people so evilly disposed as to think that some men are of an utterly ruined nature, and some of a nature which is saved, and that others are of such a disposition as their will may lead them to, either to the better, or to the worse. For that men may have a certain aptitude, one more, another less, I too admit; but not that this aptitude alone suffices for perfection, but that it is reason which calls this out, that nature may proceed to action, just as fire is produced when a flint is struck with iron.[529]

The soul is self-governed: and though the devil can suggest, he has not the power to compel against the will. He pictures to thee the thought of fornication: if thou wilt, thou acceptest it; if thou wilt not, thou rejectest. For if thou were a fornicator by necessity, then for what cause did God prepare hell? If thou were a doer of righteousness by nature and not by will, wherefore did God prepare crowns of ineffable glory? The sheep is gentle, but never was it crowned for its gentleness: since its gentle quality belongs to it not from choice but by nature.[530]

Although Gregory indicated that by his time there were some heretics who entertained such notions, the majority of church thinkers rejected them. However, one later mainstream theologian, Augustine, did go beyond his forbears in this respect. He taught that while it is true that God's grace can strengthen our will to do the right, we are utterly incapable of even willing to do good without the grace of Jesus Christ:

He operates, therefore, without us, in order that we may will; but when we will, and so will that we may act, He co-operates with us. We can, however, ourselves do nothing to effect good works of piety without Him either working that we may will, or co-working when we will. Now, concerning His working that we may will, it is said: "It is God which worketh in you, even to will." [Phil. 2:13] While of His co-working with us, when we will and act by willing, the Apostle says, "We know that in all things there is co-working for good to them that love God." [Rom. 8:28][531]

But if so, then how can *anyone* be saved? Augustine, having lost the true knowledge of the preexistence, appealed to Paul's references to "predestination" or "foreordination." In his view, these passages implied that God predestines certain people to be saved and others to be damned, and therefore gives the grace necessary to accept Christ to those in the "saved" category. What about those who would never even hear the gospel in their lifetimes? Augustine reasoned that anyone who was predestined for grace would be given that chance:

Whosoever, then, are made to differ from that original condemnation by such bounty of divine grace, there is no doubt but that for such it is provided that they should hear the gospel, and when they hear they believe, and in the faith which worketh by love they persevere unto the end . . . .[532]

Against the charge that such a thing would make God unjust, Augustine defended his doctrine by saying that God's election was based on some sort of "secret justice," known only to God.[533] And what about Paul's assertion that Jesus wills "all men to be saved, and to come unto the knowledge of the truth"? (1 Timothy 2:3-4; cf. 2 Peter 3:9) Of course, Augustine reasoned, Paul was only speaking of "all men" *who had been elected*:

> And what is written, that "He wills all men' to be saved," while yet all men are not saved, may be understood in many ways, some of which I have mentioned in other writings of mine; but here I will say one thing: "He wills all men to be saved," is so said that all the predestinated may be understood by it, because every kind of men is among them.[534]

The fundamental issue for Augustine was that if God "elected" someone to salvation before the foundation of the world, how could God's election come to nothing as a result of human sin?

> Those, then, are elected, as has often been said, who are called according to the purpose, who also are predestinated and foreknown. If any one of these perishes, God is mistaken; but none of them perishes, because God is not mistaken. If any one of these perish, God is overcome by human sin; but none of them perishes, because God is overcome by nothing.[535]

This interpretation was never accepted generally by Christianity, but centuries later John Calvin adopted the same belief.[536] However, consider the logic of this position. If God creates all men out of nothing and if God has elected certain people to salvation by grace and others to condemnation, wouldn't everything happen exactly according to His plan? If it all originated from God in the first place, how can His purposes be frustrated? Thus, strict Calvinism is logically consistent only if one ignores the belief that God wills all men to be saved. On the other hand, other mainstream Christian churches are consistent on this issue only if they ignore or water down the idea of "predestination" or "foreordination," which is clearly taught in the Bible. Therefore, we can easily see how confusion arose during the early centuries of Christianity after the doctrine of the preexistence of man came into question and as the doctrine of creation out of nothing was adopted.

Original Guilt

Mainstream Christianity has traditionally believed that not only are all human souls tainted by "original sin," but as a consequence, they are also *guilty* of Adam's transgression. Consequently, this has led those who believe in the absolute necessity of baptism to preach that infants who die without receiving the grace of baptism will be excluded from the kingdom of God.[537] On the contrary, Latter-day Saints have been taught that "the Son of God hath atoned for original guilt, wherein the sins of the parents cannot be answered upon the heads of the children, for they are whole from the foundation of the world." (Moses 6:54) Therefore, "all little children" and "those who are without the law" are "alive in Christ." (Moroni 8:22) That is, any sins that are committed solely because of the negative effects of the transgression of Adam are automatically atoned for by Jesus Christ. Therefore, little children need no baptism to be redeemed, and neither do the mentally deficient who sin in ignorance.[538]

We have seen that Jesus preached the innocence of little children, for "of such is the kingdom of heaven." (Matthew 19:14) And early writers like *Barnabas* and Hermas could not have believed in original guilt, for they believed that "all infants are honourable before God, and are the first persons with Him."[539] The Apologists of the second century concurred in this belief.[540] Similarly, Clement of Alexandria specifically stated that we come into the world without sin:

> The righteous Job says: "Naked came I out of my mother's womb, and naked shall I return there;" not naked of possessions, for that were a trivial and common thing; but, as a just man, he departs naked of evil and sin, and of the unsightly shape which follows those who have led bad lives.[541]

It is interesting to note that in Clement's time the proponents of "original guilt" were the Gnostics[542], and he argued strenuously against them:

> It is for them to tell us how the newly born child could commit fornication or in what way the child who has never done anything at all has fallen under Adam's curse. The only thing left for them to say and still be consistent, I suppose, is that birth is evil not just for the body but for the soul for which the body exists.[543]

We have seen that around the turn of the third century Tertullian *did* preach that the birth of the soul is tainted, but he *did not* preach "original guilt," even though he approved of the practice of infant baptism:

> The father should not bear the iniquity of the son, nor the son the iniquity of the father, but that every man should be chargeable with his own sin; so that the harshness of the law

having been reduced after the hardness of the people, justice was no longer to judge the race, but individuals.[544]

The situation changed further as the third century progressed. For example, C.P. Bammel notes that the notion of the succession of original guilt is to be found in Origen's *Commentary on Romans*[545], yet Origen still did not believe that infants would be condemned because of it:

> The words "I once lived without the law" in Romans 7:9 are explained as referring to the fact that every man lives without the natural law until he reaches the age of reason. During this time sin is dormant, but when he reaches the age to be able to distinguish right and wrong sin revives.[546]

By the middle of the third century, however, Cyprian connected the practice of infant baptism with the regeneration from original guilt:

> But again, if even to the greatest sinners, and to those who had sinned much against God, when they subsequently believed, remission of sins is granted -- and nobody is hindered from baptism and from grace -- how much rather ought we to shrink from hindering an infant, who, being lately born, has not sinned, except in that, being born after the flesh according to Adam, he has contracted the contagion of the ancient death at its earliest birth, who approaches the more easily on this very account to the reception of the forgiveness of sins -- that to him are remitted, not his own sins, but the sins of another.[547]

This doctrine didn't become general for some time, however, and in the fourth century Cyril of Jerusalem was still preaching the original dogma:

> And learn this also, that the soul, before it came into this world, had committed no sin, but having come in sinless, we now sin of our free-will . . . . Remember also the Scripture, which saith, even as they did not like to retain God in their knowledge: and, That which may be known of God is manifest in them; and again, their eyes they have closed.[548]

By the time Augustine wrote in the fifth century, the practice of infant baptism had become so commonplace that he could use it as proof positive that infants were born with the contagion of "original guilt." According to him "the practice of infant baptism tells us that the infant soul, not merely its flesh, stands in need of cleansing."[549]

Certainly there have been many different opinions within Christianity about the effects of Adam's transgression, many of which with the Latter-day Saint and early Church belief that unbaptized infants would not be condemned.[550] However, it should be clear by now that Joseph Smith's doctrine of the preexistence of souls restored a crucial piece of the puzzle by showing *what* exactly is inherited from Adam. And the Prophet was in line with the early Church, as well as the more enlightened mainstream Christians[551], when he preached that the effects of the Fall are freely atoned for by Jesus Christ.

The Road to Salvation in Mortality

Dispensations -- a Gospel for All Ages

Whether one believes in "original guilt" or not, all Christians agree that there is only one way to undo the effects of the Fall, as well as save mankind from their own sins, and that is through the atonement of Jesus Christ. This is true for people who lived before the advent of Christ, as well as those who lived after, but mainstream Christianity has no consistent answer to the question of how those who lived before Jesus could take advantage of His atonement. For, if those before Christ could be saved by the law they knew, why was Jesus' atonement needed?

Christianity Before Christ

Joseph Smith provided a novel answer: The gospel has been preached on earth since the beginning, starting with Adam and Eve. Thus, Adam could be termed the first Christian. (See Moses 6:52-60) Whenever the gospel has been preached, however, and the priesthood given, sooner or later apostasy has occurred and the authority and truth of God removed. Therefore, in periods of apostasy men were left with as much or as little truth for which, in God's view, they could be morally responsible. As we are told in the *Book of Mormon*: "For behold, the Lord doth grant unto all nations, of their own nation and tongue, to teach his word, yea, in wisdom, all that he seeth fit that they should have . . . ." (Alma 29:8) But when a people is ready, God plants again the seed of the true gospel and Priesthood. As Joseph Smith stated, "It is in the order of heavenly things that God should always send a new dispensation into the world when men have apostatized from the truth and lost the priesthood . . . ."[552]

The dispensation inaugurated by the revelations and ordination of Joseph Smith is the last dispensation before the Second Coming of Christ, and is termed the "dispensation of the fulness of times" because it will "bring to light the things that have been revealed in all former dispensations; also other things that have not been before revealed."[553]

According to non-Mormon scholar Heikke Raisanen wrote that the Prophet's doctrine was to him a thing of "pure logic and downright beauty," and he noted that similar concepts may be found in Clement of Rome's (ca. 96 A.D.) letter and in the Pseudepigrapha.[554]   Indeed, Joseph Smith's doctrine agrees with many early Christian writings. Paul insisted that the Lord had "preached before the gospel unto Abraham, saying, In thee shall all nations be blessed." (Galatians 3:8) And Ignatius of Antioch agreed that the prophets knew of and preached Christ:

> For the divinest prophets lived according to Jesus Christ. On this account also they were persecuted, being inspired by grace to fully convince the unbelieving that there is one God, the Almighty, who has manifested Himself by Jesus Christ His Son, who is His Word, not spoken, but essential.[555]

Tatian, Theophilus, and Eusebius all agreed that the gospel was no recent invention, but, in fact, very ancient. "Let us, then, institute a comparison between them; and we shall find that our doctrines are older, not only than those of the Greeks, but than the invention of letters."[556]

> These periods, then, and all the above-mentioned facts, being viewed collectively, one can see the antiquity of the prophetical writings and the divinity of our doctrine, that the doctrine is not recent, nor our tenets mythical and false, as some think, but very ancient and true.[557]

> If any one should assert that all those who have enjoyed the testimony of righteousness, from Abraham himself back to the first man, were Christians in fact if not in name, he would not go beyond the truth . . . . So that it is clearly necessary to consider that religion, which has lately been preached to all nations through the teaching of Christ, the first and most ancient of all religions, and the one discovered by those divinely favored men in the age of Abraham.[558]

Cardinal Daniélou mentions some of these early authors and admits that this was the position of "the earliest Christian theologians."[559]

Degrees of Truth

Clement of Alexandria's belief coincides with the philosophy found in *The Book of Mormon* that God gives as much wisdom and knowledge to a nation as it is capable of receiving:

It is He who also gave philosophy to the Greeks by means of the inferior angels. For by an ancient and divine order the angels are distributed among the nations. But the glory of those who believe is "the Lord's portion." For either the Lord does not care for all men; and this is the case either because He is unable (which is not to be thought, for it would be a proof of weakness), or because He is unwilling, which is not the attribute of a good being . . . . But in proportion to the adaptation possessed by each, He has dispensed His beneficence both to Greeks and Barbarians, even to those of them that were predestinated, and in due time called, the faithful and elect.[560]

And Eusebius taught that those who were not ready to accept the one true God were allowed to worship the heavenly bodies as a substitute:

There was but one way for those who failed of the highest religion of the Almighty to prosper, namely to choose the best of things visible in heaven . . . . So all the most beautiful visible created things were delivered to them who yearned for nothing better, since to some extent the vision of the unseen shone in them, reflected as in a mirror.[561]

The Law of Moses and the Gospel

Paul preached that the Law of Moses was a lesser or preparatory law, designed to lead Israel to Christ, added because of their transgression. "Wherefore then serveth the law? It was added because of transgressions, till the seed should come to whom the promise was made; and it was ordained by angels in the hand of a mediator." (Galatians 3:19) But Paul also insisted that the gospel was preached to the Israelites. "For unto us was the Gospel preached, as well as unto them: but the word preached did not profit them, not being mixed with faith." (Hebrews 4:2)

Joseph Smith not only accepted Paul's teachings on these matters[562], he added a striking twist. According to a revelation the Prophet received as an inspired addition to the Bible, Moses received the full gospel law on the first set of stone tablets, but then received the lower law on the next set after he broke the first when he saw the Children of Israel had reverted to idolatry.

And the Lord said unto Moses, Hew thee two other tables of stone, like unto the first, and I will write upon them also, the words of the law, according as they were written at the first on the tables which thou brakest; but it shall not be according to the first, for I will take away the priesthood out of their midst; therefore my holy order, and the ordinances thereof, shall not go before them; for my presence shall not go up in their midst, lest I destroy them. But I will give unto them the law as at the first, but it shall be after the law of a carnal commandment." (JST Exodus 34:1-2)

Consider the similarity of the preceding passage with this next one from the second-century *Epistle of Barnabas*, a thoroughly orthodox Christian work:

Yes [it is even so]; but let us inquire if the Lord has really given that testament which He swore to the fathers that He would give to the people. He did give it; but they were not worthy to receive it, on account of their sins. For the prophet declares, "And Moses was fasting forty days and forty nights on Mount Sinai, that he might receive the testament of the Lord for the people." And he received from the Lord two tables, written in the spirit by the finger of the hand of the Lord. And Moses having received them, carried them down to give to the people. And the Lord said to Moses, "Moses, Moses, go down quickly; for thy people hath sinned, whom thou didst bring out of the land of Egypt." And Moses understood that they had again made molten images; and he threw the tables out of his hands, and the tables of the testament of the Lord were broken. Moses then received it, but they proved themselves unworthy. Learn how *we* have received it. Moses, as a servant, received it; but the Lord himself, having suffered in our behalf, hath given it to us, that we should be the people of inheritance.[563]

The Loss of the Doctrine of Dispensations

At first the question of why Christianity abandoned this enlightening doctrine might seem baffling, considering how widespread it was in the first few centuries after Christ. However, since the doctrine of dispensations opened up the disconcerting possibility that the gospel may have been lost once again through all their innovations, it is understandable why later churchmen would reject it in favor of the theory of a "once for all" revelation in Christ, which affirmed their authority.[564]

Faith, Grace, and Works

When a person has the gospel of Christ preached to him, he alone has the responsibility to accept it in faith or reject it. Jesus preached that "whosoever believeth in him should not perish, but have everlasting life." (John 3:16) But what does this "saving belief or faith" imply? Conversations on this subject between Mormons and others, especially Protestants, often end up being futile exercises because many Protestants mistakenly think that Mormons believe in salvation by good works, rather than grace through faith, and many Mormons mistakenly think that all Protestants believe good works are completely unnecessary and superfluous to one's salvation. Therefore, in this section we will carefully describe the interplay of faith, grace, and works as seen by Mormons, Protestants, and the earliest Christians. (The Mormon position essentially indistinguishable from the Catholic and Orthodox doctrines on this subject, so they need not be discussed in the context of this book.)

All Have Sinned

The scriptures make absolutely clear several facts about this subject. First, every person is a sinner, and therefore cannot by his own merits attain the glory of heaven. "All have sinned, and come short of the glory of god" (Romans 3:23), said Paul. Similarly, John indicated that, "If we say that we have no sin, we deceive ourselves, and the truth is not in us." (1 John 1:8) And *The Book of Mormon* informs us that "if ye would serve [God] with all your whole souls yet ye would be unprofitable servants." (Mosiah 2:21)

Salvation by Grace

Consequently, all are in need of the atoning blood of Jesus Christ to bring them back to the presence of God and cleanse them of their transgressions. This freely given gift of Christ Jesus is part of his "grace" or divine assistance, and no amount of good works on our part can save us without Christ's help. Paul preached that, "By grace are ye saved through faith; and that not of yourselves: it is the gift of God: Not of works, lest any man should boast." (Ephesians 2:8-9) And Nephi wrote, "We labor diligently to write, to persuade our children, and also our brethren, to believe in Christ, and to be reconciled to God; for we know that it is by grace that we are saved, after all we can do." (2 Nephi 25:23)

By Grace Through Faith

Third, this saving grace is accessed by faith in the Lord Jesus Christ. Paul told the Galatians that,

> Knowing that a man is not justified by the works of the law, but by the faith of Jesus Christ, even we have believed in Jesus Christ, that we might be justified by the faith of Christ, and not by the works of the law: for by the works of the law shall no flesh be justified. (Galatians 2:16)

137

Faith and Works

Fourth, saving faith is not mere belief or intellectual assent. True faith in Christ requires a change of heart -- and a change of lifestyle. We must not only *believe in* Christ, but *believe* Christ concerning all the blessings promised the righteous. "Thou believest that there is one God; thou doest well: the devils also believe, and tremble. But wilt thou know, O vain man, that faith without works is dead?" (James 2:19-20) Therefore, true faith carries with it the motivation to do good works. Such "good works" are not to be compared to the "dead works" Paul spoke of (Hebrews 6:1), any more than living faith is to be compared to the "dead faith" James preached against.

In the late first century, Clement of Rome illustrated the difficulty in expressing the relationship between faith and works when he exhorted the Corinthians to be justified by faith rather than works, and in another passage, by works rather than words:

> And we, too, being called by His will in Christ Jesus, are not justified by ourselves, nor by our own wisdom, or understanding, or godliness, or works which we have wrought in holiness of heart; but by that faith through which, from the beginning, Almighty God has justified all men . . . [565]

> Let us clothe ourselves with concord and humility, ever exercising self-control, standing far off from all whispering and evil-speaking, being justified by our works, and not our words.[566]

So far, Mormons and most Protestants would agree. While there are a few Protestants who believe faith does not entail any moral responsibility, nearly all of them consider good works as an essential product of faith. For instance Henry Halley:

> Paul's doctrine of justification by faith, and James' doctrine of justification by works, are supplementary, not contradictory . . . . Paul preached faith as the basis of justification before God, but insisted that it must issue in the right kind of Life. James was writing to those who had accepted the doctrine of justification by faith but were not living right, telling them that such faith was no faith at all.[567]

Eternal Security? The Bible Says "No!"

Where do we differ? For one thing, many Protestants believe in "eternal security." That is, after one truly accepts Christ into his life, one is saved and cannot ever become "unsaved." Misinterpreting Paul's assertion that no outside force "shall be able to separate us from the love of God, which is in Christ Jesus our Lord" (Romans 8:39), they are persuaded that not even they themselves can reject God once they have accepted Him. Not only is this doctrine contrary to the New Testament, it was not taught in the early Church. No Christian writers can be found advocating it for centuries after the Apostolic era.

Paul insisted that salvation *could* be lost:

> If we sin wilfully after that we have received the knowledge of the truth, there remaineth no more sacrifice for sins, But a certain fearful looking for of judgment and fiery indignation, which shall devour the adversaries . . . . Of how much sorer punishment, suppose ye, shall he be thought worthy, who hath trodden under foot the Son of God, and hath counted the blood of the covenant, wherewith he was sanctified, an unholy thing, and hath done despite unto the Spirit of grace? (Hebrews 10:26-29)

Also,

> It is impossible for those who were once enlightened, and have tasted of the heavenly gift, and were made partakers of the Holy Ghost, And have tasted the good word of God, and the powers of the world to come, If they shall fall away, to renew them again unto repentance; seeing they crucify to themselves the Son of God afresh, and put him to an open shame." (Hebrews 6:4-6)

Paul entreated the Philippians to "work out [their] own salvation with fear and trembling" (Philippians 2:12), and Peter exhorted the Saints to "give diligence to make [their] calling and election sure: for if ye do these things, ye shall never fall." (2 Peter 1:10) Peter also criticized certain Christians who had forsaken the faith: "They had once escaped the world's defilements through the knowledge of our Lord and Saviour Jesus Christ; yet if they have entangled themselves in these all over again, and are mastered by them, their plight in the end is worse than before." (2 Peter 2:20 NEB) Paul counseled Timothy to "Take heed unto thyself, and unto the doctrine; continue in them: for in doing this thou shalt both save thyself, and them that hear thee." (1 Timothy 4:16) Indeed, Paul did not consider himself to be automatically saved:

> It is not to be thought that I have already achieved all this. I have not yet reached perfection, but I press on, hoping to take hold of that for which Christ once took hold of me. My friends, I do not reckon myself to have got hold of it yet. All I can say is this: forgetting what is behind me, and reaching

out for that which lies ahead, I press towards the goal to win
the prize which is God's call to the life above, in Christ
Jesus. (Philippians 3:12-14 NEB)

Eternal Security? The Fathers Say "No!"

Similarly, the Church Fathers of the second century with one accord
proclaimed that one must continue in righteousness or be condemned.
Clement of Rome, for example, told the Corinthians:

> Take heed, beloved, lest His many kindnesses lead to the
> condemnation of us all. [For thus it must be] unless we walk
> worthy of Him, and with one mind do those things which are
> good and well-pleasing in His sight.[568]

Later he asked: "For what reason was our father Abraham blessed?
was it not because he wrought righteousness and truth through faith?"[569]
Likewise, Ignatius of Antioch entreated the Magnesians:

> Lay aside, therefore, the evil, the old, the sour leaven, and be
> ye changed into the new leaven, which is Jesus Christ. Be ye
> salted in Him, lest any one among you should be corrupted,
> since by your savour ye shall be convicted.[570]

And Polycarp instructed the Philippians: "If a man does not keep
himself from covetousness, he shall be defiled by idolatry, and shall be judged
as one of the heathen."[571]

Barnabas also exhorted the Church: "Be ye taught of God, inquiring
diligently what the Lord asks from you; and do it that ye may be safe in the
day of judgment."[572] He also added: "The way of light, then, is as follows. If
any one desires to travel to the appointed place, he must be zealous in his
works."[573] The author of *2 Clement* made the same point:

> But in what way shall we confess Him? By doing what He
> says, and not transgressing His commandments, and by
> honouring Him not with our lips only, but with all our heart
> and all our mind. For He says in Isaiah, "This people
> honoureth Me with their lips, but their heart is far from Me."
> Let us, then, not only call Him Lord, for that will not save
> us. For He saith, "Not every one that saith to Me, Lord,
> Lord, shall be saved, but he that worketh righteousness."
> Wherefore, brethren, let us confess Him by our works . . .
> [574]

The angel in Hermas's vision explained that he must "endure to the
end" to sit at the right hand of God:

While I was thinking about this, and feeling vexed that she did not let me sit on the right, she said, "Are you vexed, Hermas? The place to the right is for others who have already pleased God, and have suffered for His name's sake; and you have yet much to accomplish before you can sit with them. But abide as you now do in your simplicity, and you will sit with them, and with all who do their deeds and bear what they have borne."[575]

Paul made the same point in the apocryphal *Acts of Paul*: "Blessed are they who have kept their baptism pure, for they shall rest with the Father and with the Son."[576] Irenaeus quoted the "elders who knew the Apostles" as saying that Christians should watch themselves so as not to lose their salvation: "Therefore we should . . . ourselves fear lest, after the recognition of Christ, we should do something displeasing to God, and, no longer having remission of sins, be excluded from his kingdom."[577] And Jesus, in the *Epistle of the Apostles*, proclaimed that:

If any man believe on me and do not my commandments, although he have confessed my name, he hath no profit therefrom but runneth a vain race: for such will find themselves in perdition and destruction, because they have despised my commandments.[578]

This unanimous testimony of the early Church continued for centuries, and it appears the only ones who were preaching salvation by grace alone and eternal security in the early centuries of Christianity were *the Gnostics.*[579] Therefore, it is perfectly clear that when Joseph Smith laid out the doctrines of faith, grace, and works, he was restoring the beliefs of the earliest Christians.

Baptism

Beyond the generality of "good works," Joseph Smith preached that there are certain ordinances or sacraments necessary for salvation. That is, certain rites must be performed wherein one makes covenants with God. Keeping these covenants entitles one to the grace of Jesus Christ, and hence, salvation. "We believe that through the Atonement of Christ, all mankind may be saved, by obedience to the laws and ordinances of the Gospel."[580] First on the list of essential ordinances is baptism, and Joseph Smith accordingly affirmed Jesus' teaching that one must be baptized to enter the Kingdom of God.

The Necessity of Baptism

In contrast, most Protestants have given up the idea that baptism is strictly "necessary" for salvation. For, although true faith carries with it the desire to perform good works, no particular good work, such as baptism, is necessarily required to show one's faith. A minister representing the Presbyterian Church explained:

> While baptism is urgently recommended in the Presbyterian Church, and while its omission is regarded as a grave fault, it is not held to be necessary for salvation. The Confession of Faith declares: "Grace and salvation are not so inseparably annexed unto it that no person can be regenerated or saved without it."[581]

It must be admitted that the question of whether baptism is strictly "necessary" for salvation is not clearly answered in the Bible. Although there are two passages in the New Testament where Jesus seems to give baptism as a requirement, many Protestants feel that they can legitimately interpret them otherwise.

When the resurrected Lord appeared to the disciples in Mark's account He announced: "He that believeth and is baptized shall be saved; but he that believeth not shall be damned." (Mark 16:16) But Protestants who deny the necessity of baptism point out that Jesus never said that he who believes and is not baptized will be damned. To them, belief, not baptism, is the defining characteristic of the saved person, as opposed to the damned.

Likewise, Mormons see Jesus' statement to Nicodemus, "Except a man be born of water and of the Spirit, he cannot enter into the kingdom of God" (John 3:5), as a proclamation that one must be baptized and sanctified by the Holy Spirit to be saved. On the other hand, many Protestants contend the "born of water" clause refers to birth from the water of the mother's womb. Indeed, Jesus' proclamation came in response to Nicodemus's question: "How can a man be born when he is old? can he enter the second time into his mother's womb, and be born?" (John 3:4)

Who is right? From a historical perspective, perhaps the only way to settle the question of how Jesus and the Apostles interpreted these statements is to discover how the early post-Apostolic Christian writers interpreted them. This method carries with it no guarantee, but one must grant that Christians who lived at times when there were still church members who had heard the Apostles speak, would be more likely to preserve the original teaching than some Reformer thirteen or fourteen hundred years later. And, indeed, we find that the early Christian writers unanimously insisted that to be "born of water" was to be baptized. Justin Martyr, Irenaeus, the *Clementine Homilies*, and the *Apostolic Constitutions* all testified of this fact, and the *Constitutions* also considered Jesus' statement at the end of Mark to be a command that everyone must be baptized:

For, in the name of God, the Father and Lord of the universe, and of our Saviour Jesus Christ, and of the Holy Spirit, they then receive the washing with water. For Christ also said, "Except ye be born again, ye shall not enter into the kingdom of heaven."[582]

"And dipped himself," says [the Scripture], "seven times in Jordan." It was not for nothing that Naaman of old, when suffering from leprosy, was purified upon his being baptized, but [it served] as an indication to us. For as we are lepers in sin, we are made clean, by means of the sacred water and the invocation of the Lord, from our old transgressions; being spiritually regenerated as new-born babes, even as the Lord has declared: "Except a man be born again through water and the Spirit, he shall not enter into the kingdom of heaven."[583]

And do not think, though you were more pious than all the pious that ever were, but if you be unbaptized, that you shall ever obtain hope. For all the more, on this account, you shall endure the greater punishment, because you have done excellent works not excellently. For well-doing is excellent when it is done as God has commanded. But if you will not be baptized according to His pleasure, you serve your own will and oppose His counsel. But perhaps some one will say, What does it contribute to piety to be baptized with water? In the first place, because you do that which is pleasing to God; and in the second place, being born again to God of water, by reason of fear you change your first generation, which is of lust, and thus you are able to obtain salvation. But otherwise it is impossible. For thus the prophet has sworn to us, saying, "Verily I say to you, Unless ye be regenerated by living water into the name of Father, Son, and Holy Spirit, you shall not enter the kingdom of heaven."[584]

Nay, he that, out of contempt, will not be baptized, shall be condemned as an unbeliever, and shall be reproached as ungrateful and foolish. For the Lord says: "Except a man be baptized of water and of the Spirit, he shall by no means enter into the kingdom of heaven." And again: "He that believeth and is baptized shall be saved; but he that believeth not shall be damned."[585]

Baptism by Immersion

Therefore, it is certain that baptism was considered essential by the earliest Christians, but how was it done? Jesus commanded the disciples to baptize "in the name of the Father, and of the Son, and of the Holy Ghost" (Matthew 28:19), and in general the Christian world has continued this practice. However, controversy has arisen over whether one is to be baptized by immersion or by pouring or sprinkling.

When John the Baptist restored the authority to baptize to Joseph Smith and Oliver Cowdery, he specified that baptism was to be by immersion. (D&C 13:1) And, it is clear that baptism in the New Testament was by immersion. After Jesus was baptized he "went up straightway out of the water" (Matthew 3:16), and John baptized in Aenon "because there was much water there." (John 3:23) Paul also indicated that we are "buried with [Jesus] by baptism into death." (Romans 6:4) The symbolism of the rite is clearly incomplete when pouring or sprinkling replaces immersion.

The rite of baptism began to be changed early on. Even in the first century certain communities had adopted the practice of pouring, but only when it was not possible to find enough water to immerse in. The *Didache* , which probably originated in Syria, suggests that one should be baptized in running water, but if none can be found, in still. Also, cold water is preferred over hot. "But if thou have not either, pour out water thrice upon the head into the name of Father and Son and Holy Spirit."[586] Perhaps in certain desert communities this eventuality was sometimes faced, and in time it became the practice of the Church in general to sprinkle or pour, especially when infants were baptized.

Infant Baptism

But the whole idea of baptizing infants, by immersion, sprinkling, or pouring, is seriously in question given the teachings of Christ about the innocence of children. And In fact, one could argue that such a practice betrays the very idea of the atonement. The prophet Mormon explained:

> For awful is the wickedness to suppose that God saveth one child because of baptism, and the other must perish because he hath no baptism . . . . Little children cannot repent; wherefore, it is awful wickedness to deny the pure mercies of God unto them, for they are all alive in him because of his mercy. (Moroni 8:15, 19)

And indeed, there is significant evidence that it was not the original practice of the Church to baptize infants. Not only were no infants recorded to have been baptized in the New Testament, but Jesus commanded his disciples: "Suffer little children, and forbid them not, to come unto me: for of such is the kingdom of heaven. And he laid his hands on them, and departed thence." (Matthew 19:14-15) Thus, Jesus merely blessed the children, and did not command them to be baptized, as he did adults. Mormon's contention that children cannot be baptized because they cannot repent is significant, as well, because the way to baptism is always paved with repentance. "Repent and be baptized every one of you in the name of Jesus Christ for the remission of sins, and ye shall receive the gift of the Holy Ghost" (Acts 2:38), Peter commanded.

Clement of Alexandria recorded a very ancient story about John the Apostle, where John entrusted a young boy to the care of a certain local Church leader: "[John] then departed for Ephesus. But the presbyter, taking home the youth committed to him, reared, kept, cherished, and finally baptized him."[587] If infants were to be baptized at that time, why did the cleric wait to baptize the child? Certainly he would not have neglected his duty toward this child, who had been entrusted to him by an Apostle of Jesus Christ!

The earliest reference to the practice of infant baptism was by Tertullian (ca. A.D. 200).[588] But although Tertullian gave witness to this practice among Christians, he still insisted that it was preferable to wait for baptism:

> And so, according to the circumstances and disposition, and even age, of each individual, the delay of baptism is preferable; principally, however, in the case of little children. For why is it necessary -- if (baptism itself) is not so necessary -- that the sponsors likewise should be thrust into danger? Who both themselves, by reason of mortality, may fail to fulfil their promises, and may be disappointed by the development of an evil disposition, in those for whom they stood? . . . If any understand the weighty import of baptism, they will fear its reception more than its delay: sound faith is secure of salvation.[589]

For centuries, believer baptism appears to have been the norm, even though infant baptism *was* practiced. For example, in the late fourth century Gregory of Nazianzus argued that baptism should be delayed until a child is accountable for his actions:

> For this is how the matter stands; at that time they begin to be responsible for their lives, when reason is matured, and they learn the mystery of life (for of sins of ignorance owing to their tender years they have no account to give), and it is far more profitable on all accounts to be fortified by the Font, because of the sudden assaults of danger that befall us, stronger than our helpers.[590]

The *Encyclopedia of Early Christianity* notes that the inscriptions from this early time period which mention infant baptism place the date of baptism very close to the death of the children in question, therefore, "The principal impetus for the rise and spread of infant baptism may have been the desire that the child not depart life without the safeguard of baptism."[591] But this did not necessarily imply that unbaptized infants would be damned. For instance, in the fourth century an unimpeachably "orthodox" theologian such as John Chrysostom could say that "We do baptize infants, although they are not guilty of any sins."[592]

By the fifth century, however, the rationale for infant baptism had changed. For example, Augustine saw its very existence as proof of his doctrine of original sin. But although he claimed all the unbaptized would be damned, he generously allowed that the damnation of unbaptized infants would be "the mildest punishment of all . . . ."[593] Therefore, Catholic belief from Augustine onward has been that not only may infants be baptized, but if they die without baptism they will be denied the glory of the Kingdom of God.

The Laying on of Hands for the Gift of the Holy Ghost

One more issue needs to be addressed in connection with baptism. Namely, the ordinance of baptism was not originally just a dunking. At first it included both immersion and the laying on of hands for the reception of the Holy Ghost, and only later did baptism become two separate rites. Likewise, Joseph Smith preached: "Baptism by water is but half a baptism, and is good for nothing without the other half -- that is, the baptism of the Holy Ghost."[594]

Laying on of hands always accompanied baptism in the New Testament. For example, after Philip preached to the Samaritans and baptized quite a number of them, the Apostles came and conferred the Gift of the Holy Ghost.

> Now when the Apostles which were at Jerusalem heard that Samaria had received the word of God, they sent unto them Peter and John: Who, when they were come down, prayed for them, that they might receive the Holy Ghost: (For as yet he was fallen upon none of them, only they were baptized in the name of the Lord Jesus.) Then laid they their hands on them, and they received the Holy Ghost. (Acts 8:14-17)

Certain post-Apostolic writers were anxious to preserve the form and meaning of these rites. Tertullian, for example, both confirmed that baptism was necessary and clearly defined the two parts of the ordinance:

> When, however, the prescript is laid down that "without baptism, salvation is attainable by none" (chiefly on the ground of that declaration of the Lord, who says, "Unless one be born of water, he hath not life"), there arise immediately scrupulous, nay rather audacious, doubts on the part of some . . . . Not that in the waters we obtain the Holy

Spirit; but in the water, under (the witness of) the angel, we are cleansed, and prepared for the Holy Spirit . . . . In the next place the hand is laid on us, invoking and inviting the Holy Spirit through benediction.[595]

Cyprian not only recorded the form of the rites, he identified baptism and the laying on of hands with being "born of water and the Spirit":

[After the baptisms by Philip in Samaria] that which was needed was performed by Peter and John; viz., that prayer being made for them, and hands being imposed, the Holy Spirit should be invoked and poured out upon them, which now too is done among us, so that they who are baptized in the Church are brought to the prelates of the Church, and by our prayers and by the imposition of hands obtain the Holy Spirit, and are perfected with the Lord's seal.[596]

For then finally can they be fully sanctified, and be the sons of God, if they be born of each sacrament; since it is written, "Except a man be born again of water, and of the Spirit, he cannot enter into the kingdom of God."[597]

And Bishop Cornelius of Rome disapproved of the practice of baptizing without laying on hands, for without it, how could one receive the Holy Ghost? It would only be "half a baptism," as Joseph Smith said.

Being delivered by the exorcists, he fell into a severe sickness; and as he seemed about to die, he received baptism by affusion, on the bed where he lay; if indeed we can say that such a one did receive it. And when he was healed of his sickness he did not receive the other things which it is necessary to have according to the canon of the Church, even the being sealed [laid hands on] by the bishop. And as he did not receive this, how could he receive the Holy Spirit? . . .[598]

Baptism and the laying on of hands for the reception of the Holy Ghost are necessary to enter the Kingdom of God. Joseph Smith not only got the concept right, however, he also restored the proper forms of the ordinances and the knowledge that a merciful and just God would never condemn little children for sins they never committed.

From Death to the Resurrection

The World of Spirits

If one were to ask a mainstream Christian what happens to our spirits after death, most would probably say that they go directly either to heaven or hell, even though the Bible clearly teaches the final judgment will not occur until after the millennial reign of Christ. (See Revelation 20:7-13) However, Christ taught that there is an intermediate state of the soul between death and the resurrection. In this state of action there are two main divisions, which He called Paradise, or "Abraham's bosom," and hell. For example, "Jesus said unto [the thief], Verily I say unto thee, To day shalt thou be with me in paradise." (Luke 23:43) The parable of Lazarus and the rich man makes clear that the gulf between the two divisions was impassable:

> And it came to pass, that the beggar died, and was carried by the angels into Abraham's bosom: the rich man also died, and was buried; And in hell he lift up his eyes, being in torments, and seeth Abraham afar off, and Lazarus in his bosom . . . . [Abraham says to the rich man] And beside all this, between us and you there is a great gulf fixed: so that they which would pass from hence to you cannot; neither can they pass to us, that would come from thence. (Luke 16:22, 23, 26)

But paradise, or "Abraham's bosom," cannot be equated with the kingdom of God, for at his resurrection Jesus told Mary: "Touch me not; for I am not yet ascended to my Father." (John 20:17)

The Spirit World in LDS Thought

Joseph Smith not only restored this distinction, he added many other important elements about the world of spirits, which are not clearly taught in the Bible. *The Book of Mormon* teaches that the world of spirits is divided into two parts: paradise, which is where the righteous dwell, and hell, which is where the wicked receive punishment. (Alma 40:11-14) And yet, it is all one world of spirits. As Joseph Smith taught, "Hades, sheol, paradise, spirits in prison, are all one: it is a world of spirits. The righteous and the wicked all go to the same world of spirits until the resurrection."[599] Those who enter the spirit world are capable of being instructed, and great progress may be made there toward perfection.[600] The punishment the wicked receive in hell, by which they may be purified of their sins, will have an end (D&C 19), though not until the wicked have "paid the uttermost farthing" (Matthew 5:26), as Jesus said. This world is located right here on the earth, according to Joseph Smith and Brigham Young.[601] The "great gulf" between hell and paradise was destroyed by Jesus Christ, who made it possible for the gospel to be preached to the spirits in hell, so that they may advance to paradise. (1 Peter 3:18-20; 4:6; D&C 138) Finally, when Christ was resurrected, the bodies of many of the righteous dead who had gone before were resurrected as well. (Matthew 27:52, Alma 40:20)

The Spirit World in Early Christian Thought

Several early Christian writers preached strikingly similar doctrines to the Prophet's. For example, Justin Martyr held to the belief in the two-fold division of the world of spirits:

> The souls of the pious remain in a better place, while those of the unjust and wicked are in a worse, waiting for the time of judgment. Thus some which have appeared worthy of God never die; but others are punished so long as God wills them to exist and to be punished.[602]

Irenaeus was emphatic that even believers must be taken to the underworld:

> For as the Lord "went away in the midst of the shadow of death," where the souls of the dead were, yet afterwards arose in the body, and after the resurrection was taken up [into heaven], it is manifest that the souls of His disciples also, upon whose account the Lord underwent these things, shall go away into the invisible place allotted to them by God, and there remain until the resurrection, awaiting that event.[603]

Tertullian not only preached that everyone must serve a term in the underworld, but he also taught that the spirit world is under the earth, and the fact that the souls of the wicked are punished there proves that the soul is material. He taught that the punishments in spirit hell will have an end, as well:

> By ourselves the lower regions (of Hades) are not supposed to be a bare cavity, nor some subterranean sewer of the world, but a vast deep space in the interior of the earth, and a concealed recess in its very bowels; inasmuch as we read that Christ in His death spent three days in the heart of the earth . . . . Now although Christ is God, yet, being also man, "He died according to the Scriptures," and "according to the same Scriptures was buried." With the same law of His being He fully complied, by remaining in Hades in the form and condition of a dead man; nor did He ascend into the

149

heights of heaven before descending into the lower parts of the earth, that He might there make the patriarchs and prophets partakers of Himself. (This being the case), you must suppose Hades to be a subterranean region, and keep at arm's length those who are too proud to believe that the souls of the faithful deserve a place in the lower regions.[604]

Therefore, whatever amount of punishment or refreshment the soul tastes in Hades, in its prison or lodging, in the fire or in Abraham's bosom, it gives proof thereby of its own corporeality. For an incorporeal thing suffers nothing, not having that which makes it capable of suffering; else, if it has such capacity, it must be a bodily substance. For in as far as every corporeal thing is capable of suffering, in so far is that which is capable of suffering also corporeal.[605]

All souls, therefore; are shut up within Hades: do you admit this? (It is true, whether) you say yes or no . . . . Why, then, cannot you suppose that the soul undergoes punishment and consolation in Hades in the interval, while it awaits its alternative of judgment, in a certain anticipation either of gloom or of glory? . . . What, then, is to take place in that interval? Shall we sleep? But souls do not sleep . . . . Or will you have it, that nothing is there done whither the whole human race is attracted, and whither all man's expectation is postponed for safe keeping? . . . Now really, would it not be the highest possible injustice, even in Hades, if all were to be still well with the guilty even there, and not well with the righteous even yet? . . . In short, inasmuch as we understand "the prison" pointed out in the Gospel to be Hades, and as we also interpret "the uttermost farthing" to mean the very smallest offence which has to be recompensed there before the resurrection, no one will hesitate to believe that the soul undergoes in Hades some compensatory discipline, without prejudice to the full process of the resurrection, when the recompense will be administered through the flesh besides.[606]

Origen not only taught about the division in the spirit world, but called it both a place of learning and of punishment, and indicated that it was located on the earth. The inhabitants of Paradise will receive instruction, while the inmates of hell will be punished to purify them from their sins. And if their souls can be purified, this punishment must have an end, just as Joseph Smith said.

Those who, departing this world in virtue of that death which is common to all, are arranged, in conformity with their actions and deserts -- according as they shall be deemed worthy -- some in the place which is called "hell," others in the bosom of Abraham, and in different localities or mansions.[607]

I think, therefore, that all the saints who depart from this life will remain in some place situated on the earth, which holy Scripture calls paradise, as in some place of instruction, and, so to speak, class-room or school of souls, in which they are to be instructed regarding all the things which they had seen on earth, and are to receive also some information respecting things that are to follow in the future . . . .[608]

We find a certain confirmation of what is said regarding the place of punishment, intended for the purification of such souls as are to be purified by torments, agreeably to the saying: "The Lord cometh like a refiner's fire, and like fullers' soap: and He shall sit as a refiner and purifier of silver and of gold."[609]

An End to the Torments of Hell

Jerome quoted a passage from Origen wherein he more specifically stated that hellfire would have an end, and that afterward any further punishment would consist of remorse over lost opportunities:

Hellfire, moreover, and the torments with which holy scripture threatens sinners he explains not as external punishments but as the pangs of guilty consciences when by God's power the memory of our transgressions is set before our eyes. "The whole crop of our sins grows up afresh from seeds which remain in the soul, and all our dishonourable and undutiful acts are again pictured before our gaze. Thus it is the fire of conscience and the stings of remorse which torture the mind as it looks back on former self-indulgence."[610]

Origen's teacher, Clement of Alexandria, apparently taught exactly the same doctrine in the second century:

For God's righteousness is good, and His goodness is righteous. And though the punishments cease in the course of the completion of the expiation and purification of each one, yet those have very great and permanent grief who are found worthy of the other fold, on account of not being along with those that have been glorified through righteousness.[611]

This belief seems to have died out slowly. For example, J.N.D. Kelly reports that although Basil of Caesarea (late fourth century) himself believed in the eternity of hell, he lamented that "most ordinary Christians" did not, and indeed his colleagues Gregory of Nazianzus and Gregory of Nyssa were among them.[612]

By the early fifth century a wide variety of opinions seems to have been in vogue. While some believed in an everlasting hell, others believed it would have an end, and still others believed that it *could* have an end if a saint interceded on one's behalf. And while some believed that all who had ever partaken of the Catholic sacraments of baptism and the Eucharist would be saved no matter what, others believed that only those who actually remained Catholics would be saved, even if they had lived a morally despicable life.[613] However, by the end of the fifth century, probably due to the influence of Augustine, nearly everyone had accepted the stern doctrine that hell would have no end.[614]

Bridging the Gulf of Separation

As was mentioned above, Jesus indicated that there was an inseparable gulf fixed between the two regions of the spirit world. However, according to both LDS and some early Christian teachings, Jesus broke down those barriers when he entered the world of spirits. For example, Ignatius taught that when Christ descended to the spirit world, he tore down the wall separating its two regions and arose from the dead accompanied by a multitude:

> "Many bodies of the saints that slept arose," their graves being opened. He descended, indeed, into Hades alone, but He arose accompanied by a multitude and rent asunder that means [lit. "fence" or "hedge'] of separation which had existed from the beginning of the world, and cast down its partition wall.[615]

This type of imagery is common in early Christian descriptions of Christ's descent into the spirit world. The descent is always represented as an utter sacking of the place where Christ rips apart the gates, throws down the partition walls, and leaves with the righteous dead. Thus Athanasius:

> He burst open the gates of brass, He broke through the bolts of iron, and He took the souls which were in Amente [the Egyptian name for the underworld] and carried them to His

Father . . . . Now the souls He brought out of Amente, but the bodies He raised up on the earth . . . . And the Lord died on behalf of every one, in order that every one should rise from the dead with Him.[616]

A Coptic apocryphal document attributed to Bartholomew, as well as the apocryphal *Gospel of Bartholomew* , the *Letter of Jesus to King Abgar*, and the *Gospel of Nicodemus* describe the descent in nearly identical terms:

He broke in pieces the doors, and smashed their bolts, and dragged away and destroyed the door-posts and frames. He overthrew the blazing furnaces of brass and extinguished their fires, and, removing everything from Amente, left it like a desert . . . . So Jesus went down [into Amente, and] scattered [the fiends], and cast chains on the Devil, and redeemed Adam and all his sons; He delivered man, and He shewed compassion upon His own image; He set free all creation, and all the world, and He treated with healing medicine the wound which the Enemy had inflicted on His Son. He brought back into His fold the sheep which had gone astray -- He the holy and faithful Shepherd.[617]

Then did I enter in and scourged [Hades] and bound him with chains that cannot be loosed, and brought forth thence all the patriarchs . . . .[618]

He humbled himself, and died and debased his divinity and was crucified, and descended into Hades, and burst the bars which from eternity had not been broken, and raised the dead; for he descended alone, but rose with many, and thus ascended to his Father.[619]

There came, then, again a voice saying: Lift up the gates. Hades, hearing the voice the second time, answered as if forsooth he did not know, and says: Who is this King of glory? The angels of the Lord say: The Lord strong and mighty, the Lord mighty in battle. And immediately with these words the brazen gates were shattered, and the iron bars broken, and all the dead who had been bound came out of the prisons, and we with them. And the King of glory came in the form of a man, and all the dark places of Hades were lighted up.[620]

And we shall see that Joseph Smith's doctrine that the gospel is now being preached to the spirits in hell was widespread in early Christianity, as well.

The Preaching to the Spirits in Prison

Peter, in his first general epistle, made some very strange remarks about Christ's descent to the spirit world which have haunted the Christian world for centuries:

> For Christ also hath once suffered for sins, the just for the unjust, that he might bring us to God, being put to death in the flesh, but quickened by the Spirit: By which also he went and preached unto the spirits in prison; Which sometime were disobedient, when once the longsuffering of God waited in the days of Noah . . . . (1 Peter 3:18-20)

> For for this cause was the gospel preached also to them that are dead, that they might be judged according to men in the flesh, but live according to God in the spirit. (1 Peter 4:6)

Most commentators admit the plain meaning of these passages is that after Christ died, but before He was resurrected, He visited the spirits of the disobedient of Noah's day in hell and preached the gospel to them. He did this so that they could be judged like other men who had heard the gospel, too, and be given the chance to live a godly life in the spirit.

Mainstream Christian Avoidance of the Issue

Since other Christian commentators have no knowledge of such a concept, they often try often try to come up with various alternative explanations which harmonize with their established beliefs. For example, the NIV *Study Bible* lists two other possible interpretations of this scripture:

> Some hold that in his preincarnate state Christ went and preached through Noah to the wicked generation of that time . . . . Others argue that between his death and resurrection Christ went to the prison where fallen angels are incarcerated and there preached to the angels who are said to have left their proper state and married human women during Noah's time (cf. Ge. 6:1-4) . . . . [621]

James Moffatt offers the following translation of 1 Peter 3:19, "It was in the Spirit that Enoch also went and preached to the imprisoned spirits . . .

.″[622] He justifies this blatant change in the wording by postulating that the text probably originally said "Enoch", but was changed to read "in (or by) which also" (Greek *en ho kai*) by "a scribe's blunder in dropping some repeated letters."[623] In other words, a translation is true if you drop the "anslation" and add the "ue." (Moffatt also ignores the fact that Enoch wasn't even on the earth during Noah's lifetime, see Genesis 5:22-29, so his emendation not only is completely arbitrary and out of context, but it is demonstrably untrue.)

As for 1 Peter 4:6, the translators of the *New International Version* are also guilty of inserting extra words in the text to suit their preconceptions. They translate the verse, "For this is the reason the gospel was preached even to those who are *now* dead, so that they might be judged according to men in regard to the body, but live according to God in regard to the spirit." Why do they add the word "now"? A text note explains:

> The word "now" does not occur in the Greek, but it is necessary to make it clear that the preaching was done not after these people had died, but while they were still alive. (There will be no opportunity for people to be saved after death; see Heb. 9:27.)[624]

But the verse they cite as proof only says, "And as it is appointed unto men once to die, but after this the judgment." (Hebrews 9:27) Clearly this says nothing about the time between death and the judgment, since the judgment will not take place until after the Millennial reign of Christ and the resurrection of the dead. (see Revelation 20) And wasn't it precisely Peter's point that the gospel *had* to be preached to the dead so that everyone could be judged on equal terms? If "God is no respecter of persons" (Acts 10:34), how could he condemn people for not accepting the gospel, when the vast majority of the people who have lived on the earth have never even heard of Jesus Christ?

The Early Christians on the Preaching Mission

We will find that the early Christian writers held no such narrow view, insisting that the gospel had to be preached to the spirits in prison. And they did not stop at the pitifully small amount of information Peter gave. They preached a doctrine remarkably similar to the Latter-day Saint belief that the gospel was not only preached by Christ in the spirit world, but by His disciples, as well, after they died.

Justin Martyr and Clement of Alexandria insisted that it wouldn't be right for God to condemn those who hadn't heard the gospel:

> Since those who did that which is universally, naturally, and eternally good are pleasing to God, they shall be saved through this Christ in the resurrection equally with those righteous men who were before them, namely Noah, and

Enoch, and Jacob, and whoever else there be, along with those who have known this Christ, Son of God . . . .[625]

For it is not right that these should be condemned without trial, and that those alone who lived after the advent should have the advantage of the divine righteousness. But to all rational souls it was said from above, "Whatever one of you has done in ignorance, without clearly knowing God, if, on becoming conscious, he repent, all his sins will be forgiven him."[626]

And Peter, in the *Clementine Recognitions*, derided the God of Simon Magus because he could only save those who knew of Him!

Then said Peter [to Simon Magus]: "He saves adulterers and men-slayers, if they know him; but good, and sober, an merciful persons, if they do not know him, in consequence of their having no information concerning him, he does not save! Great and good truly is he whom you proclaim, who is not so much the saviour of the evil, as he is one who shows no mercy to the good."[627]

If the definition of eternal life is to "know . . . the only true God, and Jesus Christ" (John 17:3), how can those who have not even heard of them be saved? Paul had the answer when he said that "faith cometh by hearing, and hearing by the word of God." (Romans 10:17) The only answer consistent with an all-loving and merciful God is that the gospel has to be preached to those who have not been given the chance to accept Christ in mortality. Irenaeus, Clement of Alexandria, Origen, and Hermas all testified of the fact that Jesus did, indeed, preach to the spirits in prison, some even claiming that the departed disciples of Jesus continued the preaching work:

It was for this reason, too, that the Lord descended into the regions beneath the earth, preaching His advent there also, and [declaring] the remission of sins received by those who believe in Him. Now all those believed in Him who had hope towards Him, that is, those who proclaimed His advent, and submitted to His dispensations, the righteous men, the prophets, and the patriarchs, to whom He remitted sins in the same way as He did to us, which sins we should not lay to their charge, if we would not despise the grace of God. For as these men did not impute unto us (the Gentiles) our transgressions, which we wrought before Christ was manifested among us, so also it is not right that we should lay blame upon those who sinned before Christ's coming.[628]

And it has been shown also, in the second book of the *Stromata*, that the Apostles, following the Lord, preached the Gospel to those in Hades . . . . For it was suitable to the divine administration, that those possessed of greater worth in righteousness, and whose life had been pre-eminent, on repenting of their transgressions, though found in another place, yet being confessedly of the number of the people of God Almighty, should be saved, each one according to his individual knowledge . . . . If, then, the Lord descended to Hades for no other end but to preach the Gospel, as He did descend; it was either to preach the Gospel to all or to the Hebrews only. If, accordingly, to all, then all who believe shall be saved, although they may be of the Gentiles, on making their profession there . . . .[629]

When He became a soul, without the covering of the body, He dwelt among those souls which were without bodily covering, converting such of them as were willing to Himself, or those whom He saw, for reasons known to Him alone, to be better adapted to such a course.[630]

These Apostles and teachers who preached the name of the Son of God, after falling asleep in the power and faith of the Son of God, preached it not only to those who were asleep, but themselves also gave them the seal of the preaching. Accordingly they descended with them into the water, and again ascended.[631]

This belief in Christ's preaching mission to the dead was not some incidental folk belief, but a central part of the Christian message. It was so central, in fact, that Justin Martyr accused the Jews of having removed a passage from Jeremiah about the descent and preaching to weaken the scriptural support for Christianity.

Here Trypho remarked, "We ask you first of all to tell us some of the Scriptures which you allege have been completely cancelled." [Justin quotes some passages which the Jews evidently removed from Esdras and Jeremiah.] And again, from the sayings of the same Jeremiah these have been cut out: 'The Lord God remembered His dead people of Israel who lay in the graves; and He descended to preach to them His own salvation.'[632]

The *Odes of Solomon* preserve a beautiful account of the preaching work of Christ to the dead. In one of the *Odes* the Savior says:

> Sheol saw me and was made miserable: Death cast me up and many along with me. I had gall and bitterness, and I went down with him to the utmost of his depth . . . . And I made a congregation of living men amongst his dead men, and I spake with them by living lips: Because my word shall not be void: And those who had died ran towards me: and they cried and said, Son of God, have pity on us, and do with us according to thy kindness, and bring us out from the bonds of darkness: and open to us the door by which we shall come out to thee. For we see that our death has not touched thee. Let us also be redeemed with thee: for thou art our Redeemer. And I heard their voice; and my name I sealed upon their heads: For they are free men and they are mine.[633]

God is merciful and He is just. He doesn't save some and give others no opportunity to be saved. His hand goes out to all nations and all people at all times, and Jesus' atonement breaks the bands of death and hell, so that all mankind can choose Him, and live. This is the message of Christ's preaching mission to the dead, which mainstream Christianity has lost, and God has restored through Joseph Smith.

Baptism for the Dead

"Except a man be born of water and of the Spirit, he cannot enter into the kingdom of God." How does one reconcile Jesus' statement with the fact that the unbaptized dead *can* be saved in the kingdom of God? Joseph Smith had an answer that shocked the rest of Christianity -- the living can be baptized as proxies for the dead. In this ordinance, one is baptized in behalf of a dead forbear, so that if that person decides to accept the gospel in the spirit world, the ordinance for the entrance into the kingdom of God will have been done for him.

Baptism for the Dead According to Paul

Paul mentioned this ordinance in passing as part of his argument for the reality of the resurrection: "Else what shall they do which are baptized for the dead, if the dead rise not at all? why are they then baptized for the dead?" (1 Corinthians 15:29) Commentators have long recognized that the plain meaning of the passage is that living people were being baptized for dead friends or relatives, but they usually try to get out of it by placing some other, more dubious interpretation on this verse. Thus Henry Halley:

158

This seems to mean vicarious baptism, that is, baptism for a dead friend. But there is no other Bible reference to such a practice, and no evidence that it existed in the Apostolic Church. Perhaps a better translation would be "baptized in hope of the resurrection.[634]

But Paul's statement itself is evidence that baptism for the dead existed in the Apostolic Church! The NIV *Study Bible* admits that, "The present tense suggests that at Corinth people were currently being baptized for the dead."[635] And if "baptized for the dead" really means "baptized in hope of the resurrection," it is an idiom of which translators have no knowledge, or they would have used it to sidestep the obvious meaning of the passage.

Another popular argument is that "Paul mentions this custom almost in passing, using it in his arguments substantiating the resurrection of the dead, but without necessarily approving the practice."[636] But why would Paul use some heretical practice in his arguments for the resurrection? Couldn't he find some more firm foundation for this all-important Christian doctrine? And if he mentioned it in passing, wouldn't that mean that his audience, the Corinthians, were thoroughly familiar with the practice and its implications?

A wide variety of such strange interpretations of this verse have been propagated over the centuries.[637] The basic premise of all these arguments, however, is that since they have no more information concerning the practice, it must either be illegitimate, or the verse must be interpreted in some other way, because Christianity certainly couldn't have lost such an important practice. But the information concerning this strange doctrine *has* been lost, and it took a prophet to restore it. In a recent study of the verse in question, Richard DeMaris of Valparaiso University admits that despite dozens of proposed interpretations, "the reference itself is simply so obscure and our knowledge so limited that we cannot discern just what this rite actually involved or meant."[638] However, his article makes it clear that such a rite *did* exist, even though he contends that it was probably confined to the area of Corinth.

Baptism in the Spirit World

Related to the practice of baptism for the dead is the idea that the spirits of the dead must be baptized in the spirit world after accepting the gospel there. According to Kirsopp Lake, "The idea that hearing the gospel and baptism is necessary for the salvation of the righteous dead of pre-Christian times is common . . . ."[639] For example, the *Pastor of Hermas* related that the Apostles baptized the righteous dead after preaching to them:

"They were obliged," he answered, "to ascend through water in order that they might be made alive; for, unless they laid aside the deadness of their life, they could not in any other

159

way enter into the kingdom of God. Accordingly, those also who fell asleep received the seal of the Son of God. For," he continued, "before a man bears the name of the Son of God he is dead; but when he receives the seal he lays aside his deadness, and obtains life. The seal, then, is the water: they descend into the water dead, and they arise alive.[640]

Jesus preached the same doctrine in the *Epistle of the Apostles*:

For to that end went I down unto the place of Lazarus, and preached unto the righteous and the prophets, that they might come out of the rest which is below and come up into that which is above; and I poured out upon them with my right hand the water [of] (baptism) . . . of life and forgiveness and salvation from all evil, as I have done unto you and unto them that believe on me.[641]

But if the dead receive their baptism in the world of spirits, why do they need vicarious baptism? Clement of Alexandria brought up an interesting point after quoting the passage from Hermas:

"They went down therefore into the water and again ascended . . . . But those who had fallen asleep, descended dead, but ascended alive . . . ." Then, too, the more subtle substance, the soul, could never receive any injury from the grosser element of water . . . .[642]

Of course you can't baptize a spirit in real water -- such a physically oriented ordinance must be performed in mortality. Although not strictly an official doctrine, many Latter-day Saints believe that such ordinances must be performed in the spirit world to effectualize the ordinances performed vicariously in the world of the living. After all, a spirit must *accept* the ordinances done for him. For instance, in a report requested by the First Presidency of the LDS Church, Heber Q. Hale, president of the Boise stake, related that in a vision he had seen, "Ordinances [were] performed in the spirit world effectualizing in the individual recipients the same principles of the Gospel vicariously performed here."[643]
Indeed, the idea that spirits are baptized in the spirit world may be quite relevant to our case in light of what J.R. Porter calls "the well-known [Jewish] idea of the correspondence and the simultaneity of the earthly and heavenly ritual . . . ."[644]

Baptism of Resurrected Beings -- A Variation on the Theme

In the *Gospel of Nicodemus* the concept was taken somewhat further. Two brothers were resurrected in this story after hearing Christ preach in the spirit world. Then, in their resurrected form, they were baptized in the Jordan.

> And after they had thus spoken, the Saviour blessed Adam
> with the sign of the cross on his forehead, and did this also
> to the patriarchs, and prophets, and martyrs, and forefathers;
> and He took them, and sprang up out of Hades . . . . All
> these things we saw and heard; we, the two brothers, who
> also have been sent by Michael the archangel, and have been
> ordered to proclaim the resurrection of the Lord, but first to
> go away to the Jordan and to be baptized. Thither also we
> have gone, and have been baptized with the rest of the dead
> who have risen. [645]

Baptism for the Dead Among the Cerinthians and Marcionites

Was baptism for the dead practiced in the early Church? Aside from Paul's reference there is only mention of a few heretical groups who preserved the practice. According to Fillion, the Cerinthians and Marcionites, two "heretical" sects, practiced baptism for the dead on behalf of deceased friends and relatives.[646] Epiphanius described the practice of the Cerinthians in Corinth and Galatia:

> Among them there also exists the tradition of which we have
> heard, namely that when some of them die before being
> baptized, others are baptized in place of them in their name,
> so that when they rise in the resurrection they may not pay
> the penalty of not having received baptism and become
> subject to the authority of the one who made the world. And
> this is the reason, so the tradition of which we have heard
> states, that the holy Apostle said, "If the dead are not raised
> at all, why are they baptized for them?"[647]

John Chrysostom similarly described the practice of the ancient Marcionites:

> Or will ye that I should first mention how they who are
> infected with the Marcionite heresy pervert this expression?
> And I know indeed that I shall excite much laughter;
> nevertheless, even on this account most of all I will mention
> it that you may the more completely avoid this disease: viz.,
> when any Catechumen departs among them, having
> concealed the living man under the couch of the dead, they
> approach the corpse and talk with him, and ask him if he

161

wishes to receive baptism; then when he makes no answer, he that is concealed underneath saith in his stead that of course he should wish to be baptized; and so they baptize him instead of the departed, like men jesting upon the stage.[648]

Baptism for the Dead as an Esoteric Rite

Why wasn't this practice preserved in the "orthodox" branches of the Church?[649] Peter, in the *Clementine Recognitions*, may give us a clue:

When he had thus spoken, I answered: "If those shall enjoy the kingdom of Christ, whom his coming shall find righteous, shall then those be wholly deprived of the kingdom who have died before His coming?" Then Peter says: "You compel me, O Clement, to touch upon things that are unspeakable. But so far as it is allowed to declare them, I shall not shrink from doing so . . . for not only shall they [the righteous dead] escape the pains of hell, but shall also remain incorruptible, and shall be the first to see God the Father, and shall obtain the rank of honour among the first in the presence of God."[650]

Was baptism for the dead an esoteric rite in the early church? Peter seemed to indicate that the entire subject of salvation for the dead was off limits in casual conversation.[651] However, it is certain that if the dead were to be saved, their salvation had to include baptism. In another passage, Peter intimated that the unbaptized righteous would obtain some reward in the present life, but that future rewards were reserved for those who wrought righteousness *after baptism.* "But so well pleasing . . . is chastity to God, that it confers some grace in the present life even upon those who are in error; for future blessedness is laid up for those only who preserve chastity and righteousness by the grace of baptism."[652]

The subject of secret rites and doctrines within the early Church will be discussed more fully in a later chapter, but for now it will suffice to point out that *all* the sacraments of the Church were veiled in secrecy until the third century. According to Davies, in the first two centuries of Christianity there are plenty of references to baptism and the Eucharist, but no detailed descriptions, because "the observance of the *disciplina arcani* [secret discipline] inhibited full descriptions of these rites."[653] Indeed, Tertullian's *On Baptism* (ca. 200 A.D.) is the only extant treatise on any of the sacraments from before the fourth century.[654]

Therefore, it is hardly surprising that baptism for the dead was lost early on, if it was never revealed to everyone. This is unfortunate, however, since this doctrine and practice are essential to an understanding of God's mercy and justice in action.

Objections to the LDS Practice of Baptism for the Dead

Before we move on, however, we should deal with the various objections mainstream Christians have had to the LDS practice of baptism for the dead. Although many mainstream Christian critics never bother to deal with the LDS doctrine or its justification from early Christian sources, one Catholic author, Bernard Foschini, did comment after reading Hugh Nibley's classic study, "Baptism for the Dead in Ancient Times."[655]

Foschini cites various scriptures (e.g., Hebrews 9:27, Matthew 25:13, and Luke 16:19-31) which seem to indicate that it is not possible for one to change one's ways after death.[656] But he fails to note that baptism for the dead is not considered effective for those who have already rejected Christ -- only for those who have never had a proper chance to accept or reject the truth; the audiences to whom the passages he quotes were directed *had* heard the Good News.

Ignoring the LDS belief that vicarious works must be accepted or rejected by the beneficiary, Foschini erects a straw-man argument that baptism for the dead would take away free-will:

> If we, independently from the dead, can decide or change their eternal destinies, then the fact that they are damned or saved can no longer be attributed to their faults or their merits, but to ours. It would be our responsibility! It would be impossible, if we willed it, that anyone should go to hell![657]

But this contradicts Paul's testimony that the righteous dead of Israel could not be made perfect without the Christians of his day: "God having provided some better thing for us, that they without us should not be made perfect." (Hebrews 11:40) Therefore, the salvation of the dead *must* depend in some measure upon us.

Postulating that the condition of the dead is unalterable, Foschini then reasons that Christ preached the gospel to the dead only "as an announcement of the Redemption already accomplished."[658] In other words, Christ merely went to the unbaptized dead to tell them they were damned to hell. And yet Peter insisted that the gospel was preached so that they could "live according to God in the spirit" (1 Peter 4:6), so apparently the dead *can* change their ways!

Finally, Foschini objects to Nibley's use of passages from the writings of the early Christian fathers to support the LDS belief. For, if an apostasy had occurred, as Mormons believe, why quote men who had lost the truth?

> Finally, if after the passing of the Apostles, the bankruptcy of the Church and of her true doctrine became glaringly apparent in her struggle with the gnostic so-called, why does Nibley now stress so much the words of men who had lost

the Lord's doctrine? Why does he choose a few words of the Fathers who lived in the general disaster of the Church and hold them as true?[659]

Here Foschini entirely misses the point. No Latter-day Saint ever argued that the writings of the post-Apostolic Christians were to be considered scriptural. Rather, our point is that in many cases these documents preach doctrines that are at odds with mainstream Christian interpretation, but strikingly similar to those revealed to Joseph Smith. In light of this fact, the LDS claims about the apostasy and restoration are entirely plausible. And if one admits that the LDS claims are *plausible*, he will be that much more likely to ask God whether they are, in actuality, true.

The Resurrection

As was indicated above, the spirit world is merely a waiting place for souls during the interim between death and the resurrection. The Bible is absolutely clear that the destiny of all mankind is to be resurrected and judged, as a consequence of the resurrection of the Lord Jesus Christ. Thus Paul told Felix that "there shall be a resurrection of the dead, both of the just and unjust." (Acts 24:15) Nearly all Christian denominations accept this hope. However, it should be pointed out that the type of resurrection Joseph Smith preached is somewhat different from that taught by many Christians.

The Resurrection Body in the New Testament

What will the resurrection body be like? The answer one gives to that question depends on how the seemingly contradictory scriptural passages relating to the resurrection are interpreted. For example, Paul indicated that the "natural body" would die, and a "spiritual body" would be raised up in the resurrection. (1 Corinthians 15:44) But what is a "spiritual body"? The only example of a resurrected body given in the Bible is that of Jesus, and that body was evidently very physical. He made it clear to the Apostles that he had a corporeal body by letting them touch him and watch him eat: "Handle me, and see; for a spirit hath not flesh and bones, as ye see me have." (Luke 24:39; see also John 20-21) Nevertheless, Paul insisted that "flesh and blood cannot inherit the kingdom of God." (1 Corinthians 15:50)

Christian Confusion About the Resurrected Body

It is no wonder that the Christian world lies in confusion with regard to the nature of the resurrected body. Given the presupposition that something "spiritual" is non-material, these scriptures are a confusing mess. Consequently, some mainstream Christians admit that the "spiritual body" must be material, but are noncommittal about what exactly that means, while others insist that the resurrected body is incorporeal and Jesus' resurrection body remained physical only temporarily, for evidentiary purposes. For example, Presbyterian leader John S. Bonnell explains:

> With a few exceptions, Presbyterians do not interpret the phrase in the Apostles' Creed "the resurrection of the body" as meaning the *physical* body. Saint Paul writes: "Flesh and blood cannot inherit the kingdom of God; neither doth corruption inherit incorruption." They understand "the resurrection of the body" as a reference to the *spiritual* body of the resurrection. Paul writes: "It is sown a natural body; it is raised a spiritual body" . . . . Saint John in his Gospel suggests that the resurrected body of Jesus for evidential purposes retained certain physical properties.[660]

Joseph Smith on the Nature of the Resurrected Body

In contrast, Joseph Smith revealed that the body raised up in the resurrection will be essentially the same as the mortal body: "As concerning the resurrection, I will merely say that all men will come from the grave as they lie down, whether old or young; there will not be 'added unto their stature one cubit.'"[661] And yet the human form will be perfected: "The spirit and the body shall be reunited again in its perfect form; both limb and joint shall be restored to its proper frame, even as we now are at this time . . . ." (Alma 11:43) These resurrected bodies will be "spiritual" by virtue of "having spirit in their bodies, and not blood."[662] That is, they will be bodies of flesh and bone, animated by spirit alone, and not sustained by blood.

The Early Christians on the Nature of the Resurrected Body

Certainly this in an interesting solution to the problem of how a body of "flesh and bone," as the resurrected Jesus had, could inherit the kingdom of God, and it explains how a "spiritual" body could be physical, as well. However, the test of this explanation lies with how the early Christian writers interpreted this apparent paradox.

First of all, throughout the second century, it was unanimously affirmed by mainstream Christianity that the resurrected body was essentially the same as the mortal body. Ignatius, for example, insisted that Christ not only had a physical body at his resurrection, but has one now, and will have one still at his final coming. He also testified that we will be raised up in exactly the same manner:

> And I know that He was possessed of a body not only in His being born and crucified, but I also know that He was so after His resurrection, and believe that He is so now. When, for instance, He came to those who were with Peter, He said to them, "Lay hold, handle Me, and see that I am not an

incorporeal spirit." "For a spirit hath not flesh and bones, as ye see Me have . . . ." Nor was this all; but also after He had shown Himself to them, that He had risen indeed, and not in appearance only, He both ate and drank with them during forty entire days . . . . But if they say that He will come at the end of the world without a body, how shall those "see Him that pierced Him," and when they recognise Him, "mourn for themselves?"[663]

He was also truly raised from the dead, His Father quickening Him, even as after the same manner His Father will so raise up us who believe in Him by Christ Jesus, apart from whom we do not possess the true life.[664]

Justin, Irenaeus, and Tatian all preached the resurrection of the physical body, as well. "Since we expect to receive again our own bodies, though they be dead and cast into the earth, for we maintain that with God nothing is impossible."[665] "Then, again, how can they say that the flesh, which is nourished with the body of the Lord and with His blood, goes to corruption, and does not partake of life?"[666]

And on this account we believe that there will be a resurrection of bodies after the consummation of all things . . . . Even though fire destroy all traces of my flesh, the world receives the vaporized matter ; and though dispersed through rivers and seas, or torn in pieces by wild beasts, I am laid up in the storehouses of a wealthy Lord. And, although the poor and the godless know not what is stored up, yet God the Sovereign, when He pleases, will restore the substance that is visible to Him alone to its pristine condition.[667]

In the same vein, Tertullian preached that "souls are to receive back at the resurrection the self-same bodies in which they died."[668] And Jesus, in the *Epistle of the Apostles*, preached that "the resurrection of the flesh shall come to pass with the soul therein and the spirit."[669] The author of *2 Clement* was even more emphatic:

And let no one of you say that this very flesh shall not be judged, nor rise again. Consider ye in what state ye were saved, in what ye received sight, if not while ye were in this flesh. We must therefore preserve the flesh as the temple of God. For as ye were called in the flesh, ye shall also come to be judged in the flesh. As Christ the Lord who saved us, though He was first a Spirit, became flesh, and thus called us, so shall we also receive the reward in this flesh. [670]

166

Although the early Christian writers preached the physical resurrection of the flesh, they did not teach that the dead would be raised with all their former deformities and infirmities. For example, just as the *Book of Mormon* teaches the flesh will rise "in its perfect form" (Alma 11:43), Justin Martyr insisted that all deformities would be removed in the resurrection: "For if on earth He healed the sicknesses of the flesh, and made the body whole, much more will He do this in the resurrection, so that the flesh shall rise perfect and entire."[671] On the other hand, the resurrected flesh was not thought to be superfluous, and thus Papias could insist that "There will be enjoyment of foods in the resurrection."[672]

One astonishing point in Joseph Smith's favor comes from a passage in Athenagoras' treatise on the resurrection. There he explained that the resurrected body is the same as the mortal body, except that it has no need of any type of fluids, such as blood or bile, which are strictly useful only in mortality. Compare this statement to the Prophet's, quoted above, where he described a "spiritual" body as one sustained by spirit rather than by blood. As Athenagoras stated:

> For the bodies that rise again are reconstituted from the parts which properly belong to them, whereas no one of the things mentioned is such a part, nor has it the form or place of a part. . . since no longer does blood, or phlegm, or bile, or breath, contribute anything to the life. Neither, again, will the bodies nourished then require the things they once required, seeing that, along with the want and corruption of the bodies nourished, the need also of those things by which they were nourished is taken away.[673]

The Power of Embodiment

One final fact should be noted about the doctrine of resurrection as revealed by Joseph Smith. That is, the resurrection of the flesh is not just an incidental detail in the plan of salvation, but a necessary step in the exaltation of mankind. For, if the "Father has a body of flesh and bones as tangible as man's" (D&C 130:22), and if "spirit and element, inseparably connected, receive a fulness of joy" (D&C 93:33), men must be clothed in a material body to become like their Father. And, evidently, the possession of a body entitles the bearer to greater power. "For behold, if the flesh should rise no more our spirits must become subject to that angel who fell from before the presence of the Eternal God, and became the devil, to rise no more." (2 Nephi 9:8)

This doctrine, we shall see, is entirely compatible with the worldview of ancient Judaism. And this is significant, since initially Christianity seemed indistinguishable from Judaism and was regarded by many as no more than another Jewish sect.[674] According to the ancient Jews, the spirit and body are so united that the total essence of man must include both:

To the Hebrew man has not a body, he *is* a body. There is no rigid distinction between the physical and the spiritual, because body and soul are so intimately united that they cannot be distinguished; indeed they are more than united, for the body is regarded as the soul in its outward form. Man in his totality, therefore, is not a discarnate spirit but a spiritual-corporeal entity.[675]

Indeed, the doctrine revealed to Joseph Smith that the possession of a body imparts power to a spirit[676] was also known to ancient Judaism and Jewish Christianity. For example, in the *Apocalypse of Abraham*, the patriarch saw in vision that the angels in the sixth level of heaven, who have no bodies, must obey those in the seventh:

And I looked from the height where I stood to the sixth expanse; and there I saw a multitude of spiritual angels, without bodies -- those, that is, who do the bidding of the fiery angels on the seventh firmament, on the heights of which I stood.[677]

Remarkably, the same doctrine was preached by Jesus in the *Epistle of the Apostles*: "And the Son shall become perfect through the Father who is Light, for the Father is perfect which bringeth to pass death and resurrection, and ye shall see a perfection more perfect than the perfect."[678]

How was the truth about the resurrection lost? As we discussed earlier, Christianity rejected its early materialism in favor of a Neoplatonic belief system which defined the spiritual world as something completely transcending the material. The idea of a physical resurrection would have sounded extremely crass to any educated person in the Greek-speaking world.[679] For example, when the Athenians "heard of the resurrection of the dead [from Paul], some mocked" (Acts 17:32), and the pagan Celsus objected that the Christian doctrine of resurrection is "such a hope [as] might be cherished by worms. For what sort of human soul is that which would still long for a body that had been subject to corruption?"[680] Although the dogma of a physical resurrection has survived in some quarters of mainstream Christianity even down to the present time, many have rejected it in favor of the philosophies of men.

The Millennium

It is well known that Jesus preached the doctrine of His Millennial Reign. That is, Christ will come again to earth in glory, destroy the wicked, resurrect the righteous dead, and reign on the earth for a thousand years. John the Revelator saw this event in vision:

> And I saw thrones, and they sat upon them, and judgment was given unto them: and I saw the souls of them that were beheaded for the witness of Jesus, and for the word of God, and which had not worshipped the beast, neither his image, neither had received his mark upon their foreheads, or in their hands; and they lived and reigned with Christ a thousand years. But the rest of the dead lived not again until the thousand years were finished. This is the first resurrection. (Revelation 20:4-5)

A Literal Millennial Reign

Joseph Smith taught that the scriptural descriptions of this event were to be taken literally (see Article of Faith 10 in the *Pearl of Great Price*), and indeed, the Restoration of the gospel itself is a preparation for the Second Coming of Christ. While many Christians agree that the Millennium will be a literal event, many others see it as merely a symbolic representation of the future peace that will be brought to the earth by the teachings of Christ, or something similarly vague. However, we shall see that the earliest Christian writers believed in a literal Millennial Reign, and eschewed such allegorism, until this truth was rejected on dubious grounds in the third century.

Eusebius, in the fourth century, recorded that Papias had written down the tradition of the Millennium as he had heard it from the lips of the Apostles and others who had heard the Apostles:

> The same person [Papias], moreover, has set down other things as coming to him from unwritten tradition, amongst these some strange parables and instructions of the Saviour, and some other things of a more fabulous nature. Amongst these he says that there will be a millennium after the resurrection from the dead, when the personal reign of Christ will be established on this earth.[681]

Eusebius also admitted that the great majority of second-century Christians even after Papias still expected a literal millennial reign, but he himself rejected such crass literalism and judged Papias to be mentally deficient as a result.

> Papias reproduces other stories communicated to him by word of mouth, together with some otherwise unknown parables and teachings of the Saviour, and other things of a more allegorical character. He says that after the resurrection of the dead there will be a period of a thousand

years, when Christ's kingdom will be set up on this earth in material form. I suppose he got these notions by misinterpreting the Apostolic accounts and failing to grasp what they had said in mystic and symbolic language. For he seems to have been a man of very small intelligence, to judge from his books. But it is partly due to him that the great majority of churchmen after him took the same view, relying on his early date; e.g. Irenaeus and several others, who clearly held the same opinion.[682]

Indeed, before the third century the belief in the literal fulfillment of these promises was so widespread that Irenaeus could claim it was essential to orthodoxy:

> Still in the late second century Irenaeus, who was both bishop of Lyons and a distinguished theologian, could quote Papias along with passages from the Scriptures -- and even insist that it was an indispensable part of orthodoxy to believe that these things [i.e. the Millennium] would come to pass.[683]

However, even in Justin Martyr's day doubt was beginning to spring up about this doctrine, probably because of the disillusionment of those who expected immediate fulfillment of the promises. Justin and most others still believed in the Millennium, but he could report that there were others who rejected this teaching, even though Peter warned not to expect the Second Coming immediately, for "one day is with the Lord as a thousand years, and a thousand years as one day." (2 Peter 3:8)

> I admitted to you formerly, that I and many others are of this opinion, and [believe] that such [the Millennium] will take place, as you assuredly are aware; but, on the other hand, I signified to you that many who belong to the pure and pious faith, and are true Christians, think otherwise.[684]

Spiritualizing the Millennium

According to Davies, the widespread belief in the Millennial reign was brought into general disrepute on account of its acceptance by the Montanists, and was thereafter transformed into the doctrines of purgatory and the exemption of faithful Christians from a period of waiting after death before their final appointment to the bliss of heaven.[685] Thus, without revelation, Christianity rejected a perfectly orthodox doctrine just because a heretical sect accepted it.

The extent to which the belief in a literal Millennium fell into disrepute can be illustrated by the fact that those passages which defended this doctrine in Irenaeus's *Against Heresies*, were removed from most of the manuscripts now extant by scribes in the middle ages. Roberts and Donaldson explain:

> The five following chapters [Irenaeus, *Against Heresies* 5:32-36] were omitted in the earlier editions, but added by Feuardentius. Most MSS, too, did not contain them. It is probable that the scribes of the middle ages rejected them on account of their inculcating millenarian notions, which had been long extinct in the Church.[686]

What a shame this glorious hope was lost. But its enemies could never completely drive it from Christianity, and it has had a tendency to crop up from time to time, especially during periods of political strife. Therefore, Joseph Smith's acceptance of this doctrine is not particularly remarkable, but certainly it adds weight to the already sizable mass of evidence we have collected for his claims to inspiration.

Three Degrees of Glory and Outer Darkness

The Bible makes clear that all mankind will be "judged. . . according to their works." (Revelation 20:12) And if so, won't everyone's rewards be different one from another? Jesus insisted that in His "Father's house are many mansions" (John 14:2), and Paul wrote that in the judgment a person's works might be added to his reward or burned up, but either way he might still be saved: "If any man's work abide which he hath built [upon the foundation of Jesus Christ], he shall receive a reward. If any man's work shall be burned, he shall suffer loss: but he himself shall be saved; yet so as by fire." (1 Corinthians 3:14-15) Paul also indicated that he had seen a vision of "the third heaven." (2 Corinthians 12:2) Therefore, one might logically conclude from these passages that recipients of salvation will be allotted varying rewards within at least three different "heavens" or "degrees of glory." However, it must be admitted that this fact is not really made explicit in the Bible, so it is understandable that the Christian world has for many centuries been content with the doctrine of one heaven and one hell.

The LDS Doctrine of Degrees of Glory

While pondering the significance of certain of the aforementioned passages in the Bible, Joseph Smith and Sidney Rigdon were given a most striking vision of the fate of mankind after the general resurrection and judgment, which included a description of the three principal kingdoms of glory. (D&C 76) They found that the first kingdom, called the Celestial, will be inhabited by those who have overcome by faith in Jesus Christ (D&C 76:50-70, 92-96), including children who have died and those who would have

171

accepted the gospel in this life, but were not given the chance until they reached the spirit world. (D&C 137:1-10) The second kingdom, called the Terrestrial, will be inhabited by good people who were just and kind, but were not valiant in their testimony of Jesus. Those who rejected the gospel in this life, but afterwards received it will be given a reward in this kingdom, as well. (D&C 76:71-80, 91, 97)[687] The third, or Telestial, kingdom will be given to the generally wicked masses of the earth who spent their entire residence in the Spirit World in Hell, and so were not worthy of any higher glory. (D&C 76:81-90, 98-112)

Another distinction between these kingdoms is that those who receive Celestial glory will reside in the presence of the Father Himself, while those in the Terrestrial kingdom will receive the presence of the Son, and those in the Telestial will have the Holy Ghost to minister to them. (D&C 76:62, 77, 86)

Sun, Moon, and Stars as Types of the Degrees of Glory

What marvelous light this vision has thrown upon obscure Bible passages! For example, what good does it do to know that there are three heavens if one does not know anything about them? Another example of a passage illuminated by this revelation is Paul's description of the glory of the resurrected body:

> There are also celestial bodies, and bodies terrestrial: but the glory of the celestial is one, and the glory of the terrestrial is another. There is one glory of the sun, and another glory of the moon, and another glory of the stars: for one star differeth from another star in glory. So also is the resurrection of the dead. (1 Corinthians 15:40-42)

In the vision of the kingdoms of glory, the Lord revealed that this passage is not just a comparison of earthly bodies with heavenly, but also a reference to the fact that there are three different major levels of glory to which a body can be resurrected:

> And the glory of the celestial is one, even as the glory of the sun is one. And the glory of the terrestrial is one, even as the glory of the moon is one. And the glory of the telestial is one, even as the glory of the stars is one; for as one star differeth from another star in glory, even so differs one from another in glory in the telestial world. (D&C 76:96-98)

Origen, in the early third century, revealed that the early Church interpreted this passage in essentially the same way:

> Our understanding of the passage indeed is, that the Apostle, wishing to describe the great difference among those who

172

rise again in glory, i.e., of the saints, borrowed a comparison from the heavenly bodies, saying, "One is the glory of the sun, another the glory of the moon, another the glory of the stars."[688]

He further explained that the highest of the three degrees is associated with the Father, and the second degree with the Son:

And some men are connected with the Father, being part of Him, and next to these, those whom our argument now brings into clearer light, those who have come to the Saviour and take their stand entirely in Him. And third are those of whom we spoke before, who reckon the sun and the moon and the stars to be gods, and take their stand by them. And in the fourth and last place those who submit to soulless and dead idols.[689]

We shall see that Origen's doctrine of a fourth degree for the very wicked is fairly consistent with LDS belief, as well.

John Chrysostom was another witness to the fact that the early Church considered this passage to be a reference to degrees of reward in the afterlife:

And having said this, he ascends again to the heaven, saying, "There is one glory of the sun, and another glory of the moon." For as in the earthly bodies there is a difference, so also in the heavenly; and that difference no ordinary one, but reaching even to the uttermost: there being not only a difference between sun and moon, and stars, but also between stars and stars. For what though they be all in the heaven? yet some have a larger, others a less share of glory. What do we learn from hence? That although they be all in God's kingdom, all shall not enjoy the same reward; and though all sinners be in hell, all shall not endure the same punishment.[690]

More Ancient Witnesses to the Three Degrees of Glory

This doctrine goes back much further than Origen and Chrysostom, however. Irenaeus preserved the same tradition which had supposedly come from the elders who knew the Apostles. Many think he received it from Papias:

And as the presbyters say, Then those who are deemed worthy of an abode in heaven shall go there, others shall enjoy the delights of paradise, and others shall possess the splendour of the city; for everywhere the Saviour shall be seen according as they who see Him shall be worthy. [They say, moreover], that there is this distinction between the habitation of those who produce an hundred-fold, and that of those who produce sixty-fold, and that of those who produce thirty-fold: for the first will be taken up into the heavens, the second will dwell in paradise, the last will inhabit the city; and that was on this account the Lord declared, "In My Father's house are many mansions." For all things belong to God, who supplies all with a suitable dwelling-place; even as His Word says, that a share is allotted to all by the Father, according as each person is or shall be worthy. And this is the couch on which the guests shall recline, having been invited to the wedding. The presbyters, the disciples of the Apostles, affirm that this is the gradation and arrangement of those who are saved, and that they advance through steps of this nature; also that they ascend through the Spirit to the Son, and through the Son to the Father, and that in due time the Son will yield up His work to the Father, even as it is said by the Apostle, "For He must reign till He hath put all enemies under His feet. The last enemy that shall be destroyed is death."[691]

Clement of Alexandria also expressed belief in the three degrees, and echoed the Lord's revelation to Joseph Smith that those in the highest degree "are gods, even the sons of God." (D&C 76:58)

Conformably, therefore, there are various abodes, according to the worth of those who have believed . . . . These chosen abodes, which are three, are indicated by the numbers in the Gospel--the thirty, the sixty, the hundred. And the perfect inheritance belongs to those who attain to "a perfect man," according to the image of the Lord . . . . To the likeness of God, then, he that is introduced into adoption and the friendship of God, to the just inheritance of the lords and gods is brought; if he be perfected, according to the Gospel, as the Lord Himself taught.[692]

Clement also preached that the three gradations of glory are procured by virtue of three types of actions:

[Clement of Alexandria] reckons three kinds of actions, the first of which is . . . right or perfect action, which is characteristic of the perfect man and Gnostic alone, and raises him to the height of glory. The second is the class of .

. . medium, or intermediate actions, which are done by less perfect believers, and procure a lower grade of glory. In the third place he reckons sinful actions, which are done by those who fall away from salvation.[693]

Other Systems of Multiple Heavens

Actually, there were several schemes for the structure of the heavens, with different numbers of heavens which varied also in their contents.[694] But even where three degrees were not specifically mentioned, it was maintained that various gradations of the elect exist. For example, Similitude 8 in the *Pastor of Hermas* discusses various types of elect. The editors of one collection of early Christian documents preface the chapter with this summary: "That there are many kinds of elect, and of repenting sinners: and how all of them shall receive a reward proportionable to the measure of their repentance and good works."[695]

Jesus, in the *Epistle of the Apostles*, made a distinction between the "elect" and "most elect."[696] And consistent with this, the Jewish Christian *Clementine Recognitions* reduced the number of heavens to two.[697]

One of the most popular schemes was that of seven heavens. Daniélou asserts that the idea of seven heavens was first introduced by certain Jewish Christian groups and "derives from oriental, Irano-Babylonian influences," while the older Jewish apocalyptic tradition and many other early Christian groups held to the three heavens scheme.[698] However, it appears that the seven heavens may originally have been consistent with the three heavens doctrine. For example, we have seen that Irenaeus preserved Papias's doctrine of three heavens, but in another passage he asserted that "the earth is encompassed by seven heavens, in which dwell Powers and Angels and Archangels, giving homage to the Almighty God who created all things . . . ."[699] As Daniélou points out, since the seven heavens were the dwelling places of angels, they probably were thought to have been gradations *within the second of the three principal heavens.*[700]

Outer Darkness

As we noted in the discussion of the nature of the spirit world, both the Latter-day Saints and the early Christians have taught that the "hell" associated with the spirit world will have an end. It should be noted here, however, that there will be an everlasting hell after the resurrection, and the promise of eternal punishment is very real for those who in this life and the next not only reject Christ and His Kingdom, but who consciously fight against it once they have received a witness of its truth. The Lord revealed to the Prophet that those who deny the Holy Ghost, and thus committing the unpardonable sin, will be given a kingdom of totally without glory called "outer darkness":

Thus saith the Lord concerning all those who know my power, and have been made partakers thereof, and suffered themselves through the power of the devil to be overcome, and to deny the truth and defy my power -- They are they who are the sons of perdition, of whom I say that it had been better for them never to have been born; For they are vessels of wrath, doomed to suffer the wrath of God, with the devil and his angels in eternity; Concerning whom I have said there is no forgiveness in this world nor in the world to come -- Having denied the Holy Spirit after having received it, and having denied the Only Begotten Son of the Father, having crucified him unto themselves and put him to an open shame. (D&C 76:31-35)

Similarly, both the gnostic Christian *Gospel of Philip* and the *Pastor of Hermas* describe the denizens of "outer darkness" as those who have made a conscious and specific choice to rebel against God:

An Apostolic man in a vision saw some people shut up in a house of fire and bound with fiery chains, lying in flaming ointment . . . . And he said to them, "[Why are they not able] to be saved? [They answered], "They did not desire it. They received [this place as] punishment, what is called 'the [outer] darkness,' because he is [thrown] out (into it)."[701]

From the first mountain, which was black, they that believed are the following: apostates and blasphemers against the Lord, and betrayers of the servants of God. To these repentance is not open; but death lies before them, and on this account also are they black, for their race is a lawless one.[702]

Origen taught that the wicked in outer darkness would be devoid of intelligence, and possessed of bodies stripped of all glory.

But the outer darkness, in my judgment, is to be understood not so much of some dark atmosphere without any light, as of those persons who, being plunged in the darkness of profound ignorance, have been placed beyond the reach of any light of the understanding . . . . The wicked also, who in this life have loved the darkness of error and the night of ignorance, may be clothed with dark and black bodies after the resurrection . . . .[703]

176

Finally, the Lord told Joseph Smith that He never fully reveals to men the punishments of outer darkness, but only brief visions thereof. Consider the wording of this revelation as compared to that used by Jesus in the apocryphal *Gospel of Bartholomew*:

> And the end thereof, neither the place thereof, nor their torment, no man knows; Neither was it revealed, neither is, neither will be revealed unto man, except to them who are made partakers thereof; Nevertheless, I, the Lord, show it by vision unto many, but straightway shut it up again; Wherefore, the end, the width, the height, the depth, and the misery thereof, they understand not, neither any man except those who are ordained unto this condemnation. (D&C 76:45-48)

> And the earth was rolled up like a volume of a book and the deep [hell] was revealed unto them. And when the Apostles saw it, they fell on their faces upon the earth. But Jesus raised them up, saying: Said I not unto you, "It is not good for you to see the deep." And again he beckoned unto the angels, and the deep was covered up.[704]

The Loss of the Doctrine of Degrees of Glory

We have seen that the doctrine of degrees of glory was soon confused so that a number of schemes, notably that of seven heavens, were adopted, but it was always clear to everyone that there *were* different degrees of glory in the heavens. So how was this enlightening doctrine lost? Its fate is not completely clear, but the example of Jovinian, a monk from Milan who preached around the turn of the fifth century, may be instructive. Clark describes Jovinian's teaching, and Jerome's reaction to it: "Jovinian's view, that there are only two categories, the saved and the damned, is assessed by Jerome as more akin to the philosophy of the Old Stoics than that of Christians."[705] Therefore, once again an older Christian doctrine was replaced by the speculations of a Greek philosophical school.

It is clear that Joseph Smith went far beyond the information found in the Bible concerning the degrees of glory in the resurrection. However, it is equally clear that many of those extra details he included are corroborated by the testimony of the early Christian writers -- and this to such an extent that it is hard to explain the phenomenon as mere coincidence.

Can there be any doubt that Joseph Smith preached a legitimate early Christian worldview[706], and correctly mapped out the way to salvation? This is the question that every reader must decide for himself, but in view of the evidence presented so far, it must be admitted that the suggestion is entirely plausible.

Chapter Notes

Note 1: Adam's Vision of His Posterity

Both Joseph Smith and an early Jewish legend reported that Adam had been shown a vision of his posterity. According to the Jewish *Haggadah*, Adam saw the whole history of mankind in vision immediately after his creation. "God revealed the whole history of mankind to him. He showed him each generation and its leaders; each generation and its prophets; each generation and its scholars; [etc.]"[707]

This legend is similar to the revelation given to Joseph Smith, that three years prior to his death "Adam stood up in the midst of the congregation [of his extended family]; and . . . being full of the Holy Ghost, predicted whatsoever should befall his posterity unto the latest generation." (D&C 107:56)

Note 2: Translated Beings

One final point of contact exists between the doctrine of three degrees as revealed to Joseph Smith and that preserved in ancient Christian circles. That is, Joseph Smith taught that the paradise of Eden was in a Terrestrial state, and also those persons who have been translated, or taken up to heaven without tasting death, are preserved also in a terrestrial state until they are resurrected. Compare the Prophet's doctrine of translation[708] with that preserved in another fragment attributed to Papias:

> Many have supposed that the doctrine of translation was a doctrine whereby men were taken immediately into the presence of God, and into an eternal fullness, but this is a mistaken idea. Their place of habitation is that of the terrestrial order, and a place prepared for such characters He held in reserve to be ministering angels unto many planets, and who as yet have not entered into so great a fullness as those who are resurrected from the dead.[709]

> Where, then, was the first man placed? In paradise certainly, as the Scripture declares "And God planted a garden [*paradisum*] eastward in Eden, and there He placed the man whom He had formed." And then afterwards when [man] proved disobedient, he was cast out thence into this world. Wherefore also the elders who were disciples of the Apostles tell us that those who were translated were transferred to that place (for paradise has been prepared for

178

righteous men, such as have the Spirit; in which place also Paul the Apostle, when he was caught up, heard words which are unspeakable as regards us in our present condition), and that there shall they who have been translated remain until the consummation [of all things], as a prelude to immortality.[710]

Peter preached essentially the same doctrine in the *Clementine Recognitions*:

In like manner others were dealt with, who pleased His will, that, being translated to Paradise, they should be kept for the kingdom. But as to those who have not been able completely to fulfil the rule of righteousness, but have had some remnants of evil in their flesh, their bodies are indeed dissolved, but their souls are kept in good and blessed abodes, that at the resurrection of the dead, when they shall recover their own bodies, purified even by the dissolution, they may obtain an eternal inheritance in proportion to their good deeds.[711]

Note 3: Worlds Without End

The doctrine of multiple worlds is perhaps a minor point, but it emphasizes the fact that the worldview Joseph Smith taught would have fit quite nicely within the framework of early Christian thought.

The Lord gave a vision to Joseph Smith of what Moses saw when he was caught up to a high mountain. In it, the Lord explained, "And worlds without number have I created; and I also created them for mine own purpose; and by the Son I created them, which is mine Only Begotten." (Moses 1:33) What was the purpose of all this? The Lord intimated that His eternal work and glory is to bring salvation to mankind:

And as one earth shall pass away, and the heavens thereof even so shall another come; and there is no end to my works, neither to my words. For behold, this is my work and my glory -- to bring to pass the immortality and eternal life of man. (Moses 1:38-39)

Compare this worldview to that found in many early Christian and Jewish documents. In answer to the question, "What was God doing before this world began, if this world had a beginning in time?" Origen revealed that the ancient Church held the same belief:

We say that not then for the first time did God begin to work when He made this visible world; but as, after its destruction, there will be another world, so also we believe that others existed before the present came into being. And both of these positions will be confirmed by the authority of holy Scripture. For that there will be another world after this, is taught by Isaiah, who says, "There will be new heavens, and a new earth, which I shall make to abide in my sight, saith the LORD;" and that before this world others also existed is shown by Ecclesiastes, in the words: "What is that which hath been? Even that which shall be. And what is that which has been created? Even this which is to be created: and there is nothing altogether new under the sun. Who shall speak and declare, Lo, this is new? It hath already been in the ages which have been before us."[712]

In the same vein, Clement of Rome rhapsodized: "The Creator and Father of all worlds, the Most Holy, alone knows their amount and their beauty."[713] Paul taught that the Father "made the worlds" through the agency of Jesus. (Hebrews 1:2) And an old Jewish creation legend states that: "When God made our present heavens and our present earth, 'the new heavens and the new earth' were also brought forth, yea, and the hundred and ninety-six thousand worlds which God created unto his own glory."[714]

Chapter 5: Church Organization and Life

"The Priesthood is an everlasting principle, and existed with God from eternity, and will to eternity, without beginning of days or end of years. The keys have to be brought from heaven whenever the Gospel is sent."
- Joseph Smith[715]

Perhaps none of the issues we have studied is of greater contemporary significance than the question of how the earliest Church was organized and how the business of worship was conducted in it. Catholics postulate that the priesthood was given to relatively few men who conducted a rich ritual tradition, and the governance of the Church as a whole was given to the Bishop of Rome after the death of the Apostles. Protestants, on the other hand, see the early Church as a loosely-bound community of love, administered by a "priesthood of all believers," and with a minimum of ritual.

Who is correct? Does an ordained clergy separate from the laity help or hinder the kind of personal relationship with God Jesus intended for us when he established His Church? Unfortunately, there is not enough information available on first century Christianity to completely differentiate fact from speculation, and hence Davies calls the evidence concerning the constitutional order of the earliest Church "fragmentary and ambiguous."[716] However, even though we can't piece together these fragments to get a completely coherent picture of the earliest Church, it will be possible to once again examine what evidence exists for the kind of organization and worship Joseph Smith restored.

Church Organization

Priesthood Authority

Almost everyone agrees that some kind of authority is necessary to minister in Christ's Church. However, broad disagreements exist as to the nature of that authority and as to how it is transmitted. Members of the Catholic tradition, some Protestant churches, as well as Mormons, recognize that priesthood authority must be transmitted by ordination, accomplished by the laying on of hands of those who already have the authority in question.

The Necessity of Ordination

Priesthood ordination goes back to the times of the Old Testament. For example, Aaron and his sons were consecrated as priests by Moses: "Anoint them, and consecrate them, and sanctify them, that they may minister unto me in the priest's office." (Exodus 28:41) This "consecration" was certainly accomplished by the laying on of hands, since that is the way Moses transmitted authority on other occasions. "Moses set Joshua before the congregation; he laid his hands upon him, and gave him a charge, as the Lord commanded." (Numbers 27:22-23)

In New Testament times as well, officers were ordained by those in authority. For instance, Jesus ordained His Apostles: "He ordained twelve, that they should be with him to preach, to heal sicknesses, and to cast out devils." (Mark 3:14) These men didn't volunteer for the job. Rather, they were called and ordained by Jesus Christ Himself. "Ye have not chosen me, but I have chosen you, and ordained you." (John 15:16) According to both Clement of Rome and Clement of Alexandria, the Apostles would go about preaching and organizing congregations, appointing and ordaining leaders in every locale:

> The Apostles have preached the Gospel to us from the Lord Jesus Christ; Jesus Christ [has done so] from God. Christ therefore was sent forth by God, and the Apostles by Christ. Both these appointments, then, were made in an orderly way, according to the will of God. Having therefore received their orders, and being fully assured by the resurrection of our Lord Jesus Christ, and established in the word of God, with full assurance of the Holy Ghost, they went forth proclaiming that the kingdom of God was at hand. And thus preaching through countries and cities, they appointed the first-fruits [of their labours], having first proved them by the Spirit, to be bishops and deacons of those who should afterwards believe.[717]

Referring to John, Clement of Alexandria stated:

> For when, after the tyrant's death, he returned from the isle of Patmos to Ephesus, he went away upon their invitation to the neighboring territories of the Gentiles, to appoint bishops in some places, in other places to set in order whole churches, elsewhere to choose to the ministry some one of those that were pointed out by the Spirit.[718]

Likewise, Hippolytus gave the accepted procedure for ordaining men to the offices of bishop, elder, and deacon by the laying on of hands in his *Apostolic Tradition*.[719]

182

Paul told Timothy to "neglect not the gift that is in thee, which was given thee by prophecy, with the laying on of hands of the presbytery." (1 Timothy 4:14) Notice also that these appointments were always made with the assurance of the Holy Ghost, not for any political motive, and by *ordination.* Thus Paul could say (in the present tense) of the priesthood that "no man taketh this honour unto himself, but he that is called of God, as was Aaron." (Hebrews 5:4) And we have seen that Aaron was called of God and then ordained by one in authority.

Not only did these ordinations take place, but once called, God respected his servants in their offices, and did not allow others to usurp their authority. For example, Paul found certain disciples at Ephesus and asked them if they had received the Holy Ghost. (Some missionaries at that time, e.g. Philip, had only the authority to baptize, but not to give the gift of the Holy Ghost, so higher authorities had to be called in sometimes to make sure all the proper ordinances were performed -- see Acts 8:12-17.) However, these believers hadn't even heard of the Holy Ghost.

> And he said unto them, Unto what then were ye baptized? And they said, Unto John's baptism. Then said Paul, John verily baptized with the baptism of repentance, saying unto the people, that they should believe on him which should come after him, that is, on Christ Jesus. When they heard this, they were baptized in the name of the Lord Jesus. And when Paul had laid his hands upon them, the Holy Ghost came on them; and they spake with tongues and prophesied. (Acts 19:1-6)

Was John's baptism then invalid? Obviously not, since John was an Aaronic priest, and Jesus Himself submitted to the authority of John's baptism. (Matthew 3:13-17) But since John always preached that one would come after him who would "baptize . . . with the Holy Ghost, and with fire" (Matthew 3:11), Paul had reason to suspect that they had been baptized by some well-meaning, but unauthorized, imitator of the Baptist who neglected to preach John's message about the one who would baptize with the Holy Ghost.

Likewise, the authority to perform ordinances is not conferred at baptism. Simon Magus was baptized, and then desired the power to confer the Holy Spirit, so he offered to pay for the privilege. Peter rebuked him for his temerity:

> And when Simon saw that through laying on of the Apostles' hands the Holy Ghost was given, he offered them money, Saying, Give me also this power, that on whomsoever I lay hands, he may receive the Holy Ghost. But Peter said unto him, Thy money perish with thee, because thou has thought

that the gift of God may be purchased with money." (Acts 8:13, 18-20)

Indeed, in the early Church there was always a distinction made between ordained clergy and the lay-membership. Bettenson asserts that Clement of Rome's use of the word "layman" (*laikos*) before A.D. 100 marks "the clear distinction of ministers and people."[720] Clement's exact words are as follows:

> For his own peculiar services are assigned to the high priest, and their own proper place is prescribed to the priests, and their own special ministrations devolve on the Levites. The layman is bound by the laws that pertain to laymen.[721]

The *Apostolic Constitutions* made the same distinction even more specifically:

> Neither do we permit the laity to perform any of the offices belonging to the priesthood; as, for instance, neither the sacrifice, nor baptism, nor the laying on of hands, nor the blessing, whether the smaller or the greater: for "no one taketh this honour to himself, but he that is called of God." For such sacred offices are conferred by the laying on of the hands of the bishop.[722]

Kelly reports that Clement of Rome, Ignatius, and the author of *2 Clement* (in the late first and early second centuries) all preached that the church is inseparably tied to the ordained priesthood.[723] We have already seen in Chapter 2 the immense stress Ignatius placed on loyalty to the bishops[724], and likewise the author of *2 Clement* warned that at the Judgment the wicked would cry, "Woe unto us, Thou wast He, and we did not know and did not believe, and we did not obey the presbyters [elders] when they declared unto us concerning our salvation."[725] Indeed, Wand points out that unity and authority were the hallmarks of the early Church:

> Nearly every epistle we have in the New Testament shows how anxious were the leaders to maintain the close unity of all in one body, openly exercising their own authority where necessary to that end. Unity and authority, as we have seen, were the two most characteristic notes of the primitive Church.[726]

> The Church was not only a body but a corporation, which necessarily involved organisation and a law. It is indeed doubtful whether in the mind of the Jew, stored as it was

with hopes of a coming Messianic Kingdom, any mere vague sentiment or disembodied ideal could ever have been received as a possible new religion.[727]

Ignatius of Antioch (ca. 110 A.D.) summed up the natural conclusion drawn from this information. Namely, without the ordained priesthood, *there is no Church.* "In like manner, let all reverence the deacons as an appointment of Jesus Christ, and the bishop as Jesus Christ, who is the Son of the Father, and the presbyters as the sanhedrin of God, and assembly of the Apostles. Apart from these, there is no Church."[728]

The "Priesthood of All Believers"

Some Protestants defend themselves against such charges with their doctrine of a "priesthood of all believers." That is, Peter called the Church a "chosen generation, a royal priesthood . . ." (1 Peter 2:9), so each believer is by definition ordained as a priest to God. It might be inferred from this that the priesthood was meant to be more generally spread throughout the Church than is the Catholic practice. As Irenaeus put it, "For all the righteous possess the sacerdotal rank [i.e. the priestly rank or the rank of an elder]."[729]

However, when Protestants claim that "our baptism consecrates us all without exception and makes us all priests . . .," and that all offices within the Church are merely "human callings"[730], they are every bit as out of step with the early Church as are the Catholics with their limited concept of the priesthood. As Noll points out, Peter's characterization of the Church as a "royal priesthood" must be taken in the corporate sense of an elect and holy people who had the benefit of the priesthood, just as in the ancient Israelite community:

> In conjunction with this, the faithful of that early sub-Apostolic period were also challenged by *1 Peter* and by the *Apocalypse* to see themselves as a 'priestly' people. This did not imply that each one of them was a priest, but rather that the whole community was/is made up of those who are elect and holy, and to express this fact the community was described, by adopting the covenant formula of *Exodus* 19:6, as a body of priests or a priestly community.[731]

This corporate conception of the priesthood was described by Origen: "Or are you ignorant that to you also, that is, to all the Church of God and to the people of believers, the priesthood was given? . . . [1 Peter 2:9] Therefore, you have a priesthood because you are a 'priestly nation . . . .'"[732]

Any such conception of a corporate priesthood did not make the Church hierarchy superfluous, however. Early writers such as Irenaeus and Cyprian were adamant that any schism from the "Apostolic succession" was heresy itself. The following are representative statements from these writers:

He shall also judge those who give rise to schisms, who are destitute of the love of God, and who look to their own special advantage rather than to the unity of the Church; and who for trifling reasons, or any kind of reason which occurs to them, cut in pieces and divide the great and glorious body of Christ, and so far as in them lies, [positively] destroy it, -- men who prate of peace while they give rise to war, and do in truth strain out a gnat, but swallow a camel. For no reformation of so great importance can be effected by them, as will compensate for the mischief arising from their schism.[733]

Wherefore it is incumbent to obey the presbyters who are in the Church, -- those who, as I have shown, possess the succession from the Apostles; those who, together with the succession of the episcopate, have received the certain gift of truth, according to the good pleasure of the Father. But [it is also incumbent] to hold in suspicion others who depart from the primitive succession, and assemble themselves together in any place whatsoever, [looking upon them] either as heretics of perverse minds, or as schismatics puffed up and self-pleasing, or again as hypocrites, acting thus for the sake of lucre and vainglory. For all these have fallen from the truth.[734]

There is one God, and Christ is one, and there is one Church, and one chair founded upon the rock by the word of the Lord. Another altar cannot be constituted nor a new priesthood be made, except the one altar and the one priesthood. Whosoever gathereth elsewhere, scattereth. Whatsoever is appointed by human madness, so that the divine disposition is violated, is adulterous, is impious, is sacrilegious. Depart far from the contagion of men of this kind. and flee from their words, avoiding them as a cancer and a plague, as the Lord warns you and says, "They are blind leaders of the blind."[735]

Thence, through the changes of times and successions, the ordering of bishops and the plan of the Church flow onwards; so that the Church is founded upon the bishops, and every act of the Church is controlled by these same rulers.[736]

An interesting case is that of Tertullian, who early on in his career was quite critical of heretics who separated themselves from the priesthood leadership. Note the following comments:

> But if there be any (heresies) which are bold enough to plant themselves in the midst of the Apostolic age, that they may thereby seem to have been handed down by the Apostles, because they existed in the time of the Apostles, we can say: Let them produce the original records of their churches; let them unfold the roll of their bishops, running down in due succession from the beginning in such a manner that [that first bishop of theirs] bishop shall be able to show for his ordainer and predecessor some one of the Apostles or of Apostolic men, -- a man, moreover, who continued stedfast with the Apostles.[737]

> For even on laymen do [the heretics] impose the functions of priesthood.[738]

On the other hand, after Tertullian had joined the Montanist heresy, he changed his tune. His attitude was surprisingly similar to that of modern Protestants:

> Vain shall we be if we think that what is not lawful for priests is lawful for laics [i.e. laymen]. Are not even we laics priests? It is written: "A kingdom also, and priests to His God and Father, hath He made us." Therefore, if you have the right of a priest in your own person, in cases of necessity, it behoves you to have likewise the discipline of a priest whenever it may be necessary to have the right of a priest.[739]

Therefore, it is easy to see that the "priesthood of all believers" was not the original Christian concept, but rather a convenient invention of those whom modern Protestants themselves would consider heretics. Clearly, the true Church of Christ must either have a continuation or a restoration of the original priesthood and Church leadership.

The Priesthoods of Aaron and Melchizedek

In ancient Judaism, the priesthood was held by members of only one tribe of Israel, the Levites, and certain offices could only be held by direct descendants of Aaron. The high priest was the firstborn of the sons of Aaron, and the other male descendants were priests. These priests were responsible for the sacrifices, etc., which went on at the Temple at Jerusalem, the high priest being responsible for the special services on the Day of Atonement. The rest of the Levites were basically assistants to the priests.

But all the sacrifices for the sins of the people performed by the Aaronic priests were only a type of the great sacrifice of Jesus Christ, which was still to come. Thus the Messiah was the "Great High Priest," who sacrificed Himself for the sins of all mankind. However, this sacrifice was not done under the auspices of the Aaronic priesthood, obviously, since Jesus was from the tribe of Judah. "For it is evident that our Lord sprang out of Juda[h]; of which tribe Moses spake nothing concerning priesthood." (Hebrews 7:14)

This sacrifice had to be accomplished by the authority of another priesthood -- the same priesthood that was held by the Old Testament figure, Melchizedek. Indeed, God told the Messiah, "Thou art a priest for ever after the order of Melchizedek." (Psalm 110:4) Melchizedek was the king of Salem (later Jerusalem) around 2000 B.C. He is described as a "priest of the most High God" (Genesis 14:18), to whom Abraham paid tithes.

Paul explained that this change in priesthood authority necessitated a change in the law: "For the priesthood being changed, there is made of necessity a change also of the law." (Hebrews 7:12) And instead of daily offering sacrifices, the Great High Priest after the order of Melchizedek offered a single sacrifice, which needed no repetition. "For such an high priest became us . . . who needeth not daily, as those [Aaronic] high priests, to offer up sacrifice, first for his own sins, and then for the people's: for this he did once, when he offered up himself." (Hebrews 7:26-27)

So there you have it -- essentially all the information contained in the Bible concerning the priesthood after the order of Melchizedek. Consequently, there is not much in the Bible to either prove or disprove the wealth of information Joseph Smith restored concerning both priesthoods and the relationship between them. The Lord explained:

> There are, in the church, two priesthoods, namely, the Melchizedek and Aaronic, including the Levitical Priesthood. Why the first is called the Melchizedek is because Melchizedek was such a great high priest. Before his day it was called *the Holy Priesthood, after the Order of the Son of God.* But out of respect or reverence to the name of the Supreme Being, to avoid the too frequent repetition of his name, they, the church, in ancient days, called that priesthood after Melchizedek, or the Melchizedek Priesthood. All other authorities or offices in the church are appendages to this priesthood. But there are two divisions or grand heads -- one is the Melchizedek Priesthood, and the other is the Aaronic or Levitical Priesthood . . . . The Melchizedek Priesthood holds the right of presidency, and has power and authority over all the offices in the church in

all ages of the world, to administer in spiritual things . . . .
The second priesthood is called the Priesthood of Aaron,
because it was conferred upon Aaron and his seed,
throughout all their generations. Why it is called the lesser
priesthood is because it is an appendage to the greater, or the
Melchizedek Priesthood, and has power in administering
outward ordinances. (D&C 107: 1-6, 8, 13-14)

While the extant early Christian documents make no mention of the
two priesthoods within the Church, it is at least clear that there was a hierarchy
of authority at least roughly corresponding to the distinction made by the Lord
to Joseph Smith. That is, certain officers in the Church were authorized to
perform only the "outward ordinances" while others were also able to
"administer in spiritual things." For example, Philip, who was one of the
seven ordained by the Apostles to take on the work of caring for the needy in
the Church (Acts 6:1-6), was able to baptize quite a few people in Samaria, but
the Apostles had to travel all the way there from Jerusalem to confer the gift of
the Holy Ghost on these new believers.

Now when the Apostles which were at Jerusalem heard that
Samaria had received the word of God, they sent unto them
Peter and John: Who, when they were come down, prayed
for them, that they might receive the Holy Ghost: (For as
yet he was fallen on none of them: only they were baptized
in the name of the Lord Jesus.) Then laid they their hands
on them, and they received the Holy Ghost. (Acts 8:14-17)

Likewise, members of the Aaronic priesthood among the Latter-day
Saints perform temporal functions and ordinances, including baptism, but
cannot perform the higher ordinances, such as the laying on of hands.

Specific Priesthood Offices

The Lord did not merely restore "the priesthood" through Joseph
Smith, however. Specific offices within the priesthood were also given,
forming a hierarchy of authority and function within the Church. These can be
compared to those offices known to have existed within the early Church, but
one caveat must be taken into account before we proceed with this
comparison. Specifically, this dispensation includes the priesthood and power
given in all other dispensations. "For unto you . . . is the power of this
priesthood given, for the last days and for the last time . . . in connection with
all those who have received a dispensation at any time from the beginning of
the creation . . . ." (D&C 112:30-31) It is a "welding together of
dispensations, and keys, and powers, and glories . . . ." (D&C 128:18)

Therefore, since different variations on the basic organization of God's kingdom have existed during the various dispensations, it should not be expected that the organization of the Restored Church would necessarily correspond exactly to that of the early Church. For example, the offices present in the Church in ancient America after the advent of the Savior are included in the present LDS organization, but the Restored Church also includes many additional priesthood offices. (See Moroni 2-3)

In any case, since the information we have about the organization of the early Church is somewhat ambiguous, our method will not be to compare the restored and primitive organizations side-by-side, but to list the various offices and their functions in the Restored Church and then try to marshal any scraps of evidence for their existence in the early Church. If we find that the evidence for the existence of certain offices is somewhat sketchy, however, it should come as no surprise considering the caveat noted above.

Apostles and Prophets

The necessity of Apostles and prophets in the Church was discussed in chapter 2, but not in connection with the general Church organization. In the Restored Church, there are two distinct groups of Apostles which govern the flock. The highest council of the Church is the First Presidency, consisting of three Apostles, one of which is the President of the Church. Under the First Presidency is the Council of the Twelve Apostles. All of these men are considered general officers of the Church, whose authority has no territorial boundaries, and as special witnesses of Jesus Christ they are called to receive direction for the entire Church from the Lord and to preach the gospel in every nation.

While the early Church was led by a council of twelve Apostles, as well, there seems to have been no separate presidency of three additional Apostles. However, Peter, James, and John apparently had some position of primacy among the Apostles, equivalent to a presidency within the Twelve. Jesus told Peter, "thou art Peter [*petros*], and upon this rock [*petra*] I will build my church;" (Matthew 16:18) and shortly thereafter the Lord took Peter, James, and John upto a mountain and was transfigured before them. Moses and Elias appeared, as well, and the Apostles heard the Father's voice. (Matthew 17:1-9) In addition, Clement of Alexandria claimed that these three Apostles were entrusted by the Savior with some items of "higher knowledge," which they then dispensed to the other general officers of the Church: "The Lord after his resurrection imparted knowledge to James the Just and to John and Peter, and they imparted it to the rest of the Apostles, and the rest of the Apostles to the seventy, of whom Barnabas was one."[740]

This arrangement of councils of three and twelve to lead the community of the faithful may well have been an accepted Jewish practice from which early Christianity derived its own order of government. The Essenes of the Dead Sea Scroll community, Qumran, list this arrangement in their *Manual of Discipline*, which contains their community rules. "In the

Council of the Community there shall be twelve men and three Priests, perfectly versed in all that is revealed of the Law, whose works shall be truth, righteousness, justice, loving kindness, and humility."[741]

What about "prophets"? In contemporary LDS tradition both councils of Apostles are termed "prophets" by virtue of their callings. In addition, those who are called to positions of leadership in other general and local capacities are in need of the gift of prophecy to effectively shepherd that part of the flock entrusted to them. Indeed, any member of the Church may be given the gift of prophecy, and thus effectively become a prophet, though the Lord does not direct the Church as a whole through him or her.

It is evident from the New Testament that there were people called prophets within the organization of the Church (Ephesians 4:11), as well as lay members who were given the gift of prophecy. (1 Corinthians 12:10) The first century *Didache* contains instructions on how to receive the Apostles and prophets who traveled from community to community.[742] Also, "certain prophets and teachers" who were in the Church at Antioch ordained Paul and Barnabas for a missionary labor which extended beyond the bounds of the local area, and so were undoubtedly part of the Church organization. (Acts 13:1-4)

The Seventy

Under the First Presidency and the Council of the Twelve in the Restored Church is another group of general officers called the Seventy. These men are essentially the "chief missionaries" of the Church, and they also have administrative authority under the direction of the Twelve.

During His earthly ministry, Jesus called seventy disciples for the preaching work in addition to the Twelve. "After these things the Lord appointed other seventy also, and sent them two and two before his face into every city and place, whither he himself would come." (Luke 10:1) But did the Seventy survive as a body in the post-Resurrection Church? There is some evidence that they did. For example, Clement of Alexandria was quoted above as saying that the Apostles handed down the higher knowledge given after the Resurrection to the Seventy, and in Chapter 2 we noted that Clement of Rome claimed the local officers of the Church had been appointed by the Apostles or "other eminent men."[743] Eusebius records that "After the ascension of Jesus, Judas, who was also called Thomas, sent to [King Abgar] Thaddeus, an Apostle, one of the Seventy."[744] Perhaps there aren't very many references to the Seventy after the ascension of Jesus because such officers were referred to by their general functions as "prophets" and "evangelists" (see Ephesians 4:11; 2 Tim. 4:5), rather than as "the Seventy." This would explain the order in which Paul listed the various functions or offices in the Church: "And he gave some, Apostles; and some, prophets; and some, evangelists; and some, pastors and teachers . . . ." (Ephesians 4:11)

Patriarchs

The Restored Church also includes certain ministers called patriarchs. Until recently, there was a patriarch for the entire church as well as local patriarchs in most areas where the Church is established. "This order was instituted in the days of Adam, and came down by lineage . . . from Adam to Seth [through Enoch, etc.]" (D&C 107:39-52) The main duty of patriarchs is to give "patriarchal blessings," which outline the will of the Lord for individuals, to the saints. Similarly, the patriarch Jacob, or Israel, gathered his sons together and administered blessings relating to them and their children. "And Jacob called unto his sons, and said, Gather yourselves together, that I may tell you that which shall befall you in the last days." (Genesis 49:1) Isaac gave a similar blessing to Jacob. (Genesis 27:27-30)

One might think that this office is likely not to have been included in the early Church, since it seems to belong to the first dispensations after Adam, but according to Joseph Smith the New Testament Church did include patriarchs. "An Evangelist is a Patriarch,"[745] the Prophet preached, indicating that the New Testament function or office of "evangelist" included (but perhaps was not limited to) this calling. Indeed, the word "evangelist" is a translation of the Greek "*euangelistes*," meaning "a messenger of good tidings." Can the good tidings of the gospel be preached in any more personal way than through a patriarch called to bless the saints and pronounce the will of the Lord for them?

None of this can really be considered firm evidence for the existence of patriarchs in the early Church, however, since the office of evangelist is merely mentioned, and not described, in the New Testament. On the other hand, the ultraconservative Montanists at the turn of the third century are said to have been governed by the usual bishops, elders, and deacons, as well as officers called "patriarchs" and a shadowy order known as the *koinonoi* (stewards).[746] Perhaps these officers were a holdout from the old Church order.

Local Officers

At the local level, the Restored Church is administered by the Stake Presidency, a council of three high priests who preside over a small number (generally 7 to 10) of congregations. Although there seems to be no trace of church organization at the equivalent of the stake level in the early church (there may well have been various levels of "pastors"), the offices of bishop (Greek *episcopos* = overseer), elder (Greek *presbyteros*), and deacon (Greek *diakonos* = minister) were present in the early Church. The relationship between elders and bishops is not expressly given in the New Testament, however, and therefore this has been the source of some confusion. It seems that in some communities the Church was governed by a council of elders, while in others a bishop was placed at the head of the council of elders, and as a consequence the terms "bishop" and "elder" are used almost interchangeably.[747] Perhaps the situation was similar to that in the Restored

Church, where exceptionally small congregations are administered by a "branch presidency" who may be elders rather than a bishop, who is a high priest.

By the first decade of the second century the roles of bishop, elder, and deacon were fairly well defined. Ignatius of Antioch revealed some of the specifics of this hierarchy.

> See that ye all follow the bishop, even as Christ Jesus does the Father, and the presbytery as ye would the Apostles. Do ye also reverence the deacons, as those that carry out [through their office] the appointment of God. Let no man do anything connected with the Church without the bishop. Let that be deemed a proper Eucharist, which is [administered] either by the bishop, or by one to whom he has entrusted it. Wherever the bishop shall appear, there let the multitude [of the people] also be; even as where Christ is, there does all the heavenly host stand by, waiting upon Him as the Chief Captain of the Lord's might, and the Governor of every intelligent nature. It is not lawful without the bishop either to baptize, or to offer, or to present sacrifice, or to celebrate a love-feast. But that which seems good to him, is also well-pleasing to God, that everything ye do may be secure and valid.[748]

Davies explains that a presbyter could perform all the same ordinances as a bishop, but only with the bishop's express permission.[749] This is exactly the case in the Restored Church. Elders and bishops both hold the higher priesthood, and so can perform both temporal and spiritual ordinances. However, everything must be done under the auspices of the bishop to be considered valid.

As for the offices of the Aaronic priesthood, only deacons are mentioned in the New Testament Church. Davies explains that the deacons served as messengers to the bishop, ministers to the sick and imprisoned, carriers of the sacrament (Eucharist), and collectors of offerings.[750] We might characterize the early Church deacon as roughly equivalent to a priest in the Restored Church, who is authorized to perform all the functions delegated to the Aaronic priesthood. Were there further divisions within the order of the lesser priesthood in the early Church? The Restored Church has both priests and teachers, as well as deacons, but it is unclear whether these offices existed in the Apostolic Church. At least as early as the late second and early third centuries the offices of priest and subdeacon were introduced. For example, Davies asserts that the order of subdeacons, who performed some of the functions of the deacons, must have existed at least as early as A.D. 170-180.[751]

The author of the Acts mentioned that "a great company of the priests were obedient to the faith." (Acts 6:7) Did these men then lose their callings as Aaronic priests, or were they included as priests in the new covenant community? The New Testament is silent on this matter.

Origen mentioned the presence of priests in the Church of the early third century. Interestingly, he also reveals that priests were selected by the Church hierarchy, but had to be approved by the entire Church.

> For in ordaining a priest, the presence of the people is also required that all may know and be certain that from all the people one is chosen for the priesthood who is more excellent, who is more wise, who is more holy, who is more eminent in every virtue, lest afterwards, when he stands before the people, any hesitation or any doubt should remain.[752]

Cyprian indicated that the vote of the people was required to install someone into the priesthood, but Bettenson notes that this was limited to the ratification of the choice made by the other bishops.[753] This, of course, is exactly the case in the Restored Church. "No person is to be ordained to any office in this church, where there is a regularly organized branch of the same, without the vote of that church." (D&C 20:65)

The New Testament does mention the presence of teachers (e.g. Ephesians 4:11), but the context of these passages suggests that these were merely members who had a spiritual gift for teaching. Certainly the teachers among the "prophets and teachers" at Antioch who ordained Paul and Barnabas (Acts 13:1-3) were not teachers of the Aaronic order.

High Priests after the Order of Melchizedek

Another local priesthood quorum in the Restored Church is that of the high priests. These men hold the Melchizedek priesthood just as the elders do, but their office is higher, and consequently one must be a high priest to hold certain administrative positions, including that of bishop. As was mentioned earlier in this chapter, the New Testament identifies Christ as the great High Priest after the order of Melchizedek, but says nothing more on the subject. Were there other high priests after this order? It seems obvious that Melchizedek was one, at least, and it is called an "order," after all. Theophilus of Antioch taught that Melchizedek was the first of many priests of his order:

> And at that time there was a righteous king called Melchisedek, in the city of Salem, which now is Jerusalem. This was the first priest of all priests of the Most High God; and from him the above-named city Hierosolyma was called Jerusalem. And from his time priests were found in all the earth.[754]

Again, it is unclear whether an actual office of "high priest" existed in the early Church, but many early Christian documents other than the New Testament do refer to prophets and bishops as "high priests." However, it is not completely evident whether this was just a literary device to compare them to the old order of Aaronic High Priests or a reference to their specific office.

Both Ignatius and Hippolytus called bishops "high priests": "And say I, Honour thou God indeed, as the Author and Lord of all things, but the bishop as the high-priest, who bears the image of God -- of God, inasmuch as he is a ruler, and of Christ, in his capacity of a priest."[755] "Grant unto this Thy servant whom Thou has chosen for the episcopate to feed Thy holy flock and serve as Thine high priest . . . ."[756] Clement of Alexandria called each man who had been entrusted with the mysteries of God a "truly kingly man; he is the sacred high priest of God."[757] Likewise, the *Didache* referred to prophets and Apostles, as "high priests." "Every first-fruit, therefore, of the products of wine-press and threshing-floor, of oxen and of sheep, thou shalt take and give to the prophets, for they are your high priests."[758]

Origen called the Apostles and their successors "priests after the great High Priest." "In the same way the Apostles also and their successors, priests according to the *great High Priest* . . . ."[759] On the other hand, Origen insisted that only Christ can be a High Priest after the order of Melchizedek:

> But to this we reply that the Apostle clearly defined his meaning, and declared the prophet to have said about the Christ, "Thou art a priest for ever, according to the order of Melchisedek," and not according to the order of Aaron. We say accordingly that men can be high-priests according to the order of Aaron, but according to the order of Melchisedek only the Christ of God.[760]

It is clear from the foregoing citations, however, that bishops and others were considered "priests" after the order of Melchizedek, if not "high priests." We have also seen that the New Testament Church may not have made a distinction between offices corresponding to the Aaronic priesthood. Therefore, if there were no office of Aaronic priest, there may not have been a need to distinguish priests of the higher priesthood by calling them "high priests." That is, the office of "priest after the order of Melchizedek" in the early Church may have been equivalent to the office of "high priest after the order of Melchizedek" in the Restored Church.

The Purpose of Priesthood Offices

What can we say about the organization of the Restored Church as compared to that of the early Church? Simply that they are quite similar, although certain offices present in the Restored Church may or may not have been present in the Church of the former dispensation. But as was pointed out earlier, one need not expect the early Christian Church to have had all the same offices as the Restored Church because Joseph Smith claimed to have restored priesthood offices from all former dispensations.

The most important thing to note is that Joseph Smith restored the basic structure of the early Church "For the perfecting of the saints, for the work of the ministry, for the edifying of the body of Christ." (Ephesians 4:12) Not just human inventions, the offices in the Church reflect these purposes Paul listed and were meant to endure in God's Church "till we all come in the unity of the faith, and of the knowledge of the Son of God, unto a perfect man, unto the measure of the stature of the fulness of Christ," so that "we henceforth be no more children, tossed to and fro, and carried about with every wind of doctrine . . . ." (Ephesians 4:13-14) Therefore, these same offices of "Apostles; . . . prophets; . . . evangelists; . . . pastors and teachers" (Ephesians 4:11) and others for which there is some evidence in the records of the early Church were restored by God through the Prophet Joseph Smith after a long period of apostasy had left Christianity without inspired leadership.

Church Life

Just as the LDS Church has a similar organization to the early Christian Church, several peculiarities of LDS worship, church government, and sacramental practice have early Christian analogues as well.

The Lord's Day

Along with most of the rest of Christianity, Latter-day Saints conduct their regular worship services on the first day of the week, Sunday, rather than following the Old Testament custom of celebrating the Sabbath on the seventh day. On the other hand, some other millenarian movements which started around Joseph Smith's time, notably the Seventh Day Adventists, have claimed that Christians should continue the Jewish custom, since the New Testament never explicitly states that the original Sabbath had been superseded.

However, the evidence from early Christian documents weighs heavily in favor of those who celebrate the Sabbath on Sunday. And while this is not particularly striking confirmation of the Prophet's inspiration, it is nevertheless solid evidence when placed in context with the rest of this study. Therefore, a brief presentation of this evidence is in order.

While it has already been pointed out that the New Testament never explicitly states that the Old Testament Sabbath had been superseded, it does show that after the Lord was resurrected on the first day of the week, the Apostles and other Christians began gathering together on that day:

In the end of the sabbath, as it began to dawn toward the first day of the week, came Mary Magdalene and the other Mary to see the sepulchre. And, behold, there was a great earthquake: for the angel of the Lord descended from heaven, and came and rolled back the stone from the door, and sat upon it. His countenance was like lightning, and his raiment white as snow: And for fear of him the keepers did shake, and became as dead [men]. And the angel answered and said unto the women, Fear not ye: for I know that ye seek Jesus, which was crucified. He is not here: for he is risen, as he said. Come, see the place where the Lord lay. (Matthew 28:1-6)

Then the same day at evening, being the first day of the week, when the doors were shut where the disciples were assembled for fear of the Jews, came Jesus and stood in the midst, and saith unto them, Peace be unto you. (John 20:19)

And upon the first day of the week, when the disciples came together to break bread, Paul preached unto them, ready to depart on the morrow; and continued his speech until midnight. (Acts 20:7)

The first day of the week was called "the Lord's day" by Christians thereafter, because they celebrated the day of the Lord's resurrection. (E.g. John indicated that he "was in the Spirit on the Lord's day" when he received his revelation -- Revelation 1:10.) And while the scriptures themselves are not especially explicit on this point, other very early Christian documents are. Both *Barnabas* and the *Didache* indicate that the Sabbath was to be celebrated on Sunday:

Ye perceive how He speaks: Your present Sabbaths are not acceptable to Me, but that is which I have made, [namely this,] when, giving rest to all things, I shall make a beginning of the eighth day, that is, a beginning of another world. Wherefore, also, we keep the eighth day with joyfulness, the day also on which Jesus rose again from the dead. And when He had manifested Himself, He ascended into the heavens.[761]

But every Lord's day do ye gather yourselves together, and break bread, and give thanksgiving after having confessed your transgressions, that your sacrifice may be pure. But let no one that is at variance with his fellow come together with you, until they be reconciled, that your sacrifice may not be profaned. For this is that which was spoken by the Lord: In every place and time offer to me a pure sacrifice.[762]

Ignatius told the Magnesians to go forward, "no longer observing the Sabbath, but living in the observance of the Lord's day, on which also our life has sprung up again by Him and by His death.[763] Clearly this practice was initiated very early on in Christian history, most probably immediately after the Ascension of the Lord.

Worship

An examination of early Christian worship reveals that it was manifestly dissimilar to the ornate displays which grew up as part of the medieval mass. The earliest Christians had simple worship services which more resembled those of the Latter-day Saints and many Protestant denominations. That is, the believers gathered on Sunday to participate in the sacrament of the Lord's Supper and to preach the gospel to one another, pray, sing hymns, etc. Davies asserts that there was a remarkable amount of freedom exercised in the organization of these early services, nevertheless, there were certain fixed liturgical forms such as the sacrament.[764]

Justin Martyr described a typical Christian worship service in the second century:

> And on the day called Sunday, all who live in cities or in the country gather together to one place, and the memoirs of the Apostles or the writings of the prophets are read, as long as time permits; then, when the reader has ceased, the president verbally instructs, and exhorts to the imitation of these good things. Then we all rise together and pray, and, as we before said, when our prayer is ended, bread and wine and water are brought, and the president in like manner offers prayers and thanksgivings, according to his ability . . . . But Sunday is the day on which we all hold our common assembly, because it is the first day on which God, having wrought a change in the darkness and matter, made the world; and Jesus Christ our Saviour on the same day rose from the dead.[765]

The bishop or president was not the only one who could give sermons in such a meeting. Bishops Alexander and Theoctistus of Jerusalem and Caesarea, respectively, insisted that it was the practice of many churches in their day (3rd century), as it is in many contemporary churches, to allow qualified laymen to preach:

For whenever persons able to instruct the brethren are found, they are exhorted by the holy bishops to preach to the people. Thus in Laranda, Euelpis by Neon; and in Iconium, Paulinus by Celsus; and in Synada, Theodorus by Atticus, our blessed brethren. And probably this has been done in other places unknown to us.[766]

The Sacrament of the Lord's Supper

Water, Wine, or Water and Wine?

It is interesting to note that Justin indicated the use of wine and water in the sacrament of the Lord's Supper. Similarly, Latter-day Saints usually use water in the sacrament, although they at one time used wine. This practice was started as a result of a revelation to Joseph Smith, wherein an angel warned him not to purchase wine from his enemies for communion, since it could easily be poisoned. The Lord explained that the exact substances used in this ordinance didn't matter, as long as it was done in remembrance of Christ's body and blood:

> For, behold, I say unto you, that it mattereth not what ye shall eat or what ye shall drink when ye partake of the sacrament, if it so be that ye do it with an eye single to my glory -- remembering unto the Father my body which was laid down for you, and my blood which was shed for the remission of your sins. (D&C 27:2)

And while some anti-Mormon critics charge that Latter-day Saints substitute water because they "reject the full value of Christ's blood,"[767] it can be shown that some early Jewish Christians used water in this ordinance, as well. One of the very early (first or second century) *Odes of Solomon* referred to this practice. The hymn asserts, "Blessed then are the ministers of that draught who are entrusted with that water of His . . . ."[768] Commenting on this passage, Carl Jung points out that the use of water shows that, like the Mormons, these early Christians were more interested in the symbolism behind the ordinance than in the use of any particular ritual substance: "The fact that the Eucharist was also celebrated with water shows that the early Christians were mainly interested in the symbolism of the mysteries and not in the literal observance of the sacrament."[769]

The principal reason many Jewish Christians opted to use water in the sacrament was that some of them had taken Nazarite vows; that is, they had vowed to abstain from wine[770], from cutting their hair, and from contact with the dead. The second-century writer Hegesippus claimed that James the brother of Jesus had taken such a vow:

James, the brother of the Lord, succeeded to the government of the Church in conjunction with the Apostles. He has been called the Just by all from the time of our Saviour to the present day; for there were many that bore the name of James. He was holy from his mother's womb; and he drank no wine nor strong drink, nor did he eat flesh. No razor came upon his head; he did not anoint himself with oil, and he did not use the bath. He alone was permitted to enter into the holy place ; for he wore not woolen but linen garments.[771]

The *Acts of Thomas* also described the Apostle Thomas as one who drank only water[772], so when one Mygdonia brought him some bread and wine for the sacrament, he refused it and "He brake bread and took a cup of water . . . ."[773]

As early as the late second and early third centuries, however, this practice was called into question by those who insisted on using water mixed with wine. Therefore, Irenaeus, Clement of Alexandria, and Cyprian all condemned the Ebionites and other Jewish Christian "heretics" who used only water:

Therefore do [the Ebionites] reject the commixture of the heavenly wine, and wish it to be water of the world only . . . [774]

And those destitute of prudence, that is, those involved in heresies, "I enjoin," remarks Wisdom, saying, "Touch sweetly stolen bread and the sweet water of theft;" the Scripture manifestly applying the terms bread and water to nothing else but to those heresies, which employ bread and water in the oblation, not according to the canon of the Church. For there are those who celebrate the Eucharist with mere water.[775]

Thus, therefore, in consecrating the cup of the Lord, water alone cannot be offered, even as wine alone cannot be offered. For if any one offer wine only, the blood of Christ is dissociated from us; but if the water be alone, the people are dissociated from Christ; but when both are mingled, and are joined with one another by a close union, there is completed a spiritual and heavenly sacrament.[776]

Changes in the Doctrine of the Sacrament

This attention to symbolic meaning rather than empirical reality by the Jewish Christians was a product of the Hebrew roots of the early Church.

It was the loss of this attitude that led to the adoption of the strange doctrine of "transubstantiation," which was foreign to the Hebrew mind. Davies explains:

> The Hebrew, unlike the Greek, was not interested in things in themselves but only in things as they are called to be. He was not concerned with an object as such but with what it becomes in relation to its final reference according to the divine purpose. The meaning of an object therefore does not lie in its analytical and empirical reality but in the will that is expressed by it. Hence Jesus could say of a piece of bread: 'This is my body.' The bread does not cease to be bread, but it becomes what it is not, namely the instrument and organ of his presence, because through his sovereign word he has given it a new dimension.[777]

Thus, Edwin Hatch asserts that "it is among the Gnostics that there appears for the first time an attempt to realize the change of the elements to the material body and blood of Christ."[778]

This unfortunate trend of formalization in sacramental practice and changes in the doctrine of the sacrament continued into the Middle Ages, as various pagan concepts and formulae were adopted into the Catholic and Orthodox liturgies. And as we have seen, this type of thing was an inescapable consequence of the loss of revelation in the Church.

Anointing the Sick

It is common for Latter-day Saints to follow the admonition of James: "Is any sick among you? let him call for the elders of the church; and let them pray over him, anointing him with oil in the name of the Lord: And the prayer of faith shall save the sick . . . ." (James 5:14-15) Accordingly, Latter-day Saint elders consecrate olive oil for use in blessing the sick. And while people of other denominations also anoint the sick on occasion, the *consecration* of the oil in early Christianity is not found in the New Testament, but is consistent with LDS practice.

Specifically, there was a clear demarcation in the early church as to who could and who could not bless the oil. While bishops and elders could consecrate oil, those in the lower echelons of the priesthood, such as deacons, could not. The *Apostolic Constitutions* described the practice:

> Concerning the water and the oil, I Matthias make a constitution. Let the bishop bless the water, or the oil. But if he be not there, let the presbyter bless it, the deacon standing by. But if the bishop be present, let the presbyter and deacon stand by, and let him say thus: O Lord of hosts,

the God of powers, the creator of the waters, and the supplier of oil, who art compassionate, and a lover of mankind, who hast given water for drink and for cleansing, and oil to give man a cheerful and joyful countenance; do Thou now also sanctify this water and this oil through Thy Christ, in the name of him or her that has offered them, and grant them a power to restore health, to drive away diseases, to banish demons, and to disperse all snares through Christ our hope, with whom glory, honour, and worship be to Thee, and to the Holy Ghost, for ever. Amen.[779]

Gradually the rite of anointing the sick was corrupted. For example, John Chrysostom advocated using oil taken from church lamps and from martyrs' shrines, while some others suggested the use of oil filtered through martyrs' relics.[780] Finally, J. Halliburton notes that after the patristic period, anointing of the sick became restricted to those who were deemed incurably ill and needed a ritual preparation for purgatory.[781]

Tithes, Offerings, and the United Order

All churches need money to function in the world, and the Restored Church is no exception. Inspired by God, Joseph Smith restored correct, biblically based principles for the collection of church revenue. The principles restored fall into two categories which we will call the "law of consecration" and the "law of tithes and offerings."

Consecration and Tithing

The law of consecration concerns the consecration of all one's time, talents, and substance to the building of the Kingdom of God. In the spirit of this law members of the New Testament Church renounced the practice of "serving Mammon" and lived with common ownership of all their substance.

And the multitude of them that believed were of one heart and of one soul: neither said any of them that ought of the things which he possessed was his own; but they had all things in common. (Acts 4:32)

Similarly, the Lord instituted a program called "the United Order" in the Restored Church, and at one time the Saints lived with all things in common. Various revelations to Joseph Smith delineated exactly how this order was to be administered. (e.g. see D&C 51, 82, 104) Unfortunately, the Saints proved themselves unready to live such a lofty law and therefore it was held in abeyance and the lesser law of tithes and offerings was instituted:

> Behold, now it is called today until the coming of the Son of Man, and verily it is a day of sacrifice, and a day for the tithing of my people; for he that is tithed shall not be burned at his coming. (D&C 64:23)

The law of tithes and offerings is basically that one should give one tenth of one's income to the Lord, as well as offerings for the poor. This law was practiced in the Old Testament, as evidenced by the following passage from Malachi:

> Will a man rob God? Yet ye have robbed me. But ye say, Wherein have we robbed thee? In tithes and offerings . . . . Bring ye all the tithes into the storehouse, that there may be meat in mine house, and prove me now herewith, saith the Lord of hosts, if I will not open you the windows of heaven, and pour you out a blessing, that there shall not be room enough to receive it. (Malachi 3:8, 10)

Although it is obvious, the "United Order" in the early Christian Church didn't last long, the New Testament is not clear about what replaced that system. Consequently, some have criticized the Latter-day Saints for practicing the law of tithes and offerings, which they say is a holdover from the Mosaic Law. This law was terminated by the death of Jesus, they say, and therefore should not be required.[782] However, the *Apostolic Constitutions* make it clear that the law of tithes and offerings was practiced in the early Church:

> Let him [the Bishop] use those tenths and first-fruits, which are given according to the command of God, as a man of God; as also let him dispense in a right manner the free-will offerings which are brought in on account of the poor . . . .[783]

In fact, it can be shown that tithing was thought to have replaced consecration as a lower law. In the third decade of the third century Pope Urban I claimed that some Christians, especially clergy, still attempted to live the law of consecration:

> We know that you are not ignorant of the fact that hitherto the principle of living with all things in common has been in vigorous operation among good Christians, and is still so by the grace of God; and most of all among those who have been chosen to the lot of the Lord, that is to say, the clergy, even as we read in the Acts of the Apostles: "And the multitude of them that believed were of one heart and of one

203

soul: neither said any of them that ought of the things which he possessed was his own; but they had all things common."[784]

In 251 A.D. Cyprian looked back with nostalgia at the time when the early saints lived with everything in common, and complained that the Christians of his day were for the most part unwilling to even pay tithes:

> But in us unanimity is diminished in proportion as liberality of working is decayed. Then they used to give for sale houses and estates; and that they might lay up for themselves treasures in heaven, presented to the Apostles the price of them, to be distributed for the use of the poor. But now we do not even give the tenths from our patrimony; and while our Lord bids us sell, we rather buy and increase our store. Thus has the vigour of faith dwindled away among us; thus has the strength of believers grown weak.[785]

Fast Offerings

In addition to tithes, free-will offerings are given in the Restored Church in conjunction with a monthly fast. That is, the members of the Church fast, and then give at least the amount of money they saved by not eating to the Bishop for distribution to the poor. A passage in Isaiah indicates that the Israelites of the Old Testament had a similar practice:

> Is this the fast that I have chosen? to loose the bands of wickedness, to undo the heavy burdens, and to let the oppressed go free, and that ye break every yoke? Is it not to deal thy bread to the hungry, and that thou bring the poor that are cast out to thy house? (Isaiah 58:6-7)

Once again, the early Christian documents are clear that Joseph Smith restored a genuine early Christian practice in this case. Davies explains that in the second century, "fasting was closely linked with almsgiving."[786] For example, *Barnabas* and Hermas advocated a practice nearly identical to that which the Prophet restored:

> Behold, this is the fast that I have chosen, saith the Lord, not that a man should humble his soul, but that he should loose every band of iniquity, untie the fastenings of harsh agreements, restore to liberty them that are bruised, tear in pieces every unjust engagement, feed the hungry with thy bread, clothe the naked when thou seest him, bring the homeless into thy house, not despise the humble if thou

behold him, and not [turn away] from the members of thine own family. [787]

Offer to God a fasting of the following kind: Do no evil in your life, and serve the Lord with a pure heart: keep His commandments, walking in His precepts, and let no evil desire arise in your heart; and believe in God . . . . Having fulfilled what is written, in the day on which you fast you will taste nothing but bread and water; and having reckoned up the price of the dishes of that day which you intended to have eaten, you will give it to a widow, or an orphan, or to some person in want . . . . [788]

Chapter 6: The Temple

"The order of the house of God has been, and ever will be, the same, even after Christ comes; and after the termination of the thousand years it will be the same; and we shall finally enter into the celestial kingdom of God, and enjoy it forever.
- Joseph Smith[789]

Although it was not mentioned in Chapter 4, the ordinance of baptism for the dead is performed by the Latter-day Saints in buildings they call temples. Various other ordinances, notably the Endowment and marriage for eternity, are also performed there, both for the living and the dead. Therefore, in keeping with the theme of this book, this last chapter will be devoted to the presentation of evidence that similar ordinances were practiced in ancient Christianity. It is hoped that along the way the reader will get a sense of the beauty and majesty of these ordinances and the principles they symbolize -- in this way coming to realize that the restoration of temple worship is indeed the crowning achievement of the Prophet Joseph Smith.

The reinstitution of temple worship was an integral part of the "Restoration of All Things," and yet the content of these ordinances is so shocking to much of the rest of the Christian world that they are routinely labeled as satanic in anti-Mormon literature.[790] A large part of the information purveyed in these "exposés" is patently false, however, so perhaps the average Christian would be less shocked by LDS temple ordinances if he or she could be disabused of the wild notions about what goes on in them. This is easier said than done, unfortunately, since Latter-day Saints do not speak openly about certain aspects of these sacred ordinances, especially the Endowment.

Esotericism and the Latter-day Saints

Why Secrecy?

The esotericism involved with the Temple is the crux of the problem encountered by a book such as this, which seeks to present parallels to LDS beliefs and practices in ancient Christianity. As a Latter-day Saint who has participated in these rites, I am bound not to discuss certain aspects of them outside of our temple walls. This is no attempt on the part of Mormons to make their rituals seem more mysterious and impressive. Rather, Latter-day Saints do not discuss certain things in order to follow Jesus' admonition that

207

certain aspects of the gospel are too sacred to be spoken about to those who are not prepared to appreciate or understand them. (Matthew 7:6) That is, even though many may be curious about certain aspects of the gospel, they are probably not willing to take on the added responsibility which goes along with that knowledge. For anyone who is willing to learn the mysteries of God "precept upon precept; line upon line, . . . here a little, and there a little" (Isaiah 28:10), and to make such commitments, the doors to the knowledge of the temple are soon opened. (Latter-day Saints may qualify to enter the temple only after one year of membership, as long as they have been living in accordance with their covenants.) As Jesus said immediately after he charged his disciples not to cast their pearls before swine, "Ask, and it shall be given you; seek, and ye shall find; knock, and it shall be opened unto you . . . ." (Matthew 7:7) *The Book of Mormon* explains this principle clearly:

> And now Alma began to expound these things unto him, saying: It is given unto many to know the mysteries of God; nevertheless they are laid under a strict command that they shall not impart only according to the portion of his word which he doth grant unto the children of men, according to the heed and diligence which they give unto him. And therefore, he that will harden his heart, the same receiveth the lesser portion of the word; and he that will not harden his heart, to him is given the greater portion of the word, until it is given unto him to know the mysteries of God until he know them in full. And they that will harden their hearts, to them is given the lesser portion of the word until they know nothing concerning his mysteries . . . . (Alma 12:9-11)

Esoteric Doctrines and the Latter-day Saints

There are both esoteric doctrines and rites within Mormonism. These can take a variety of forms. The esoteric doctrines, for the most part, are of a personal nature. That is, God may reveal certain mysteries to a prophet, Apostle, or any other member of His Church, but unless direction comes to reveal it through the President of the Church, one is to keep it to himself. Brigham Young summarized:

> If the Lord Almighty should reveal to a High Priest, or anyone other than the head, things that are true . . . or a new doctrine that will be, in five, ten or twenty years hence become the doctrine of this Church and Kingdom, but which has not yet been revealed to this people, and reveal it to him by the same Spirit, the same messenger, the same voice, the same power that gave revelations to Joseph when he was

living, it would be a blessing to that High Priest or individual; but he must rarely divulge it to a second person on the face of this earth, until God reveals it through the proper source to become the property of the people at large.[791]

On rare occasions, the prophets have taught from the pulpit in such a way that only those who were prepared could understand it.[792]

The Endowment

The esoteric rites in Mormonism are associated with the Temple, and especially with the ritual known as the "Endowment." And yet, the temple rites are not unknown, because Latter-day Saint authors have spoken about them in general terms and because some disaffected Latter-day Saints have revealed some of the more esoteric aspects to the public. Why do Latter-day Saints refuse to speak openly about certain aspects of the temple rites? The main reason is that those who enter the temple make covenants not to speak about temple worship and ordinances outside the temple. Also, the rites of the Temple are conveyed in symbolic forms so that only those who are spiritually prepared can discern their sacred meanings. Thus, one may know something of the form of the ritual but be completely in the dark as to its meaning. LDS scholar Hugh Nibley makes exactly this point:

> Even though everyone may discover what goes on in the temple, and many have already revealed it, the important thing is that I do not reveal these things; they must remain sacred to me. I must preserve a zone of sanctity which cannot be violated whether or not anyone else in the room has the remotest idea what the situation really is . . . . No matter what happens, it will, then, always remain secret: only I know exactly the weight and force of the covenants I have made -- I and the Lord with whom I have made them-- unless I choose to reveal them. If I do not, then they are secret and sacred no matter what others may say or do. Anyone who would reveal these things has not understood them, and therefore that person has not given them away. You cannot reveal what you do not know![793]

In keeping with the sacred nature of the Temple we will give an explanation of the temple Endowment which will consist exclusively of the information available in publicly published statements of various Latter-day Saint general authorities. I will neither go beyond the substance of these statements in my commentary nor comment very much on those parts of ancient ceremonies presented which parallel the Endowment. That is, certain aspects of the ancient ceremonies I will present are very similar to the temple ceremony, and certain aspects are not. (Very little doctrine or practice was transmitted through the apostasy without changes or corruptions, and given their esoteric nature the temple ceremonies would probably have been among the first ordinances to become corrupted or lost.)

In large part I will leave it up to the reader to judge the significance of each area of information presented. Thus, those readers who have participated in the Endowment will necessarily be better equipped in their judgment than those who have not. However, much of the information presented will be related to those parts of the temple ceremony which are public knowledge, so even one who is only cursorily familiar with this aspect of Mormonism will be in a position to examine much of the evidence.

The temple Endowment is primarily a vehicle to present greater light and knowledge about the gospel to those who seek them. In the temple, the Plan of Salvation is presented to the participants in symbolic form, reminding them of their covenants before God and the way to eternal life. By gaining this knowledge *and living by it* one receives the keys one needs to come into the presence of God in the world to come. The public descriptions and explanations of the Endowment by prophets and Apostles of the LDS Church which follow should give the reader some idea of what constitutes this sacred ordinance.

Elder John A. Widtsoe, formerly an Apostle in the Restored Church, outlined the Endowment thus:

> The endowment and the temple work as revealed by the Lord to the Prophet Joseph Smith fall clearly into four distinct parts: The preparatory ordinances; the giving of instruction by lectures and representations; covenants; and, finally, tests of knowledge. I doubt that the Prophet Joseph Smith, unlearned and untrained in logic, could of himself have made the thing so logically complete.[794]

Elder Boyd K. Packer, of the Quorum of the Twelve, explains that the first phase of the Endowment ceremony deals with preparatory or "initiatory" ordinances wherein the participant is washed and anointed. He points out that these ordinances are "mostly symbolic in nature."[795]

The Lord has said concerning these ordinances: "I say unto you, how shall your washings be acceptable unto me, except ye perform them in a house which you have built to my name?" (D&C 124:37) Also: "I say unto you, that your anointings, and your washings . . . are ordained by the ordinance of my holy house." (D&C 124:39) Elder Packer goes on to explain that in connection with the washings and anointings, candidates are officially clothed in a symbolic white garment and promised certain blessings.[796] Indeed, throughout the Endowment various symbolic white vestments are used.[797]

210

The next phase consists of Christ-centered instruction about one's place in the Plan of Salvation. Apostle James E. Talmage gave the following description:

> The Temple Endowment, as administered in modern temples, comprises instruction relating to the significance and sequence of past dispensations, and the importance of the present as the greatest and grandest era in human history. This course of instruction includes a recital of the most prominent events of the creative period, the condition of our first parents in the Garden of Eden, their disobedience and consequent expulsion from that blissful abode, their condition in the lone and dreary world when doomed to live by labor and sweat, the plan of redemption by which the great transgression may be atoned, the period of the great apostasy, the restoration of the Gospel with all its ancient powers and privileges, the absolute and indispensable condition of personal purity and devotion to the right in present life, and a strict compliance with Gospel requirements.[798]

Elder Packer explains that much of the instruction in the temple is given in symbolic fashion. This should come in no surprise, since so much of the teaching in the scriptures is done symbolically as well.[799]

Associated with this instruction are various covenants the participants make in relation to their daily conduct. Elder Talmage made the following observations about this phase of the ceremony:

> The ordinances of the endowment embody certain obligations on the part of the individual, such as covenant and promise to observe the law of strict virtue and chastity, to be charitable, benevolent, tolerant and pure; to devote both talent and material means to the spread of truth and the uplifting of the race; to maintain devotion to the cause of truth; and to seek in every way to contribute to the great preparation that the earth may be made ready to receive her King,—the Lord Jesus Christ. With the taking of each covenant and the assuming of each obligation a promised blessing is pronounced, contingent upon the faithful observance of the conditions.

> No jot, iota, or tittle of the temple rites is otherwise than uplifting and sanctifying. In every detail the endowment ceremony contributes to covenants of morality of life, consecration of person to high ideals, devotion to truth,

patriotism to nation, and allegiance to God. The blessings of the House of the Lord are restricted to no privileged class; every member of the Church may have admission to the temple with the right to participate in the ordinances thereof, if he comes duly accredited as of worthy life and conduct.[800]

In relation to the final phase of the endowment, the tests of knowledge, not much can be said beyond the following statement by the prophet Brigham Young:

> Let me give you a definition in brief. Your endowment is, to receive all those ordinances in the house of the Lord, which are necessary for you, after you have departed this life, to enable you to walk back to the presence of the Father, passing the angels who stand as sentinels, being enabled to give them the key words, the signs and tokens, pertaining to the holy Priesthood, and gain your eternal exaltation in spite of earth and hell.[801]

As President Young seems to indicate, the Endowment as a whole symbolizes and prepares one for the celestial ascent, or as President David O. McKay described, the "step-by-step ascent into the eternal presence." Thus, the ceremony also includes a symbolic "prayer circle," which, along with the rest of the Endowment "precedes the symbolic entrance into the celestial world and the presence of God."[802]

In addition to the above, there are a significant number of specific ritual aspects of the Endowment which I have not mentioned. However, those familiar with the ceremony will recognize many of these elements in the descriptions of the ancient rites that follow.

The temple Endowment is a profound experience for those who participate in it seeking light and knowledge from above, so one could say that its own fruits justify it, no matter whether it was ever practiced by the ancient Church, or not. However, significant evidence does exist that the ancient Christians practiced similar rituals and had a rich esoteric tradition. Therefore the next task at hand is to describe various of these rites in the context of the people who practiced them.

Esotericism in Early Christianity

Esoteric Doctrines

Secrecy in the New Testament

When critics of the Restoration speak of the secrecy involved in the Endowment, they never fail to bring up Jesus' statement to the high priest at His trial: "I spake openly to the world; I ever taught in the synagogue, and in the temple, whither the Jews always resort; and in secret have I said nothing." (John 18:20) Certainly no Latter-day Saint would say that Jesus lied when he said this, but certain facts must be pointed out in relation to this statement in order to assess the impact it should have on our appraisal of the Endowment.

First, while Jesus' teaching was for the most part public before his death, it may not have been when he appeared to the Apostles and some others after his resurrection. Luke begins the Acts with this statement:

> The former treatise have I made, O Theophilus, of all that Jesus began both to do and teach, Until the day in which he was taken up, after that he through the Holy Ghost had given commandments unto the Apostles whom he had chosen: To whom also he shewed himself alive after his passion by many infallible proofs, being seen of them forty days, and speaking of the things pertaining to the kingdom of God . . . . (Acts 1:1-3)

What were these things that Jesus spoke of during the forty days? The New Testament is strangely silent about what must have been the most important teaching to ever take place in the Savior's earthly ministry. It is highly unlikely that it was just a repetition of what Jesus had already said. Shortly before his death, Christ insisted to the Apostles that he hadn't taught them everything: "I have yet many things to say unto you, but ye cannot bear them now." (John 16:12)

Second, although Jesus taught in public, he usually did it in such a way that those who were not prepared to hear the gospel would misunderstand. The Savior's parables certainly were useful tools to bring His lofty teachings down to the level of the common man, but it is not often recognized that these symbolic stories also served the function of veiling the truth from those who were not seeking it. When His disciples asked Him the purpose of speaking in parables, Jesus gave them a most instructive answer:

> And the disciples came, and said unto him, Why speakest thou unto them in parables? He answered and said unto them, Because it is given unto you to know the mysteries of the kingdom of heaven, but to them it is not given. For

whosoever hath, to him shall be given, and he shall have more abundance: but whosoever hath not, from him shall be taken away even that he hath. Therefore speak I to them in parables: because they seeing see not; and hearing they hear not, neither do they understand. (Matthew 13:9-13)

Apparently not many of His hearers understood Jesus' parables, for it was His standard practice to take His disciples aside after reciting a parable and explain it to them clearly. (See Matthew 13)

Professor Joachim Jeremias delineates this pattern of secrecy in the New Testament by listing the items of information which Jesus apparently did not divulge to the public at large. He also shows that in doing so, Jesus was completely at home in the religious environment of the time, for the "whole environment of primitive Christianity knows the element of the esoteric." As one of his examples he cites the Essenes of Qumran, who buried the Dead Sea Scrolls. This sect of Jews apparently required that at his admission, a new member would swear terrible oaths to never reveal the secret teachings of the order to outsiders.

The classes of information Jeremias claims made up the esoteric teaching of Jesus before the Resurrection are: 1) Jesus' messiahship, 2) the prediction of Jesus' crucifixion, 3) prophecies about the signs of the end times, and 4) individual items of instruction. Jesus revealed His messiahship to his disciples before the passion, but always enjoined them to secrecy about it (Mark 8:30; 9:9). He publicly proclaimed His position only once, when he revealed it to the Sanhedrin just before his death (Mark 14:62). His predictions of His own death were exclusively given to close disciples (Mark 8:31; 9:31; 10:32-34), as were his predictions for the end of the world (Mark 13:3). Items of individual instruction were usually given in enigmatic terms, followed by some hint that a deeper meaning was implied. ("He who is able to receive this, let him receive it" [Matthew 19:12], or "He who has ears to hear, let him hear" [Matthew 9:15].) In addition to all this, Jeremias claims that Jesus hinted in general terms about a secret teaching which was to be made public in the future (Matthew 10:27; Mark 4:22).[803]

Morton Smith, of Harvard University, concurs with Jeremias that the religious environment of Judaism was permeated with secrecy -- not only the Essenes, but the priests of the temple at Jerusalem and the Samaritan priests had "a large body of secret traditions and practices." There were, in addition, a large number of secret sects in Judaism, including the well-known Pharisees. The Pharisees had a large body of secret doctrines which they not only were sworn to keep secret from outsiders, but from less reliable members of their own sect.[804]

This practice of revealing the higher truths only to the mature in the gospel was continued in the Apostolic Church. The writings of Paul, in particular, are replete with oblique references to secret teachings. Jeremias[805] quotes the following passages (among others) to show that Paul possessed some body of esoteric doctrine which was only to be imparted to the "mature" (Greek *teleioi*):

> Let a man so account of us, as of the ministers of Christ, and stewards of the mysteries of God. (1 Corinthians 4:1)

> Howbeit we speak wisdom among them that are perfect: yet not the wisdom of this world, nor of the princes of this world, that come to nought: But we speak the wisdom of God in a mystery, even the hidden wisdom, which God ordained before the world unto our glory . . . . (1 Corinthians 2:6-7)

> I have fed you with milk, and not with meat: for hitherto ye were not able to bear it, neither yet now are ye able. (1 Corinthians 3:2)

Many similar passages could be cited, but emphasis has been placed on those addressed to the Corinthians because, as Jeremias points out, these were people who had been Christians for years!

Secrecy in the Post-Apostolic Church

As was mentioned above, esoteric trends entered Christianity not through pagan channels, but through its parent Judaism. "Whether oral or recorded in apocryphal works, the esoteric traditions transmitted within Christianity during the first centuries often seem to be of Jewish origin."[806] Accordingly, Jewish-Christian texts like the *Pseudo-Clementine* literature are replete with references to the secret tradition. For example, in the *Clementine Homilies* Peter explained that certain "hidden truths" were to be kept from the wicked.

> And Peter said: "We remember that our Lord and Teacher, commanding us, said, 'Keep the mysteries for me and the sons of my house.' Wherefore also He explained to His disciples privately the mysteries of the kingdom of heaven. But to you who do battle with us, and examine into nothing else but our statements, whether they be true or false, it would be impious to state the hidden truths."[807]

In the *Recognitions* Peter explained further that sometimes certain subtle tactics had to be used to make sure the hidden wisdom was not spoken in front of the unworthy:

> But if he remains wrapped up and polluted in those sins which are manifestly such, it does not become me to speak

to him at all of the more secret and sacred things of divine knowledge, but rather to protest and confront him, that he cease from sin, and cleanse his actions from vice. But if he insinuate himself, and lead us on to speak what he, while he acts improperly, ought not to hear, it will be our part to parry him cautiously. For not to answer him at all does not seem proper, for the sake of the hearers, lest haply they may think that we decline the contest through want of ability to answer him, and so their faith may be injured through their misunderstanding of our purpose."[808]

Meantime Peter, rising at the crowing of the cock, and wishing to rouse us, found us awake, the evening light still burning; and when, according to custom, he had saluted us, and we had all sat down, he thus began. "Nothing is more difficult, my brethren, than to reason concerning the truth in the presence of a mixed multitude of people. For that which is may not be spoken to all as it is, on account of those who hear wickedly and treacherously; yet it is not proper to deceive, on account of those who desire to hear the truth sincerely. What, then, shall he do who has to address a mixed multitude? Shall he conceal what is true? How, then, shall he instruct those who are worthy? But if he set forth pure truth to those who do not desire to obtain salvation, he does injury to Him by whom he has been sent, and from whom he has received commandment not to throw the pearls of His words before swine and dogs, who, striving against them with arguments and sophisms, roll them in the rand of carnal understanding, and by their barkings and base answers break and weary the preachers of God's word. Wherefore I also, for the most part, by using a certain circumlocution, endeavour to avoid publishing the chief knowledge concerning the Supreme Divinity to unworthy ears." Then, beginning from the Father, and the Son, and the Holy Spirit, he briefly and plainly expounded to us, so that all of us hearing him wondered that men have forsaken the truth, and have turned themselves to vanity.[809]

This tradition of keeping certain teachings secret was continued for hundreds of years after the passing of the Apostles. For example, Ignatius of Antioch, at the beginning of the second century, insisted to the Roman Christians that he knew certain truths about the government and hierarchy of the heavens, but he could not reveal them because the Roman Saints might be harmed by knowledge they weren't ready for:

I am able to write to you of heavenly things, but I fear lest I should do you an injury. Know me from myself. For I am cautious lest ye should not be able to receive [such knowledge], and should be perplexed. For even I, not because I am in bonds, and am able to know heavenly things, and the places of angels, and the stations of the powers that are seen and that are not seen, am on this account a disciple; for I am far short of the perfection which is worthy of God.[810]

In the late second and early third centuries Clement of Alexandria and his pupil Origen were quite specific about a secret tradition that existed in the Church in their day.[811] For example, against the charges of the pagan Celsus, Origen retorted that the Christians weren't the only ones with a set of esoteric doctrines:

In these circumstances, to speak of the Christian doctrine as a *secret* system, is altogether absurd. But that there should be certain doctrines, not made known to the multitude, which are (revealed) after the exoteric ones have been taught, is not a peculiarity of Christianity alone, but also of philosophic systems, in which certain truths are exoteric and others esoteric.[812]

However, Origen distinguished the pagan mysteries from the Christian mysteries in that the Christians required that one be purified from evil for a period of time before initiation:

And since the grace of God is with all those who love with a pure affection the teacher of the doctrines of immortality, whoever is pure not only from all defilement, but from what are regarded as lesser transgressions, let him be boldly initiated in the mysteries of Jesus, which properly are made known only to the holy and the pure. The initiated of Celsus accordingly says, "Let him whose soul is conscious of no evil come." But he who acts as initiator, according to the precepts of Jesus, will say to those who have been purified in heart, "He whose soul has, for a long time, been conscious of no evil, and especially since he yielded himself to the healing of the word, let such an one hear the doctrines which were spoken in private by Jesus to His genuine disciples." Therefore in the comparison which he institutes between the procedure of the initiators into the Grecian mysteries, and the teachers of the doctrine of Jesus, he does not know the difference between inviting the wicked to be healed, and initiating those already purified into the sacred mysteries![813]

At the turn of the third century Tertullian chided certain heretics, not for having esoteric teachings, but for making the higher teachings available to everyone:

> I must not omit an account of the conduct also of the heretics -- how frivolous it is, how worldly, how merely human, without seriousness, without authority, without discipline, as suits their creed. To begin with, it is doubtful who is a catechumen, and who a believer; they have all access alike, they hear alike, they pray alike -- even heathens, if any such happen to come among them. "That which is holy they will cast to the dogs, and their pearls," although (to be sure) they are not real ones, "they will fling to the swine."[814]

Lactantius lamented the fact that Christian silence concerning the mysteries of the Kingdom engendered suspicion and base rumors among the pagans:

> This is the doctrine of the holy prophets which we Christians follow; this is our wisdom, which they who worship frail objects, or maintain an empty philosophy, deride as folly and vanity, because we are not accustomed to defend and assert it in public, since God orders us in quietness and silence to hide His secret, and to keep it within our own conscience; and not to strive with obstinate contention against those who are ignorant of the truth, and who rigorously assail God and His religion not for the sake of learning, but of censuring and jeering. For a mystery ought to be most faithfully concealed and covered, especially by us, who bear the name of faith. But they accuse this silence of ours, as though it were the result of an evil conscience; whence also they invent some detestable things respecting those who are holy and blameless, and willingly believe their own inventions.[815]

As late as the fourth century, Basil of Caesarea reported that there was still a strong unwritten and secret tradition that he believed originated with the Apostles:

> Of the beliefs and practices whether generally accepted or publicly enjoined which are preserved in the Church some we possess derived from written teaching; others we have

received delivered to us "in a mystery" by the tradition of
the Apostles . . . .[816]

> In the same manner the Apostles and Fathers who laid down
> laws for the Church from the beginning thus guarded the
> awful dignity of the mysteries in secrecy and silence, for
> what is bruited abroad random among the common folk is no
> mystery at all. This is the reason for our tradition of
> unwritten precepts and practices, that the knowledge of our
> dogmas may not become neglected and contemned by the
> multitude through familiarity. "Dogma" [doctrine] and
> "Kerugma" [preaching] are two distinct things; the former is
> observed in silence; the latter is proclaimed to all the world.
> One form of this silence is the obscurity employed in
> Scripture, which makes the meaning of "dogmas" difficult to
> be understood for the very advantage of the reader . . . .[817]

Also, a fourth century Mesopotamian Christian document divides
members of the Church into the "just" and the "perfect." And Guy Stroumsa
of Hebrew University takes it for granted that "each category of believers
receives a different type of teaching."[818]

The Content of the Secret Tradition

We have discussed in detail the fact that *there was* an esoteric
tradition within early Christianity, but now the question of *what that tradition
included* naturally arises. Clement of Alexandria claimed that the true
"gnostic" tradition was concerned primarily with cosmogony and theology. In
other words, it was concerned with the creation and the nature of God:

> The science of nature, then, or rather observation, as
> contained in the gnostic tradition according to the rule of the
> truth, depends on the discussion concerning cosmogony,
> ascending thence to the department of theology. Whence,
> then, we shall begin our account of what is handed down,
> with the creation as related by the prophets, introducing also
> the tenets of the heterodox, and endeavouring as far as we
> can to confute them. But it shall be written if God will, and
> as He inspires; and now we must proceed to what we
> proposed, and complete the discourse on ethics.[819]

Jean Daniélou finds that the esoteric teachings attributed to the
Apostles by the Apocrypha and the traditions of the elders who knew the
Apostles had primarily to do with the "celestial voyage" or the journey from
earth to heaven. [820]

This, then, was the content of the early esoteric tradition -- creation, theology, and celestial voyage. And although the *specifics* of the tradition changed with the variations in belief of the various Christian movements, the *form* remained the same. For example, the Gnostics borrowed this form of the "gnosis" from original Jewish Christianity, as we shall see later in this chapter, but scholars such as Jean Daniélou claim they substituted the original content with "foreign oriental or Hellenistic conceptions." [821]

Secret Rites

It is not enough to prove that there was a body of esoteric doctrine in ancient Christianity. In order to show a more complete correspondence to Mormonism, it must be shown that these secret doctrines were connected in some way to secret rituals analogous to those practiced in modern LDS temples.

Baptism and Eucharist as "Mysteries"

In our discussion of baptism for the dead, it was shown that the early Church guarded *all* of its ordinances, including baptism and the Eucharist, in a shroud of secrecy. Davies reports that in the first two centuries of Christianity, there are a number of references to baptism and the Eucharist, but no detailed descriptions, because "the observance of the *disciplina arcani* [secret discipline] inhibited full descriptions of these rites."[822] Indeed, very early on (ca. A.D. 110) Ignatius also referred to the Eucharist as one of "the mysteries":

> It is fitting also that the deacons, as being [the ministers] of the mysteries of Jesus Christ, should in every respect be pleasing to all. For they are not ministers of meat and drink, but servants of the Church of God. They are bound, therefore, to avoid all grounds of accusation [against them], as they would do fire.[823]

The early second-century *Epistle to Diognetus* claimed that an outsider must not expect to be able to learn anything about the worship of the Christians: "You must not hope to learn the mystery of their peculiar mode of worshipping God from any mortal."[824] And Tertullian refuted charges of immorality in Christian meetings by saying that since no Christian would reveal what goes on there, strangers must be making the charges.[825]

In the fourth century, Athanasius spoke of this tradition of secrecy and referred to these rites as "the mysteries":

> We ought not then to parade the holy mysteries before the uninitiated, lest the heathen in their ignorance deride them, and the Catechumens being over-curious be offended.[826]

Why the emphasis on guarding the ordinances from the profane? Actually, the word "mystery" [Greek *mysterion*] is a technical religious term equivalent to the Latin *sacramentum*, which simply means "ordinance."[827] The term was normally used in the context of the Greek "mystery religions" which were common in the ancient world, and included various secret doctrines and rites.[828] Therefore, when Paul and later Christian writers spoke of "the mysteries," they were borrowing a technical term loaded with meaning, and may well have been referring not only to certain doctrines, but to various rites associated with them.[829]

Indeed, "D.W.B. Robinson argues that *teleioi* [as used by Paul] is employed in the mystery-initiate sense [in Phil. 3:15 (cf. 1 Cor. 2:6; Col. 1:28)]; Hebrew believers were 'the first initiates into God's hidden mystery.'"[830] That is, the Greek word *teleioi* is another technical term associated with the mystery religions, and when Paul used it to denote the "mature in the faith," he could also have meant, more specifically, "those who have been initiated into the mysteries."[831]

Were There Other "Mysteries"?

It is quite possible, then, that even from the beginning Christians associated their esoteric doctrines with certain rituals. As Guy Stroumsa observes, "In fact there is a manifest connection between ritual and doctrine."[832] But were baptism and the Eucharist the only rituals ever referred to as "mysteries" in early Christianity? A clue might have been given by a certain statement of Hippolytus (ca. A.D. 200):

> But if there is any other matter which ought to be told, let the bishop impart it secretly to those who are communicated. He shall not tell this to any but the faithful and only after they have first been communicated. This is the white stone of which John said that there is a new name written upon it which no man knows except him who receives.[833]

R.P.C. Hanson insists that it "is not clear what the matter delivered through this secret rule was. It obviously could not have had any reference to baptism and Eucharist."[834]

We shall see that not only were there rituals other than baptism and the Eucharist in early Christianity, but in some ways they were strikingly similar to the LDS Endowment. Later much of the symbolism of these rites was adopted into the liturgies of baptism and the Eucharist. (This could have been a natural consequence of the fact that all the early Christian rituals were considered more or less part of the esoteric tradition.)

"Orthodox" Christian Rites: The Mysteries of Clement

There are perhaps dozens of allusions to the secret rites of the ancient Church in early Christian documents, but two descriptions of these rites stand out from the rest as more complete and clear. First, Clement of Alexandria described in various places in his writings a rite he called a "mystery," which was an initiation ceremony not necessarily connected with baptism. Second, Cyril of Jerusalem, in the fourth century, described in detail the liturgies of baptism and the Eucharist, which by that time included a variety of ritual actions, some of which are recognizable in Clement's earlier "mystery."

The Secret Tradition Transmitted in a "Mystery"

According to Mosheim, Clement of Alexandria claimed to possess a secret tradition of knowledge (Greek *gnosis*) handed down from the Savior to the Apostles and on to Clement himself by way of certain of his teachers.

> Clement represents this secret discipline, to which he gives the title of *gnosis*, as having been instituted by Christ himself . . . . It appears that he considered this *gnosis*, or gift of knowledge, as having been conferred by our Lord, after his resurrection, on James the Just, John, and Peter, by whom it was communicated to the other Apostles; and that by these this treasure was committed to the seventy disciples, of whom Barnabas was one . . . . Clement makes it a matter of boast that the secret discipline thus instituted by Christ was familiar to those who had been his masters and preceptors, whom he very lavishly extols, and seems to exult not a little in having, under their tuition, enjoyed the advantage of being instructed in it himself.[835]

Clement represented the true *gnosis* as having been transmitted to initiates in the form of a "mystery," which, as we have seen, probably meant in a ritual enactment or symbolic ordinance. He also stipulated that certain "purifications and previous instructions" were given before the mysteries were revealed:

> But since this tradition is not published alone for him who perceives the magnificence of the word; it is requisite, therefore, to hide in a mystery the wisdom spoken, which the Son of God taught.[836]

> Wherefore also all men are His; some through knowledge, and others not yet so; and some as friends, some as faithful servants, some as servants merely. This is the Teacher, who trains the Gnostic by mysteries, and the believer by good

222

hopes, and the hard of heart by corrective discipline through sensible operation.[837]

Thence the prophecies and oracles are spoken in enigmas, and the mysteries are not exhibited incontinently to all and sundry, but only after certain purifications and previous instructions.[838]

The teachings of these mysteries were probably quite symbolic, and Clement wrote that the Lord teaches in "enigmas" so that one has to work to get at the truth:

Dreams and signs are all more or less obscure to men, not from jealousy (for it were wrong to conceive of God as subject to passions), but in order that research, introducing to the understanding of enigmas, may haste to the discovery of truth.[839]

What form did this "mystery" take? Clement made several allusions to the initiation rite in his *Stromata* and his *Exhortation to the Heathen*. Another possible reference was made in Clement's recently discovered letter to a certain Theodore, in which he quoted a lost *Secret Gospel of Mark*.

The "Drama of Truth"

In the *Exhortation to the Heathen* Clement invited the Greeks to abandon their mystery religions and participate in the true mysteries of God. He represented the Christian mystery as a "drama of truth" and an "initiation," lighted by torches and including a hymn sung about the altar in imitation of the choir of angels around the throne of God:

Come, O madman, not leaning on the thyrsus, not crowned with ivy; throw away the mitre, throw away the fawn-skin; come to thy senses. I will show thee the Word, and the mysteries of the Word, expounding them after thine own fashion. This is the mountain beloved of God . . . consecrated to dramas of the truth, -- a mount of sobriety, shaded with forests of purity . . . . O truly sacred mysteries! O stainless light! My way is lighted with torches, and I survey the heavens and God; I become holy whilst I am initiated. The Lord is the hierophant [teacher of mysteries], and seals while illuminating him who is initiated, and presents to the Father him who believes, to be kept safe for ever. Such are the reveries of my mysteries. If it is thy wish, be thou also initiated; and thou shall join the choir along with angels around the unbegotten and indestructible and the only true God, the Word of God, raising the hymn with us.[840]

The "Ring-Dance" or "Prayer Circle"

E. Louis Backman, of the Royal University of Upsala, Sweden, indicates that this hymn was probably sung as part of a "ring-dance" performed in many religions, including early Christianity:

> Let me first emphasize that the closing words [of the hymn] must not be regarded as referring only to that which awaits in the future a person inducted into the Christian mysteries. These remarkable final words should also, perhaps mainly, be interpreted quite literally. If you are inducted into the Christian mysteries, then you must perform a ring-dance round the altar . . . not only with the other novitiates but also with the angels! For they are present and participate in the mystery.[841]

The idea that the "ring-dance" was performed in imitation of the angels around God's throne may be significant for the interpretation of a certain remark Jesus made in the *Epistle of the Apostles*. There Jesus alluded to a certain "service" or rite which was performed daily at the "altar of the Father."[842] Hennecke and Schneemelcher speculate: "Is this a projection into heaven of a practice of the Christian community?"[843] If so, the practice of such "mysteries" extended back at least several decades before Clement.

This "ring-dance" was an act of praise and included a prayer. Backman[844] cites a passage from the *Stromata* in which Clement reveals that the initiates raised their hands in prayer during the dance: "So also we raise the head and lift the hands to heaven, and set the feet in motion at the closing utterance of the prayer . . . ."[845]

References to the mystery of the ring-dance/prayer circle in early Christianity can also be found in the writings of Gregory Thaumaturgus (A.D. 210-260), bishop of Pontus, and Basileios (A.D. 344-407), bishop of Caesarea:

> We do find the following [in Gregory's writings]: 'He who has done everything preserved and prescribed by Providence in its secret mysteries, reposes in Heaven in the bosom of the Father and in the cave in the bosom of the Mother (Christ Jesus). The ring-dance of the angels encircles him, singing his glory in Heaven and proclaiming peace on earth.' In his *Four Sermons* (10:1146) he quotes a curious legend, 'Today (Christ's birthday) Adam is resurrected and performs a ring-dance with the angels, raised up to heaven'.[846]

In [Basileios's] writings there are several references to the existence of the dance in early Christianity. Thus he says of one who has died in blessedness (Letter 40): 'We remember those who now, together with the Angels, dance the dance of the Angels around God, just as in the flesh they performed a spiritual dance of life and, here on earth, a heavenly dance.' Thus life in this temporal world, where it is lived in righteousness, may be described as a spiritual heavenly dance. In another letter (ad 1:2) he writes '*Could there be anything more blessed than to imitate on earth the ring-dance of the angels* and at dawn to raise our voices in prayer and by hymns and songs glorify the rising creator.'[847]

One might think it strange that the prayer described by Clement was given with arms raised, but J. G. Davies explains that this was the natural posture for one consumed with the thought of the risen Lord.[848] A passage from the first-century *Odes of Solomon* explains that this posture was adopted in imitation of the Savior on the cross: "I stretched forth my hands and sanctified my Lord: For the extension of my hands is His sign: And my expansion is the upright tree [or cross]."[849] An Egyptian Christian work of unknown date, called the *First Book of Adam and Eve*, intimates that Adam and Eve were believed to be the first to adopt this posture in prayer: "Then Adam and Eve spread their hands unto God, praying and entreating Him to drive Satan away from them . . . ."[850] This or a similar gesture is still practiced in a number of Christian churches. It is also part of the LDS temple ceremony.

The Linen Garment

Clement's letter to Theodore also sheds some light on the early Christian mysteries. In this document, Clement wrote to a certain local church leader who had asked several questions about a document called the *Secret Gospel of Mark*, which a libertine Gnostic group called the Carpocratians had corrupted to suit their agenda. Clement decried the fact that the Gnostics had corrupted the text and described the document as an expansion of Mark's canonical gospel written after Peter died:

> [Thus] he composed a more spiritual Gospel for the use of those who were being perfected. Nevertheless, he yet did not divulge the things not to be uttered, nor did he write down the hierophantic teaching of the Lord, but to the stories already written he added yet others and, moreover, brought in certain sayings of which he knew the interpretation would, as a mystagogue [teacher of mysteries], lead the hearers into the innermost sanctuary of that truth hidden by seven [veils]. Thus, in sum, he prearranged matters, neither grudgingly nor incautiously, in my opinion,

225

and, dying, he left his composition to the church in Alexandria, where it even yet is most carefully guarded, being read only to those who are being initiated into the great mysteries.[851]

Even though the fragments we have of the *Secret Gospel of Mark* do not reveal the secret teachings, it may give us one more detail about what Clement called "the great mysteries." Clement includes a passage from the *Secret Gospel* in his letter which tells of Jesus teaching the mysteries to a young man whom he had recently raised from the dead:

> And after six days Jesus told him what to do and in the evening the youth comes to him, wearing a linen cloth over [his] naked [body]. And he remained with him that night, for Jesus taught him the mystery of the Kingdom of God.[852]

Therefore, it may be inferred that people participating in the "great mysteries" were dressed in linen robes.[853] Certainly it would have been standard procedure to call for special ritual clothing in such an important rite, just as was done for the rites of the temple at Jerusalem. And indeed, references to special symbolic garments or robes abound in early Christian literature. Note, for example, that the *Shepherd of Hermas* includes a description "of a marked secret and symbolic nature" of twelve virgins clothed in white linen. The angel told Hermas that nobody can enter the Kingdom of God unless he is clothed in their garments.[854]

Origen insisted, in a sermon on the book of Leviticus, that the faithful must have garments kept apart from the common clothing of the world:

> Therefore, you have a priesthood because you are 'a priestly nation,' and for this reason 'you ought to offer an offering of praise to God,' an offering of prayers, an offering of mercy, an offering of purity, an offering of justice, an offering of holiness. But in order to offer these things worthily, you must have clean clothes separated from the common clothing of the rest of humanity . . . .[855]

In these sermons Origen compared the Christian garment (whether it was real or figurative) to the garments given to the Temple priests, and likened these to the skin tunics given to Adam and Eve by God:

> But before we begin to say something about this kind of garment, I want to compare those miserable garments, with which the first man was clothed after he had sinned, with these holy and faithful garments. Indeed, it is said that God made those. "For God made skin tunics and clothed Adam

and his wife." Therefore, those were tunics of skins taken from animals. For with such as these, it was necessary for the sinner to be dressed. It says, "with skin tunics," which are a symbol of the mortality which he received because of his skin and of his frailty which came from the corruption of the flesh. But if you have been already washed from these and purified through the Law of God, then Moses will dress you with a garment of incorruptibility so that "your shame may never appear" and "that this mortality may be absorbed by life."[856]

The Secret Teaching

We have already seen several of the ritual elements included in Clement's "Great Mysteries," but we are left to speculate about the specific teaching enacted in the "drama of truth." Given that the esoteric traditions seem to have normally included cosmogony (creation), theology, and the cosmic journey, we may infer that aspects of these subjects were symbolically reenacted in Clement's drama. For instance, Wagner speculates that this initiation may have included a ritual enactment of certain aspects of the creation:

> Perhaps the initiation was a nocturnal rite which included human gnostic teachers breathing the Spirit into the candidates as Jesus breathed upon his disciples in their special room after the resurrection (John 20) and in harmony with the creation of humanity (Gen. 2).[857]

The reenactment of the "cosmic journey" or heavenly ascent most likely followed the pattern of the ascension narratives common in ancient Judaism and Christianity. These ascension narratives usually included a ritual clothing in the heavenly garment and anointing.[858] The heavenly garment is obtained after one ascends through the various spheres of heaven, giving the appropriate passwords along the way.[859] The *Ascension of Isaiah* includes a good example of this motif:

> And then many of the righteous will ascend with him, whose spirits do not receive their garments till the Lord Christ ascends and they ascend with him. Then indeed will they receive their garments and thrones and crowns when he shall have ascended into the seventh heaven . . . . And again I beheld when he descended into the second heaven, and again he gave the password there, for the doorkeepers demanded it and the Lord gave it.[860]

In the account of Enoch's ascension in *2 Enoch* the prophet was also anointed before he was clothed in the garment:

> And the Lord said to his servants tempting them: 'Let Enoch stand before my face into eternity,' and the glorious ones bowed down to the Lord, and said: 'Let Enoch go according to Thy word.' And the Lord said to Michael: 'Go and take Enoch from out his earthly garments, and anoint him with my sweet ointment, and put him into the garments of My glory.'[861]

These ascension narratives often included ritual handclasps, such as were included in the Christian Gnostic, Jewish Gnostic, and Greek mysteries, as we shall see.[862] Whoever was being conducted through the heavens was lifted along after grasping the right hand of the guiding angel or God. For example, in the *Gospel of Nicodemus*, Jesus descends into Hades after His death, grasps the right hand of Adam, and leads him to paradise with all the saints following:

> The King of glory stretched out His right hand, and took hold of our forefather Adam, and raised him . . . . And setting out to paradise, He took hold of our forefather Adam by the hand, and delivered him, and all the just, to the archangel Michael.[863]

A similar occurrence was also described in *1 Enoch*: "And the angel Michael, . . . seizing me by my right hand and lifting me up, led me out into all the secrets of mercy; and he showed me all the secrets of righteousness."[864]

It must be remembered that these apocryphal narratives were often centered around ritual forms that were practiced on earth, as well as in heaven. For example, J.R. Porter uses the example of Levi's heavenly anointing in the *Testament of Levi* as an example of the close relationship between earthly and heavenly rituals:

> Another heavenly anointing is found in the Testament of Levi 8.4-5 where the patriarch Levi is invested, according to the ritual for the installation of the high-priest, by seven angels, one of whom anoints him with holy oil. This reflects the well-known idea of the correspondence and the simultaneity of the earthly and heavenly ritual and it raises the question as to whether the actual high priest may have been considered in Israel to be raised by his anointing to the heavenly sphere and to have become an angelic being thereby.[865]

"Orthodox" Christian Rites: The Later Rituals of Baptism and the Eucharist

By the third and fourth centuries much of the symbolism of the "great mysteries" had been incorporated into the liturgies of baptism and the Eucharist.[866] Those who had not been initiated were kept out and strict silence in regard to the mysteries was required of the initiates. Mosheim explains:

> The multitude professing Christianity were therefore divided by them into the "profane," or those who were not yet admitted to the mysteries, and the "initiated," or faithful and perfect . . . . and as none were permitted to be present at these "mysteries," as they were termed, save those whose admission into the fellowship of the church was perfect and complete, so likewise was it expected that, as a matter of duty, the most sacred silence should be observed in regard to everything connected with the celebration of them, and nothing whatever relating thereto to be committed to the ears of the profane.[867]

The most complete description of these rites now extant was given by Cyril of Jerusalem, who wrote a series of catechetical lectures designed to instruct investigators (or "catechumens") and the newly baptized in the late fourth century. The last five of these lectures are called the "Lectures on the Mysteries," and were intended for those who had been recently baptized and given the Eucharist. A description of these rites follows.

The Renunciation of Satan

In an effort to mimic the design of the Jerusalem Temple, the basilicas of this era were divided into three parts: the atrium or forecourt, the church proper for the congregation, and the holy place where the clergy officiated at the altar.[868] "The Christian sanctuary, insofar as it was a temple, recalled in some way the holy of holies, in the temple of Jerusalem."[869] The initiate was first taken to the forecourt of the baptistry where facing West, he extended his arm and renounced Satan using the following formula: "I renounce thee, Satan. And all thy works. And all thy pomp. And all thy service." The initiate then turned to the East. Cyril explained that this action constituted a symbolic re-entrance into the Garden of Eden: "When therefore thou renouncest Satan, utterly breaking all thy covenant with him, that ancient league with hell, there is opened to thee the paradise of God, which He planted towards the East, whence for his transgression our first father was banished; and a symbol of this was thy turning from West to East, the place of lights." Then the initiate recited another formula: "I believe in the Father, and in the Son, and in the Holy Ghost, and in one Baptism of repentance."[870]

229

Initial Anointing and Baptism

The initiate was then conducted to the inner chamber where he was stripped naked, anointed with oil, and baptized. Cyril described this process:

> As soon, then, as ye entered, ye put off your tunic; and this was an image of putting off the old man with his deeds. Having stripped yourselves, ye were naked; in this also imitating Christ, who was stripped naked on the Cross, and by His nakedness put off from Himself the principalities and powers, and openly triumphed over them on the tree . . . . O wondrous thing! ye were naked in the sight of all, and were not ashamed; for truly ye bore the likeness of the first-formed Adam, who was naked in the garden, and was not ashamed. Then, when ye were stripped, ye were anointed with exorcised oil, from the very hairs of your head to your feet, and were made partakers of the good olive-tree, Jesus Christ . . . . After these things, ye were led to the holy pool of Divine Baptism, as Christ was carried from the Cross to the Sepulchre which is before our eyes And each of you was asked, whether he believed in the name of the Father, and of the Son, and of the Holy Ghost, and ye made that saving confession, and descended three times into the water, and ascended again; here also hinting by a symbol at the three days burial of Christ . . . .[871]

The Catholic editors of another English translation of Cyril's works explain that the "tunic was the garment worn by both sexes next to the skin. The candidates would already have removed their shoes and outer garments . . . ."[872] Who performed the anointing over the whole body? "For the men, no doubt, priests, deacons and the lower clergy. But for the women? . . . [*Apostolic Constitutions*] 3:15-16 says that the deaconesses completed the anointing after a deacon had begun it on the forehead."[873]

Second Anointing

After baptism the initiate was anointed again, and Cyril gave a more complete description this time:

> [The] ointment is symbolically applied to thy forehead and thy other senses; and while thy body is anointed with the visible ointment, thy soul is sanctified by the Holy and life-giving Spirit. And ye were first anointed on the forehead . . . . Then on your ears; that ye might receive the ears which are quick to hear the Divine Mysteries . . . . Then on the nostrils . . . . Afterwards on your breast; that having put on the

breast-plate of righteousness, ye may stand against the wiles of the devil . . . .[874]

In some churches the initiate's feet were washed at this time, as well.[875]

The White Garment

A subsequent passage in Cyril's lectures indicates that the initiate was symbolically clothed in white after the baptism:

> Let thy garments be always white, for the Lord is well pleased with thy works; for before thou camest to Baptism, thy works were vanity of vanities. But now, having put off thy old garments, and put on those which are spiritually white, thou must be continually robed in white: of course we mean not this, that thou art always to wear white raiment; but thou must be clad in the garments that are truly white and shining and spiritual . . . .[876]

According to Arthur McCormack, the initiate was required to wear the white garments for the rest of the day, and he also received a new name after the clothing.[877]

The officiating bishop also wore white priestly garb reminiscent of the priestly robes worn in the Jerusalem Temple. Wharton B. Marriott writes that "the dress appropriate to the most solemn offices of the holy ministry, during the primitive age, was white."[878] He also reports that the bishops anciently "wore mitres or priestly caps, after the model of the Jewish priests."[879] Jerome described the mitres of the Jewish priests:

> The fourth of the vestments is a small round cap . . . much as though a sphere were to be divided through the centre, and one half thereof to be put upon the head . . . . It has no peak at the top, nor does it cover the whole head as far as the hair extends, but leaves about a third of the front part of the head uncovered. It is attached by a band onto the back of the head, so as not to be liable to fall off.[880]

There are other articles the Catholic clergy have historically worn as part of their sacred vestments, including a girdle or sash and a stole worn over the shoulders. The stole is worn on different sides, depending on the degree within the priesthood, and is said to represent "the Stole of immortality," lost through the transgression of Adam and Eve.[881]

The Prayer Circle

Cyril went on to describe the liturgy of the Eucharist. First the deacon gave the officiating priest water to wash his hands and the elders

231

positioned themselves to stand around the altar in a circle.[882] "Then the Deacon . . . cried aloud, 'Receive ye one another; and let us kiss one another . . . .' The kiss therefore is reconciliation, and for this reason holy . . . ."[883] A prayer was then offered by the priest in behalf of those in the circle and the others attending which included the giving of thanks, petition for blessing to be pronounced upon the Eucharist, and petition "for the common peace of the Churches, for the welfare of the world (1); for kings; for soldiers and allies; for the sick; for the afflicted; and, in a word, for all who stand in need of succour . . . ."[884]

Cyril then went on to explain that the prayer included petitions in behalf of the dead, who were expected to derive some benefit therefrom. (Perhaps this is a remnant of other ordinances for the dead?)

> Then we commemorate also those who have fallen asleep before us, first Patriarchs, Prophets, Apostles, Martyrs, that at their prayers and intercessions God would receive our petition. Then on behalf also of the Holy Fathers and Bishops who have fallen asleep before us, and in a word of all who in past years have fallen asleep among us, believing that it will be a very great benefit to the souls, for whom the supplication is put up, while that holy and most awful sacrifice is set forth . . . . For if a king were to banish certain who had given him offence, and then those who belong to them should weave a crown and offer it to him on behalf of those under punishment, would he not grant a remission of their penalties?[885]

Charles Walker writes, "Formerly the names of those to be prayed for in the Liturgy were written on tablets, or parchments, which, from being folded twice, were called diptychs."[886] The editors of the Catholic edition explain that there was probably more to this prayer which Cyril does not repeat and which was "recited by the celebrant in a low voice and perhaps behind a curtain (veil, screen)."[887]

Passwords and Signs

Next the priest chanted the Lord's Prayer and invited the participants to share in the sacrament of the Eucharist.[888] It is interesting to note that the Lord's prayer also served as a sort of password for the initiates:

> As those who were admitted to the inner sights of the mysteries had a formula or pass-word . . ., so the catechumens had a formula which was only entrusted to them in the last days of their catechumenate -- the baptismal formula itself and the Lord's Prayer."[889]

As the faithful approached the priest they put forward their hands in the shape of a cup to receive the bread:

> In approaching therefore, come not with thy wrists extended, or thy fingers spread; but make thy left hand a throne for the right, as for that which is to receive a King. And having hollowed thy palm, receive the Body of Christ, saying over it, Amen.[890]

Third Anointing

Finally the participant took a sip from the cup and anointed his sense organs with the wine:

> Then after thou hast partaken of the Body of Christ, draw near also to the Cup of His Blood; not stretching forth thine hands, but bending, and saying with an air of worship and reverence, Amen, hallow thyself by partaking also of the Blood of Christ. And while the moisture is still upon thy lips, touch it with thine hands, and hallow thine eyes and brow and the other organs of sense.[891]

The Sacraments Become Exoteric

Little of these rites now remain in the liturgies of the Christian churches of today, so one might wonder what became of them. C.W. Heckethorne asserts that the secret tradition of early Christianity was lost after the Church became the dominant religion and there really weren't very many people around from whom one could keep secrets:

> The number of the faithful having greatly increased -- the Christians from being persecuted having become persecutors, and that of the most grasping and barbarous kind -- the Church in the seventh century instituted the minor orders, among whom were the doorkeepers, who took the place of the deacons. In 692 everyone was ordered thenceforth to be admitted to the public worship of the Christians, their esoteric (secret) teaching of the first ages was entirely suppressed, and what had been pure cosmology and astronomy was turned into a pantheon of gods and saints. Nothing remained of the mysteries but the custom of secretly reciting the canon of the Mass. Nevertheless in the Greek Church the priest celebrates divine worship behind a curtain, which is only removed during the elevation of the host, but since at that moment the worshippers prostrate themselves, they are supposed not to see the holy sacrament.[892]

233

Gnostic Christian Rites

The True Gnosis

It bears repeating that there was, indeed, a true *gnosis*, or hidden knowledge. J.N.D. Kelly points out that such a strain had existed in the other branches of Christianity since the earliest times:

> There was a powerful strain in early Christianity which was in sympathy with Gnostic tendencies. We can see it at work in the Fourth Gospel, with its axiom that eternal life consists in knowledge of God and of Christ, and even more clearly in such second-century works as *2 Clement* and Theophilus's *Ad Autolycum*. As we noticed above, Clement of Alexandria freely applied the title 'gnostics' to Christians who seemed to have a philosophic grasp of their faith. It is the existence of a genuinely Christian, orthodox 'gnosis' side by side with half-Christian versions which in part accounts for the difficulty in defining Gnosticism precisely.[893]

According to Morton Smith, the fact that there existed an esoteric tradition in the earliest forms of Christianity goes a long way to explain why there was such a great profusion of Gnostic Christian sects, although gnosticism had existed in other forms previous to the advent of Christ:

> But it seems likely that the primitive secret tradition of Christianity will prove the most important single factor in solving one of the major problems of the history of gnosticism: Why did so very many gnostic sects spring up so early in so many parts of the Christian Church? Groups that seem gnostic occasionally appear in paganism or Judaism, but nowhere else is there anything like the quantity and vigor of the Christian development. This has to be explained, and the explanation must be something in Christianity. What else but the secret tradition?[894]

Although a Gnostic strain was present in post-Apostolic Catholic Christianity, that doesn't necessarily mean that their *gnosis* was the true one! Clement and Origen's *gnosis* apparently included various quasi-Platonic speculations of their own which were not present in the original Church,[895] and earlier "orthodox" writings with a Gnostic flair, such as the *Epistle of the Apostles*, soon fell out of favor because they were "too heavily loaded with strange views and no longer had any contemporary significance."[896]

We are not so much interested in the content of the secret *doctrine* as we are in the content of the secret *rituals* that went along with them. H.J. Rose explains that it has always been standard procedure to keep rituals, but change the doctrines associated with them to suit the times. Thus rituals are among the most conservative elements of religion.[897] Therefore, even though the Gnostics held to some doctrines that are repugnant to Latter-day Saints and mainstream Christians alike, it is still instructive to investigate their rituals to determine whether they might have been remnants of an earlier esoteric tradition within Apostolic Christianity.

In Gnostic Christianity we find rituals very similar to the mysteries of other branches of the early Church.[898] Indeed, as was discussed above, Clement claimed that the Carpocratian Gnostics had obtained a copy of the *Secret Gospel of Mark* and had corrupted it to suit their own libertine tendencies. Therefore, since this document was associated with the "Great Mysteries," it should not be surprising that the Gnostics had similar rites.[899] In order to provide a survey of these rites, they will be briefly discussed in connection with three documentary sources: 1) the *Gospel of Philip*, 2) the *Books of Jeu* , the *Pistis Sophia*, and related documents, and 3) the *Acts of John.*

The Gospel of Philip

The Coptic Gnostic *Gospel of Philip* was discovered in 1945 in Egypt as part of the Nag Hammadi texts. J.J. Buckley claims that this document is in essence a preparatory manual for an esoteric initiation rite.[900] Although the descriptions of the rites practiced by those who accepted this document are somewhat vague, they are of great interest to Latter-day Saints. The text describes five successive rites: "The Lord [did] everything in a mystery, a baptism and a chrism and a Eucharist and a redemption and a bridal chamber."[901] Considering anointing (chrism) and the Eucharist to be related to baptism, the text goes on to compare baptism, the rite called the "redemption," and marriage to the three levels of the sanctuary in the Temple at Jerusalem: "Baptism is 'the Holy' building. Redemption is 'the Holy of the Holy.' 'The Holy of the Holies' is the bridal chamber."[902]

Some more details of the marriage ceremony are given, as well, which will be discussed later in this chapter. At least one of these rites undoubtedly included the teaching of various "mysteries." Hennecke and Schneemelcher discuss the content of the esoteric teaching, and reveal that certain passwords designed to allow the soul to ascend through the heavens were included:

> The gospel [of Philip] must therefore have contained revelations imparted by Jesus to another person (probably Philip) and reported by him. The instruction here bears upon a subject familiar to Gnosis: the manner of the ascent of the soul. By means of ritual formulae, which are at the

same time passwords, the soul ascending after death to its heavenly fatherland obtains from the planetary Archons, the hostile 'powers' of destiny who oppose its return, free passage through the seven successive spheres of the visible firmament.[903]

Clues about the nature of the ritual formulas required were given by Irenaeus, who noted that some Gnostic sects referred to the redemption as "The name which is hidden from every deity."[904] He also observed that "others still repeat certain Hebrew words, in order the more thoroughly to bewilder those who are being initiated."[905]

In connection with the ritual enactment of the heavenly ascent, it is also interesting to note that certain Gnostic ascension narratives also contained ritual handclasps. For example, in one Manichean narrative, the Primeval Man is drawn up to heaven by celestial messengers:

> The Living Spirit, who was accompanied by the Mother of Life, extended his right hand to Primeval Man. The latter seized it and thus was drawn up out of the depths of the world of darkness. Together with the Mother of Life and the Living Spirit he rose up and up, soared like victorious light out of darkness, till he was returned to the paradise of light, his celestial home, where his kin awaited him.[906]

The Pistis Sophia, the Two Books of Jeu, and Related Documents

Other Coptic Gnostic works contain information about the "mysteries" the Gnostics practiced. Two good examples are the *Pistis Sophia* and the *Two Books of Jeu*. In these documents the Apostles and some female disciples gather together somewhere to receive instruction in the mysteries from the risen Lord. The *Pistis Sophia* relates that after clothing themselves in linen garments, the participants situated themselves in a circle about Jesus, who stood at the altar. Then Jesus offered a rather strange prayer in behalf of his disciples:

> Thomas, Andrew, James and Simon the Canaanite were in the west, with their faces turned towards the east, but Philip and Bartholomew were in the south (with their faces) turned towards the north, but the other disciples and the women disciples stood behind Jesus. But Jesus stood beside the altar. And Jesus cried out, turning towards the four corners of the world with his disciples, who were all clothed in linen garments, and said: *iao, iao, iao* . . . . But when Jesus had said this, he said: Thou Father of all Fatherhood of the Infinite hearken unto me for my disciples' sake . . . .[907]

In all of these documents Jesus answered various questions his disciples asked. Although the answers given usually reflected some rather strange Gnostic doctrines, the general subjects covered can be inferred from a related document called the *Sophia Jesu Christi*:

> After he had risen from the dead, when they came, the twelve disciples and seven women who had followed him as disciples, into Galilee . . . where they were now at a loss in regard to the true nature of the universe, the plan of salvation, the holy providence, the excellency of the powers, about all that the Redeemer did with them, the secrets of the holy plan of salvation, then there appeared to them the Redeemer . . . .[908]

In the *Two Books of Jeu* the Savior also gave various "seals" and passwords necessary to ascend to the highest heaven, just as were given in the *Gospel of Philip*:

> Here also are imparted the secret names of the aeons, their several numbers, the "seals" and "pass-words," the formulae which allow free passage through each of their spheres, on after the other, and ensure escape from their grasp and power.[909]

It is interesting to note that one of the formulae given in the *Pistis Sophia* is the statement: "He is I, and I am he." Jean Doresse explains that this is "the mystery whose words are of an extraordinary power, and thanks to which each of the Perfect ones will be absorbed, in the end, into the person of Jesus himself . . . ."[910] Remember that Ignatius had a similar formula he considered necessary, "Thou art I and I am thou,"[911] which may have been part of the "orthodox" Christian esoteric tradition.

Then, of course, the discourse was concluded with a charge to keep the mysteries secret:

> These mysteries which I shall give you, preserve, and give them to no man except he be worthy of them. Give them not to father nor to mother, to brother or to sister or to kinsman, neither for food nor for drink, nor for woman-kind, neither for gold nor for silver, nor for anything at all of this world. Preserve them, and give them to no one whatsoever for the sake of the good of this whole world.[912]

The Acts of John

The *Acts of John* was a common Gnostic document which relates a similar initiation ceremony including the familiar ring-dance/prayer circle.

According to Max Pulver, this document was always believed to refer to an initiation rite, and certain clues are given about some of the paraphernalia used in the ceremony:

> Thus, as late as the fourth century the hymn from the Acts of St. John was still regarded as a ritual of initiation; here Christ is a mystagogue . . . . That is, Christ was held to have delivered a secret initiation and to have left a secret tradition to his disciples, and above all to John . . . .[913]

> In the last four verses of the hymn [in the Acts of St. John] Christ refers to himself as a torch, a mirror, a door, and a way. These are not only familiar symbols but also probably instruments of initiation.[914]

A passage from the *Acts of John* itself describes the ring-dance/prayer circle practiced as part of the initiation:

> But before he was arrested by the lawless Jews, whose lawgiver is the lawless serpent, he assembled us all and said, 'Before I am delivered to them, let us sing a hymn to the Father, and so go to meet what lies before (us).' So he told us to form a circle, holding one another's hands, and himself stood in the middle and said, 'Answer Amen to me'. So he began to sing the hymn and to say . . . . [A long hymn follows, which includes the following injunction:] 'Now if you follow my dance, see yourself in Me who am speaking, and when you have seen what I do, keep silence about my mysteries.'[915]

The overarching purpose of this initiation, according to Pulver, was once again to give certain symbols, marks of recognition, and passwords to the disciples so they could ascend to the highest heaven and become deified:

> The initiates [in the Acts of John] have entered into the godhead, fused with it. And the mystery god has no longer any outward form but only a voice . . . . This voice imparts to them the symbols, the marks of recognition and passwords . . . .[916]

The End of Esotericism

It has been established beyond doubt that an esoteric tradition of both doctrines and rituals existed in the early Church. However, it is equally clear that these esoteric trends eventually were modified or disappeared altogether. What happened to the esoteric doctrines and rituals in early Christianity, and why did they fall out of favor?

The Fight Against Gnosticism

The devaluation of the esoteric traditions started in the second century with the "orthodox" fight against Gnosticism. Guy Stroumsa explains:

> A more convincing answer lies with the fight of the Church Fathers against Gnosticism. Various Gnostic groups seem to have accepted and developed, sometimes in baroque fashion, early Jewish-Christian esoteric traditions. The appropriation of these traditions by the Gnostics made them suspect for "orthodox" Christian intellectuals. In their merciless fight against the Gnostics, the Church Fathers felt the need to reject these esoteric traditions, which had accompanied Christianity since its beginning, but which had become an embarrassing burden. Victory over Gnosticism thus meant the eradication of esotericism from Christian doctrine.[917]

Obviously, it would have been very difficult for the Church hierarchy to combat such claims to an esoteric tradition, unless they denied its existence altogether.[918] On the other hand, certain Jewish Christian groups felt that the way to fight pretensions to the hidden wisdom was by secretly teaching the *true* gnosis. Peter explained the principle in the *Clementine Homilies*:

> And thus, as the true Prophet has told us, a false prophet must first come from some deceiver; and then, in like manner, after the removal of the holy place, the true Gospel must be secretly sent abroad for the rectification of the heresies that shall be.[919]

Of course, Jewish Christianity was not very successful as a movement, and was soon absorbed into the Catholic tradition. The more successful Catholic tradition responded, as was mentioned above, by either downplaying or denying the secret tradition,[920] and even by denying the authenticity of apocryphal writings that had formerly been considered orthodox.[921]

From Gnosticism to Mysticism

In both the East and West by the fourth century the vocabulary of the esoteric traditions was appropriated to describe the new "mystical" traditions of the monks.[922] The beginnings of this trend can be found in Origen[923], and its culmination in Gregory the Great, who wrote that the mysteries imparted to the faithful not only *should not* be spoken, but *cannot* be spoken.[924] The point

239

of this mystical tradition was to "experience the divinity" by means of the "interior senses," thus obtaining a knowledge of the divine that could not be obtained in any other way, and could not be expressed by means of human language.[925]

Naturally, the mystical tradition was much more acceptable to the Church hierarchy than the esoteric tradition. After all, if the hidden wisdom *cannot* be expressed in human language, it would be difficult for heretics to exploit it.

Trivialization of the Esoteric Doctrine

As Stroumsa points out, the cultic practices associated with the esoteric tradition survived much longer than the secret *doctrines* in the form of the secret discipline associated with baptism and the Eucharist.[926] The esoteric doctrines were gradually either replaced by mysticism or trivialized. Whereas the original "gnosis" had to do with the great mysteries of theology, cosmology, and creation, when Basil of Caesarea described the secret tradition, he named only trivial practices such as praying toward the east and signing initiates with the cross after baptism:

> For instance, to take the first and most general example, who is thence who has taught us in writing to sign with the sign of the cross those who have trusted in the name of our Lord Jesus Christ? What writing has taught us to turn to the East at the prayer? Which of the saints has left us in writing the words of the invocation at the displaying of the bread of the Eucharist and the cup of blessing? For we are not, as is well known, content with what the Apostle or the Gospel has recorded, but both in preface and conclusion we add other words as being of great importance to the validity of the ministry, and these we derive from unwritten teaching.
>
> Moreover we bless the water of baptism and the oil of the chrism, and besides this the catechumen who is being baptized. On what written authority do we do this? Is not our authority silent and mystical tradition? Nay, by what written word is the anointing of oil itself taught? And whence comes the custom of baptizing thrice? And as to the other customs of baptism from what Scripture do we derive the renunciation of Satan and his angels? Does not this come from that unpublished and secret teaching which our fathers guarded in a silence out of the reach of curious meddling and inquisitive investigation?[927]

Stroumsa also suggests that Basil may have been protecting the more important points of the esoteric tradition in this way[928], but assuming he had nothing more to offer, it would help to explain why the esoteric tradition was completely dropped soon after Basil's lifetime.

Augustine and the End of Esotericism

It is difficult to say exactly how long the secret tradition survived in Christianity.[929] With the fight against Gnosticism and the Peace of the Church in the fourth century[930], a new religious sensibility developed within Christianity so that only isolated groups of heretics retained any esoteric doctrines and rites.[931] By far the most perfect representative of the new ethos was Augustine, who lived in the late fourth and early fifth centuries, and in this section we will examine his thought on the subject of esotericism.

Augustine summarized his position while commenting on a certain statement Jesus made, recorded in the Gospel of John. "I have yet many things to say unto you, but ye cannot bear them now." (John 16:12) Apparently the Gnostic heretics had appropriated this passage to show that they were in possession of the teachings Jesus declined to tell His disciples at that time, and Augustine justly pointed out that just because Jesus declined to say something doesn't give anyone license to claim he has those very teachings:

> Do we on that account know what it is that He would not say, as we should know it were we reading or hearing it as uttered by Himself? For it is one thing to know whether we or you could bear it; but quite another to know what it is, whether able to be borne or not. But when He Himself was silent about such things, which of us could say, It is this or that? Or if he venture to say it, how will he prove it? For who could manifest such vanity or recklessness as when saying what he pleased to whom he pleased, even though true, to affirm without any divine authority that it was the very thing which the Lord on that occasion refused to utter? Which of us could do such a thing without incurring the severest charge of rashness, -- a thing which gets no countenance from prophetic or Apostolic authority?[932]

Next Augustine simply assumed that the Catholic Church was in possession of the teachings Jesus declined to preach, and asked why the catechumens (investigators) of his day could bear all the teachings and sacramental practices of the Church, but the disciples of Jesus couldn't. The answer? It wasn't really that those without the Holy Spirit *couldn't bear* such things, but they were kept from the neophytes for a time so that they would *"more ardently desire them"*:

> How then, could not the disciples bear any of those things which were written after the Lord's ascension, even though the Holy Spirit was not yet sent to them, when now they are

all borne by catechumens prior to their reception of the Holy Spirit? For although the sacramental privileges of believers are not exhibited to them, it does not therefore happen that they cannot bear them; but in order that they may be all the more ardently desired by them, they are honorably concealed from their view.[933]

Augustine explained further that anyone can *bear* the teachings of the Church, but without the aid of the Holy Spirit, they cannot *understand* them. For example, he excused the incomprehensibility of his doctrine of God by claiming that anyone could immediately see its truth with the aid of the Holy Spirit:

So shall the result be, that not from outward teachers will you learn those things which the Lord at that time declined to utter, but be all taught of God; so that the very things which you have learned and believed by means of lessons and sermons supplied from without regarding the nature of God, as incorporeal, and unconfined by limits, and yet not rolled out as a mass of matter through infinite space, but everywhere whole and perfect and infinite, without the gleaming of colors, without the tracing of bodily outlines, without any markings of letters or succession of syllables, -- your minds themselves may have the power to perceive.[934]

And although no one keeps silence about Him, who is there that apprehends Him as He is to be understood, although He is never out of the mouths and the hearing of men? Who is there, whose keenness of mind can even get near Him? Who is there that would have known Him as the Trinity, had not He Himself desired so to become known? And what man is there that now holds his tongue about that Trinity; and yet what man is there that has any such idea of it as the angels? The very things, therefore, that are incessantly being uttered off-hand and openly about the eternity, the truth, the holiness of God, are understood well by some, and badly by others: nay rather, are understood by some, and not understood at all by others.[935]

Finally, Augustine gave the most compelling reason for his prejudice against esoteric traditions. That is, many of the heretical groups who made use of esoteric doctrines actually preached a "hidden knowledge" that was contradictory to the exoteric doctrines taught in the scriptures:

Accordingly, when the Lord says, "I have yet many things to say unto you, but ye cannot bear them now," He means that what they were still ignorant of had afterwards to be supplied to them, and not that what they had already learned was to be subverted.[936]

Here again we see the influence of the early fight against Gnosticism. As a result of their indiscriminate appeals to the secret tradition to defend their wild speculations, *all* esotericism became suspect to their enemies.

Heavenly Marriage

Eternal Marriage

LDS Belief and Practice

The crowning ordinance of the temple is the Celestial Marriage ceremony. In this rite a husband and wife are joined together not just till death separates them, but for eternity, as part and parcel of the exaltation or deification bestowed on those who reach the highest level of the Celestial kingdom. Those "sealed" together in this rite will be able to participate in the creative work of God in the world to come. The Lord explained this principle to Joseph Smith:

> Therefore, if a man marry him a wife in the world, and he marry her not by me nor by my word, and he covenant with her so long as he is in the world and she with him, their covenant and marriage are not of force when they are dead, and when they are out of the world; therefore, they are not bound by any law when they are out of the world. Therefore, when they are out of the world they neither marry nor are given in marriage; but are appointed angels in heaven, which angels are ministering servants, to minister for those who are worthy of a far more, and an exceeding, and an eternal weight of glory. For these angels did not abide my law; therefore, they cannot be enlarged, but remain separately and singly, without exaltation, in their saved condition, to all eternity; and from henceforth are not gods, but are angels of God forever and ever. (D&C 132:15-17)

The Reticence of Jesus

This is a bold and wonderful promise, and one which none of the mainstream Christian sects can give. In fact, Latter-day Saints receive endless criticism for this belief because the sects interpret a certain answer Jesus gave to the Sadducees to mean that there is no marriage in heaven. Matthew reports the conversation thus:

> The same day came to him the Sadducees, which say that there is no resurrection, and asked him, Saying, Master, Moses said, If a man die, having no children, his brother shall marry his wife, and raise up seed unto his brother. Now there were with us seven brethren: and the first, when he had married a wife, deceased, and, having no issue, left his wife unto his brother: Likewise the second also, and the third, unto the seventh. And last of all the woman died also. Therefore in the resurrection whose wife shall she be of the seven? for they all had her. Jesus answered and said unto them, Ye do err, not knowing the scriptures, nor the power of God. For in the resurrection they neither marry, nor are given in marriage, but are as the angels of God in heaven. (Matthew 22:23-30)

It must be admitted that the doctrine of eternal marriage is not explicitly taught in the New Testament. However, Latter-day Saints normally reply that there is evidence that Christian marriage was among the early esoteric traditions (see below), so it is not surprising that Jesus would not have explained the doctrine in detail to the Sadducees, who did not even believe in a resurrection and were only trying to trap Jesus in his words. From an LDS viewpoint, Jesus' reply to the Sadducees was technically correct, since the people in question were Sadducees themselves ("there were *with us* seven brethren"), and hence were not on the path to the highest degree of salvation. (D&C 132:15-16)[937]

Early Christian Evidence

Details of the earliest Christian concept of marriage were undoubtedly left out of the New Testament, and R.M. Grant reports that Christian marriage was considered "a great mystery" by Paul, and therefore was probably part of the esoteric teaching:

> In Ephesians 5:22-33 the prophecy of Genesis 2:24 ["the two shall become one flesh."] is described as "a great mystery" and is referred not only to Christ and the church but also to Christian marriage in general.[938]

Paul also taught that "neither is the man without the woman, neither the woman without the man, in the Lord." (1 Corinthians 11:11)

In the early third century Origen reported that certain Christians, apparently considered orthodox, believed in marriage after the resurrection. Interestingly, he asserted that they thought this way because they understood the scriptures in a "Jewish sense," and we have seen that many of the great changes came in Christianity through the adoption of Greek philosophical tenets in place of Jewish beliefs.

> Certain persons . . . are of the opinion that the fulfillment of the promises of the future are to be looked for in bodily pleasure and luxury . . . . And consequently they say, that after the resurrection there will be marriages, and the begetting of children, imagining to themselves that the earthly city of Jerusalem is to be rebuilt . . . . Such are the views of those who, while believing in Christ, understand the divine Scriptures in a sort of Jewish sense, drawing from them nothing worthy of the divine promises.[939]

Another more subtle reference to this subject may be found in the second century sermon, *2 Clement*:

> For the Lord Himself, being asked by one when His kingdom would come, replied, "When two shall be one, and that which is without as that which is within, and the male with the female, neither male nor female."[940]

As was stated in our discussion of Gnostic Christian rites similar to the Endowment, certain Gnostic groups considered marriage to be their most holy mystery. We have already seen this in the *Gospel of Philip*, and Irenaeus charged a Gnostic group called the Marcosians with a similar practice, as well:

> For some of [the Marcosians] prepare a nuptial couch, and perform a sort of mystic rite (pronouncing certain expressions) with those who are being initiated, and affirm that it is a spiritual marriage which is celebrated by them, after the likeness of the conjunctions above.[941]

The *Gospel of Philip* states that "those who have united in the bridal chamber will no longer be separated."[942] One aspect of the ceremony is revealed when the bridal chamber is referred to as "mirrored": "One receives them [the male and female powers] from the mirrored bridal chamber."[943] As with the LDS sealing ceremony, this Gnostic rite could not be rejected in mortality and then accepted later: "If anyone becomes a son of the bridal chamber, he will receive the light. If anyone does not receive it while he is in these places, he will not be able to receive it in the other place."[944] Note that the result of this mystic marriage was believed to be children! "The heavenly man has many more sons than the earthly man. If the sons of Adam are many, although they die, how much more the sons of the perfect man, they who do not die but are always begotten."[945]

Although no proof has been presented here that eternal marriage was the original Christian practice, it cannot be denied that this belief was held in one form or another by a significant number of early Christians.

Changes in the Marriage Doctrine

But whether or not eternal marriage was the original doctrine, it can be shown that significant changes in the ideal of Christian marriage took place over the first few centuries after Christ. Confusion started early, and the reason for the misunderstanding can be traced to some enigmatic and seemingly contradictory statements of Paul in his first letter to the Corinthians. As we mentioned above, Paul told the Corinthians that "neither is the man without the woman, neither the woman without the man, in the Lord." (1 Corinthians 11:11) On the other hand, while answering certain unknown questions the Corinthians had posed to Paul, he advised against marriage:

> Now concerning the things whereof ye wrote unto me: It is
> good for a man not to touch a woman . . . . I say therefore to
> the unmarried and widows, It is good for them if they abide
> even as I. But if they cannot contain, let them marry: for it
> is better to marry than to burn. (1 Corinthians 7:1, 9)

And yet, later in the chapter Paul made clear that this was not a general principle, but special counsel in unusual circumstances: "I suppose therefore that this is good for the present distress, I say, that it is good for a man so to be." (1 Corinthians 7:26) Paul never let us know what the "present distress" was, but clearly there *are* circumstances in which it is better not to marry, and indeed there are many in the Restored Church who live celibate lives for various reasons.

In some quarters, however, Paul's general counsel about marriage was forgotten, and neither marriage nor celibacy was considered a superior state. For example, both Clement of Rome and Ignatius, around the turn of the second century, apparently considered celibacy to be a viable alternative to marriage, and advised celibate Christians not to boast about their strength: "Let him that is pure in the flesh not grow proud of it, and boast, knowing that it was another who bestowed on him the gift of continence."[946]

> If any one can continue in a state of purity, to the honour of
> Him who is Lord of the flesh, let him so remain without
> boasting. If he begins to boast, he is undone; and if he
> reckon himself greater than the bishop, he is ruined.[947]

Apparently some had adopted the ideals of the pagan ascetics, who considered celibacy a higher way of life, and they were so proud of their "purity" that some of them considered themselves outside their bishops' jurisdiction. (Alternatively, it should be noted that Clement and Ignatius may have advised celibacy for the same reason Paul did, or because of some other special circumstance. This cannot be known with certainty, however.)

Others retained the knowledge that the sexes are not without each other "in the Lord." For example, Clement of Alexandria felt that marriage "was good practice for life as a god."[948] D.G. Hunter summarizes Clement's thought:

> Clement insists that marriage and procreation are an intrinsic and positive part of God's plan for the human race. He frequently cites Gen. 1:28 ("Increase and multiply") and regards human procreation as an act of co-creation with God: "In this way the human being becomes the image of God, by cooperating in the creation of another human being" . . . . Indeed, Clement is even capable of regarding marriage as, in some respects, superior to celibacy. The celibate who is concerned only for his salvation is "in most respects untried." By contrast, the married man who must devote himself to the administration of a household is a more faithful reflection of God's own providential care.[949]

By the third century, mainstream writers such as Methodius and Lactantius could claim that while marriage was proper, celibacy was a higher way of life.[950] This attitude has persisted in the Catholic tradition to this day.

Plural Marriage

Undoubtedly the Latter-day Saint practice that has generated the most publicity is plural marriage. Some Mormons practiced this during the nineteenth century until it was forbidden by order of the First Presidency. This has often been construed as a change in *doctrine* by outsiders, but to Latter-day Saints it has always been viewed rather as a change in *policy* consistent with principles found in both the Bible and the *Book of Mormon*. For instance, it is well known that many Old Testament figures practiced plural marriage, but later Paul directed that bishops and deacons, at least, should be the "husbands of one wife." (1 Tim 3:2, 12) Similarly, the *Book of Mormon* prophet Jacob gave a stinging rebuke to those who were practicing plural marriage, because it had been forbidden to them at that time, but then gave a caveat: "For if I will, saith the Lord of Hosts, raise up seed unto me, I will command my people; otherwise they shall hearken unto these things." (Jacob 2:30) Therefore, the doctrine of the LDS Church has been from the beginning that usually the Lord commands monogamy, but sometimes He commands polygamy to "raise up seed" to Himself.

It is interesting to note that when the Christian world was confronted with LDS practice of plural marriage, they reacted with the utmost abhorrence in spite of the many Biblical figures who practiced it as well. Biblical polygamy has normally been characterized as something which God simply overlooked for a while until Jesus came to set things straight. However, some very prominent early Christian writers held views on this issue that were strikingly similar to the LDS perspective. For example, Tertullian claimed that monogamy was preferable, but the Lord had allowed polygamy at certain times to "replenish the world":

> As I think, moreover, each pronouncement and arrangement is (the act) of one and the same God; who did then indeed, in the beginning, send forth a sowing of the race by an indulgent laxity granted to the reins of connubial alliances, until the world should be replenished, until the material of the new discipline should attain to forwardness: now, however, at the extreme boundaries of the times, has checked (the command) which He had sent out, and recalled the indulgence which He had granted; not without a reasonable ground for the extension (of that indulgence) in the beginning, and the limitation of it in the end.[951]

And Augustine wrote that polygamy was only forbidden at that time because of the laws and customs of the time:

> Again, Jacob the son of Isaac is charged with having committed a great crime because he had four wives. But here there is no ground for a criminal accusation: for a plurality of wives was no crime when it was the custom; and it is a crime now, because it is no longer the custom. There are sins against nature, and sins against custom, and sins against the laws. In which, then, of these senses did Jacob sin in having a plurality of wives? As regards nature, he used the women not for sensual gratification, but for the procreation of children. For custom, this was the common practice at that time in those countries. And for the laws, no prohibition existed. The only reason of its being a crime now to do this, is because custom and the laws forbid it.[952]

Polygamy and the Mystery of Marriage

We discussed above the fact that Christian marriage was referred to by Paul as "a great mystery" in itself, which also symbolized the union of Christ and the Church. Accordingly, Justin Martyr not only defended the polygamy of Old Testament figures, but referred to it as a "mystery" as well:

> "And this one fall of David, in the matter of Uriah's wife, proves, sirs," I said, "that the patriarchs had many wives, not to commit fornication, but that a certain dispensation and all mysteries might be accomplished by them; since, if it were

248

allowable to take any wife, or as many wives as one chooses, and how he chooses, which the men of your nation do over all the earth, wherever they sojourn, or wherever they have been sent, taking women under the name of marriage, much more would David have been permitted to do this."[953]

Although the evidence is far from conclusive, a form of plural marriage may have been practiced by some of the Apostles and prophets in the early Church. The following passage from the Didache speaks of prophets who "work unto the mystery of the church," which "mystery" we have already seen was marriage -- and possibly plural marriage.

> And every prophet, proved true, working unto the mystery of the Church in the world, yet not teaching others to do what he himself doeth, shall not be judged among you, for with God he hath his judgment; for so did also the ancient prophets."[954]

Jean Daniélou links this mystery to the type of "spiritual marriages" that groups like the Marcosians practiced:

> The expression 'cosmic mystery of the Church' seems to stand in opposition to a 'heavenly mystery of the church'. This heavenly mystery is the celestial marriage of Christ to the Church, which also finds its expression in this world. The allusion in this passage would therefore seem to be to those spiritual unions which existed in Jewish Christianity between prophet-Apostles and a sister. Hermas also appears to allude to this custom (*Sim.* IX, 10:6-11:8), while a similar reference may underlie *I Cor.* 7:36ff. The custom endured in the institution of Virgins. The relation of these unions to their heavenly ideal is explicitly stated by the Gnostics: 'Some of them prepare a nuptial couch and perform a sort of mystic rite (*mystagogia*) . . . affirming that what is performed by them is a spiritual marriage after the likeness of the unions . . . above' (*Adv. haer.* I, 21:3).[955]

And although Daniélou sees no connection here with plural marriage, it is evident that this "mystery" was something that the "ancient prophets" practiced, but which was forbidden for ordinary Christians. Considering Paul's prohibition against plural marriage for bishops and deacons, it may well have been polygamy.

Heavenly Mother

Related to the doctrine of eternal marriage in LDS theology is the belief in a Heavenly Mother as well as a Father. Mormons do not worship this being, and actually know little about Her beyond that She is "married" to the Father, participated in creation, and is co-equal with the Father. Therefore, this could be another doctrine likely not to have been revealed in former dispensations, but there is some evidence that it may have been.

The Hebrew Goddess

It is well known that the Israelites worshipped a goddess, from time to time, who was believed to be the consort of "Yahweh" or Jehovah. Theodore Robinson explains:

> From our Old Testament alone we should never have guessed that Israel associated a goddess with Yahweh, even popularly, but the conclusion is irresistible, and we are justified in assuming that she played her part in the mythology and ritual of Israel.[956]

Widengren also reports that in Jeremiah's day a goddess called the "Queen of Heaven" received officially sanctioned worship in Jerusalem. He sees this as connected to the year-rites, in which a sacred marriage was performed for the god and goddess, who then gave birth to a Savior-King:

> In much later times there was a goddess called the Queen of Heaven(s), to whom official sacrifices were offered by kings and princes, both in Jerusalem and in other cities of Judah, Jer. xliv. 17 . . . . That the sacred marriage should bring as its fruit the birth of the Savior-King is in accordance with the general myth and ritual pattern . . . .[957]

The worship of the Queen of Heaven was forbidden by Jeremiah, but this also is consistent with LDS practice, since Mother-worship is not permitted for Mormons, either.[958] In fact, Margaret Barker notes that the evidence points to the conclusion that the goddess had a long-standing relationship with the Temple cult itself.[959]

This tradition survived in Judaism until the time of Christ, when Philo the Jew could speak of a Mother in Heaven as the personification of "Wisdom": "[Moses'] father being God, who is likewise Father of all, and his mother Wisdom, through whom the universe came into existence."[960]

Could there have been a legitimate and divinely sanctioned Hebrew Goddess? The first chapter of Genesis may give us a clue: "And God said, Let us make man in our image, after our likeness . . . . So God created man in his image, in the image of God created he him; male and female created he them." (Genesis 1:26-27) Given the fact that the Israelites and the earliest Christians believed in an anthropomorphic God, it is significant that God said "Let *us* make man in *our* image," and that the image of God is defined as "male and female."

Heavenly Mother in Jewish Christianity

There is no strong evidence from the New Testament of any belief in a Heavenly Mother, but some post-Apostolic Jewish Christians explicitly stated this belief. For example, the Jewish Christian *Gospel of the Hebrews* apparently taught that the Holy Spirit was Jesus' Mother. It is interesting to note that Origen quoted this passage from the lost *Gospel* and treated it as an authoritative source, finding it necessary to offer a rather fanciful interpretation to explain away the verse:

> If any one should lend credence to the Gospel according to the Hebrews, where the Saviour Himself says, "My mother, the Holy Spirit took me just now by one of my hairs and carried me off to the great mount Tabor," he will have to face the difficulty of explaining how the Holy Spirit can be the mother of Christ when it was itself brought into existence through the Word. But neither the passage nor this difficulty is hard to explain. For if he who does the will of the Father in heaven is Christ's brother and sister and mother [see Matthew 12:47-50], and if the name of brother of Christ may be applied, not only to the race of men, but to beings of diviner rank than they, then there is nothing absurd in the Holy Spirit's being His mother, every one being His mother who does the will of the Father in heaven.[961]

The Gnostic "Sophia"

Gnostic Christians believed in a Mother in Heaven as well, and the Father, Mother, and Son were considered a sort of Gnostic Trinity by them. For instance, the *Secret Book of John* speaks of "the three: the Father, the Mother, and the Son, the perfect power."[962] In the *Hymn of the Pearl*, a document which may have been written as early as the first century and may not be Gnostic at all[963], the hero is sent a heavenly message which begins: "From thy father the King of Kings, and from thy mother, mistress of the East, and from thy brother, our next in rank . . . ."[964] The *Gospel of Philip* calls the Mother "Wisdom" (Greek *Sophia*)[965], and Hennecke and Schneemelcher report that Wisdom was presented as a celestial being, who in fact was "the female aspect of the creative power," in such documents as the *Sophia Jesu Christi.*[966]

Finally, the *Gospel of Philip* taught that the existence of the world depends on the mystery of marriage: "Great is the mystery of marriage! For [without] it the world would [not have existed]. Now the existence of [the

251

world depends on man], and the existence [of man on marriage]."[967] I doubt a Mormon could have phrased it any better.

The Female Aspect of God in Catholic Tradition

Margaret Barker posits that the "gnostic Sophia is all that remains of Israel's goddess."[968] But what happened to the goddess in the "orthodox" tradition? Most likely it was quickly modified or dropped because of its close association with Gnosticism. For example, a modified form of the doctrine can be found in the writings of Clement of Alexandria. Wagner summarizes:

> Clement then pressed the scripture and his gnostic traditions to make the church *Ekklesia*, a heavenly female who was one of a threesome that originated in God's mind. God's will became Cosmos, God's Wisdom was Logos, and God's Purpose (*Boulema*) appeared as *Ekklesia*.[969]

Certainly this was another echo of the ancient Hebrew goddess.

Chapter Notes

Note 1: Jewish Esoteric Rites

Of related interest is the fact that various Jewish groups may have had similar mystery rites. While the Essenes, whose community at Qumran wrote the Dead Sea Scrolls, had their own peculiar rites, the ancient Jews in general also participated in ceremonies called "year rites" and other initiation ceremonies, which were common throughout the ancient Near East and included some elements in common with the rites we have already discussed.

Essene Initiation

The writings of the Essenes are replete with references to the mysteries of God. What did these mysteries include? J.J. Gunther explains that the basic "mystery" of the Essenes had to do with the plan of salvation:

> In the Qumran writings there are many references to the mysteries or secrets (raz) which have been revealed. Some are recorded on heavenly tablets (Cave 4 fragments). The basic raz concerns the wonders of God: His grace, mercy, wisdom and truth. These attributes are expressed through the mysteries of the divine plan of history.[970]

Gunther also quotes the ancient historian Pliny to show that the Essenes instructed their initiates in the mysteries "in accordance with an ancient method of inquiry . . . by means of symbols"[971]

Hippolytus intimated that in the Essene rituals the initiate swore to "tell nothing (of their secrets) to others even if he shall suffer violence unto death. Besides this, he swears to them to impart none of the doctrines [of the sect] otherwise than as he himself received them."[972]

Year Rites

In early Judaism certain rituals called "year rites" in which the epic of creation in Genesis was used as a liturgical text were performed annually.

> The creation story of Genesis is enacted during seven days and this fact has been compared to the seven tablets of the Babylonian Epic of Creation as well as with the seven days of the Israelitic Festival of Booths. It has been surmised by Humbert that the Hebrew story of creation was used as a cult text or at least served 'a liturgical purpose'.[973]

This practice was common to all Near Eastern cultures including those of the Babylonians, Hittites, and others.[974] Associated with the creation ritual was a rite involving a dying god and a ritual marriage between the god and his consort. This symbolized the yearly change of the seasons and insured the continued fertility of the earth for the subsequent year. Theodore Robinson reports that the scholarly consensus is that the Israelites had such rites, just as their neighbors did:

> This subject has been closely studied in recent years, and it is generally (though not universally) agreed that a ritual involving a dying God, a divine marriage, and a ceremonial procession, was found in Israel. It would be strange if it were not so, for some such ceremonial is almost universal among agricultural peoples, though in many instances it has lost one or more of its characteristic features.[975]

Did the Hebrews have any rituals analogous to the ring-dance/prayer circle described in many of the other texts we have examined? Backman, in his book on religious dances, speculates that the Israelites used a ring-dance in their worship around the Golden Calf, described in Exodus 32. He considers this evidence that the ring-dance was so common in antiquity that the Israelites chose it as a matter of course.[976]

Instruction in the Mysteries

Another strange mystery ritual is recounted in the apocryphal *Testament of Job*. In this document, Job gathered his children together to instruct and bless them before he died. In one section he gave his daughters certain articles of clothing, variously described as fiery cords, ropes, or robes. He explained that these robes were given to him by the Lord as a cure for the diseases he was afflicted with during his great trial, and he instructed his daughters to wear them as a protection against Satan. The daughters put on the garments and began worshipping and speaking in the heavenly language. Then they discussed together "the heavenly mysteries." The narrator, Job's brother, went on to say that he wrote down everything that went on "except for the hymns and signs of the word, for these are the mysteries of God."[977]

What were the identities of these "signs of the word?" Perhaps they relate to the familiar motif of the journey of the soul through the spheres of heaven. Ernst Müeller explains:

> In this Hechaloth literature [ancient Jewish mystical documents], as in the kindred passages in the Talmud and Midrash, we meet with angelic beings in boundless profusion . . . . In the works which relate journeys of the soul there appear at the gates of the various heavens special gatekeepers (porters), who also hand over the "seals" to those who are to be initiated.[978]

And indeed, such rites were divided into parts corresponding to the different stages in a soul's progress: "A passage from a Hechaloth tractate quoted by Sholem makes it clear that to each stage of initiation corresponded a stage in religious and moral progress."[979]

It was probably common in Jewish initiation rites to use sacred robes or vestments, such as those given to Job's daughters. Müeller reports that various ancient Jewish mystical documents describe this practice:

> From the description in the Zohar cited above we may conclude that already in the talmudical period there were formal initiations. Sholem mentions a special initiation rite which is described in the "Sefer ha-Malbush" as an "investing with the divine Name," and in which the candidate has to put on a robe with the name of God woven into it.[980]

Finally, the early Christian writer Origen asserted that the Temple cult itself had been used by the priests to relate the mysteries to initiates:

> In conformity to which the Jewish priests "served unto the example and shadow of heavenly things," explaining enigmatically [i.e. in secret] the object of the law regarding the sacrifices, and the things of which these sacrifices were the symbols.[981]

Unfortunately, not much else is known about such ancient Jewish initiation rites. However, it should be clear that such rites existed, and they were similar in form to those we have discussed already.

Note 2: Gnostic Jewish Esoteric Rites

Jewish gnosticism was much less prevalent than its Christian counterpart, but amazingly, the only Gnostic sect to survive to the present time is a Jewish Gnostic group called the Mandaeans. ("Mandaean" simply means "Gnostic" in their dialect.) This strange sect has survived in southern Iraq and southern Iran since approximately the third century A.D., when they migrated from Palestine.[982]

This sect was originally studied by E.S. Drower, who reports that their mystery rites were based on the creation story and other elements of the plan of salvation:

> The Mandaean system includes 'Mysteries', i.e. sacraments to aid and purify the soul, to ensure her rebirth into a spiritual body, and her ascent from the world of matter. These are often adaptations of existing seasonal and traditional rites to which an esoteric interpretation is based on the Creation story . . . , especially on the Divine Man, Adam, as crowned and anointed King-priest."[983]

In fact, Jean Doresse indicates that Adam played a leading part in many Judeo-Gnostic rituals.[984]

The Mandaeans call themselves "Nasoraeans," which "today indicates not only one who observes strictly all rules of ritual purity, but one who understands the secret doctrine."[985] Dr. Drower goes on to explain that each mystery is given in the form of a drama: "Each raza, 'each mystery,' is a drama, . . . but they are still couched in the language of parable and symbol, so obscure in expression that none but a "true Nasorean" can interpret its meaning."[986] Each mystery also includes a ritual handclasp called a *kusta*:

> The creation of Adam is related in the third person, and it begins, like all divine acts, with immersion (i.e. baptism?) and prayer. As *kusta* [i.e. the act of exchanging the ritual handclasp symbolic of good faith and of covenant] is in the Nasoraean church a rite which must precede and conclude every sacramental rite, personified Ether is called upon to be present for the ritual handclasp symbolical of truth and good faith.[987]

Note 3: Greek Mystery Religions

Given the LDS doctrine of dispensations, Mormons should not be surprised to find that many pagan cultures and religions had rituals similar to the mystery rites discussed above. After all, if the Endowment were given to Adam, it is possible that remnants of the ceremony would be found in a wide variety of places. Of particular interest to us, however, are the "mystery religions" of ancient Greek culture, because they existed concurrently with the ancient Christian mysteries.

According to Edwin Hatch, the "mysteries were probably the survival of the oldest religions of the Greek races and of the races which preceded them." The main ritual elements of these religions were "the initiation, the sacrifice, and the scenic representation of the great facts of natural life and human life, of which the histories of the gods were themselves symbols . . . ." The purpose of the initiation was purification, and was accomplished by the confession of sins and a symbolic washing similar to baptism.[988] The initiate approached this sacrament in the hope of becoming a new creature, "twice-born," in mystic harmony with the savior-god to whom the ritual was dedicated. "All the Mystery-gods were primarily saviour-gods."[989] This union was believed to ultimately result in the deification of the initiate.[990] Samuel Angus reports that the emphasis was not on any specific teaching, however, but on the exhibition of the divine symbols.[991] After the public and private sacrifices, the mysteries concluded with a dramatic representation of the cosmic plan of history calculated to teach the doctrine of the immortality of the soul.[992]

Certain mystery religions also incorporated other elements familiar to us. For example, the Eleusinian Mysteries included a ring-dance[993] and many others included a sacred meal as a sacrament of union with the savior-deity.[994] Ritual handclasps such as those used by the Mandaeans were employed in the Sabazian mysteries[995] and the mysteries of Mithras.[996] The purpose of the mysteries of Mithras, in particular, was to prepare the soul to "ascend through the seven planetary spheres to Paradise."[997] Indeed, a ritual enactment of this ascension was performed by the initiate, "clad in holy garments and led by the High Priest."[998] All of the mysteries were esoteric and initiates were impressed with an "awful obligation to perpetual secrecy as to what was said and transacted behind closed doors in the initiation proper . . . ."[999]

It should be obvious to anyone at this point that many ritual elements of the Mysteries were very analogous to elements of Christian ritual, including the Eucharist, baptism, and the "great mysteries." In addition, the motif of a dying and rising savior-god was common to both traditions. Bruce Metzger points out that these parallels have been recognized since the early centuries of Christianity:

> That there *are* parallels between the Mysteries and
> Christianity has been observed since the early centuries of

the Church, when both Christian [e.g. Justin Martyr, *Apol. I*, 66:4, and *Dial.* 70:1; and Tertullian, *de Corona*, 15, and *de Praescript.*, 40,] and non-Christian [e.g. Celsus, in Origen's, *Contra Celsum*, 6:22,] alike commented upon certain similarities.[1000]

Is this proof that Christian rituals and doctrine were merely spin-offs or copies of models found in the popular religions of the day? Some scholars have come to this conclusion, but Jesuit scholar Hugo Rahner of the University of Innsbruck points out that religious symbols are the common heritage of mankind, and if a certain amount of borrowing was done it is of no consequence, since the doctrine transmitted through these symbols is essentially different.[1001] Also, Rahner recognizes that it may not have been an accident that there were so many points of contact between ancient Christianity and the popular religions of the day. God Himself may well have prepared the culture of the Roman Empire to receive Christ by exactly those means.[1002]

However, as was mentioned above, Latter-day Saints see an additional possibility -- that the mystery religions were corrupted remnants of the true doctrine, which had been long since lost. This possibility seems likely in light of the fact that the "Mysteries preserved much in ritual that was archaic, the original significance of which was lost in antiquity . . . ."[1003]

Note 4: Masonry & Mormonism

It is a well-known fact that certain symbols used in the LDS Endowment have counterparts in the ritualism of the Freemasons. Since Joseph Smith was himself a Mason for a short time, anti-Mormon writers often charge that he stole the Endowment from that fraternity. The correspondence is hardly surprising, however, since the Prophet confided in several people that he believed the Masonic rituals were incomplete remnants of the ancient Endowment. Apparently, the ceremony was revealed to him after he had asked the Lord about the status of the Masonic teachings.[1004]

Therefore, the question at hand is not whether the Prophet borrowed some symbolism from the Masonic rites, but whether similar rites were found in ancient Christianity. Indeed, the symbols Joseph Smith made use of are not exclusive to the Masons, but go back thousands of years. So even if the Prophet borrowed some symbols, just as the early Christians apparently borrowed from the mystery religions, it is entirely possible that these were exactly *the right symbols*, handed down from a time when the rituals were not yet corrupted. Furthermore, the Prophet restored symbolism in the Endowment which is *not* found in the Masonic rite, but which was to be found, as we have seen, in the liturgies of the various mystery rites we have discussed.

Note 5: Mixing of Ritual Elements

We have seen that the later rites of baptism and the Eucharist included elements quite similar to those found in the earlier "orthodox" and Gnostic mysteries. But while Cyril of Jerusalem's and related accounts make clear that these rites had become quite complicated by the fourth century, the New Testament accounts suggest rather simple ritual patterns.[1005] As was mentioned above, the hypothesis being advanced here is that the ritual elements of the higher ordinances were adopted into baptism and the Eucharist. But how and why did this happen?

The confusion probably began with the Gnostics, who apparently took elements of the higher ordinances for use in the baptismal rite, and elements of the baptismal rite for use in the higher ordinances. For example, Hippolytus described the "Redemption" rite of one Gnostic group and indicated that they had incorporated a second baptism into it:

> And subsequent to the (first) baptism, to these they promise another, which they call Redemption. And by this (other baptism) they wickedly subvert those that remain with them in expectation of redemption, as if persons, after they had once been baptized, could again obtain remission.[1006]

And whereas there is no solid evidence for baptismal anointing in New Testament[1007] or in "orthodox" Christianity until Tertullian (ca. 200 A.D.)[1008] Irenaeus described certain Gnostic groups who had introduced anointing into the baptismal rite. "Others, again, lead them to a place where water is, and baptize them . . . . After this they anoint the initiated person with balsam; for they assert that this unguent is a type of that sweet odour which is above all things."[1009] J. John argues that the Gnostics may have introduced anointing into baptism to express their superiority over ordinary Christians:

> If, as Lampe believes, [the Gnostics] were the first Christians to introduce [anointing], the motive of the rite may well have been to express and emphasize their spiritual superiority over ordinary Christians who as yet practiced only water-baptism. Dix, agreeing that the earliest unambiguous evidence for chrismation is Gnostic, argues that it is unthinkable that the Church should have taken over from its doctrinal enemies.[1010]

But if there is no solid evidence for baptismal anointing in first and second-century "orthodox" liturgy, and it is "unthinkable" that they would have adopted the practice from the Gnostics, how did it come about that the Catholic baptismal liturgy *did* eventually incorporate anointing? Perhaps the answer is that anointing existed from the beginning in the higher ordinances.

However, as the higher ordinances fell out of favor and as the various branches of Christianity drifted further from the truth, elements of these rites were incorporated into baptism and the Eucharist and the higher ordinances were set aside.

Chapter 7: Mormonism in the Early Jewish Christian Milieu

Author's Note: Shortly after the original print version of this book was published, I was asked to address the theme of the book at the 1st annual FAIR Conference in Ben Lomond, CA. Instead of just summarizing the contents, I decided to follow up on a pattern I had begun to notice. The main function of the book was to describe and catalogue early Christian beliefs and practices similar to those of the Latter-day Saints, but I had begun to notice that those similarities could often be traced to groups of early Jewish Christians. This was quite striking, because early Christianity was heterogeneous enough that it was inevitable some groups would have held beliefs similar to the Latter-day Saints, so finding that many of them could be traced back to the most primitive and enigmatic early Christians greatly enhanced the value of the evidence detailed in the book. The following chapter is the text of my FAIR Conference address. I have included it in this edition to give readers an idea of what further research could be done in this area. (Also note that the treatment of the identity of Jehovah is more developed here than in Ch. 3.)

Roman Catholic apologist Patrick Madrid recently posed a challenging question for Latter-day Saints. That is, if Mormonism is essentially a "restoration" of primitive Christianity, where can we find historical evidence for some ancient Christian group that "was identical to the Mormon Church of today"? He goes on, "We have records of many controversies that raged in the early days of the Church, and there just is no evidence-none at all-that Mormonism existed prior to the 1830s."[1011] Whether Mr. Madrid is adequately informed about LDS claims and the state of the evidence concerning them, is beside the point. If Latter-day Saints want to make a rigorous historical case for our faith, we need to demonstrate at least some probability that a group of "Former-day Saints" really existed. What evidence for such a group should we expect to find, and what evidence is there? In this paper I attempt to answer these questions, at least in part, and show a high probability for the proposition that a group of "Former-day Saints" existed within the early Jewish Christian milieu.

The Spectrum of Early Christian Belief

What was the "early Jewish Christian milieu" and what was its relationship to other forms of Christianity? It is an irrefutable fact that the first Christians were Jewish Christians, and consequently their theology made use of Jewish thought-forms and Jewish categories. Since the discovery of the Dead Sea Scrolls, it has become increasingly apparent that the Christianity of the New Testament had clear ties to the kind of Apocalyptic Judaism1012 represented by the Essenes of Qumran.1013 In his landmark study of Jewish Christian theology, Jean Danièlou writes, "The thesis is that there was a first form of Christian theology expressed in Jewish-Semitic terms."1014 And with reference to the first Christians, J.N.D. Kelly writes that their theology "was taking shape in predominantly Judaistic moulds."1015

The Jews of the diaspora "provided the initial basis for church growth during the first and early second centuries."[1016] However, by the mid-second century we can speak of three major movements within Christianity-Jewish Christianity, Hellenistic or "Gentile" Christianity, and Gnosticism. It must be remembered that these are artificial categories, and in reality there was a spectrum of belief. That is, there were Jewish Gnostic Christians, Gentile Christians with Gnostic tendencies, Gentile Christians who retained many Jewish Christian traditions, etc. In Latter-day Saint belief, all of these groups participated in or fell victim to the general apostasy. How did this happen?

The Apostasy in Jewish Christianity

The New Testament gives evidence that certain factions within Jewish Christianity rebelled against the authority of the Apostles, and refused to accept the fact that Christ had fulfilled the Law of Moses. As the missionary efforts of the Church moved beyond Palestine, the question came up as to whether Gentile converts should be circumcised and be subject to the Law of Moses. Acts 15 describes a council in Jerusalem where the "Apostles and elders" considered the matter and decided that the converts *did not* have to keep the ritual requirements of the Law. However, many of those who had originally insisted on the continuity of the Law would not accept this decision, and insisted on preaching their views to the churches. For instance, Paul complained that the Galatians had turned to "another Gospel" (Galatians 1:6), and specifically censured those who desired "to be under the law." (Galatians 4:21) Paul also dealt with this issue in other letters, such as his Epistle to the Romans, and he further warned Titus against "giving heed to Jewish fables." (Titus 1:14) It is clear that New Testament Christianity grew from the soil of Apocalyptic Judaism, but there were a great number of competing and contradictory apocalyptic traditions which some Jewish Christians may have inherited and been unwilling to give up.

Danièlou[1017] describes a host of Jewish Christian heretical sects, including the Ebionites, Elkesaites, Cerinthians, and others. These ranged from strictly Jewish groups who merely believed in Jesus as the greatest of the prophets-the son of Joseph and Mary[1018], to quasi-Gnostic speculations that drew heavily on miscellaneous Jewish apocalyptic traditions. Apart from these were more moderate strains of Jewish Christianity known to us from the New Testament, miscellaneous apocryphal texts, as well as such writings as *Barnabas*, the *Pastor of Hermas*,[1019] and miscellaneous traditions scattered throughout the writings of more Hellenized Christians. Gradually, these groups lost their vitality and were melded into the Hellenized congregations.[1020]

The Gnostic Heretics

For a few centuries there existed alongside the Catholic Christian tradition various heretical groups categorized as "Gnostic."[1021] This name comes from *gnosis*, the Greek word for "knowledge." Hans Jonas explains that Gnostics believed they were saved by knowledge, specifically the knowledge of God, or that knowledge was the form of salvation itself.[1022]

While it may be tempting to equate this sentiment to Jesus 'statement: "Ye shall know the truth, and the truth shall make you free" (John 8:32) or to Joseph Smith's that "a man is saved no faster than he gets knowledge,"[1023] upon further reflection it becomes obvious that the Gnostic belief was very different from the original Christian teaching. Knowledge itself cannot save without the atonement of Jesus Christ. On the other hand, in Gnostic circles Christ's incarnation and atonement were thought to have been illusory, since Gnosticism radicalized the common Hellenistic notion that matter is a lesser reality into the doctrine that matter is evil. (If matter is evil, how could a divine being associate himself with it?) And while true Christians viewed the physical body as necessary, the Gnostics thought of it as a prison into which the pre-existent spirit had fallen and from which it must escape.[1024] In order to promote their reputations as masters of hidden knowledge, the Gnostic teachers put together a bewildering array of eclectic theologies utilizing a hodgepodge of "oriental mythologies, astrological doctrines, Iranian theology, elements of Jewish tradition, Christian salvation-eschatology, [and] Platonic terms and concepts."[1025]

The birth of the Gnostic Christian movement took place during the Apostolic period, but Gnostics probably never became terribly prevalent at that time because the Apostles actively combated this heresy, calling it the "knowledge falsely so called." (1 Timothy 6:20) John condemned these "docetists" (from the Greek *dokein* = "to seem") who claimed Jesus only "seemed" to come in the flesh as antichrists. "And every spirit that confesseth not that Jesus Christ is come in the flesh is not of God: and this is that spirit of antichrist." (1 John 4:3) But according to Eusebius (a fourth century Catholic historian), Gnostic teachers came out of the woodwork in great profusion after the Apostles were all gone.[1026]

The "Hellenization" of Christianity

Hellenized Christianity grew out of the original Jewish Christianity as the faith moved more and more into a Gentile world saturated by Greek, or "Hellenistic" culture and thought. As Adolf von Harnack observed, this move catalyzed "the greatest transformation which the new religion ever experienced."[1027]

Certainly the entire Mediterranean world was touched to one degree or another by Hellenistic culture and thought, and Israel was no exception, but the Palestinian Jews proved to be a particularly resistant group, and in large part retained their own distinctive thought-forms and traditions.[1028] Therefore, when Gentiles and Hellenized Jews outside of Palestine came to form the majority of the Christians, it was natural that some would attempt to make the Christian message more palatable to the Greek mind by building bridges with the popular philosophy of the day, which was an amalgamation of the thought of various Greek philosophical schools, especially the Middle Platonists and the Stoics.

At first, Christian thought was quite foreign to Greek philosophy, although there were certainly important points of contact upon which the Christian missionaries capitalized.[1029] As Harnack notes, "Yet we cannot say that the earliest Christian writings, let alone the gospel, show, to any considerable extent, the presence of a Greek element."[1030] For instance, Paul warned, "Beware lest any man spoil you through philosophy and vain deceit, after the tradition of men, after the rudiments of the world, and not after Christ." (Colossians 2:8) Referring to this passage, James Shiel of the University of Sussex writes, "Saint Paul's letters [contain] a severe warning against Greek philosophy as a dangerous deception"[1031] Cardinal Danièlou writes that "If we now examine the forms of thought and philosophical systems current at the time when Christianity first made its appearance in the world, it is clear that they were by no means ready to assimilate this Christian conception: on the contrary, they were wholly antagonistic thereto."[1032] However, Shiel notes that a few generations after the Apostles, one "comes upon a reversed situation. The religious message is now framed in philosopher's language, reminiscent at every turn of Heraclitus or Plato or Aristotle or Cleanthes or Epictetus. Indeed, the Christian religion is now occasionally called a philosophy and its founder described as a philosopher."[1033]

Beginning in the mid-second century, this shift in attitude was accomplished thanks to the efforts of a class of Christian writers later historians have dubbed the "Apologists." These included Aristides, Justin, Tatian, Athenagoras, and others. Intellectuals themselves, they sought to express their faith in intellectually respectable terms, but the net result of their labors was not just to translate Christian ideas into a Hellenistic idiom. Rather, they imported philosophical ideas into their thought that had been anathema to the original Christians.[1034] One can certainly understand the temptation to make such accommodations, since the Greeks normally saw the Christians as intellectually feeble barbarians, but in the end Rebecca Lyman notes that "the efforts of the apologists succeeded in enabling Christianity to be labeled a third-rate philosophy rather than a first-rate superstition."[1035]

The philosophical assumptions and definitions these early Apologists adopted have profoundly affected Christian theology to this day. Edwin Hatch summarizes:

> A large part of what are sometimes called Christian doctrines, and many usages which have prevailed and continue to prevail in the Christian Church, are in reality Greek theories and Greek usages changed in form and colour by the influence of primitive Christianity, but in their essence Greek still.[1036]

It should be clear from the foregoing discussion that the various branches of early Christianity based their thinking upon fundamentally different sets of axioms, and each branch was not entirely homogenous. However, if Joseph Smith was correct in his claim to restore the original Christian theology, we must look for historical confirmation among the specifically Jewish Christian documents and traditions. As DaniÈlou stated, Jewish Christian teaching was the "first form of Christian theology".

Limitations of This Study

There are certainly limitations to our inquiry. Few Jewish Christian documents have survived, and those that have are from a range of different groups within that milieu. In any case Joseph Smith said that things would be revealed in this dispensation which have been "kept hid from before the foundation of the world," (D&C 124:41) so some LDS doctrines may *not* have been taught by the ancient Saints. We should also expect some *cultural* differences to affect some matters of interpretation and practice. The prophet Alma wrote, "For behold, the Lord doth grant unto all nations, of their own nation and tongue, to teach his word, yea, in wisdom, all that he seeth fit that they should have; therefore we see that the Lord doth counsel in wisdom, according to that which is just and true." (Alma 29:8) Nevertheless, it is clear that in most of the basics, at least, our hypothetical "Former-day Saints" would have to have been very much like the Latter-day Saints, so we can expect to find a good deal of Latter-day Saint doctrine and practice within the ancient documents. The balance of this paper will demonstrate that this is, indeed, the case.

Jewish Christian and LDS Theology/Anthropology

W.D. Davies of Duke University observed that "Mormonism is the Jewish-Christian tradition in an American key. What it did was to re-Judaize a Christianity that had been too much Hellenized."[1037] This is true with respect to any number of issues, but in order to keep this study to an acceptable length, we will restrict ourselves to matters of theology and anthropology. It is our doctrines regarding the nature of God, the nature of man, and the relationship between the two, that differentiate LDS thought most strikingly from mainstream Christianity. While there are many important commonalities, close analysis reveals a chasm between the two worldviews that profoundly affects many other areas of doctrine. And yet, nearly every major tenet of LDS theology and anthropology can be found within the early Jewish Christian milieu.

The Anthropomorphic God

What kind of being is God? How can He be described? Joseph Smith preached that "if you were to see [God] today, you would see him like a man in form,"[1038] and that "the Father has a body of flesh and bones as tangible as man's; the Son also." (D&C 130:22)

On the other hand, mainstream Christians generally accept definitions such as that promulgated by the Vatican Council, where God was said to be "eternal, immense, incomprehensible, Öwho, being a unique spiritual substance by nature, absolutely simple and unchangeable, must be declared distinct from the world in fact and by essence."[1039] This sort of definition was readily accepted among second-century Gentile Christians because it exactly coincided with those being taught by the contemporary Greek philosophers. For instance, the Middle Platonist philosopher Plutarch wrote the following:

> Socrates and Plato held that (God is) the One, the single self-existent nature, the monadic, the real Being, the good: and all this variety of names points immediately to mind. God therefore is mind, a separate species, that is to say what is purely immaterial and unconnected with anything passible.[1040]

Gentile Christian thinkers frankly admitted this correspondence, and in fact promoted the doctrine as a ready defense against the attacks of pagan critics. Tertullian wrote, "Whatever attributes therefore you require as worthy of God, must be found in the Father, who is invisible and unapproachable, and placid, and (so to speak) the God of the philosophers."[1041]

This was not, however, the case for the Jews or the Jewish Christians, except insofar as they had been influenced by Hellenistic thought. Thus, even in the third century Origen could say, "The Jews indeed, but also some of our people, supposed that God should be understood as a man, that is, adorned with human members and human appearance. But the philosophers despise these stories as fabulous and formed in the likeness of poetic fictions."[1042] Notice that Origen did not appeal to unanimous Christian tradition to establish his doctrine of the incorporeality of God, but to the philosophers. Indeed, in another passage Origen admitted this was the subject of some confusion among Christians. "For it is also to be a subject of investigation how God himself is to be understood-whether as corporeal, and formed according to some shape, or of a different nature from bodies-a point which is not clearly indicated in our teaching."[1043]

A second-century Jewish Christian document, the *Clementine Homilies*, explicitly taught anthropomorphism. The following is part of a conversation that is said to have occurred between Simon Magus and Peter. "And Simon said: 'I should like to know, Peter, if you really believe that the shape of man has been moulded after the shape of God.' And Peter said: 'I am really quite certain, Simon, that this is the case. It is the shape of the just God.'"[1044]

The anthropomorphic teaching of the Jews and Jewish Christians was based upon a literal interpretation of the Bible. Many examples of anthropomorphic Bible passages could be cited, but for now a few explicit statements will suffice. Ezekiel's vision of the heavenly throne is described thus: "Above the vault over their heads there appeared, as it were, a sapphire in the shape of a throne, and high above all, upon the throne, a form in human likeness." (Ezekiel 1:26 NEB) Just prior to his martyrdom, Stephen said, "Behold, I see the heavens opened, and the Son of man standing on the right hand of God." (Acts 7:56) John reported a similar vision of God. "And immediately I was in the spirit: and, behold, a throne was set in heaven, and one sat on the throne." (Revelation 4:2) Edmond LaB. Cherbonnier of Trinity College summarizes this phenomenon as follows: "In short, to use the forbidden word, the biblical God is clearly anthropomorphic-not apologetically so, but proudly, even militantly."[1045] Christopher Stead of the Cambridge Divinity School agrees that, "The Hebrews pictured the God whom they worshipped as having a body and mind like our own, though transcending humanity in the splendour of his appearance, in his power, his wisdom, and the constancy of his care for his creatures."[1046]

Mainstream Christians usually interpret the Biblical statements allegorically, and offer two major points of scriptural evidence. First, they cite John 4:24, "God is Spirit" or "God is a Spirit." If God is a Spirit, they say, He cannot have a body. However, John's statement "God is Spirit" is parallel to two passages in his first epistle, "God is light" (1 John 1:5) and "God is love" (1 John 4:8) In context, all of these passages seem to be referring to God's activity toward men rather than to the nature of His "Being". Furthermore, Christopher Stead explains how such statements would have been interpreted within ancient Judaism. "By saying that God is spiritual, we do not mean that he has no body but rather that he is the source of a mysterious life-giving power and energy that animates the human body, and himself possesses this energy in the fullest measure."[1047]

Second, mainstream Christians appeal to passages like John 1:18. "No man hath seen God at any time." Latter-day Saints can harmonize these passages with those that describe visions of the Father by referring to Moses' vision of God, as described in the Pearl of Great Price. "And he saw God face to face, and he talked with him, and the glory of God was upon Moses; therefore Moses could endure his presence. [Moses said] For behold, I could not look upon God, except his glory should come upon me, and I were transfigured before him." (Moses 1:2, 14) An identical solution is offered by Peter in the Jewish Christian *Clementine Homilies.*

> For I maintain that the eyes of mortals cannot see the incorporeal form of the Father or Son, because it is illumined by exceeding great light. For he who sees God cannot live. For the excess of light dissolves the flesh of him who sees; unless by the secret power of God the flesh be changed into the nature of light, so that it can see light.[1048]

The point of these passages is not that no one has or will have a vision of God's person, but rather that men cannot see God as He is. We must be changed and protected by the grace of God to withstand His presence. However, this will not always be the case. As John further wrote, "Beloved, now are we the sons of God, and it doth not yet appear what we shall be: but we know that, when he shall appear, we shall be like him; for we shall see him *as he is*." (1 John 3:2, emphasis added)

The Unity of the Godhead

One feature of the New Testament all Christians must come to terms with is the fact that in some passages the Father is represented as "the only true God" (John 17:3), while in others the Son and Holy Spirit are also called "God" (John 1:1; John 14:26; Acts 13:2). How can this apparent contradiction be resolved? It can readily be seen that the two disparate definitions of God discussed above must lead to different conclusions regarding this question.

In harmony with their definition of God as an indivisible, eternal, unchanging spiritual "essence", mainstream Christians say that the members of the Trinity are separate "persons" who share a single "Divine Being". All three persons have always existed in the same relationship to one another, and there is no hierarchy within the Trinity. That is, the Father, Son, and Holy Spirit do not differ in rank or glory. On the other hand, Latter-day Saints believe the members of the Godhead are separate beings, and so in a sense we believe in more than one God. However, Latter-day Saints also speak of "one God" in two senses. First, the Godhead is "one" in will, purpose, love, and covenant. Second, the Father is the absolute monarch of the known Universe, and all others are subject to Him.

In order to find a historical basis for the Latter-day Saint doctrine of the Divine Unity, we need not look exclusively among the Jewish Christians, because it was almost universally accepted among Christians before the Nicene Council of 325 A.D. that the Father, Son, and Holy Ghost were united in will, but separate in rank and glory. J.N.D. Kelly of Oxford University notes that even at the Council of Nicea the majority party believed "that there are three divine hypostases [or "persons"], separate in rank and glory but united in

268

harmony of will."[1049] This doctrine is called "subordinationism", and R.P.C. Hansen writes, "Indeed, until Athanasius began writing, every single theologian, East and West, had postulated some form of Subordinationism. It could, about the year 300, have been described as a fixed part of catholic theology."[1050] Henry Bettenson writes that "'subordinationism' was pre-Nicene orthodoxy."[1051] Paul wrote that the Father is "the God and Father of our Lord Jesus Christ" (Romans 15:6, NEB), and revealed that *after* the resurrection Jesus will "be subject unto him [the Father] that put all things under him, that God may be all in all." (1 Corinthians 15:24-28) Indeed, Jesus Himself said, "My Father is greater than I." (John 14:28)

This doctrine took various forms, depending on the particular concept of God involved. Within Jewish Christianity, where God was often conceived of as having a body in human form, Jesus and the Holy Spirit were described both as gods, worthy of worship, and the chief among the archangels.[1052] While Latter-day Saints generally do not refer to the Son and Spirit as "angels", such a designation is consistent with our belief that Jesus, the Holy Spirit, and all angels and men are "sons of God" (Job 38:7), differing in degree and power, but not in essential nature. This belief is graphically illustrated in the Jewish Christian apocryphal text, *The Ascension of Isaiah*:

> Then the angel who conducted me said to me, "Worship this one"; so I worshiped and praised. And the angel said to me, "This is the Lord of all glory whom you have seen". And while the angel was still speaking, I saw another glorious one, like to him, and the righteous drew near to him, worshiped, and sang praise. And I saw the Lord and the second angel, and they were standing; but the second one whom I saw was on the left of my Lord. And I asked, "Who is this?" and he said to me, "Worship him, for this is the angel of the Holy Spirit". So my Lord drew near to me, and the angel of the Spirit and said, "Behold, now it is granted to you to behold God, and on your account is power given to the angel with you." And I saw how my Lord worshiped, and the angel of the Holy Spirit, and how both together praised God.[1053]

An early second century Jewish Christian document, the *Shepherd of Hermas* spoke of "the angel of the prophetic Spirit"[1054] and Jesus as the "'glorious angel' or 'most venerable angel'."[1055] Justin Martyr, a converted philosopher who lived in Rome in the mid-second century, was no Jewish Christian, but Robert M. Grant suggests that in passages like the following, he was influenced by the Jewish Christian writings of Hermas, who lived in the same congregation.[1056] Justin Martyr wrote that the "first-begotten," the Logos, is the "first force after the Father:" he is "a second God, second numerically but not in will," doing only the Father's pleasure.[1057] He designated the Son as "this power which the prophetic word calls God and Angel"[1058], and in the same vein stated the following. "We reverence and worship Him and the Son who came forth from Him and taught us these things, and the host of other good angels who are about Him and are made quite like Him, and the Prophetic Spirit."[1059] He also maintained that the Son is "in the second place, and the prophetic Spirit in the third."[1060] Finally, the Jewish Christian *Clementine Recognitions* had this to say regarding Jesus' status:

> For the Most High God, who alone holds the power of all things, has divided all the nations of the earth into seventy-two parts, and over these He hath appointed angels as princes. But to the one among the archangels who is greatest, was committed the government of those who, before all others, received the worship and knowledge of the Most High God. Thus the princes of the several nations are called gods. But Christ is God of princes, who is Judge of all.[1061]

The Names of God

The above-mentioned text from the *Clementine Recognitions* brings up the issue of how Latter-day Saints use the names of God in the Bible. Four names or titles are commonly used to connote God in the Old Testament-El ("God"), Elohim ("God" or "gods"), Elyon ("Most High"), and Yahweh (equivalent to "Jehovah").[1062] Most mainline Christians see all these designations as referring to one divine being. However, the Latter-day Saint usage is much more complicated. On one hand, the Divine names can refer to specific Persons, i.e. El or Elohim usually refers to the Father, and "Yahweh" usually refers to the Son. On the other hand, they have also been used as titles in reference to more than one Divine Person. Both the Father and the Son have been called "Jehovah" or Yahweh (D&C 109:34, 42, 68; D&C 110:3)[1063], and it is believed that the Bible passages which link Yahweh with Elohim or Elyon (e.g. Isaiah 43:12-13; Isaiah 45:21-22 NEB) refer to a "divine investiture of authority", where the Son is allowed to speak in the first person as the Father.[1064]

When one examines the context of passages such as the foregoing reference to the *Clementine Recognitions*, it becomes clear that the usage of the Divine Names/Titles was similarly complicated in the Jewish Apocalyptic and Jewish Christian traditions. The *Recognitions* was referring to a particular passage which occurs in both the Septuagint and Dead Sea Scrolls manuscripts of Deuteronomy. "When the Most High parceled out the nations, when he dispersed all mankind, he laid down the boundaries of every people according to the number of the sons of God; but the LORD's [Yahweh's] share was his own people, Jacob was his allotted portion." (Deuteronomy 32:8-9 NEB) Based on this and other passages, some Biblical scholars now conclude that the Israelites originally believed El to be the high God, and Yahweh to be the chief among the "sons of El"-the second God and chief archangel who had special responsibility for Israel.[1065]

Certainly this is a debated point, and beyond the scope of this paper, but it is beyond debate that this was a standard early Christian interpretation of the passage. As late as the fourth century, the great historian and bishop, Eusebius of Caesarea, could write:

> In these words [Deut. 32:8] surely he names first the Most High God, the Supreme God of the Universe, and then as Lord His Word, Whom we call Lord in the second degree after the God of the Universe. And their import is that all the nations and the sons of men, here called sons of Adam, were distributed among the invisible guardians of the nations, that is the angels, by the decision of the Most High God, and His secret counsel unknown to us. Whereas to One beyond comparison with them, the Head and King of the Universe, I mean to Christ Himself, as being the Only-begotten Son, was handed over that part of humanity denominated Jacob and Israel, that is to say, the whole division which has vision and piety.[1066]

According to Alan Segal, in a number of Jewish Apocalyptic texts there were actually two Yahwehs. Both the High God and principal angel were so designated.[1067] Similarly, in the Jewish Christian *Apocalypse of Abraham*, preserved only in the Slavonic language, God is designated both as El and "Jaoil", and in some manuscripts the angel accompanying Abraham is also named "Jaoil".[1068] Indeed, Segal notes that during the first Christian centuries, the rabbis engaged in debates with various sects, including the Christians, who all seem to have claimed there was a second God, in many cases identifying him with Yahweh or "the bearer of the divine name."[1069] Significantly, Jean Daniélou writes that "the Name of God" was one of the principal designations of the Son within Jewish Christianity.[1070]

Creation from Unformed Matter

The idea that there are multiple Divine Beings who have material bodies with human form is sharply at odds with the axiom of the theologians that God's "Essence" is "wholly other" than the rest of the universe. This assumption on the part of mainstream Christians is based on the doctrine of *creatio ex nihilo* – creation from nothing. In his 1990 Presidential address to the British Association for Jewish Studies, Peter Hayman asserted the following:

> Nearly all recent studies on the origin of the doctrine

of *creatio ex nihilo* have come to the conclusion that this doctrine is not native to Judaism, is nowhere attested in the Hebrew Bible, and probably arose in Christianity in the second century C.E. in the course of its fierce battle with Gnosticism. The one scholar who continues to maintain that the doctrine is native to Judaism, namely Jonathan Goldstein, thinks that it first appears at the end of the first century C.E., but has recently conceded the weakness of his position in the course of debate with David Winston.[1071]

The Apostle Peter was quite explicit about his belief in creation from a watery chaos, rather than from nothingness. He wrote, "There were heavens and earth long ago, created by God's word out of water and with water." (2 Peter 3:5 NEB) The background for this passage is the first two verses of Genesis: "In the beginning of creation the earth was without form and void, with darkness over the face of the abyss, and a mighty wind that swept over the surface of the waters." (Genesis 1:1-2 NEB) David Winston writes that the Rabbis presupposed the same watery chaos. For instance, he notes that *Mekilta, Shirta* 8 states that "to make a roof man requires wood, stones, dirt, and water, whereas God has made a roof for his world out of water. God's first act of creation thus presupposes the existence of water."[1072] Similarly, the *Sefer Yesira* states, "He formed substance from chaos and made it with fire and it exists, and he hewed out great columns from intangible air."[1073] In the *Bereshit Rabba* we find, "R. Huna said, 'If it were not written explicitly in Scripture, it would not be possible to say it: *God created the heaven and the earth*. From *the earth was chaos*, etc.'"[1074]

However, the interpretation of some of the early texts can be confusing, and indeed, a few seemingly contradict creation from chaos. In the Apocrypha, 2 Maccabees asserts that "God made [the sky and the earth] out of nothing, and man comes into being in the same way." (2 Maccabees 7:28 NEB) On the other hand, the *Wisdom of Solomon* says, "For thy almighty hand, which created the world out of formless matter, was not without further resource." (Wisdom of Solomon 11:17 NEB) Paul seemed to imply creation out of nothing: "God summons things that are not yet in existence as if they already were" (Romans 4:17 NEB), and yet we saw that Peter's language recalled the Genesis account of creation from a watery chaos. Indeed, in the very same verse Paul wrote that God "fashioned" (Greek *katertisthai* = "adjusted, put in order again, restored, repaired") the universe, but in such a way that "the visible came forth from the invisible." (Hebrews 11:3 NEB) The second-century *Pastor of Hermas* asserted that God "made out of nothing the things that exist,"[1075] but in another passage clearly presupposed creation from a watery chaos: "By His strong word [He] has fixed the heavens and laid the foundations of the earth upon the waters."[1076]

Gerhard May has convincingly shown that where these early texts say God created out of "nothing" or "non-being", etc., they were using a common ancient idiom to say that "something new, something that was not there before, comes into being; whether this something new comes through a change in something that was already there, or whether it is something absolutely new, is beside the question."[1077] For instance, the Greek writer Xenophon wrote that parents "bring forth their children out of non-being'.[1078] Philo of Alexandria wrote that Moses and Plato were in agreement in accepting a pre-existent material, but also that God brings things "out of nothing into being" or "out of non-being".[1079] Therefore, in view of this common usage, and the many explicit statements by ancient authors regarding the pre-existent matter, we must rule out a belief in *creatio ex nihilo* unless it is explicitly stated otherwise.

We do not find such explicit statements anywhere until the mid-second century with the Gnostic teacher Basilides and later the Christian apologists Tatian and Theophilus of Antioch.[1080] Even as late as the turn of the third century, Tertullian had to take the more ancient usage into account when arguing for the new doctrine. "And even if they were made out of some (previous) matter, as some will have it, they are even thus out of nothing, because they were not what they are."[1081]

Given the state of the evidence, we can be fairly certain that when Joseph Smith said matter is eternal, and that God fashioned the earth from pre-existent matter[1082], he was restoring the earliest Jewish Christian belief.

The Pre-Mortal Existence of Souls

Latter-day Saints not only reject the notion that the material world was created from nothing, but that the spiritual world was so created. Joseph Smith taught that the "intelligence" of man is eternal, and at some point God organized this "intelligence" into the spirits of men. (Abraham 3:22-23) Thus, the spirits of men pre-existed their bodies.

R.G. Hammerton-Kelly, professor of New Testament at McCormick Theological Seminary, reports that "the idea that certain things pre-exist in the mind of God or in heaven has a long history in the Biblical and early Jewish traditions."[1083] For instance, "in Job 15:8 the primal man is pictured in the council of the gods before the world was made."[1084] David Winston reports that the *Bereshith Rabba* and *Ruth Rabba* tell of God consulting the souls of the righteous before deciding to create the world[1085] *The Wisdom of Solomon*, in the Apocrypha, states: "As a child I was born to excellence, and a noble soul fell to my lot; or rather, I myself was noble; and I entered into an unblemished body." (Wisdom of Solomon 8:19-20 NEB) The *Midrash Kee Tov* says that all the souls of the righteous, including Adam, Noah, Abraham, Moses, etc. "were with God before the creation of the world."[1086] And an important Jewish theologian at about the time of Christ, Philo, taught that "the heavenly man is God's offspring while the earthly man is merely the work of an artificer."[1087]

Origen quoted a Jewish apocryphal document called the *Prayer of Joseph*, which asserted that Jacob was one of the archangels in his premortal existence:

> Thus Jacob says: "I, Jacob, who speak to you, arid Israel, I am an angel of God, a ruling spirit, and Abraham and Isaac were created before every work of God; and I am Jacob, called Jacob by men, but my name is Israel, called Israel by God, a man seeing God, because I am the first-born of every creature which God caused to live."[1088]

The Enoch texts also contain the common element of the pre-existence. (This is significant, since the early Christians apparently took at least one of these documents very seriously. Indeed, Jude referred to one of them in his general epistle. (See Jude 1:14) 2 *Enoch* states that, "all souls are prepared to eternity, before the formation of the world,"[1089] and cites Adam as the prime example:

> And I placed on the earth, a second angel, honorable, great and glorious, and I appointed him as ruler to rule on earth and to have my wisdom, and there was none like him of earth of all my existing creatures. I called his name Adam.[1090]

1 Enoch relates that before God created the world he held a consultation with the souls of the righteous.[1091]

Clearly the pre-existence of souls, and even their identification with the angels of God, was a commonplace in the soil of Apocalyptic Judaism from which Christianity sprang. But did the Jewish Christians continue this tradition? Certainly the pre-existence of Christ is explicitly taught in the New Testament (John 1:1; 1 Peter 1:19-20; Colossians 1:12-15), but what about the rest of us? Hammerton-Kelly writes that the pre-existence of the Church, at least, is everywhere presupposed in the New Testament.[1092] For instance, Paul wrote to Titus, "In hope of eternal life, which God, that cannot lie, promised before the world began." (Titus 1:2) Similarly, two of the earliest Jewish Christian writings, the *Shepherd of Hermas* and 2 *Clement* say the following about the Church. "She was created first of all and for her sake was the world made."[1093] "Moreover, the books and the Apostles declare that the Church belongs not to the present, but existed from the beginning."[1094] However, it must be remembered that some of the ancients believed the creation pre-existed in the mind of God, rather than as a number of distinct entities. Which concept formed the background of the New Testament anthropology? Commenting on Paul's doctrine of foreordination as expounded in Romans 8:28-30, Hammerton-Kelly explains that the Greek verb for "foreknow" used in the passage means "'to take note of', 'to fix regard upon' something, preliminary to selecting it for some special purpose." But when did this selection occur? "Most commentators believe that it took place in the eternal counsels of God, before the creation of the world."[1095] Thus, it is clear that, according to Paul, in the eternal counsels of God we existed as specific entities.

This belief continued within Jewish Christianity even after the Apostolic age. For instance, in the Jewish Christian *Clementine Recognitions* Peter states, "after all these things He made man, on whose account He had prepared all things, whose internal species is older, and for whose sake all things that are were made."[1096] Regarding the "internal species" of man mentioned here, the Presbyterian translators of this passage declare in the footnote: "That is, his soul, according to the doctrine of the pre-existence of souls." Even more striking, from a Latter-day Saint point of view, is Abraham's vision of the pre-existent host as reported in the Jewish Christian *Apocalypse of Abraham*, also called the *Book of Abraham* in some manuscripts. Compare the following to Abraham's vision of the pre-existent host in the Pearl of Great Price, Abraham 3.

> And everything I had planned to be came into being: it was already pre-figured in this, for all the things and all the people you have seen stood before me before they were created. And I said, Mighty and Eternal Ruler, who then are the people in this picture on this side and on that? And he said to me, Those on the left side are the many peoples which have existed in the past, and after you are appointed, some for judgment and restoration, some for vengeance and perdition, until the end of the age. And those on the right side of the picture, they are the people set apart for me from the people with Azazil [Satan]. These are the people who are going to spring from you and will be called my people.[1097]

The Deification of Man

At this point it should be clear that within both Jewish Christianity and Mormonism, men are thought to be more than some "rational animal", brought into existence out of nothing by God. Joseph Smith went on to teach that those who fully keep God's law will "be gods, because they have no end; therefore shall they be from everlasting to everlasting, because they continue; then shall they be above all, because all things are subject unto them." (D&C 132:20) For the Prophet, this went hand in hand with the doctrine of pre-existence. Humans are the same species as God, and hence have the potential to become like Him.

When we search for similar deification doctrines within early Christianity, we are deluged with examples. Within Gentile Christianity, we find numerous texts like the following from Justin Martyr (ca. 150 A.D.), who wrote that "all men are deemed worthy of becoming 'gods,' and of having power to become sons of the Highest."[1098] Hans Jonas writes that the ultimate object of the Gnostics was to obtain the knowledge of God, and become a partaker in the divine essence.[1099] One text states, "This is the good end of those who have attained gnosis: to become God."[1100] There is also considerable support for this doctrine in the New Testament. For example, John wrote, "Beloved, now are we the sons of God, and it doth not yet appear what we shall be: but we know that, when he shall appear, we shall be like him; for we shall see him as he is." (1 John 3:2.) And Jesus Christ told John that, "To him that overcometh will I grant to sit with me in my throne, even as I also overcame, and am set down with my Father in his throne." (Revelation 3:21) Also, "He that overcometh shall inherit all things; and I will be his God, and he shall be my son." (Revelation 21:7) Paul wrote to the Romans, "The Spirit itself beareth witness with our spirit, that we are the children of God: And if children, then heirs; heirs of God, and joint-heirs with Christ." (Romans 8:16-17) Such statements would not have been out of place in Apocalyptic Judaism, for in the Dead Sea Scrolls we find the appellations "*el*" and "*elohim*" applied to Melchizedek. "A godlike being has taken his place in the council of God; in the midst of the divine beings [*elohim*] he holds judgment."[1101] Similarly, the *War Scroll* says that God will "exalt the authority of Michael among the gods and the dominion of Israel among all flesh."[1102]

The question, therefore, is not *whether* the primitive Church believed men could become gods, but what that meant to them. The fourth century theologian Gregory of Nazianzus gave us an interpretive key: "I too might be made God so far as He is made Man."[1103] Within early Christianity there were any number of views about who Christ was in relation to the Father, and with respect to men. However, given the Hellenistic assumptions of the Gentile Christians, it was usually thought that men could become "gods" in a different sense than the Father, though not necessarily in a different sense than the Son. The idea was that there are two classes of beings – God, who is an eternal, unchangeable, simple, spiritual "essence", and everything else, which is created out of nothing. And those who are created out of nothing can only approach the status of the Eternal God, but never reach it.

We have already seen, however, that within the Jewish Christian milieu, the following precepts were taught: 1) the Father has a body in human form; 2) there is more than one Divine Being, though they are united in will under the monarchy of the "only true God", the Father; 3) creation out of pre-existent materials; 4) the pre-existence of the human soul, and the identification of human souls, the Son, and the Spirit with the angels of God. But are humans really "the offspring of God" (Acts 17:28), as Paul put it, in the sense that we are the same "species"? Christopher Stead writes, "In a Palestinian milieu it was still possible to picture the heavenly Father in human form and to see the contrast between heaven and earth as one of light and glory against relative darkness and indignity."[1104] Thus, among the Jews God was thought to be above every other being, but still fundamentally akin to mankind. This concept is brought out clearly in a fascinating passage in the Jewish

Christian *Clementine Homilies.*

> Learn this also: The bodies of men have immortal souls, which have been clothed with the breath of God; and having come forth from God, they are of the same substance, but they are not gods. But if they are gods, then in this way the souls of all men, both those who have died, and those who are alive, and those who shall come into being, are gods. But if in a spirit of controversy you maintain that these also are gods, what great matter is it, then, for Christ to be called God? for He has only what all have.[1105]

Several things should be noted about this passage. First, it is maintained that the Father is "the only true God". (John 17:3) All others, including Jesus, can be called gods in a subsidiary sense. Second, the "immortal souls" of men are said to "come forth from God" and are "of the same substance" as God. Prior to the fourth century, phrases such as "of one substance" or "of the same substance" implied a generic unity of species, meaning something like "made of the same kind of stuff".[1106] Finally, Jesus is said to have exactly the same kind of soul as the rest of humanity.

On the other hand, why is Jesus called God's "only begotten Son" in the New Testament (John 1:18; 3:16; 3:18; Hebrews 11:17; 1 John 4:9) if we are all the children of God? The answer lies in what was meant by the word "begotten". Within modern mainstream Christianity, it has been held that the Son was eternally generated, or "begotten", from the Father since before the beginning of time, hence there was never a time when the Father was not a Father, and the Son was not a Son. However, Jean Daniélou points out that Origen (early third century) was the first Catholic Christian to explicitly state a doctrine of eternal generation, although some Gnostics had expressed a similar view in the second century.[1107] Commenting on a passage from the writings of Ignatius of Antioch (ca. 110 A.D.), J.N.D. Kelly notes the following:

> His divine Sonship dates from the incarnation.... In tracing His divine Sonship to His conception in Mary's womb, he was simply reproducing a commonplace of pre-Origenist theology; the idea did not convey, and was not intended to convey, any denial of His pre-existence. So far as Ignatius is concerned, he definitely states that He "existed with the Father before the ages", and that He "came forth from the unique Father, was with Him and has returned to Him".[1108]

This is completely in harmony with the LDS teaching that all are the spiritual children of God, but Jesus is the only one begotten by God *in the flesh.* Given all this, it is also clear that in the early Jewish Christian milieu, deified men would have been considered subordinate to the Father, but not fundamentally different than Him in nature.

Eternal Marriage

In Latter-day Saint thought, deification is intimately related to marriage. That is, in order to obtain the highest degree of heaven and be deified, "a man must enter into this order of the priesthood [meaning the new and everlasting covenant of marriage]." (D&C 131:2) Men and women are deified together, and their marriage, performed in an LDS Temple, is an eternal covenant. (D&C 132:15-17) This principle is not clearly taught in the New Testament, but as we shall see, it is not incompatible with it. Consider the following account of a conversation Jesus had with some of his detractors:

> The same day came to him the Sadducees, which say that there is no resurrection, and asked him... Now there were with us seven brethren: and the first, when he had married a wife, deceased, and, having no issue, left his wife unto his brother: Likewise the second also, and the third, unto the seventh. And last of all the woman died also. Therefore in the resurrection whose wife shall she be of the seven? for they all had her. Jesus answered and said unto them, Ye do err, not knowing the scriptures, nor the power of God. For in the resurrection they neither marry, nor are given in marriage, but are as the angels of God in heaven. (Matthew 22:23-30)

At first glance, this passage seems to contradict the LDS doctrine, but several points can be made to show that this is not necessarily so. First, Latter-day Saints believe Jesus' answer was strictly true, since the apostate Sadducees said the seven brothers "were with us".

> If a man marry him a wife in the world, and he marry her not by me nor by my word, Öwhen they are out of the world they neither marry nor are given in marriage; but are appointed angels in heaven, which angels are ministering servants, to minister for those who are worthy of a far more, and an exceeding, and an eternal weight of glory. (D&C 132:15-16)

But why didn't Jesus, or at least the writers of the New Testament, explain the doctrine in its entirety? In fact, it was common practice within early Christianity and Judaism to preserve the highest and holiest doctrines for the ears of mature disciples.[1109] Jesus commanded, "Give not that which is holy unto the dogs, neither cast ye your pearls before swine, lest they trample them under their feet, and turn again and rend you." (Matthew 7:6) Paul told the Corinthians, who had been Christians for years, "I have fed you with milk, and not with meat: for hitherto ye were not able to bear it, neither yet now are ye able." (1 Corinthians 3:2) Peter explained the same principle to the apostate Simon Magus in the *Clementine Homilies*:

> And Peter said: "We remember that our Lord and Teacher, commanding us, said, 'Keep the mysteries for me and the sons of my house.' Wherefore also He explained to His disciples privately the mysteries of the kingdom of heaven. But to you who do battle with us, and examine into nothing else but our statements, whether they be true or false, it would be impious to state the hidden truths."[1110]

Robert M. Grant notes that, "In Ephesians 5:22-33 the prophecy of Genesis 2:24 {'the two shall become one flesh.'} is described as "a great mystery" and is referred not only to Christ and the church but also to Christian marriage in general."[1111] And Paul may have hinted at this mystery when he said, "Neither is the man without the woman, neither the woman without the man, in the Lord." (1 Corinthians 11:11) Thus, it seems doubtful that Jesus would have explained His doctrine of marriage in full to the Sadducees.

Second, we must ask what Jesus was referring to when he said, "Ye do err, not knowing the scriptures." Which scriptures? John Tvedtnes argues that Jesus was referring to a passage in the book of Tobit, in the Apocrypha.

> In the Apocrypha… we read of a young woman, Sarah, who had been married to seven husbands (all brothers), each of whom was killed on the wedding night by a demon. But in the story (*Tobit* 6:10-8:9), Sara ultimately marries an eighth husband, Tobias, son of Tobit, who, following instructions from the archangel Raphael, manages to chase the demon away and is therefore not slain. Of special interest is the fact that the archangel (who, according to *Tobit* 3:17, had been sent to arrange the marriage) tells the young man that his wife had been appointed to him "from the beginning" (*Tobit* 6:17). This implies that she had not been sealed to any of her earlier husbands, which would explain why none of them would claim her in the resurrection, as Jesus explained. But if she were sealed to Tobias, the situation changes. Assuming that the Sadducees (whose real issue was one of resurrection, not of eternal marriage) were alluding to this story but left off part of it, this would explain why Jesus told them, "Ye do err, *not knowing the scriptures*, nor the power of God" [1112]

Finally, many Jewish Christians *did* practice a form of celestial marriage, and this can be traced back to the first century. The Christian philosopher Origen complained in the third century about the Jewish Christians and others who believed in a literal millennial reign of Christ, and he added this:

> Certain persons are of the opinion that the fulfillment of the promises of the future are to be looked for in bodily pleasure and luxury. And consequently they say, that after the resurrection there will be marriages, and the begetting of children. Such are the views of those who, while believing in Christ, understand the divine Scriptures in a sort of Jewish sense, drawing from them nothing worthy of the divine promises. [1113]

Cardinal Daniélou infers a similar interpretation from an enigmatic passage in the *Didache*, a first-century Jewish Christian document, where prophets are mentioned as performing something called "the cosmic mystery of the Church".[1114] Daniélou links this mystery to the type of "spiritual marriages" some Gnostic groups practiced:

> The expression "cosmic mystery of the Church" seems to stand in opposition to a "heavenly mystery of the church". This heavenly mystery is the celestial marriage of Christ to the Church, which also finds its expression in this world. The allusion in this passage would therefore seem to be to those spiritual unions which existed in Jewish Christianity between prophet-apostles and a sister. . . The relation of these unions to their heavenly ideal is explicitly stated by the Gnostics: "Some of them prepare a nuptial couch and perform a sort of mystic rite (mystagogia) affirming that what is performed by them is a spiritual marriage after the likeness of the unions above" (Adv. haer. I, 21:3). [1115]

The Gnostic rite is described in the *Gospel of Philip* as being performed in "the mirrored bridal chamber",[1116] and "those who have united in the bridal chamber will no longer be separated."[1117] Stuart George Hall writes that Melito, Bishop of Sardis in the late second century, may have preserved a fragment of the ancient bridal chamber ceremony in his writings, as well.[1118]

Heavenly Mother

If men and women are deified together as husband and wife, the question naturally arises, "Does God the Father have a wife?" Latter-day Saints believe this to be the case, and it was also the case among the ancient

Israelites and Jewish Christians.

It is well known that the Israelites worshipped a goddess, from time to time, who was believed to be the consort of "Yahweh" or Jehovah. Theodore Robinson explains:

> From our Old Testament alone we should never have guessed that Israel associated a goddess with Yahweh, even popularly, but the conclusion is irresistible, and we are justified in assuming that she played her part in the mythology and ritual of Israel.[1119]

Widengren also reports that in Jeremiah's day a goddess called the "Queen of Heaven" received officially sanctioned worship in Jerusalem. He sees this as connected to the year-rites, in which a sacred marriage was performed for the god and goddess, who then gave birth to a Savior-King:

> In much later times there was a goddess called the Queen of Heaven(s), to whom official sacrifices were offered by kings and princes, both in Jerusalem and in other cities of Judah, [Jer. 44:17]Ö. That the sacred marriage should bring as its fruit the birth of the Savior-King is in accordance with the general myth and ritual pattern.[1120]

The worship of the Queen of Heaven was forbidden by Jeremiah, but this also is consistent with LDS practice, since Mother-worship is not permitted for Mormons, either.[1121]

All of this is consistent with the creation account in Genesis. "And God said, Let us make man in our image, after our likeness. So God created man in his image, in the image of God created he him; male and female created he them." (Genesis 1:26-27) Given the fact that the Israelites and the earliest Christians believed in an anthropomorphic God, it is significant that God said "Let *us* make man in *our* image," and that the image of God is defined as "male and female".

Origen quoted a lost Jewish Christian *Gospel According to the Hebrews*, where the Savior Himself says, "My mother, the Holy Spirit took me just now by one of my hairs and carried me off to the great mount Tabor,"[1122] Melito of Sardis (late second century), who was not a Jewish Christian, but believed the Jewish Christian doctrine of an anthropomorphic deity, preserves this fragment, which may have come from the liturgy of the bridal chamber ritual. "Hymn the Father, you holy ones; sing to your Mother, virgins." [1123] In many Gnostic documents, as well, there is a Trinity of Father, Mother, and Son. For instance, the *Secret Book of John* speaks of "the three: the Father, the Mother, and the Son, the perfect power."[1124]

Certainly there are differences in detail here with the LDS belief, but it is perfectly clear that a Heavenly Mother played a role in ancient Israelite and Jewish Christian thought.

God as a Deified Man

At the end of his prophetic career, Joseph Smith revealed one final point that sheds brilliant light on all the other doctrines we have examined here. Namely, "God himself was once as we are now, and is an exalted man, and sits enthroned in yonder heavens!"[1125] Unfortunately, the above quotation summarizes essentially all we know about this truth. We do not necessarily expect this doctrine to have been known among the ancient Christians, since Joseph Smith taught that "things that have not been before revealed" would be known in this dispensation. (D&C 124:41) This marvelous key lies at the pinnacle of the Prophet's teaching, and at the very outskirts of our knowledge about God. Two questions must be answered in this context, however. That is, does the doctrine contradict previously revealed scripture, and did anyone hold such a view among the ancient Jewish Christians?

Our detractors constantly point out Bible verses concerning God's unchanging and eternal nature to show that the scriptures do contradict the Prophets teachings. Even the *Book of Mormon* states, "I know that God is not a partial God, neither a changeable being; but he is unchangeable from all eternity to all eternity." (Moroni 8:18) However, it can easily be shown that the LDS interpretation of the scriptures is in harmony with the mindset of the ancient Hebrews, while mainstream Christians apply Hellenistic assumptions to the text.

The ancient Greeks were absolutely enamored with metaphysics-with "being," "essence," "eternity," etc. The Greek philosophers pondered incessantly about how the material world relates to the true reality, whereas for the Hebrews the material world *was* reality. When they wrote about God, they didn't obsess about his "being" or "essence," but rather focused on His relationship to men and the world. Likewise, when they spoke of God's nature and eternity, they used *relative* terms — relative, that is, *to them*. For example, many of the Biblical passages which speak of God's immutability do so in terms of His honesty, justice, mercy, and constancy. (See Titus 1:2; Numbers 23:19; 1 Samuel 15:29; Hebrews 6:18; Genesis 18:25; Ezekiel 18:14-32; Isaiah 46:10-11; Mark 13:31; Matt. 24:35; Luke 1:20; James 1:17; Daniel 6:26: Hebrews 6:18-19) Christopher Stead explains, "The Old Testament writers sometimes speak of God as unchanging. In Christian writers influenced by Greek philosophy this doctrine is developed in an absolute metaphysical sense. Hebrew writers are more concrete, and their thinking includes two main points: (1) God has the dignity appropriate to old age, but without its disabilities; and (2) God is faithful to his covenant promises, even though men break theirs."[1126] (Cf. Isaiah 40:28; Exodus 34:9-10) When God is described as "From everlasting to everlasting" (Psalm 41:13 NEB), the word translated as "everlasting" is the Hebrew *olam*, which means "(practically) eternity" or "time out of mind."[1127] Another Psalm (104:5 NASB) says that God "established the earth upon its foundations, so that it will not totter forever and ever." And yet Isaiah (24:20 NEB) saw a future time when "the earth reels to and fro like a drunken man." To the Hebrew mind these passages were not contradictory, because terms like "everlasting" and "forever" were relative terms, and they had no conception of "eternity" and "infinity" as modern people see them.

So it is with the Latter-day Saints. We see such scriptural statements about the "everlasting" and "unchanging" God as an indication of God's perfect and unchanging moral character, as well as God's eternity *relative* to men. God is spoken of as the "only true God," because *in relation to us* this is perfectly true. Given this Hebrew mindset, it is easy to see how Latter-day Saints can accept the biblical statements about God and also believe that God was once a man, having a Father Himself. And as it turns out, some early Christians may have believed the same type of doctrine. Consider the reasoning of Irenaeus of Lyons (ca. 180 A.D.) while arguing against the Gnostic belief that the Creator was only a secondary God.[1128] Irenaeus pounded home the fact that the true God *is* the Creator, but what about the possibility that there is a God above God? And what was God doing before the creation of the world? Irenaeus cited Matthew 24:36, where Christ indicates that only the Father knows the time of the Second Coming, and asserted that since even Jesus doesn't know everything, we ought to leave such unrevealed questions to God.

> If, for instance, any one asks, "What was God doing before He made the world?" we reply that the answer to such a question lies with God Himself. For that this world was formed perfect by God, receiving a beginning in time, the Scriptures teach us; but no Scripture reveals to us what God was employed about before this event. The Father, therefore, has been declared by our Lord to excel with respect to knowledge; for this reason, that we, too, as long as we are connected with the scheme of things in this world, should leave perfect knowledge, and such questions [as have been mentioned], to God, and should not by any chance, while we seek to investigate the sublime nature of the Father, fall into the danger of starting the question whether there is another God above God.

Certainly Irenaeus, as a Gentile Christian with a philosophical viewpoint, believed no such thing. Irenaeus was not shy at all about labeling the Gnostic heresies as damnable and ridiculous falsehoods, yet in this case his language was strangely subdued. It is not clear whether this particular doctrine had been revealed to the early Christians, but certainly the Hebrew conception of God had not died out in all quarters of the Church, and in this mindset these "speculations" could be seen as a distinct possibility. There were some

Christians – probably Jewish Christians — who were "speculating" about these things, or Irenaeus would have said things differently.

Conclusions

In the preface to his book, *On First Principles*, the early Christian theologian Origen listed several questions for which he said there was no uniform answer in the Church of his time. These included the origin of the Holy Spirit, the origin of the soul and of angels, what existed before the creation of the world and what will exist after, whether God has a body, and some others also of interest to Latter-day Saints. Robert M. Grant comments on Origen's list, "If one takes all these questions together, it is obvious that they are concerned with the basic question as to what kind of philosophical-theological framework is to be provided for the apostolic preaching."[1129] It should be clear from the information presented here that one of the competing philosophical frameworks was very similar to that taught by the Prophet Joseph Smith.

What are we to make of this fact? Detractors often point to various disparate sources contemporary with Joseph Smith as the inspiration for this or that doctrine. But wherever he got his ideas, Joseph Smith put them together in a coherent and complete system, which can be found almost in its entirety within ancient Jewish Christianity. Finally, he went beyond what we now find in the ancient documents with striking insight and clarity. How did he accomplish this amazing feat at a time when very little was known about the Jewish origins of the Church? Personally, I can think of no other reasonable explanation than the one Joseph Smith gave, and to which the Holy Spirit testifies. The Church of Jesus Christ of Latter-day Saints is a divinely ordained Restoration of the ancient Apostolic Church.

Chapter 8: Conclusions

"Where is your wise man now, your man of learning or your subtle debater --
limited, all of them, to this passing age? God has made the wisdom of this
world look foolish."
- 1 Corinthians 1:20-21 NEB

The great historian of Christianity, Adolf von Harnack, assessed the
state of modern Christianity in the following way:

> There are only two possibilities here: either the Gospel is in
> all respects identical with its earliest form, in which case it
> came with its time and has departed with it; or else it
> contains something which, under differing historical forms,
> is of permanent validity.[1130]

Notice that Harnack takes for granted the fact that the "primitive" Church has
come and gone, because modern mainstream Christianity is demonstrably far
different from it. Latter-day Saints believe that much of the New Testament
church with its basic doctrines and ordinances forms the fabric of most modern
Christian churches, but they also hold that "many plain and precious" things
have been lost or changed over the two centuries since Christ was crucified
and the church fell into apostasy. Latter-day Saints claim that those lost or
altered elements were restored by God in these latter days through the Prophet
Joseph Smith.

Since he claimed to restore ancient Christian truths at a time when not
much was known about that era, we have tested his claim by showing that
these restored doctrines and practices were for the most part indeed present in
early Christianity. If Joseph Smith taught a number of esoteric doctrines that
were unknown to have existed in the early church during his time but which
research and uncovered documents now show were part of early Christianity,
one has to conclude that he was either inspired or impossibly lucky.

In other words, the Church which Joseph Smith claims to have
restored is much closer to the original church of Christ, as revealed in the
many documents of the first three centuries after Christ, than any other modern
Christian church. Had Joseph Smith created a church which differed from the
other churches of his day and which had no relation to what we now know of
the primitive church, his claim to be a restorer would be blatantly fraudulent,
but since support for his teachings and ideas is so abundant from early
documents, not in a general way, but in numerous specifics, one has to
conclude that there was some source other than his own imagination for these
striking parallels.

Appendix: Descriptions of Ancient Documents and Writers

Descriptions of various early Christian and Jewish writers and documents are provided in this appendix. Document titles are given in italics.

The Acts of Paul was written around A.D. 185-195 by a presbyter in Asia Minor, according to Tertullian. The writer was apparently expelled from the Church for his work, although it contains nothing that would have been considered overtly heretical, except one passage where a female heroine, Thecla, baptized herself.[1131]

The Apocalypse of Abraham was probably written in the first century A.D., and is most likely of Jewish origin, although there may have been some Christian interpolations in the text. This document has been preserved only in the Slavonic language, and was first published 1863. It is an account of some events in the patriarch Abraham's life, including various revelations.[1132]

Apolinarius of Hierapolis was a bishop in that city sometime during the reign of the emperor Marcus Aurelius (A.D. 161-180). His writings have been lost, but fragments are preserved by such writers as Eusebius.[1133]

The Apostolic Constitutions are a fourth century compilation of the teachings and practices of the Christian Church. However, the material included in the work is of varying age and some of it may be based on documents, such as the *Didache,* going back to the first century.[1134]

Arians: see "Arius."

Aristides (early to mid-second century) wrote the earliest preserved Christian apology, which was addressed to the Roman Emperor. Nothing further is known about him.[1135]

Arius was a presbyter (elder) at the Church in Alexandria ca. A.D. 320. His opposition to Bishop Alexander on the doctrine of the Trinity was the spark that ignited the doctrinal controversy which ultimately led to the Council of Nicea in A.D. 325 and 13 subsequent councils culminating with the Council of Constantinople of A.D. 381. Arius downplayed the divinity of the Son and insisted Jesus was merely a created being. Followers of this doctrine were called "Arians."[1136]

The Ascension of Isaiah is a work of early Christian Apocrypha, probably written in the first and second centuries A.D. The first section, which deals with the martyrdom of Isaiah, is probably of Jewish origin and was written at least as early as the first century. The second section deals with Isaiah's vision and journey into the heavens. This probably had its origin in second century Christianity.[1137]

Athanasius (ca. A.D. 300-373) was bishop of Alexandria from A.D. 328 to 373. He led the fight against the Arians at the Council of Nicea (A.D. 325) while a deacon under bishop Alexander. Active in this controversy till the end of his life, Athanasius, was exiled and readmitted as bishop several times during his career as the political winds changed in favor of either the Arians or Nicenes.[1138]

Athenagoras (ca. A.D. 177) was an Athenian philosopher who converted to Christianity. His only surviving works are a defense of Christianity which was presented to the Roman Emperor, and a treatise on the Christian doctrine of the resurrection.[1139]

Augustine (A.D. 354-430) was bishop of Hippo in North Africa. Although his mother was a Christian, he did not convert until he was over thirty. One of the most prolific writers of early Christian, Augustine was also one of its most important theologians.[1140] His life's work was essentially to put Christian theology on what he saw as the solid foundation of Platonic philosophy.

Barnabas (first or early second century) is an early epistle by an unknown author attacking Judaism. It has been attributed by many to Barnabas, the companion of Paul, but others doubt this.[1141]

Basil of Caesarea (A.D. 330-379) was bishop of that see starting in A.D. 360 and is considered a most important theologian, especially in the Eastern Orthodox Churches.[1142]

Book of the Secrets of Enoch: see "Enoch Literature."

Cerinthians: The followers of Cerinthus (first half of the second century), who was a Jewish-Christian Gnostic, characterized as a "pseudo-Apostle" by Epiphanius. This sect flourished in Asia Minor.[1143]

The Christian Sibyllines are a work of Christian Apocrypha dating from the middle of the second century A.D. Parts of the text may have had their origin at a later time. "Sibyls" in Greek legend were women who prophesied in a state of ecstasy.[1144]

1 Clement: see "Clement of Rome."

2 Clement, the oldest complete Christian sermon now extant, was written around A.D. 150. Although the author is unknown (and it certainly was not Clement of Rome), this document came to be associated with *1 Clement* by the fourth century.[1145]

Clementine Homilies: see "*Pseudo-Clementines*."

Clementine Recognitions: see " *Pseudo-Clementines*."

Clement of Alexandria (A.D. 160-215) headed the official Christian catechetical school in Alexandria. One of his pupils was, apparently, Origen. Heavily influenced by Greek philosophical speculations, Clement tried to present the gospel in a manner that would be acceptable to the Greek mind. His work had a significant impact on later theologians.[1146]

Clement of Rome was the bishop of Rome from about A.D. 88-97. He reportedly knew Peter and had significant influence even outside his own see. His letter, known as *1 Clement*, was written to exhort the Corinthian saints to resist certain factions which had arisen in opposition to the leadership of the Corinthian Church. A plausible date for its composition is ca. A.D. 96.[1147]

Cyprian (ca. A.D. 200-258) was elected bishop of Carthage in A.D. 248 or 249. He was involved in various schisms which afflicted the Christianity of his day, persuading the various factions to preserve unity.[1148]

Cyril of Jerusalem (d. A.D. 387) was bishop of Jerusalem from about A.D. 349 till his death. His beliefs are known to us from his *Catechetical Lectures*, which were designed to explain the faith to catechumens (those who were studying to join the Church) and to explain the sacraments (mysteries) of baptism and the Eucharist to those who had just participated in them for the first time.[1149]

The Didache dates from somewhere between A.D. 70 and the early second century, and was probably written in Syria or Egypt. Its full title translates as "The Teaching of the Lord Through the Twelve Apostles to the Nations." Its contents include moral teaching and instructions on various aspects of Church practice.[1150]

Dionysius of Corinth (A.D. 110-180) was bishop of that city, and wrote several important letters to various other churches. Fragments of some of these letters have been preserved by Eusebius.[1151]

1 Enoch: see "Enoch Literature."

2 Enoch: see "Enoch Literature."

Enoch Literature: Manuscripts of a body of literature based on the life and revelations of the biblical prophet Enoch have lately come to light, revealing that he was a favorite hero in Jewish apocalyptic literature. It has also become clear that many early Christian documents, including those in the New Testament, relied heavily on the language and teachings of these texts. The most well-known examples of this genre are *1 Enoch* and *2 Enoch (Secrets of Enoch)*; both documents are thought to have been written in the first two centuries before Christ. *1 Enoch* in particular was very respected in the early Church. Not only did Jude quote from it in the New Testament, but it was considered canonical by many early Christians, including the author of *Barnabas*, Clement of Alexandria, Irenaeus, and Tertullian.[1152]

Epiphanius (ca. A.D. 315-403) was bishop of Salamis in Cyprus. In his *Panarion* he attempted to refute every heresy known to him.[1153]

The Epistle of the Apostles is an apocryphal work dating from about 150 A.D. The beginning is worded as a letter, but the overall form of the work is that of a post-resurrection dialogue between Jesus and his Apostles. This was a literary form used extensively in Gnostic writings, but apparently the author of this work used it as a vehicle to propagate strongly anti-Gnostic views. For example, the work argues for the full humanity of Christ, the resurrection of the flesh, and the necessity of literal water baptism.[1154]

Epistula Apostolorum: see *"The Epistle of the Apostles."*

Eusebius (ca. A.D. 260-339) was bishop of Caesarea. His most famous work was his *Ecclesiastical History*, and indeed, he was the first major historian of Christianity. Many fragments of early writings that are otherwise lost can be found in Eusebius's writings.[1155]

The Gospel of Bartholomew is an apocryphal document from the third century which describes Jesus' crucifixion and descent into Hades.[1156]

The Gospel of Philip is a collection of statements concerning ordinances and ethics. It probably originated with the Valentinian Gnostics in third century A.D. Syria, and was most likely used to prepare investigators for initiation rites.[1157]

The Gospel of Thomas is a collection of sayings of Jesus which many scholars feel is closely related to the hypothetical source of the gospel narratives in the New Testament. Many of the parables and sayings of Jesus found in the Gospels appear in the Gospel of Thomas, as well, but in an apparently more primitive form. It was probably written in the second half of the first century A.D., but the version available today may not be original. Clearly some Gnostic influence has been exerted on the text, but the extent of this influence is not clear.[1158]

Gregory of Nazianzus (ca. A.D. 329-390) was bishop of Constantinople. His father actually forced ordination on him and he never really enjoyed his ecclesiastical duties, but Gregory was an able theologian and orator. He was instrumental, along with Hilary, Basil, and Gregory of Nyssa, in ironing out the final Trinitarian position and related issues.[1159]

Gregory of Nyssa (ca. A.D. 331-395) was bishop of that city from 372 until his death. An extremely influential theologian, he was heavily involved in the fight against extreme forms of Arianism. He was very acquainted with the Greek philosophy of the day, especially Middle Platonism and Neoplatonism, and he put this education to use in his theological speculations. His major theological accomplishment was to elaborate on the concept of the fundamental distinction between God and created beings and to exclude from mainstream Christian belief any concept of subordinationism. His brother, Basil of Caesarea, was also a noted theologian.[1160]

Gregory Thaumaturgus (ca. A.D. 210-260), known as the "wonder worker," was bishop of Neocaesarea. He studied under Origen at the catechetical school at Alexandria.[1161]

Hegesippus (ca. 110-180]) was an early Christian Greek author who was mainly concerned with Apostolic succession and the origin of heresies. Fragments of his work are preserved by Eusebius.[1162]

Hermas lived in Rome and was the author of the document known as the *Shepherd of Hermas* or the *Pastor of Hermas*. Written in stages between A.D. 90 and 150, this work is a chronicle of a series of visions given to Hermas in which an angel sometimes appeared as a shepherd. This document was extremely important in the early Church and was even considered canonical by many Christians for centuries after its composition.[1163]

Hippolytus (ca. A.D. 170-236) was a presbyter (elder) at Rome and an important theologian. In consequence of a theological dispute with the bishop of Rome, he became the bishop of a rival, schismatic community. In A.D. 235 the emperor exiled both Hippolytus and his rival bishop and later had them put to death. Apparently he and the other bishop were reconciled before their martyrdom.

Ignatius of Antioch (d. ca. A.D. 110) was bishop of that city and a martyr. He was arrested during the reign of Trajan, and on the way to Rome for judgment he wrote seven letters -- six to various churches and one to Polycarp, bishop of Smyrna. One of the main purposes of many of these letters seems to have been to establish the authority of the bishops.[1164]

Irenaeus **of Lyons** (ca. A.D. 115-202), the first great Catholic theologian, was bishop of Lyons and a student of Polycarp. Irenaeus's major concern was to stop the spread of gnosticism in Christianity, and this is the theme of his most famous work, *Against all Heresies.*[1165]

Jeu, Two Books of: This Gnostic work was probably composed in Egypt around the beginning of the third century. It is supposedly a record of some conversations of Jesus with His disciples and some women after his resurrection. The Coptic manuscript was discovered in 1769, and was published in 1891.[1166]

John Chrysostom (ca. A.D. 347-407) was bishop of Constantinople from 398 to shortly before his death. "Chrysostom," meaning "golden-mouthed," refers to John's extraordinary preaching ability. He was known as the greatest preacher in early Christianity. His writings were very popular, especially in the East, and hundreds of manuscript copies have been preserved. John took some uncompromising moral stances, and even criticized the empress for the opulent life of the court. He overstepped his authority, however, when he deposed several bishops who were not under his jurisdiction for selling church offices and embezzling church money. This gave his enemy, Theophilus, bishop of Alexandria, an opening to hold a synod and depose John on the basis of a series of trumped up charges. He lived out his final few years in exile.[1167]

Justin Martyr (d. ca. A.D. 163) was a most important apologist for the early Church. Educated in philosophy, he was converted to Christianity and wrote several tracts calculated to win favor for the Christian cause. He established a school in Rome, where he continued to wear his philosopher's cloak. Tatian was one of his students. Justin was condemned, scourged, and beheaded by the Romans when he would not deny his faith and sacrifice to the pagan gods.[1168]

Lactantius (ca. A.D. 250-325) was a Christian apologist from North Africa. Lactantius was more of a rhetorician than a theologian, and his works were more calculated to persuade than inform.[1169]

Marcionites were followers of Marcion (d. ca. A.D. 154), who was a Gnostic heretic expelled from the church at Rome. Marcion believed that the Gods of the Old and New Testaments were separate and only the New Testament deity was worthy to be called God. This sect was extremely successful and survived at least into the late fourth century.[1170]

Melito (ca. A.D. 170) was bishop of Sardis. He was one of the most voluminous writers of the second century, but only fragments of his works survive.[1171]

Methodius (d. ca. A.D. 311) was bishop of Olympus and an opponent of Origen's theology. Only fragments of his writings are now available.[1172]

Montanism was an ecstatic Christian prophetic movement (in some ways comparable to today's Pentecostals) which flourished in Asia Minor from the late second century until the fourth century. This sect was named after its founder and first prophet, Montanus (ca. A.D. 170), who supposedly received revelation while in an unconscious ecstasy. He was joined by two prophetesses, Priscilla and Maximilla. They were fairly mainstream in their theology, but differed from other Christians in asserting that a prophet is not in control of his faculties when he prophesies. The first councils of the Church, in the late second century, were called in order to excommunicate the Montanists. The most famous convert to this movement was Tertullian.[1173] R.M. Grant comments: "Suffice it to say that it was by no means a return to primitive Christianity."[1174]

Montanus: see "Montanism."

Novatian (mid-third century) was a presbyter in Rome who led a schism because he believed the holiness of the Church was threatened by the readmission of apostates. He was ordained counter-bishop by three other Italian bishops. He had a formidable reputation as a theologian, and his treatise on the Trinity is considered the greatest Christian theological treatise from the West before 350.[1175]

The Odes of Solomon are a collection of beautiful songs or poems dedicated to Christ, which, paradoxically, never mention the name of Christ. One of the most plausible explanations of their origin is that they were written by newly baptized Christians in the first century.[1176]

Origen (ca. A.D. 185-251) was one of the most important theologians of the early Church, and produced some 2000 works, including commentaries on almost every book in the Bible. He was born of Christian parents in Alexandria. He eventually succeeded Clement as the head of the catechetical school there. Origen was an incurable speculator at a time when orthodoxy was not strictly defined, and later councils judged some of his doctrines heretical.[1177] On the other hand, Hatch calls Origen's *De Principiis* ("On First Principles") the first complete system of dogma in Christianity, and recommends the study of it because "of the strange fact that the features of it which are in strongest contrast to later dogmatics are in fact its most archaic and conservative elements."[1178]

The Pastor of Hermas: see "Hermas."

Papias (ca. A.D. 70-155), bishop of Hierapolis, wrote a series of five books about the gospel, of which only fragments have been preserved. He made a special effort to collect items of doctrine preserved orally by those who had actually heard the Apostles speak.[1179]

The Pistis Sophia is a group of Gnostic documents composed at various times during the third century in Egypt. Included in this work is a supposed conversation between Jesus and His disciples after His resurrection.

Polycarp (d. ca. A.D. 156) was bishop of Smyrna. Irenaeus claimed that he had been appointed to that post by the Apostles themselves, and was taught by the Apostle John. Polycarp apparently wrote several letters to neighboring congregations, but only his letter to the Philippian saints remains. An early account of his martyrdom is also preserved, which describes various miracles accompanying that event.[1180]

Pseudo-Clementines: These documents, whose main constituents are the *Clementine Homilies* and the *Clementine Recognitions*, are pseudonymously attributed to Clement of Rome, and are in the form of biographical novels. In their present form, these works had their origin in fourth century Syria, but probably they were derived from a common second century source, and are quite valuable as a window into second-century Christian life and thought. Indeed, R.M. Grant calls the *Recognitions* "a favourite piece of 'Sunday afternoon literature'" of the second century.[1181] They describe various travels of Clement, his conversion, and conversations with Peter the Apostle. They were originally written in Greek, but the only extant version of the *Recognitions* is a Latin translation by Rufinus, who apparently made some "corrections" to the text. These documents, however, contain considerable conservative and Jewish elements, and many scholars consider them to be a product of a widespread branch of Jewish-Christianity of which we have no other witness.[1182]

Rufinus of Aquileia (ca. A.D. 345-410) was a monk who translated many earlier Christian documents into Latin, and also defended the doctrines of Origen against detractors. Many of Origen's writings survive only in Rufinus's translations, which is unfortunate, since Rufinus felt that certain "unorthodox" doctrines Origen preached were later insertions, so he felt free to delete them in his translations.[1183]

Secrets of Enoch: see "Enoch Literature."

The Shepherd of Hermas: see "Hermas."

Tatian (mid-second century) was born a pagan and lived the life of a wandering Sophist before he was converted to Christianity about A.D. 150. He was a student of Justin, but later left the Catholic church to found a Gnostic group called the Encratites.

Tertullian (ca. A.D. 155-225) was born to heathen parents in Carthage, and was trained to become a lawyer. When he became a Christian, he used his training to write tracts in defense of the Church. Tertullian was an ordained presbyter (elder), but eventually defected to the Montanist camp and wrote several bitter attacks against the Catholics.[1184]

The Testament of Job is a work of Jewish apocrypha most likely dating from the first century A.D.; however, its original form may have been older. It contains an account of the discourse the biblical figure Job gave to his children just before he died.[1185]

Theophilus of Antioch (second century) was bishop of Antioch about A.D. 180. Versed in Greek philosophy and rhetoric, he used his skills to defend Christianity and attack idolatry, in particular, emperor worship.[1186]

Key to Abbreviations

ACW: Quasten, Johannes, and J.C. Plumpe, eds. *Ancient Christian Writers: The Works of the Fathers in Translation.* Washington, D.C.: The Catholic University of America.

ANF: Roberts, Alexander, and James Donaldson, eds. *The Ante-Nicene Fathers*, 10 vols. Buffalo: The Christian Literature Publishing Company, 1885-1896.

ANT: James, Montague R. *The Apocryphal New Testament.* Oxford: Clarendon Press, 1983.

ECD: Kelly, J.N.D. *Early Christian Doctrines*, Revised ed. San Francisco: Harper Collins, 1978.

EEC: Ferguson, E. Encyclopedia *of Early Christianity*, 2nd ed. New York: Garland Publishing, 1997.

FC: *The Fathers of the Church: A New Translation.* Washington D.C.: The Catholic University of America Press.

JD: Watt, J., ed. *Journal of Discourses*, 26 vols. Liverpool: 1854-1886.

NEB: *The New English Bible With the Apocrypha.* Oxford: Oxford University Press, 1970.

NPNF Series 1: Schaff, Philip., ed. *The Nicene and Post-Nicene Fathers*, Series 1, 14 vols. New York: The Christian Literature Publishing Company, 1886-1890.

NPNF Series 2: Schaff, Philip., and Henry Wace, eds. *The Nicene and Post-Nicene Fathers*, Series 2, 14 vols. New York: The Christian Literature Publishing Company, 1890-1900.

NTA: Schneemelcher, Wilhelm, ed. *New Testament Apocrypha*, 2 vols. Translated by A.J.B. Higgins and others. Philadelphia: The Westminster Press, 1963.

TOB: Barnstone, Willis, ed. *The Other Bible.* San Francisco: Harper & Row, 1984.

TPJS: Smith, Joseph Fielding, ed. *Teachings of the Prophet Joseph Smith,* Salt Lake City: Deseret Book, 1976.

Selected Bibliography

Amidon, Philip. R., tr. *The Panarion of St. Epiphanius, Bishop of Salamis*. New York: Oxford University Press, 1990.

Amis, Robin. *A Different Christianity: Early Christian Esotericism and Modern Thought*. Albany: State University of New York Press, 1995.

Angus, Samuel. *The Mystery-Religions*. New York: Dover Publications, 1975.

Arnold, Eberhard. *The Early Christians After the Death of the Apostles*. Rifton, NY: Plough Publishing House, 1970.

Backman, E. Louis. *Religious Dances in the Christian Church and in Popular Medicine*. Westport, CT: Greenwood Press, 1977.

Barclay, John, and John Sweet, eds. *Early Christian Thought in its Jewish Context*. Cambridge: Cambridge University Press, 1996.

Barker, James L. *The Divine Church*, 3 vols. Salt Lake City: Deseret News Press, 1951.

Barker, Margaret. *The Great Angel: A Study of Israel's Second God*. Louisville, KY: Westminster/John Knox Press, 1992.

Barnstone, Willis, ed. *The Other Bible*. San Francisco: Harper & Row, 1984.

Beisner, E. Calvin. *God in Three Persons*. Illinois: Tyndale House Publishers, 1978.

Bercot, David W. *Will the Real Heretics Please Stand Up: A New Look at Today's Evangelical Church in the Light of Early Christianity*. Henderson, TX: Scroll Publishing Co., 1989.

_____. *Common Sense: A New Approach to Understanding Scripture*. Tyler, TX: Scroll Publishing Co., 1992.

_____. *What the Early Christians Believed*, audio tape set. Tyler, TX: Scroll Publishing Co., 1994.

Bettenson, Henry. *The Early Christian Fathers*. London: Oxford University Press, 1956.

_____. *The Later Christian Fathers*. London: Oxford University Press, 1970.

Blumenthal, H.J., and Robert A. Markus, eds. *Neoplatonism and Early Christian Thought*. London: Variorum Publications Ltd., 1981.

Bowman, Robert M., Jr. "'Ye Are Gods?' Orthodox and Heretical Views on the Deification of Man." *Christian Research Journal* (Winter/Spring 1987): 18ff.

Brantl, George. *Catholicism*. New York: George Braziller, 1962.

Brough, R. Clayton. *Teachings of the Prophets*. Bountiful, UT: Horizon Publishers, 1993.

Buckley, J.J. "A Cult Mystery in the Gospel of Philip." *Journal of Biblical Literature* 99 (1980): 569-581.

Budge, E.A. Wallace. *Coptic Homilies*. London, Longmans and Co., 1910.

_____. *Coptic Apocrypha*. London: Longmans and Co., 1913.

Campbell, Joseph, ed. *The Mysteries*, Princeton, NJ: Princeton University Press, 1955.

Cartwright, Richard. *Philosophical Essays*. Cambridge, MA: The MIT Press, 1987.

Chadwick, Henry. *Early Christian Thought and the Classical Tradition*. New York: Oxford University Press, 1966.

Charlesworth, James H., ed. *The Old Testament Pseudepigrapha*, 2 vols. New York: Doubleday, 1983.

Clark, Elizabeth A. *The Origenist Controversy: The Cultural Construction of an Early Christian Debate*. Princeton, NJ: Princeton University Press, 1992.

Clement of Alexandria, *Stromateis* 1-3, FC 85. Translated by J. Ferguson. Washington, D.C.: The Catholic University of America Press, 1991.

Cohn, Norman, *Cosmos, Chaos and the World to Come*. New Haven: Yale University Press, 1993.

Colson, F.H., and G.H. Whitaker, tr. *Philo*, 10 vols. and 3 supplementary vols. Cambridge, MA: Harvard University Press, 1934.

Crowther, Duane S. *Life Everlasting*. Salt Lake City: Bookcraft, 1967.

Cullman, Oscar. *The Christology of the New Testament*. Translated by Shirley C. Guthrie, and Charles A.M. Hall. Philadelphia, 1959.

Cyril of Alexandria. *Letters* 1-50, FC 76. Translated by John I. McEnerney. Washington D.C.: The Catholic University of America Press, 1987.

Cyril of Jerusalem. *The Works of Saint Cyril of Jerusalem*, vol. 2. FC 64. Translated by Leo P. McCauley, and Anthony A. Stephenson. Washington, D.C.: The Catholic University of America Press, 1970.

Daniélou, Jean. *The Lord of History: Reflections on the Inner Meaning of History*. Translated by N. Abercrombie. Chicago: Henry Regnery, 1958.

_____. *The Theology of Jewish Christianity*. Translated by John A. Baker. Philadelphia: The Westminster Press, 1964.

_____. *Gospel Message and Hellenistic Culture*. Translated by John A. Baker. Philadelphia: The Westminster Press, 1973.

Davies, John G. *The Early Christian Church*. New York: Anchor Books, 1965.

Decker, Ed, and Dave Hunt. *The God Makers*. Eugene, OR: Harvest House Publishers, 1984.

DeMaris, R.E. "Corinthian Religion and Baptism for the Dead (1 Corinthians 15:29): Insights from Archaeology and Anthropology." *Journal of Biblical Literature* 114 (1995): 661-682.

Doresse, Jean. *The Secret Books of the Egyptian Gnostics*. London: Hollis and Carter, 1960,

Draper, Richard D. *Opening the Seven Seals: The Visions of John the Revelator*. Salt Lake City: Deseret Book, 1991.

Drower, E.S. *The Secret Adam*. London: Oxford University Press, 1960.

Dudley, Martin, and Geoffrey Rowell, eds. *The Oil of Gladness: Anointing in the Christian Tradition.* London: SPCK, 1993.

Dunn, James D.G. *The Partings of the Ways: Between Christianity and Judaism and their Significance for the Character of Christianity.* London: SCM Press, 1991.

Ehrman, Bart D. *The Orthodox Corruption of Scripture: The Effect of Early Christological Controversies on the Text of the New Testament.* New York: Oxford University Press, 1993.

Eissfeldt, Otto. "El and Yahweh." *Journal of Semitic Studies* 1 (1956): 25-30.

Eliade, Mircea., and Ioan P. Couliano. *The Eliade Guide to World Religions.* San Francisco: Harper Collins, 1991.

Elliot, J.H. *The Elect and the Holy: An Exegetical Examination of I Peter 2:4-10 and the Phrase "Basileion hierateuma".* Leiden: E.J. Brill, 1966.

Eusebius. *The History of the Church from Christ to Constantine.* Translated by G.A. Williamson. New York: Penguin Books, 1965.

_____. *Preparation for the Gospel.* Translated by E.H. Gifford. Oxford: The Clarendon Press, 1903.

_____. *The Proof of the Gospel,* 2 vols. Translated by W.J. Ferrar. New York: The Macmillan Company, 1920.

Fergusen, Everett, ed. *Encyclopedia of Early Christianity,* New York: Garland Publishing, 1990.

Fergusen, Sinclair B., David F. Wright, and J.I. Packer, eds. *New Dictionary of Theology.* Downers Grove, Illinois: InterVarsity Press, 1988.

Foschini, Bernard M. "'Those Who Are Baptized for the Dead' 1 Cor. 15:29." *Catholic Biblical Quarterly* 13 (1951): 46-78, 172-198, 276-283.

Freemantle, Anne. *The Age of Belief.* New York: Penguin Books, 1982.

Gilson, Etienne. *Reason and Revelation in the Middle Ages.* New York: Scribner's, 1938.

Goldstein, Jonathan. "The Origins of the Doctrine of Creation Ex Nihilo." *Journal of Jewish Studies* 35 (1984): 127-135.

_____. "Creation Ex Nihilo: Recantations and Restatements." *Journal of Jewish Studies* 38 (1987): 187-194.

Goodenough, Erwin R. *Jewish Symbols in the Greco-Roman Period*, 13 vols. New York: Bollingen/Pantheon, 1953-1958.

Grant, Robert M. *Second Century Christianity*, London: Society for Promoting Christian Knowledge, 1946.

_____. *After the New Testament*. Philadelphia: Fortress Press, 1967.

_____, ed. *The Apostolic Fathers*, 6 vols. New York: Thomas Nelson & Sons, 1964-1968.

Green, R.L. *C.S. Lewis*. London: *The Bodley Head*, 1963.

Griffith, Michael T. *Signs of the True Church of Christ*. Bountiful, UT: Horizon Publishers & Distributors, 1989.

_____. *One Lord, One Faith: Writings of the Early Christian Fathers as Evidences of the Restoration*. Bountiful, UT: Horizon Publishers & Distributors, 1996.

Guillaumont, Antoine, H.-Ch. Puech, G. Quispel, W. Till, and Y. A. Al Masih. *The Gospel According to Thomas*. New York: Harper & Brothers, 1959.

Gunther, John J. *St. Paul's Opponents and Their Background*. Leiden: E.J. Brill, 1973.

Halley, Henry H. *Halley's Bible Handbook*. Grand Rapids: Zondervan, 1965.

Hammerton-Kelly, Robert G. *Pre-Existence, Wisdom, and the Son of Man*. Cambridge: Cambridge University Press, 1973.

Hanson, R.P.C. *Tradition in the Early Church*. London: SCM Press, 1962.

Harnack, Adolf von. *What is Christianity?* Translated by Thomas B. Saunders. Philadelphia: Fortress Press, 1957.

_____. *History of Dogma*, 7 vols. Translated by Neil Buchanan. New York: Dover, 1961.

Haroldson, E. "Good and Evil Spoken of." *Ensign* 25 (August 1995): 8-11.

Harvey, V.A. *A Handbook of Theological Terms*. New York: Macmillan, 1964.

Hatch, Edwin. *The Influence of Greek Ideas and Usages Upon the Christian Church*. London: Williams and Norgate, 1914.

Hayman, Peter. "Monotheism -- A Misused Word in Jewish Studies?" *Journal of Jewish Studies* 42 (1991): 1-15.

Heckethorn, Charles W. *The Secret Societies of all Ages and Countries*, 2 vols. New Hyde Park, New York: University Books, 1965.

Hippolytus. *The Apostolic Tradition*. Edited by Gregory Dix, and Henry Chadwick. Ridgefield, CT: Morehouse Publishing, 1991.

Hooke, Samuel H., ed. *Myth and Ritual*. Oxford: Oxford University Press, 1933.

_____, ed. *Myth, Ritual, and Kingship*. Oxford: Clarendon Press, 1958.

Hopkins, Richard R. *How Greek Philosophy Corrupted the Christian Concept of God*. Bountiful, UT: Horizon Publishers & Distributors, Inc., 1998.

Hunter, David G. *Marriage in the Early Church*, Minneapolis: Fortress Press, 1992.

Hurtado, Larry W. "What Do We Mean by 'First-Century Jewish Monotheism'?" In E.H. Lovering, Jr., ed. *Society of Biblical Literature 1993 Seminar Papers*. Atlanta: Scholars Press, 1993, 348-368.

Irenaeus. *Proof of the Apostolic Preaching*, ACW 16. Translated by Joseph P. Smith. Westminster, MD: Newman Press, 1953.

Jackson, Kent P. *From Apostasy to Restoration*. Salt Lake City: Deseret Book Co., 1996.

James, Montague R. *The Apocryphal New Testament*. Oxford: Clarendon Press, 1983.

Jantzen, Grace. *God's World, God's Body*. Philadelphia: The Westminster Press, 1984.

Jaspers, Karl. *The Great Philosophers*, 4 vols. New York: Harcourt Brace & Company, 1981.

Jeremias, Joachim. *The Eucharistic Words of Jesus*. Philadelphia: Fortress Press, 1966.

Jerome. *The Homilies of Saint Jerome*, vol. 1, FC 48. Translated by M.L. Ewald. Washington, D.C.: The Catholic University of America Press, 1964.

Jonas, Hans. *The Gnostic Religion*. Boston: Beacon Press, 1963.

Jurgens, William A. *The Faith of the Early Fathers*. Collegeville, MN: The Liturgical Press, 1970.

Kelly, J.N.D. *Early Christian Doctrines*, Revised ed. San Francisco: Harper Collins, 1978.

Klimkeit, Hans-Joachim. *Gnosis on the Silk Road*. San Francisco: Harper Collins, 1993.

Krauth, Charles P. *The Conservative Reformation and Its Theology*. Minneapolis: Augsburg Publishing House, 1963.

Lake, Kirsopp. *The Apostolic Fathers*, 2 vols. Cambridge, Mass.: Harvard University Press, 1912-13.

Lash, Nicholas, and Joseph Rhymer, eds. *The Christian Priesthood*. London: Darton, Longman & Todd, 1970.

Le Guillou, M.J. *The Spirit of Eastern Orthodoxy*. Translated by Donald Attwater. New York: Hawthorn Books, 1962.

Leith, John H. *Creeds of the Churches--A Reader in Christian Doctrine From the Bible to the Present*. New York: Anchor Books, 1963.

Lewis, C.S. *Mere Christianity*. New York: Macmillan Company, 1952.

The Lost Books of the Bible. New York: Bell Publishing Company, 1979.

Lortz-Kaiser, *History of the Church*, translated from the German, 2nd ed. Milwaukee, 1939.

Ludlow, Daniel H., ed. *Encyclopedia of Mormonism*, 4 vols. New York: Macmillan, 1992.

Lundquist, John M., Steven D. Ricks, eds. *By Study and Also by Faith*, vol. 1. Salt Lake City: Deseret Book and F.A.R.M.S., 1990.

Luther, Martin. *The Bondage of the Will*. Translated by Henry Cole. Grand Rapids: Baker Book House, 1976.

Lyman, J. Rebecca. *Christology and Cosmology: Models of Divine Activity in Origen, Eusebius, and Athanasius*. Oxford: Clarendon Press, 1993.

Madsen, Truman G., ed. *Reflections on Mormonism: Judaeo Christian Parallels*. Provo, UT: Religious Studies Center, Brigham Young University, 1978.

Markus, Robert A. *The End of Ancient Christianity*. New York: Cambridge University Press, 1990.

Marriott, Wharton B. *Vestiarum Christianum, the Origin and Gradual Development of the Dress of Holy Ministry in the Church*. London: Rivingtons, 1868.

McConkie, Bruce R. *Mormon Doctrine*, 2nd Ed. Salt Lake City: Bookcraft, 1966.

McCormack, Arthur. *Christian Initiation*. New York: Hawthorn Books, 1969.

Metzger, Bruce M. *Historical and Literary Studies: Pagan, Jewish, and Christian*. Grand Rapids: Wm. B. Eerdmans, 1968.

Metzger, Bruce M., and Michael D. Coogan, eds. *The Oxford Companion to the Bible*. New York: Oxford University Press, 1993.

Miller, John H. *Fundamentals of the Liturgy*. Notre Dame, Ind.: Fides Publishers Association, 1959.

Moffatt, James. *The Moffatt New Testament: Parallel Edition*. New York: Harper & Brothers Publishers, 1922.

Mosheim, Johann L. *Historical Commentaries on the State of Christianity*, 2 vols. New York: S. Converse, 1854.

"The Mormon Church: A Restoration of All Things?" *Awake!* (November 8, 1995): 19-25.

"Mormonism: Christian or Cult?" Saints Alive Tract.

Müeller, Ernst. *A History of Jewish Mysticism.* New York: Barnes and Noble, 1995.

Mullen, E. Theodore. *The Assembly of the Gods: The Divine Council in Canaanite and Early Hebrew Literature.* Chicago: Scholars Press, 1980.

Murray, Gilbert. *Five Stages of Greek Religion.* Garden City, NY: Doubleday Anchor Books, 1955.

The New English Bible With the Apocrypha. Oxford: Oxford University Press, 1970.

Nibley, Hugh W. *Mormonism and Early Christianity.* Salt Lake City: Deseret Book and F.A.R.M.S., 1987.

_____. *The World and the Prophets.* Salt Lake City: Deseret Book and F.A.R.M.S., 1987.

_____. *Temple and Cosmos.* Salt Lake City: Deseret Book and F.A.R.M.S., 1992, p. 64.

The NIV Study Bible. Grand Rapids: Zondervan, 1985.

Noll, Ray R. *Christian Ministerial Priesthood: A Search for its Beginnings in the Primary Documents of the Apostolic Fathers.* San Francisco: Catholic Scholars Press, 1993.

Norman, Keith. "Ex Nihilo: The Development of the Doctrines of God and Creation in Early Christianity." *BYU Studies* 17 (Spring 1977): 291-318.

O'Connell, Robert J. *The Origin of the Soul in St. Augustine's Later Works.* New York: Fordham University Press, 1987.

Origen. *Prayer; Exhortation to Martyrdom,* ACW 19. Translated by John J. O'Meara. New York: Newman Press, 1954.

Origen. *Homilies on Genesis and Exodus,* FC 71. Translated by Ronald E. Heine. Washington D.C.: The Catholic University of America Press, 1982.

Origen. *Homilies on Leviticus,* FC 83. Translated by Gary W. Barkley. Washington D.C.: The Catholic University of America Press, 1990.

Packer, Boyd K. *The Holy Temple.* Salt Lake City: Bookcraft, 1980.

Paulsen, David L. "Early Christian Belief in a Corporeal Deity: Origen and Augustine as Reluctant Witnesses." *Harvard Theological Review* 83 (1990): 105-116.

_____. "The Doctrine of Divine Embodiment: Restoration, Judeo-Christian, and Philosophical Perspectives." *BYU Studies* 35 (1995-1996): 7-94.

Pelikan, Jaroslav. *The Emergence of the Catholic Tradition 100-600.* Chicago: University of Chicago Press, 1971.

Platt, Rutherford H., Jr., ed. *The Forgotten Books of Eden.* New York: Random House, 1980.

Prestige, G.L. *God in Patristic Thought.* London: Oxford University Press, 1956.

Quasten, Johannes. *Patrology,* 4 vols. Westminster, MD: Christian Classics, Inc., 1983-1986.

Quasten, Johannes, and J.C. Plumpe, eds. *Ancient Christian Writers: The Works of the Fathers in Translation.* Washington, D.C.: The Catholic University of America.

Roberts, Alexander, and James Donaldson, eds. *The Ante-Nicene Fathers,* 10 vols. Buffalo: The Christian Literature Publishing Company, 1885-1896.

Robinson, James M., ed. *The Nag Hammadi Library in English.* San Francisco: Harper & Row, 1977.

Robinson, Steven E. *Are Mormons Christians?* Salt Lake City: Bookcraft, Inc., 1991.

Rose, H.J. *Ancient Greek Religion.* New York: Barnes and Noble, 1995.

Rosten, Leo. *Religions of America.* New York: Simon and Schuster, 1975.

Rykwert, Joseph. *Church Building.* New York: Hawthorn Books, 1966.

Schaff, Philip., ed. *The Nicene and Post-Nicene Fathers,* Series 1, 14 vols. New York: The Christian Literature Publishing Company, 1886-1890.

Schaff, Philip., and Henry Wace, eds. *The Nicene and Post-Nicene Fathers,* Series 2, 14 vols. New York: The Christian Literature Publishing Company, 1890-1900.

Schneemelcher, Wilhelm, ed. *New Testament Apocrypha,* 2 vols. Translated by A.J.B. Higgins and others. Philadelphia: The Westminster Press, 1963.

Schweitzer, Albert. *The Mysticism of Paul the Apostle.* Translated by William Montgomery. London, 1931.

Segal, Alan F. *Two Powers in Heaven: Early Rabbinic Reports About Christianity and Gnosticism.* Leiden: E.J. Brill, 1977.

Seiss, J.A. *The Apocalypse,* 3 vols. New York: Charles C. Cook, 1901.

Shiel, James. *Greek Thought and the Rise of Christianity.* London: Longmans, Green and Co., Ltd., 1968.

Shipps, Jan. *Mormonism: The Story of a New Religious Tradition.* Urbana: University of Illinois Press, 1985.

Smith, Joseph Fielding. *Doctrines of Salvation,* 3 vols. Salt Lake City: Bookcraft, 1955.

_____, ed. *Teachings of the Prophet Joseph Smith,* Salt Lake City: Deseret Book, 1976.

Smith, Morton. *The Secret Gospel,* New York: Harper and Row, 1973.

Snyder, Graydon. *The Apostolic Fathers: A New Translation and Commentary.* Camden, NJ: Thomas Nelson and Sons, 1968.

Sparks, H.F.D., ed. *The Apocryphal Old Testament.* Oxford: Clarendon Press, 1984.

Stark, Rodney. *The Rise of Christianity: A Sociologist Reconsiders History.* Princeton, NJ: Princeton University Press, 1996.

Stead, Christopher. *Divine Substance.* Oxford: Clarendon Press, 1977.

_____. *Philosophy in Christian Antiquity.* Cambridge: Cambridge University Press, 1994.

Strong, Augustus H. *Systematic Theology.* Old Tappan, NJ: Fleming H. Revell Company, 1970.

Strong, James. *The New Strong's Complete Dictionary of Bible Words.* Nashville: Thomas Nelson Publishers, 1996.

Stroumsa, Guy G. *Hidden Wisdom: Esoteric Traditions and the Roots of Christian Mysticism.* New York: E.J. Brill, 1996.

Talmage, James E. *The House of the Lord.* Salt Lake City: Bookcraft, 1962.

Towns, Elmer. *Theology for Today.* Dubuque, IA: Kendall Hunt Publishing Company, 1989.

Tvedtnes, John. "A Much-Needed Book That Needs Much." Review of *One Lord, One Faith*, by Michael T. Griffith. *FARMS Review of Books* 9 (1997): 33-42.

The Universal Jewish Encyclopedia, 10 vols. New York: Universal Jewish Encyclopedia Co., Inc., 1939-1943.

Urban, Linwood. *A Short History of Christian Thought.* Oxford: Oxford University Press, 1995.

Vermaseren, M.J. *Mithras: The Secret God.* Translated by T. Megaw, and V. Megaw. London: Chatto and Windus, 1963.

Vermes, Geza. *The Dead Sea Scrolls in English.* New York: Penguin Books, 1975.

Wagner, Walter H. *After the Apostles: Christianity in the Second Century.* Minneapolis: Fortress Press, 1994.

Walker, Charles. *The Ritual "Reason Why".* Oxford: A.R. Mowbray & Co., 1901.

Wand, J.W.C. *A History of the Early Church to A.D. 500.* London: Methuen & Co., 1937.

Watt, J., ed. *Journal of Discourses*, 26 vols. Liverpool: 1854-1886.

Wellnitz, Marcus von. "The Catholic Liturgy and the Mormon Temple." *BYU Studies* 21-22 (Winter 1981 - Fall 1982): 3-35.

Wernick, Nissim, "A Critical Analysis of the Book of Abraham in the Light of Extra-Canonical Jewish Writings." Ph.D. diss., Brigham Young University, 1968.

Widtsoe, John A. "Temple Worship." *The Utah Genealogical and Historical Magazine* 12 (1921): 58.

_____, ed. *Discourses of Brigham Young.* Salt Lake City: Deseret Book Company, 1954.

Wiles, Maurice. *The Making of Christian Doctrine*, Cambridge: Cambridge University Press, 1967.

Williams, Rowan, ed. *The Making of Orthodoxy: Essays in honour of Henry Chadwick,* New York: Cambridge University Press, 1989.

Winston, David. "The Iranian Component in the Bible, Apocrypha and Qumran." *History of Religions* 5 (1965): 212.

_____. "Creation Ex Nihilo Revisited: A Reply to Jonathan Goldstein," *Journal of Jewish Studies* 37 (1986): 88-91.

Winter, Michael M. *Saint Peter and the Popes.* Westport, CT: Greenwood Press, 1960.

Wolfson, Harry A. *The Philosophy of the Church Fathers*, vol. 1. Cambridge, Mass.: Harvard University Press, 1964.

Wright, G.E. *God Who Acts.* London: SCM Press, 1952.

Yamauchi, Edwin M. *Pre-Christian Gnosticism.* London: Tyndale Press, 1973.

Young, Brigham. "For this is Life Eternal," Discourse given in General Conference, October 8, 1854, Ms. Brigham Young Papers, d 1234ff marked: Addresses—1854, July - Oct. Editing spelling, punctuation, grammatical corrections and scriptural references by Elden J. Watson, April 1974.

Young, Frances. "'Creatio ex Nihilo': A Context for the Emergence of the Christian Doctrine of Creation." *Scottish Journal of Theology* 44 (1991): 139-151.

Endnotes

[1] R.L. Green, C.S. Lewis (London: The Bodley Head, 1963), 9.

[2] Hugh Nibley has written extensively about the connection between Mormonism and Early Christianity in his books, *The World and the Prophets*, *Mormonism and Early Christianity*, and various others. These are excellent sources for the interested student, but Nibley treats the subject in bits and pieces, and I found that I needed some background in early Christian history to completely understand many of his points. James Barker's *The Divine Church* contains an excellent discussion of the apostasy as a historical process, but glosses over many of the theological aspects. Michael Griffith's books, *One Lord, One Faith* and *Signs of the True Church of Christ*, have some useful information on early Christianity, but tend to quote LDS authors too frequently and cover the subject matter inadequately. However, Griffith intended these books only as short sketches pointing the reader to sources for further study.

[3] David Bercot, a member of the Society of the Good Shepherd, which seeks to reestablish the faith of the pre-Nicene Church, makes the following criticism:

> We should either honestly accept the historical evidence of the early Christian writings, or we should quit quoting them altogether. Either these people were orthodox Christians -- or they were heretics. To quote them when they support our denomination's beliefs, and then call them heretics when they don't, is hypocritical. David W. Bercot, *Common Sense: A New Approach to Understanding Scripture* (Tyler, TX: Scroll Publishing Co., 1992), 108.

However, at least from an LDS perspective, this is impractical. Since we believe the post-apostolic Church had fallen away, we fully expect these documents to include views contrary to ours. But we also expect that the earlier we go, the more true doctrine we are likely to find. Therefore, it is perfectly legitimate for us to use early Christian writings to support our practices and beliefs, as long as it is recognized that these same documents also contain false doctrine.

[4] C.S. Lewis, *Mere Christianity* (New York: Macmillan Company, 1952), 56.

[5] Ed Decker and Dave Hunt, *The God Makers* (Eugene, OR: Harvest House Publishers, 1984), 12

[6] "Mormonism: Christian or Cult?," Saints Alive tract, 1.

[7] Jan Shipps, *Mormonism: The Story of a New Religious Tradition* (Urbana: University of Illinois Press, 1985).

[8] ECD 4.

[9] Truman G. Madsen, ed., *Reflections on Mormonism: Judaeo-Christian Parallels* (Provo, UT: Religious Studies Center, Brigham Young University, 1978), xvi.

[10] For more complete reviews of the evidence for an apostasy, see Kent P. Jackson, "'Watch and Remember': The New Testament and the Great Apostasy," in John M. Lundquist and Steven D. Ricks, eds., *By Study and Also By Faith*, vol. 1 (Salt Lake City: Deseret Book and F.A.R.M.S., 1990), 81-117; Hugh W. Nibley, "The Passing of the Primitive Church: Forty Variations on an Unpopular Theme," in *Mormonism and Early Christianity* (Salt Lake City: Deseret Book and F.A.R.M.S., 1987), 168-208.

[11] John G. Davies, *The Early Christian Church* (New York: Anchor Books, 1965), 86.

[12] Kent P. Jackson, *From Apostasy to Restoration* (Salt Lake City: Deseret Book Co., 1996), 9.

[13] See Chapter Note 1 for a refutation of this line of reasoning.

[14] One might object that Paul implied the belief that some in his generation would remain living until Christ's return in 1 Thess. 4:15, but if Paul gave that impression in his first letter to the Thessalonians, he corrected this misconception within a year or two when he wrote his second letter. 2 Thess. 2:1-3 reads, "Now we beseech you. . . That ye be not soon shaken in mind, or be troubled . . . as that the day of Christ is at hand. Let no man deceive you by any means: for that day shall not come, except there come a falling away first . . . ."

[15] Richard D. Draper, *Opening the Seven Seals: The Visions of John the Revelator* (Salt Lake City: Deseret Book, 1991), 37.

[16] Certain of the earliest non-canonical Christian writings also testified of the coming apostasy. The *Didache* (Greek "teaching" -- short for "Teaching of the Twelve Apostles,") which was probably written in the first century, recorded:

> For in the last days false prophets and corrupters shall be multiplied, and the sheep shall be turned into wolves, and love shall be turned into hate; for when lawlessness increaseth, they shall hate and persecute and betray one another, and then shall appear the world-deceiver as Son of God, and shall do signs and wonders, and the earth shall be delivered into his hands, and he shall do iniquitous things which have never yet come to pass since the beginning. *Didache* 16, in ANF 7:382.

In an early second-century apocryphal document, the *Epistle of the Apostles*, the resurrected Jesus told his apostles:

> There shall come forth another doctrine, and a confusion, and because they shall strive after their own advancement, they shall bring forth an unprofitable doctrine. And therein shall be a deadly corruption (of uncleanness,) and they shall teach it, and shall turn away them that believe on me from my commandments and cut them off from eternal life. *Epistle of the Apostles* 50, in ANT, 503.

[17] Robert M. Grant, *Second Century Christianity* (London: Society for Promoting Christian Knowledge, 1946), 9.

[18] "With the apostles James the brother of the Lord received the succession in the church." Hegesippus, quoted in Grant, *Second-Century Christianity*, 58.

[19] Polycrates, Bishop of Ephesus, in Grant, *Second-Century Christianity*, 82.

[20] *1 Clement* 44, in ANF 1:17, brackets in original.

[21] *1 Clement* 44, in ANF 1:17. Notice that Clement indicated the bishops were chosen by the apostles, or "other eminent men." So perhaps even after the apostles disappeared there were some men left over who had general, rather than merely local, authority in the Church, such as Jesus' seventy disciples. (See Luke 10:1) In any case, there is no indication of any provision for the people themselves to choose a bishop, or for other bishops to ordain them, as later became the custom.

[22] *1 Clement* 46, in ANF 1:17.

[23] Ignatius, *Magnesians* 4, in ANF 1:61.

[24] See Ignatius, *Trallians* 7, in ANF 1:68-69; *Ephesians* 2, in ANF 1:50., *Magnesians* 6-7, *Philadelphians* 3, and *Smyrnaeans* 8.

[25] Ignatius, *Smyrnaeans* 11, in ANF 1:91, brackets in original.

[26] Walter H. Wagner, *After the Apostles: Christianity in the Second Century* (Minneapolis: Fortress Press, 1994), 142.

[27] Ignatius, *Romans* 9, in ANF 1:77.

[28] Ignatius, *Trallians* 3, in ANF 1:67.

[29] Ignatius, *Ephesians* 11, in ANF 1:54.

[30] *Pastor of Hermas*, Sim. 9:31, in ANF 2:53-54.

[31] Hippolytus, *The Apostolic Tradition* 1:4, edited by Gregory Dix and Henry Chadwick (Ridgefield, CT: Morehouse Publishing, 1991), 2.

[32] Hippolytus, *The Apostolic Tradition* 38:4, p. 72.

[33] The Apostolic Fathers were Christian writers from the generation just after the apostles.

[34] Johannes Quasten, *Patrology*, 4 vols., (Westminster, MD: Christian Classics, Inc., 1983-1986), 1:92-93.

[35] ECD 60. A number of prominent early Christian writers, including Irenaeus, Tertullian, and Origen quoted the *Pastor* as one of the books of Holy Scripture. Quasten, *Patrology*, 1:103; cf. Origen, *De Principiis* 2:1:5, in ANF 4:270.

[36] Quasten, *Patrology*, 1:97-99.

[37] *Pastor of Hermas*, Vision 3:8, in Kirsopp Lake, tr., *The Apostolic Fathers*, 2 vols. (Cambridge, Mass.: Harvard University Press, 1912-13), 2:49. See also Grayden Snyder, *The Apostolic Fathers: A New Translation and Commentary* (Camden, NJ: Thomas Nelson and Sons, 1968), 6:50. Some other translations (e.g. see ANF 2:16, where Hermas asks if it is the "end of the ages") seem to imply that Hermas was asking if the world was about to end, but the more literal translations of Lake and Snyder leave a number of interpretations open, and certainly the other

passages quoted make it clear that it was the end of the Church being spoken of, not the end of the world. For the Greek text of the passage, see 48 of Lake's volume.

[38] *Pastor of Hermas*, Vision 3:5, in ANF 2:14.

[39] *Pastor of Hermas*, Vision 2:2, in ANF 2:11.

[40] *Pastor of Hermas*, Vision 3:9, in ANF 2:16.

[41] *Pastor of Hermas*, Vision 3:7, in ANF 2:15.

[42] Eusebius, *The History of the Church from Christ to Constantine*, translated by G.A. Williamson (New York: Penguin Books, 1965), 13.

[43] ECD 237.

[44] J.W.C. Wand, *A History of the Early Church to A.D. 500* (London: Methuen & Co., 1937), 256-257.

[45] Wand, *A History of the Early Church to A.D. 500*, 244.

[46] *Apostolic Constitutions* 47:31, in ANF 7:501.

[47] David Bercot, a member of the Society of the Good Shepherd, which seeks to reestablish the faith of the pre-Nicene Church, noted that the only possible candidates for an episcopal succession unsullied by the political authorities are a few of the Oriental Orthodox churches, such as the Orthodox Church of India. See David W. Bercot, "Apostolic Succession," in *What the Early Christians Believed*, audio tape set (Tyler, TX: Scroll Publishing Co., 1994), tape 4. Take, for instance, the popes. From 867 to 962 A.D. the papacy was virtually controlled by some powerful Italian families. Roman Catholic historian Lortz-Kaiser comments, "The papacy, which had many immoral incumbents at this time, sank to its lowest depth." *Lortz-Kaiser, History of the Church*, translated from the German, 2nd ed. (Milwaukee, 1939), 183. Another Roman Catholic historian, Poulet-Raemers, notes that for more than fifty years the powerful family of the Roman vestiary Theophylactus, especially his daughter Marozzia, "dominated Rome and imposed the candidates of their choice upon clergy and people." When John X, who owed his election as Pope to Marozzia, shook off her yoke, Marozzia stirred up a revolt in Rome and had the Pope killed. "Marozzia was now able to control the papacy. She gave it in turn to her puppets, Leo VI (928-929,) Stephen VII (929-931,) and finally to her own son John XI." Poulet-Raemers, *Histoire de l'Eglise*, (Paris, 1926,) 1:418-419, translated in Barker, *The Divine Church*, 3 vols. (Salt Lake City: Deseret News Press, 1951), 3:136-137.

[48] Jaroslav Pelikan, *The Emergence of the Catholic Tradition (100-600)* (Chicago: University of Chicago Press, 1971), 108-109

[49] Jean Daniélou, *Gospel Message and Hellenistic Culture*, translated by John A. Baker (Philadelphia: The Westminster Press, 1973), 140.

[50] Wand, *A History of the Early Church to A.D. 500*, 379-280; note also this comment by Edwin Hatch: "The theory [upon which the ecumenical councils were based] assumes that God never speaks to men except through the voice of the majority. It is a large assumption." Edwin Hatch, *The Influence of Greek Ideas and Usages Upon the Christian Church* (London: Williams and Norgate, 1914), 331.

[51] Hansen, R., "The Achievement of Orthodoxy in the Fourth Century AD," in Williams, ed., *The Making of Orthodoxy*, 143-144.

[52] Athanasius, *De Synodis* 1:2-3, in NPNF Series 2, 4:451-452.

[53] Cyril of Jerusalem, *Catechetical Lecture* 15:9, in NPNF Series 2, 7:106-107.

[54] Grant, *Second-Century Christianity*, 13.

[55] Grant, *Second-Century Christianity*, 57.

[56] Grant, *Second-Century Christianity*, 15-16.

[57] Catholic scholar and apologist Michael Winter admits, "In the first place it appears, from the records which have survived, that of the thirteen bishops who ruled in Rome from the death of St. Peter until the end of the second century, only two of them exerted their authority outside the city in a manner which could be called papal." Michael M. Winter, *Saint Peter and the Popes* (Westport, CT: Greenwood Press, 1960), 113. The two popes here referred to were Clement of Rome (ca. 96 A.D.,) who wrote a letter exhorting the Corinthians not to eject their priesthood officers, and Victor (ca. 190 A.D.,) who threatened to excommunicate the Asian Churches for refusing to follow the Roman tradition of when to celebrate Easter. However, Clement claimed only the authority of the Holy Spirit in his letter (*1 Clement* 63, in ANF 10:248), and the Asians paid no attention to Victor's threats. Funk-Hemmer, *Histoire de l'Eglise*, Paris, 1904, 1:294, 194; translated in Barker, *The Divine Church*, 1:170. Winter goes on,

> In the face of this strong probability of a popedom, the events of the first two centuries present an unexpected enigma. It must be admitted that the activities of the early bishops of Rome do not harmonize with this expectation. . . . Winter, *Saint Peter and the Popes*, 116.

That is, it seems probable that if there were a central authority in the New Testament Church (Peter,) there should have been one in the post-apostolic Church, so the fact that no one exerted or even claimed such authority during this period is baffling.

[58] ECD 6; "The thesis is that *there was a first form of Christian theology expressed in Jewish-Semitic terms.*" Jean Daniélou, *The Theology of Jewish Christianity*, translated by John A. Baker (Philadelphia: The Westminster Press, 1973), 10, emphasis in original; cf. Adolf von Harnack, *History of Dogma*, 7 vols., translated by Neil Buchanan (New York: Dover, 1961), 1:287.

[59] Rodney Stark, *The Rise of Christianity: A Sociologist Reconsiders History* (Princeton, NJ: Princeton University Press, 1996), 49.

[60] Davies, W.D., "Israel, the Mormons and the Land," in Madsen, ed., *Reflections on Mormonism: Judaeo-Christian Parallels*, 91.

[61] Daniélou, *The Theology of Jewish Christianity*, 55-85.

[62] Daniélou, *The Theology of Jewish Christianity*, 8.

[63] Kelly (ECD 26) points out that Gnosticism was not really a movement, as such, since although there were a multitude of Gnostic teachers, there was no single Gnostic organization or church.

[64] Hans Jonas, *The Gnostic Religion* (Boston: Beacon Press, 1963), 32, 34.

[65] Joseph Smith, in TPJS 217.

[66] Jonas, *The Gnostic Religion*, 49-51.

[67] Hans-Joachim Klimkeit, *Gnosis on the Silk Road* (San Francisco: Harper Collins, 1978), 149.

[68] See 2 John 7 for John's warning to reject those who did not confess that Jesus had come in the flesh.

[69] Eusebius, *Ecclesiastical History* 3:32, in NPNF Series 2, 1:164.

[70] Jonas, *The Gnostic Religion,* 25.

[71] Harnack, *What is Christianity?*, 191-192.

[72] Stark, *The Rise of Christianity*, 58.

[73] Harnack, *What is Christianity?,* 200.

[74] James Shiel, *Greek Thought and the Rise of Christianity* (London: Longmans, Green and Co., Ltd., 1968), 1.

[75] Daniélou, J., *The Lord of History: Reflections on the Inner Meaning of History*, translated by N. Abercrombie (Chicago: Henry Regnery, 1958), 1.

[76] Shiel, *Greek Thought and the Rise of Christianity*, 1.

[77] Wagner, *After the Apostles*, 138. "Do you accept of the vain and silly doctrines of those who are deemed trustworthy philosophers?" *Mathetes to Diognetus* 8, in ANF 1:28.

[78] Harry A. Wolfson, *The Philosophy of the Church Fathers*, vol. 1 (Cambridge, Mass.: Harvard University Press, 1964), 1:9-10.

[79] Harnack fixes the first real influx of specifically Greek thought into Christianity to about A.D. 130. Harnack, *What is Christianity?*, 201.

[80] Harry Wolfson of Harvard University gives three reasons for the rise of this "philosophized Christianity."

> First, it came about through the conversion to Christianity of pagans who had been trained in philosophy. . . . Second, philosophy was used by Christians as a help in their defense against accusations brought against them [by the pagans]. . . . Third, philosophy. . . was found to be of still greater usefulness as an immunization or an antidote against the heresy of Gnosticism. The Gnostics happened to have done what Paul said he was not going to do: they adorned the faith of the New Testament with 'persuasive words of wisdom'. . . . [Therefore, some of the Fathers] undertook to set up a new Christian philosophy in opposition to that of the Gnostics. . . . Wolfson, *The Philosophy of the Church Fathers*, 1:11-14.

[81] J. Rebecca Lyman, *Christology and Cosmology: Models of Divine Activity in Origen, Eusebius, and Athanasius* (Oxford: Clarendon Press, 1993), 10.

[82] Hatch, *The Influence of Greek Ideas and Usages Upon the Christian Church*, 130-131.

[83] Hatch, *The Influence of Greek Ideas and Usages Upon the Christian Church*, 126. R.M. Grant points out that the Apologists devoted large portions of their writings to proving that the philosophers actually *stole* their ideas from the Jews. Grant, *Second-Century Christianity*, 15. Note also Theophilus of Antioch's strange comparison of the Hebrew prophets to the Greek Sibyls, a class of pagan female oracles. Theophilus, *To Autolycus* 2:9, in ANF 2:97. Wolfson shows that the Fathers at different times used all three of the explanations proposed by Philo the Jew -- namely that certain true principles could have been borrowed from the Jews, discovered by the native reason of the philosophers, or given them by God as a gift. Wolfson, *The Philosophy of the Church Fathers*, 1:21-23.

[84] Hatch, *The Influence of Greek Ideas and Usages Upon the Christian Church*, 133-134.

[85] Harnack, *What is Christianity?,* 200.

[86] Hatch, *The Influence of Greek Ideas and Usages upon the Christian Church*, 350.

[87] Wolfson, *The Philosophy of the Church Fathers*, 1:15-23.

[88] Harnack, A., quoted in Jonas, *The Gnostic Religion*, 36.

[89] Etienne Gilson, *Reason and Revelation in the Middle Ages* (New York: Scribner's, 1938), 16, 22.

[90] Augustine, *Confessions* 9:10, in NPNF Series 1, 1:137-138. Compare the other pillar of Catholic doctrine, St. Thomas Aquinas, who reinterpreted Christianity in light of the philosophy of Aristotle. Before completing his great theological treatise, the *Summa Theologica*, Thomas had some sort of revelation or spiritual experience that convinced him to stop writing. Anne Fremantle writes:

> Some time before he died, St. Thomas himself stopped writing, leaving his greatest work, the *Summa Theologica*, forever unfinished, because he said it had been granted him to experience such things as made all he had ever written seem to him to be "of straw." Anne Fremantle, *The Age of Belief* (New York: Penguin Books, 1982), 148.

[91] Wand, *A History of the Early Church to A.D. 500*, 38-39.

[92] Justin Martyr, *Dialogue with Trypho* 3, in ANF 1:196; cf. *Clementine Recognitions* 10:51, in ANF 8:205.

[93] NTA 2:607.

[94] Justin Martyr, *Dialogue with Trypho* 82, in ANF 1:240.

[95] Eusebius's exact words were:

> And in another place the same author [Irenaeus] writes: "As also we hear that many brethren in the Church possess prophetic gifts, and speak, through the Spirit, with all kinds of tongues, and bring to light the secret things of men for their good, and declare the mysteries of God." So much in regard to the fact that various gifts remained among those who were worthy even until that time. Eusebius, *Ecclesiastical History* 5:7, in NPNF Series 2, 1:222.

[96] Robert A. Markus describes the appeal of Eusebius's approach to his contemporaries:

> It's [Eusebius's Church History's] form and it's choice of themes both set the pattern for all the Church historians at least until the end of the sixth century, even though the Church's history as it was taking shape was beginning to press on the conventions uncomfortably. In the very genre they adopted, its unchanging consistency and almost monolithic uniformity, the Church historians were proclaiming the identity of the Church of the fourth, the fifth and the sixth centuries with the persecuted Church of the first three. Reading Eusebius and the translations and continuations of his *Ecclesiastical history* was thus one way by which later Christians could convince themselves that they were the true descendants of the martyrs. Robert A. Markus, *The End of Ancient Christianity* (New York: Cambridge University Press, 1990), 92.

[97] Irenaeus, *Against Heresies* 3:24:1, in ANF 1:458.

[98] Origen, *Against Celsus* 2:8, in ANF 4:433.

[99] ANF 4:433.

[100] Apolinarius of Hierapolis, quoted in Eusebius, *Ecclesiastical History* 5:16, in NPNF Series 2, 1:231.

[101] Apolinarius of Hierapolis, quoted in Eusebius, *Ecclesiastical History* 5:17, in NPNF Series 2, 1:234. So also Origen:

> Moreover, it is not the part of a divine spirit to drive the prophetess into such a state of ecstasy and madness that she loses control of herself. For he who is under the influence of the Divine Spirit ought to be the first to receive the beneficial effects; and these ought not to be first enjoyed by the persons who consult the oracle about the concerns of natural or civil life, or for purposes of temporal gain or interest; and, moreover, that should be the time of clearest perception, when a person is in close intercourse with the Deity. Origen, *Against Celsus* 7:3, in ANF 4:612.

Compare this remark by Tertullian, who converted to Montanism:

> For when a man is rapt in the Spirit, especially when he beholds the glory of God, or when God speaks through him, he necessarily loses his sensation, because he is overshadowed with the power of God. Tertullian, *Against Marcion* 4:22, in ANF 3:383. Cf. Maurice Wiles, *The Making of Christian Doctrine* (Cambridge: Cambridge University Press, 1967), 46.

[102] Apolinarius of Hierapolis, quoted in Eusebius, *Ecclesiastical History* 5:17, in NPNF Series 2, 1:234.

[103] Hippolytus, at least, claimed the presence of the gift of healing at the turn of the third century. See Hippolytus, *The Apostolic Tradition* 15, p. 22.

[104] Tertullian, *On Modesty* 21, in ANF 4:99-100.

[105] For one attempt at replacing the gifts, see Chapter Note 2.

[106] Davies, *The Early Christian Church*, 135.

[107] For example, John Chrysostom "repeatedly deals with the nature and purpose of miracles. . . and points out that it is better to suffer for Christ and to cast out sin than to expel a demon." Quasten, *Patrology*, vol. 3, 440-441. Certainly this is true, but it completely evades the issue at hand.

[108] Wand, *A History of the Early Church to A.D. 500*, p.59. Harnack makes the same point:

> The New Testament, though not all at once, put an end to the composition
> of works which claimed an authority binding on Christendom (inspiration);
> but it first made possible the production of secular Church literature and
> neutralised the extreme dangers attendant on writings of this kind.
> Harnack, *History of Dogma*, 2:62.

Harnack also gives the following unflattering description of the motives of those who closed the canon:

> Men, however, conceal from themselves their own defects, by placing the
> representatives of the past on an unattainable height, and forming such an
> estimate of their qualities as makes it unlawful and impossible for those of
> the present generation, in the interests of their own comfort, to compare
> themselves with them. Harnack, *History of Dogma*, 2:53.

[109] Van Unnik, Willem Cornelis, "De la Regle *mete prostheinai mete aphelein* dans l'histoire du canon," *Vigiliae Christianae* 3 (1949): 1-2, quoted in Hugh W. Nibley, *The World and the Prophets* (Salt Lake City: Deseret Book and F.A.R.M.S., 1987), 202.

[110] ECD 60. A number of prominent early Christian writers, including Irenaeus, Tertullian, and Origen quoted the *Shepherd* as one of the books of Holy Scripture. Quasten, *Patrology*, 1:103; cf. Origen, *De Principiis* 2:1:5, in ANF 4:270.

[111] *The Pastor of Hermas* Vision 5, in ANF 2:19.

[112] du Toit, A.B., "Canon," in Bruce M. Metzger and Michael D. Coogan, eds., *The Oxford Companion to the Bible* (New York: Oxford University Press, 1993), 103.

[113] Clement of Alexandria, *Selections from the Prophets* 11:27, in Eberhard Arnold, *The Early Christians After the Death of the Apostles*, (Rifton, NY: Plough Publishing House, 1970), 116.

[114] ECD 54.

[115] ECD 59-60.

[116] Davies, *The Early Christian Church*, 85.

[117] In the case of the Old Testament canon, Jews, Protestants, and some Orthodox churches follow the Hebrew Bible, while Roman Catholics and some Orthodox churches accept fourteen or fifteen extra books known as the "Apocrypha" found in the Septuagint. The New Testament canon is more standardized, with some minor exceptions. For instance, the canon of the Ethiopian Church consists of 38 books to this day. Metzger and Coogan, eds., *The Oxford Companion to the Bible*, 102-104.

[118] Justin Martyr, *Dialogue with Trypho* 71-72, in ANF 1:234-235. Irenaeus also gives witness to this reading:

> And in Jeremias He thus announces His death and descent into hell, in the words: "And the Lord the Holy One of Israel bethought Him of His dead, who in the past had slept in the dust of the earth, and went down unto them, to bring the good news of salvation, to deliver them." Here He also gives the reason for His death; for His descent into hell was salvation for the departed. Irenaeus, *Proof of the Apostolic Preaching* 78, translated by Joseph P. Smith (Westminster, MD: Newman Press, 1953), ACW 16:97.

It is also interesting that the *Clementine Homilies* maintained that certain inaccurate statements about God had been allowed to creep into scripture. Latter-day Saints would disagree with the *Homilies* about exactly which passages had been corrupted, but it is interesting to note that it was commonplace in the second century to represent the scriptures as having sustained some deletions and corruptions. *Clementine Homilies* 2:38-39, in ANF 8:236. Note also Origen's assessment of the Old Testament texts available to him: "And in many other of the sacred books I found sometimes more in our copies than in the Hebrew, sometimes less." Origen, *Letter to Africanus* 3, in ANF 4:386.

[119] Daniel-Rops, *L'Eglise des Apotres et des Martyrs*, 313, translated in Barker, *The Divine Church*, 1:16. A non-Mormon scholar of Church History confirmed Barker's translation for me, although the quotation appeared on 309 of his copy of Daniel-Rops. Unfortunately, Daniel-Rops gave no reference for his quotation of Origen, and I have been unable to locate it in any of the extant English translations of Origen's writings. (Since some of Origen's works have never been translated into English, it may well be that it is from an untranslated work.)

[120] Harnack, *History of Dogma*, 2:47.

[121] ANF 2:571.

[122] Dionysius of Corinth, quoted in Eusebius, *Ecclesiastical History* 4:23, in NPNF Series 2, 1:201-202.

[123] Bart D. Ehrman, *The Orthodox Corruption of Scripture: The Effect of Early Christological Controversies on the Text of the New Testament* (New York: Oxford University Press, 1993), xi-46. Many of these changes might seem to us to be minor, but Ehrman shows how even simple variations such as "Jesus" vs. "Christ" were of great significance in the theological debates of the second and third centuries. (See 137-165.)

[124] M.J. Le Guillou, *The Spirit of Eastern Orthodoxy*, translated by Donald Attwater, (New York:

Hawthorn Books, 1962), 20.

[125] *Clementine Recognitions* 1:16, in ANF 8:81; cf. *Clementine Recognitions* 10:42, in ANF 8:203.

[126] *Clementine Recognitions* 3:53, in ANF 8:128. Although critics of the LDS Church often urge people *not* to pray about the message of Mormonism (e.g. see Decker and Hunt, *The God Makers*, 170,) the Latter-day Saints are again in harmony with early Christianity when they ask investigators to study *and* pray to confirm their message.

[127] Ignatius, *Philadelphians* 8, in ANF 1:84.

[128] Papias, *Fragment* 1, in ANF 1:153. ". . . . which things were indeed plainly spoken by Him, but are not plainly written; so much so, that when they are read, they cannot be understood without an expounder, on account of the sin which has grown up with men, as I said before." Peter, in *Clementine Recognitions* 1:21, in ANF 8:83.

[129] Irenaeus, *Against Heresies* 4:32:1, in ANF 1:506.

[130] Justin Martyr, *Address to the Greeks* 8, in ANF 1:196.

[131] E.g. see Gilson, *Reason and Revelation in the Middle Ages*. Likewise, in his penetrating study of the influence of philosophy in ancient Christianity, Cambridge Divinity Professor Christopher Stead calls the influx of Platonic philosophy "a godsend for the Church, whether by fortunate chance or literally by a divine dispensation . . . ." However, he admits that "it formed no part of the original message of Christ or his Apostles," and he suggests that Christian theology has reached the point where it ought to move beyond the limits imposed by the Platonists. Christopher Stead, *Philosophy in Christian Antiquity* (Cambridge: Cambridge University Press, 1994), 243-244.

[132] Bruce R. McConkie, *Mormon Doctrine,* 2nd ed. (Salt Lake City: Bookcraft, 1966), 221.

[133] Hippolytus, *Treatise on Christ and Anti-Christ* 44-46, in ANF 5:214.

[134] Justin Martyr, *Dialogue with Trypho* 49, in ANF 1:219.

[135] John Chrysostom, *Homilies on the Gospel of Matthew* 37:4, in NPNF Series 1, 10:245.

[136] J.A. Seiss, *The Apocalypse*, 3 vols. (New York: Charles C. Cook, 1901), 2:192-193.

[137] Joseph Smith, in TPJS 345.

[138] Jerome (quoting Origen,) *Letter* 124:13, in NPNF 2, 6:243; see also Origen, *De Principiis* 4:1:25, in ANF 4:375.

[139] Origen, *Commentary on John* 14, in ANF 10:305

[140] *The Pastor of Hermas*, Vis. 2:4, in ANF 2:12.

[141] *2 Clement* 14:2, in Robert M. Grant, ed., *The Apostolic Fathers*, 6 vols. (New York: Thomas Nelson & Sons, 1964-1968), 2:126.

[142] Tertullian, *On the Soul* 58, in ANF 3:234-235.

[143] The verse is actually rendered thus in some modern translations, notably the *Revised Standard Version* and the NEB.

[144] Winter, *Saint Peter and the Popes*, 17.

[145] *Discourse of Apa Athanasius Concerning the Soul and the Body*, in E.A.W. Budge, *Coptic Homilies* (London, Longmans and Co., 1910), 271-272.

[146] An alternate opinion was expressed to me by one of the reviewers of this book. In his view, this passage refers symbolically to the earthly Church, but the phrase, "the gates of hades shall not prevail against it" suggests that the Church would at some future time be located *behind* the gates of hades, but would not remain there. Thus the passage is actually a prediction of the future apostasy and Restoration.

[147] Le Guillou, *The Spirit of Eastern Orthodoxy*, 60.

[148] Harnack notes:

> We find nothing in the apostolic age which suggests a community of men who were ascetics on principle; on the contrary, we find the conviction prevailing everywhere that it is within the given circumstances, in the calling and position in which he finds himself, that a man is to be a Christian. Harnack, *What is Christianity?*, 83.

[149] R.A. Markus asserts the following:

> The ideal of the philosophic life was among the most important of the sources which nourished Christian monasticism. It was especially well suited for this because it was often associated with some degree of self-denial. In contrast with Judaism, where asceticism played only a minor role and one largely confined to the fringes of orthodox circles, the whole Hellenistic and Roman philosophical tradition offered a rich store-house of commonplaces extolling the ascetic life. Markus, *The End of Ancient Christianity*, 73.

An example of the adoption of these pagan ideals in the second century can be found in Justin's writings, where he extolled a certain young Christian man who tried to get a surgeon to remove his testicles. The Roman governor wouldn't allow it, so the young man contented himself with living a celibate life intact. See Justin Martyr, *First Apology* 29, in ANF 1:172.

[150] Note this comment by Tertullian near the turn of the third century:

> We are not Indian Brahmins or Gymnosophists, who dwell in woods and exile themselves from ordinary human life. We do not forget the debt of gratitude we owe to God, our Lord and Creator; we reject no creature of His hands, though certainly we exercise restraint upon ourselves, lest of any gift of His we make an immoderate or sinful use. So we sojourn with you in the world, abjuring neither forum, nor shambles, nor bath, nor booth, nor workshop, nor inn, nor weekly market, nor any other places of commerce. We sail with you, and fight with you, and till the ground with

you; and in like manner we unite with you in your traffickings -- even in the various arts we make public property of our works for your benefit. Tertullian, *Apology* 42, in ANF 3:49.

[151] Davies, *The Early Christian Church*, 185.

[152] Robin Amis, *A Different Christianity: Early Christian Esotericism and Modern Thought* , (Albany: State University of New York Press, 1995), 21.

[153] Davies, *The Early Christian Church*, 184-185.

[154] Le Guillou, *The Spirit of Eastern Orthodoxy*, 60.

[155] Amis, *A Different Christianity*, 19.

[156] *Didache* 11, in ANF 7:380-381.

[157] *Barnabas* 4, in ANF 1:139, brackets in original.

[158] Davies, *The Early Christian Church*, 185.

[159] Markus, R.A., *The End of Ancient Christianity*, 17.

[160] Joseph Smith, in TPJS 324.

[161] E. Calvin Beisner, *God in Three Persons* (Illinois: Tyndale House Publishers, 1978), 19.

[162] Decker and Hunt, *The God Makers*, 11, 31.

[163] Some who doubt the Trinitarian doctrine point out that the Greek "*theos en ho logos*" may be translated "the Word was God" or "the Word was *a* God." While this is demonstrably true, it is not an issue for Latter-day Saints, so I mention this fact only in passing.

[164] Joseph Smith, in TPJS 370-371, emphasis in original.

[165] Joseph Smith, in TPJS 370.

[166] See also Ignatius, *Ephesians* 4, in ANF 1:51.

[167] Joseph Smith, in TPJS 372-373.

[168] Joseph Smith, in TPJS 312.

[169] Joseph Smith, in TPJS 345.

[170] Joseph Smith, in TPJS 345-346.

[171] *Nicene Creed*, in NPNF Series 1, 14:3, brackets in original.

[172] From the Greek *ousia*. The Nicene Creed uses the word *homoousios*, meaning "of the same substance or essence." The common notion of the Trinity as a single person who dons three different masks in order to relate to humanity is actually a heresy called *modalism*, which was condemned by Catholic councils. Beisner, *God in Three Persons*, 18.

[173] Wiles, *The Making of Christian Doctrine*, 144.

[174] For an excellent summary of how this terminology was used by different parties at different times, see Christopher Stead, *Divine Substance* (Oxford: Clarendon Press, 1994).

[175] ECD 15-16.

[176] ECD 15-16.

[177] Karl Jaspers, *The Great Philosophers*, 4 vols. (New York: Harcourt Brace & Company, 1981), 3:13. Compare these statements by Xenophanes and Empedocles with those in the *Westminster Confession of Faith* (written in 1646 as a creed for the "Reformed" churches which originated with the work of Zwingli and Calvin,) and with the Vatican Council of 1871. The *Westminster Confession* defines God as "infinite in being and perfection, a most pure spirit, invisible, without body, parts, or passions, immutable, immense, eternal, incomprehensible. . . ." *The Westminster Confession of Faith* in John H. Leith, *Creeds of the Churches -- A Reader in Christian Doctrine From the Bible to the Present* (New York: Anchor Books, 1963), 197. Similarly, the Vatican Council explained that God is "eternal, immense, incomprehensible,. . . . who, being a unique spiritual substance by nature, absolutely simple and unchangeable, must be declared distinct from the world in fact and by essence. . . ." George Brantl, *Catholicism* (New York: George Braziller, 1962), 41.

[178] Empedocles, in Jaspers, *The Great Philosophers*, vol. 3, 51.

[179] Stead, *Divine Substance*, 187-188. See also, V.A. Harvey, *A Handbook of Theological Terms* (New York: Macmillan, 1964), 129.

[180] Edwin Hatch asserts:

> The earliest forms of Christianity were not only outside the sphere of Greek philosophy, but they also appealed, on the one hand, mainly to the classes which philosophy did not reach, and, on the other hand, to a standard which philosophy did not recognize. Hatch, *The Influence of Greek Ideas and Usages upon the Christian Church*, 124.

[181] For a more complete discussion of the influence of Greek philosophy on Christian theology, as well as an excellent biblically-based defense of related LDS doctrines, see Richard R. Hopkins, *How Greek Philosophy Corrupted the Christian Concept of God* (Bountiful, UT: Horizon Publishers & Distributors, Inc., 1998).

[182] Plutarch, quoted in Eusebius, *Preparation for the Gospel* 14:16, translated by E.H. Gifford (Oxford: The Clarendon Press, 1903), 812.

[183] Numenius, quoted by Eusebius, *Preparation for the Gospel* 11:10, p. 566.

[184] Athenagoras, *A Plea Regarding Christians* 10, in ANF 2:133.

[185] Clement of Alexandria, *Stromata* 5:12, in ANF 2:464.

[186] Irenaeus, *Against Heresies* 2:13:3, in ANF 1:374. In the case of Irenaeus, mainstream Christians often object that he was taught by Polycarp, who was a hearer of John, and Irenaeus was supremely concerned with preserving the "tradition" he had inherited against the heretics. Certainly this is true, but it is not clear how well Irenaeus was instructed by Polycarp, and it is completely clear that he was guilty of importing Greek philosophical tenets into the Christian faith. In a postscript to his translation of Cardinal Daniélou 's *Gospel Message and Hellenistic Culture*, John Austin Baker summarizes Daniélou 's findings on Irenaeus: "Devoted as he was to the detailed content of the Tradition, he was nevertheless profoundly original in the large perspectives within which he organised that content." Daniélou, *Gospel Message and Hellenistic Culture*, 503.

[187] Tertullian, *Against Marcion* 2:27, in ANF 3:319.

[188] anthropomorphic = "in the form of man"

[189] Grace Jantzen, *God's World, God's Body* (Philadelphia: The Westminster Press, 1984), 23. An example of this bias can be seen in the following quotation of the Greek poet, Aeshylus: "Afar from mortals place the holy God, nor ever think that He, like to thyself, in fleshly robes is clad; for all unknown is the great God to such a worm as thou." Aeshylus, quoted by Justin Martyr, *On the Sole Government of God* 2, in ANF 1:290.

[190] Cherbonnier, E. LaB., "In Defense of Anthropomorphism," in Madsen, ed., *Reflections on Mormonism: Judaeo-Christian Parallels*, 162; cf. G.E. Wright, *God Who Acts* (London: SCM Press, 1952), 49-50.

[191] Stead, *Philosophy in Christian Antiquity*, 120.

[192] Alan F. Segal, *Two Powers in Heaven: Early Rabbinic Reports About Christianity and Gnosticism* (Leiden: E.J. Brill, 1977), 149.

[193] *Clementine Homilies* 16:19, in ANF 8:316. The *Clementine Recognitions* also seem to imply that God is cognizable only through the senses:

> Then said Peter: "Give us then, as I have often said, as being yourself a new God, or as having yourself come down from him, some new sense, by means of which we may know that new God of whom you speak; for those five senses, which God our Creator has given us, keep faith to their own Creator, and do not perceive that there is any other God, for so their nature necessitates them." Peter, in *Clementine Recognitions* 2:60, in ANF 8:114.

[194] *Clementine Homilies* 17:7, in ANF 8:319-320. The *Homilies* also address the problem raised by John 1:18: "No man hath seen God at any time. . . ." How could anyone know what shape the Father has, if no one has ever seen Him? And what of Joseph Smith's claim to have seen the Father? The LDS explanation is that one may see the face of God only if one is protected by the "glory of the Lord." Otherwise one cannot endure His presence. See Moses 1:2, 13-14. Peter, in the *Homilies*, offers a similar explanation:

> For I maintain that the eyes of mortals cannot see the incorporeal form of the Father or Son, because it is illumined by exceeding great light. . . .
> For he who sees God cannot live. For the excess of light dissolves the flesh

of him who sees; unless by the secret power of God the flesh be changed into the nature of light, so that it can see light. . . . *Clementine Homilies* 17:16, in ANF 8:322-323.

[195] *The Gospel of Bartholomew*, in ANT, 172.

[196] Wand, *A History of the Early Church to A.D. 500*, 209-210.

[197] Elizabeth A. Clark, *The Origenist Controversy: The Cultural Construction of an Early Christian Debate* (Princeton, NJ: Princeton University Press, 1992), 66.

[198] Wand, *A History of the Early Church to A.D. 500*, 181.

[199] Daniélou, *The Theology of Jewish Christianity*, 50.

[200] Origen, *Against Celsus* 7:27, in ANF 4:621.

[201] David L. Paulsen, "Early Christian Belief in a Corporeal Deity: Origen and Augustine as Reluctant Witnesses," *Harvard Theological Review* 83 (1990): 111-112. Certainly the learned Melito could not have been one of the simpletons Origen referred to in *Against Celsus*. Gennadius recorded that not only did Melito write a large number of theological books, including one *On the Corporeality of God*, but "he was considered a prophet by many of us." Gennadius, in NPNF Series 2, 3:368-369.

[202] Origen, *De Principiis* Preface 9, in ANF 4:241.

[203] Origen, *Homilies on Genesis* 3:1, translated by Ronald E. Heine (Washington D.C.: The Catholic University of America Press, 1982), FC 71:89.

[204] Augustine, *Confessions* 5:10, in NPNF Series 1, 1:86.

[205] Augustine, *Confessions* 5:14 and 6:3, in NPNF Series 1, 1:88, 91.

[206] Augustine, quoted in David L. Paulsen, "The Doctrine of Divine Embodiment: Restoration, Judeo-Christian, and Philosophical Perspectives," *BYU Studies* 35 (1995-1996): 76.

[207] Justin Martyr, *Dialogue With Trypho* 127, in ANF 1:263. Interestingly enough, Justin chided the Jews for believing that it *was* the Father himself who appeared to men:

> And again, when He says, "I shall behold the heavens, the works of Thy fingers," unless I understand His method of using words, I shall not understand intelligently, but just as your teachers suppose, fancying that the Father of all, the unbegotten God, has hands and feet, and fingers, and a soul, like a composite being; and they for this reason teach that it was the Father Himself who appeared to Abraham and to Jacob. Justin Martyr, *Dialogue With Trypho* 114, in ANF 1:256.

[208] Justin Martyr, *On the Resurrection* 7, in ANF 1:297.

[209] Justin Martyr, *Dialogue with Trypho* 113, in ANF 1:255.

[210] Irenaeus, *Against Heresies* 4:3:1, in ANF 1:465, brackets in original. This quotation is interesting because here Irenaeus was arguing against the Valentinian Gnostics, who believed in a high God as "the One" and a lower demiurge or creator god who was responsible for the evil of the material world. Irenaeus attempted to prove that the Father *was* the creator, so that is why he took issue with their belief in an anthropomorphic creator god, but in essence the Gnostic position on anthropomorphism was no different from his, for they both posited a high God as "the One" and a lower anthropomorphic God.

[211] Irenaeus, *Proof of the Apostolic Preaching* 11, in ACW 16:54; cf. *Against Heresies* 5:6:1, in ANF 1:531.

[212] Irenaeus, *Against Heresies* 4:7:2-4, in ANF 1:470, brackets in original. Notice that here, like Justin, Irenaeus acknowledged that the Jews, for the most part, still accepted the anthropomorphic character of the Most High God.

[213] E.g. the New King James Version, the New English Bible, the Bible in Basic English, the Revised Standard Version, the New Revised Standard Version, and the New American Standard Version; cf. Dodd, *The Interpretation of the Fourth Gospel*, 225; also Brown, *The Gospel According to John (i-xii,)* 167, 172.

[214] E.g. see Dodd, *The Interpretation of the Fourth Gospel*, 225; also Brown, *The Gospel According to John (i-xii,)* 167, 172. For an example of a translation which utilizes this wording, see the NEB.

[215] Stead, *Philosophy in Christian Antiquity*, 98.

[216] "Scripture does say, of course, that God is Spirit (*pneuma*.) But *pneuma*, in the Greek text of that time, did not necessarily indicate incorporeality as we would expect; in fact, it was sometimes taken to imply the reverse." Jantzen, *God's World, God's Body*, 22.

[217] Harnack, *History of Dogma*, 1:180 n. 1.

[218] I.e. his concept of God has been described as a "thinking gas." Hansen, R., "The Achievement of Orthodoxy in the Fourth Century AD," in Rowan Williams, ed., *The Making of Orthodoxy: Essays in Honour of Henry Chadwick* (New York: Cambridge University Press, 1989), 151-152.

[219] Tertullian, *Against Praxeas* 7, in ANF 3:602.

[220] Origen, *De Principiis* 1:1:1, in ANF 4:242; cf. *De Principiis* 2:8:5, in ANF 4:289. "It is evident from this remark that one very natural interpretation of the word *pneuma* to the reader of the New Testament in Origen's time might not have been 'incorporeal' but the very opposite." Jantzen, *God's World, God's Body*, 22-23. Indeed, it is now being recognized that even "Origen had a subtle and often unappreciated understanding of the 'spiritual body'." Clark, *The Origenist Controversy*, 93. Roberts and Donaldson reveal that although he was a thoroughgoing Platonist, even Origen believed that God had a body. This sentiment was so repugnant to later generations that it was apparently removed from a passage in Origen's *De Principiis* in the fourth century by Rufinus, who translated it into Latin. "Since it seems to follow that God possesses a body, although of extreme tenuity, Rufinus has either suppressed this view, or altered the meaning of Origen's words." ANF 4:348.

[221] Augustine, *On Christian Doctrine* 3:10, in NPNF Series 1, 2:560.

[222] Hatch, *The Influence of Greek Ideas on Christianity*, 65.

[223] "Allegories are an after-thought [to the earliest Christians], they said sometimes, a mere pious gloss over unseemly fables." Hatch, *The Influence of Greek Ideas and Usages Upon the Christian Church*, 79.

[224] Aristides, *Apology* 13, in ANF 10:275. The same point is made by Clement's brother Niceta in *Clementine Recognitions* 10:35, in ANF 8:201-202.

[225] "The reasons given for believing that the Old Testament had an allegorical meaning were precisely analogous to those which had been given in respect to Homer." Hatch, *The Influence of Greek Ideas and Usages Upon the Christian Church*, 70-71. A.H. Strong summarizes the situation in modern theological circles:

> Those passages of Scripture which seem to ascribe to God the possession
> of bodily parts and organs, as eyes and hands, are to be regarded as
> anthropomorphic and symbolic. When God is spoken of as appearing to
> the patriarchs and walking with them, the passages are to be explained as
> referring to God's temporary manifestations of himself in human form --
> manifestations which prefigured the final tabernacling of the Son of God in
> human flesh. Augustus H. Strong, *Systematic Theology* (Old Tappan, NJ:
> Fleming H. Revell Company, 1970), 250.

[226] Cherbonnier, E. LaB., "In Defense of Anthropomorphism," in Madsen, ed., *Reflections on Mormonism*, 163-164.

[227] Whittaker, John, "Plutarch, Platonism, and Christianity," in H.J. Blumenthal and Robert A. Markus, eds., *Neoplatonism and Early Christian Thought* (London: Variorum Publications Ltd., 1981), 50

[228] Davies, *The Early Christian Church*, 251.

[229] Augustine, *The Trinity* 7:4, in NPNF Series 1, 3:109.

[230] The concept of the unknowability of God seems to have infiltrated Christianity first through the Gnostics. Ignatius castigated these heretics because "They introduce God as a Being unknown. . . ." Ignatius, *Trallians* 6, in ANF 1:68. "Do ye, therefore, notice those who preach other doctrines, how they affirm that the Father of Christ cannot be known." Ignatius, *Smyrnaeans* 6, in ANF 1:89.

[231] Le Guillou, *The Spirit of Eastern Orthodoxy*, 31.

[232] Hatch, *The Influence of Greek Ideas and Usages upon the Christian Church*, 251-254. Compare the following statement by Peter in the *Clementine Recognitions*:

> But also the philosophers say that God is not angry, not knowing what they
> say. For anger is evil, when it disturbs the mind, so that it loses right
> counsel. But that anger which punishes the wicked does not bring
> disturbance to the mind; but it is one and the same affection, so to speak,
> which assigned rewards to the good and punishment to the evil; for if He
> should bestow blessings upon the good and the evil, and confer equal
> rewards upon the pious and the impious, He would appear to be unjust

rather than good. *Clementine Recognitions* 10:48, in ANF 8:205.

[233] Hatch, *The Influence of Greek Ideas and Usages Upon the Christian Church*, 239.

[234] Origen, *Homilies on Numbers* 33:2, in Henry Bettenson, *The Early Christian Fathers* (London: Oxford University Press, 1956), 187.

[235] Osborn, *The Emergence of Christian Theology*, 113. Christopher Stead writes that there is no escaping the conclusion Plotinus drew. That is, an absolutely simple God cannot understand or control the influence He exerts on the world. Stead, C., "Divine Simplicity as a Problem for Orthodoxy," in Williams, ed., *The Making of Orthodoxy*, 266.

[236] Westminster Confession of Faith, in *Creeds of the Churches -- A Reader in Christian Doctrine From the Bible to the Present*, 197.

[237] Hatch, *The Influence of Greek Ideas and Usages upon the Christian Church*, 195-196.

[238] Peter Hayman, "Monotheism -- A Misused Word in Jewish Studies?," *Journal of Jewish Studies* 42 (1991): 3. After a debate with David Winston, Goldstein admitted that his position was weak. See Jonathan Goldstein, "The Origins of the Doctrine of Creation Ex Nihilo," *Journal of Jewish Studies* 35 (1984): 127-135 and Jonathan Goldstein, "Creation Ex Nihilo: Recantations and Restatements," *Journal of Jewish Studies* 38 (1987): 187-194. For David Winston's reply see David Winston, "Creation Ex Nihilo Revisited: A Reply to Jonathan Goldstein," *Journal of Jewish Studies* 37 (1986): 88-91.

[239] Frances Young, "'Creatio ex Nihilo': A Context for the Emergence of the Christian Doctrine of Creation, " *Scottish Journal of Theology* 44 (1991): 139-151.

[240] The Jewish Apocryphal book of *Wisdom* preaches creation from formless matter, as well: "For thy almighty hand, which created the world out of formless matter, was not without further resource." (*Wisdom of Solomon* 11:17 NEB) It should be remembered that many Jewish apocryphal books, including *Wisdom* were accepted as inspired by Christians in the first two centuries after Christ. ECD 54. Consider also the same doctrine in some other ancient Jewish texts. "He formed substance from chaos and made it with fire and it exists, and he hewed out great columns from intangible air." *Sefer Yesira*, quoted in Hayman, "Monotheism -- A Misused Word in Jewish Studies?," 2. "R. Huna said, in the name of Bar Qappara: 'If it were not written explicitly in Scripture, it would not be possible to say it: *God created the heaven and the earth. From what? From the earth was chaos. . .*, etc." *Bereshit Rabba*, quoted in Hayman, "Monotheism -- A Misused Word in Jewish Studies?," 2.

[240] ECD 54.

[241] Justin Martyr, *First Apology* 10, in ANF 1:165.

[242] Clement of Alexandria, *The Instructor* 3:12, in ANF 2:296; cf. *Excerpts of Theodotus* 2, in ANF 8:43.

[243] Origen, *De Principiis* 2:1:4, in ANF 4:269, brackets in original. Origen complained in another passage that "very many, indeed" had held this opinion:

> Very many, indeed, are of opinion that the matter of which things are made is itself signified in the language used by Moses in the beginning of

Genesis: "In the beginning God made heaven and earth; and the earth was invisible, and not arranged:" for by the words "invisible and not arranged" Moses would seem to mean nothing else than shapeless matter. Origen, *De Principiis* 4:1:33, in ANF 4:379.

[244] Theophilus, *Theophilus to Autolycus* 2:4, in ANF 2:95.

[245] Winston, "Creation Ex Nihilo Revisited: A Reply to Jonathan Goldstein," 89.

[246] Young, "'Creatio ex Nihilo': A Context for the Emergence of the Christian Doctrine of Creation," 150.

[247] *Wisdom of Solomon* 11:17 NEB.

[248] 2 Maccabees 7:28 NEB.

[249] *Pastor of Hermas*, Vision 1:1, in ANF 2:9, brackets in original. Origen mistakenly interpreted this passage from Hermas, as well as a similar one from one of the Books of the Maccabees in this way:

> But that we may believe on the authority of holy Scripture that such is the case, hear how in the book of Maccabees, where the mother of seven martyrs exhorts her son to endure torture, this truth is confirmed; for she says, "I ask of thee, my son, to look at the heaven and the earth, and at all things which are in them, and beholding these, to know that God made all these things when they did not exist." In the book of the Shepherd also, in the first commandment, he speaks as follows: "First of all believe that there is one God who created and arranged all things, and made all things to come into existence, and out of a state of nothingness." Origen, *De Principiis* 2:1:5, in ANF 4:270.

[250] *Pastor of Hermas*, Vision 1:3, in ANF 2:10.

[251] Young, F., 1991, "'Creatio ex Nihilo': A Context for the Emergence of the Christian Doctrine of Creation," *Scottish Journal of Theology*, vol. 44, 141.

[252] Young, "'Creatio ex Nihilo': A Context for the Emergence of the Christian Doctrine of Creation," 149.

[253] Note how Tertullian, who accepted creation *ex nihilo*, found it necessary to take into account the older usage as employed by those who believed in creation from chaos:

> The Creator's works testify at once to His goodness, since they are good, as we have shown, and to His power, since they are mighty, and spring indeed out of nothing. And even if they were made out of some (previous) matter, as some will have it, they are even thus out of nothing, because they were not what they are. Tertullian, *Against Marcion* 2:5, in ANF 3:301.

[254] Young, "'Creatio ex Nihilo': A Context for the Emergence of the Christian Doctrine of Creation," 139-151.

[255] For a more complete examination of the early Christian evidence by an LDS scholar, see Keith

Norman, "Ex Nihilo: The Development of the Doctrines of God and Creation in Early Christianity," *BYU Studies* 17 (Spring 1977): 291-318.

[256] Joseph Smith, in TPJS 350-352.

[257] Hippolytus, *Refutation of All Heresies* 10:29, in ANF 5:151.

[258] ECD 83.

[259] Margaret Barker, *The Great Angel: A Study of Israel's Second God* (Louisville, KY: Westminster/John Knox Press, 1992), 162. For a good summary of the current scholarly debate, see Larry W. Hurtado, "What Do We Mean by 'First-Century Jewish Monotheism'?," in E.H. Lovering, Jr., ed. *Society of Biblical Literature 1993 Seminar Papers* (Atlanta: Scholars Press, 1993), 348-368.

[260] Cf. Emerton, J.A., "Names of God in the Hebrew Bible," in Metzger and Coogan, eds., *The Oxford Companion to the Bible*, 548-549.

[261] See Chapter Note 1.

[262] Otto Eissfeldt, "El and Yahweh," *Journal of Semitic Studies* 1 (1956): 25-30.

[263] Barker, *The Great Angel*, 198-199.

[264] Barker, *The Great Angel*, 34.

> Parallels are found in descriptions of glorious angelic figures acting as principal agents on behalf of God -- a notion finally going back to the OT figure of 'the angel of the Lord' representing God himself, and (in practice) identified with him in contacts with human beings (see e.g. Exod. 3; Judg. 13.) De Jonge, M., "Monotheism and Christology," in John Barclay and John Sweet, eds., *Early Christian Thought in its Jewish Context*, Cambridge: Cambridge University Press, 1996), 233.

[265] *War Rule* 17, in Geza Vermes, *The Dead Sea Scrolls in English* (New York: Penguin Books, 1975), 146.

[266] Barker, *The Great Angel*, 19.

[267] Barker, *The Great Angel*, 43-44.

[268] Barker, *The Great Angel*, 70.

[269] Barker, *The Great Angel*, 81.

[270] Segal, *Two Powers in Heaven*, 262. "We should also note how frequently subsequent rabbinic polemic against the minim consists in a defense of monotheism, the unity of God." James D.G. Dunn, *The Partings of the Ways: Between Christianity and Judaism and their Significance for the Character of Christianity* (London: SCM Press, 1991), 225.

[271] Segal, *Two Powers in Heaven*, 149.

[272] Philo, *Questions and Answers on Genesis* 2:62, in F.H. Colson and G.H. Whitaker, tr.., *Philo*, Suppl. 1:150.

[273] Philo, *On the Confusion of Tongues* 146, in Colson and Whitaker, trans., *Philo*, 4:89.

[274] Philo, *Questions and Answers on Genesis* 3:39, in Colson and Whitaker, tr., *Philo*, Suppl. 1:226; cf. Segal, *Two Powers in Heaven*, 162.

[275] Philo, *Leg.* 3:81, quoted in Segal, *Two Powers in Heaven*, 166.

[276] Barker, *The Great Angel*, 114.

[277] Barker, *The Great Angel*, 116.

[278] Hurtado, "What Do We Mean by 'First-Century Jewish Monotheism'?," 366.

[279] See Barker, *The Great Angel*, 219. An apparent exception to the rule is Psalm 110:1, where the Psalmist says, "The LORD [Yahweh] said unto my Lord, Sit thou at my right hand, until I make thine enemies thy footstool." In Acts 2:34-36 Peter said this referred to the Father speaking to Christ. This may be another case where the "Yahweh Only" party altered the scripture, but there is another possible explanation. That is, the king of Israel is often described as the son of Yahweh Barker, *The Great Angel*, 9, and therefore the psalm may have been speaking of Yahweh's relationship to the king, but symbolically also representing the relationship between Elohim and Yahweh. See the Codex Sainaiticus reading of the *Epistle of Barnabas* 12, in ANF 1:145 footnote 18. Also, the Septuagint has "The Lord said unto Cyrus," indicating that this passage represented the relationship between Yahweh and Cyrus, king of Persia, who delivered the Israelites from bondage in Babylon. The parallel relationship between Elohim and Yahweh, as Jesus Christ, is obvious.

[280] Justin Martyr, *Dialogue with Trypho* 36, in ANF 1:212-213.

[281] Justin Martyr, *Second Apology* 6, in ANF 1:190.

[282] Daniélou, *The Theology of Jewish Christianity*, 146.

[283] Hatch, *The Influence of Greek Ideas and Usages upon the Christian Church*, 268.

> Then I replied, "I shall attempt to persuade you, since you have understood the Scriptures,[of the truth] of what I say, that there is, and that there is said to be, another God and Lord subject to the Maker of all things; who is also called an Angel, because He announces to men whatsoever the Maker of all things--above whom there is no other God--wishes to announce to them.... I shall endeavour to persuade you, that He who is said to have appeared to Abraham, and to Jacob, and to Moses, and who is called God, is distinct from Him who made all things,--numerically, I mean, not[distinct] in will." Justin Martyr, *Dialogue with Trypho* 56, in ANF 1:223, brackets in original.

[284] Justin Martyr, *Dialogue With Trypho* 127, in ANF 1:263.

[285] Justin Martyr, *First Apology* 13, ANF 1:167.

[286] *The Pastor of Hermas*, Commandment 11, in ANF 2:27-28.

[287] Specifically, Hermas seems to have identified Jesus with Michael. *Daniélou, The Theology of Jewish Christianity,* 123-124. However, this may not be particularly significant, since other Jewish Christian texts speak of Jesus appearing to mortals disguised as one of the archangels. *Daniélou, The Theology of Jewish Christianity,* 131.

[288] *Ascension of Isaiah*, in TOB, 528.

[289] Other possible adherents to such an "angel Christology" are Irenaeus and Ignatius. See Lanne, E., quoted in Daniélou, *The Theology of Jewish Christianity,* 138; Wagner, *After the Apostles,* 146.

[290] Clement of Alexandria, *Stromata* 7:3, in ANF 2:527.

[291] Peter, in *Clementine Recognitions* 2:42, in ANF 8:109.

[292] Hippolytus, *The Apostolic Tradition* 4:4, p. 7.

[293] Tertullian, *Against Praxeas* 7, in ANF 3:602.

[294] Tertullian, *Against Praxeas* 13, in ANF 3:607-608.

[295] Origen, *Against Celsus* 5:39, in ANF 4:561.

[296] Origen, *Dial Heracl.* 2:3, quoted in Segal, *Two Powers in Heaven*, 231.

[297] Origen, *Against Celsus* 8:12, in ANF 4:643-644.

[298] Origen, *De Principiis* 1:3:4, in ANF 4:253.

[299] Novatian, *On the Trinity* 19, in ANF 5:630; cf. *On the Trinity* 18, in ANF 5:628.

[300] Novatian, *On the Trinity* 12, in ANF 5:621.

[301] Novatian, *On the Trinity* 16, in ANF 5:625.

[302] Novatian, *On the Trinity* 27, in ANF 5:637-638.

[303] Novatian, *On the Trinity* 20, in ANF 5:631.

[304] Novatian, *On the Trinity* 31, in ANF 5:644.

[305] Lactantius, *Divine Institutes* 4:6, in ANF 7:105.

[306] *Fruit* 216-219, quoted in Barker, *The Great Angel*, 203.

[307] Methodius, *The Banquet of the Ten Virgins* 3:4, in ANF 6:318.

[308] Eusebius, *The Proof of the Gospel* 1:5, 2 vols., translated by W.J. Ferrar (New York: The Macmillan Company, 1920), vol. 1, 26; cf. *Preparation for the Gospel* 7:15, p. 351.

[309] Eusebius, *The Proof of the Gospel* 4:7, vol. 1, 176.

[310] Eusebius, *Preparation for the Gospel* 7:15, pp. 351-352.

[311] Basil of Caesarea, *On the Holy Spirit* 45, in NPNF Series 2, 8:28.

[312] Bettenson, *The Early Christian Fathers*, 330. See also Urban, *A Short History of Christian Thought*, 54.

[313] Hippolytus, *Scholia on Daniel* 7, in ANF 5:189; cf. Davies, *The Early Christian Church*, 122.

[314] Irenaeus, *Against Heresies* 2:27:8, in ANF 1:402. The same point is made by Peter in the *Clementine Recognitions*:

> But no one ought to be ashamed of this, because there is no man who ought to profess that he knows all things; for there is only One who knows all things, even He who also made all things. For if our Master declared that He knew not the day and the hour whose signs even He foretold, and referred the whole to the Father, how shall we account it disgraceful to confess that we are ignorant of some things, since in this we have the example of our Master? *Clementine Recognitions* 10:14, in ANF 8:196.

[315] Clement of Alexandria, *Stromata* 4:25, in ANF 2:438.

[316] Irenaeus, *Against Heresies* 3:9:1, in ANF 1:421. Christopher Stead points out that Irenaeus may have considered the Son and Spirit to be coequal, in harmony with his description of the Son and Spirit as 'the two hands of God,' "but his image hardly suggests the later view that *all three* Persons are coequal." Stead, *Philosophy in Christian Antiquity*, 157, emphasis in original.

[317] Origen, *De Principiis* 1:3:7, in ANF 4:255; Origen, *De Principiis* 1:3:7, in ANF 4:255.

[318] Athenagoras, *Legatio* 10:5, in Osborn, *The Emergence of Christian Theology*, 175.

[319] Athenagoras, *Legatio* 10:2, in Osborn, *The Emergence of Christian Theology*, 175.

[320] Lyman, *Christology and Cosmology*, 13.

[321] Plotinus, quoted in Osborn, *The Emergence of Christian Theology*, 57.

[322] Origen, *Commentary on John* 8:25, in Bettenson, *The Early Christian Fathers*, 233.

[323] Wagner, *After the Apostles*, 46.

[324] Wagner, *After the Apostles*, 48.

[325] Harnack, *What is Christianity?*, 202-203.

326 ECD 95-101; Hatch, *The Influence of Greek Ideas and Usages Upon the Christian Church*, 264.

327 Tertullian, *Against Praxeas* 5-6, in ANF 3:600-601.

328 Tertullian, *Against Hermogenes* 3, in ANF 3:478; cf. Novatian, *On the Trinity* 31, in ANF 5:643; Hippolytus, *Refutation of All Heresies* 10:29, in ANF 5:150-151; Tatian, *Address to the Greeks* 5, in ANF 2:67.

329 Origen, *De Principiis* 1:2:10, in ANF 4:249-250. Origen was not original in this, however. Cardinal Daniélou notes that the theory of eternal generation had already been formulated in the Gnostic text, *Treatise of the Three Natures*, found at Nag Hammadi. Daniélou, *Gospel Message and Hellenistic Culture*, 378.

330 Tertullian, *Against Praxeas* 9, in ANF 3:603-604, brackets in original; cf. Novatian, *On the Trinity* 31, in ANF 5:644.

331 Stead, *Philosophy in Christian Antiquity*, 188.

332 ECD 21.

333 Eusebius, *Ecclesiastical History* 1:2:8, in NPNF Series 2:1:83.

334 Origen, *Against Celsus* 4:15, in ANF 4:503; cf. Methodius, *Homily on the Cross and Passion of Christ* Fragment 3, in ANF 6:400; Eusebius, *The Proof of the Gospel* 4:13, vol. 1, 188-189; Irenaeus, *Against Heresies* 3:19:3, in ANF 1:449; Gregory of Nazianzus, *Epistle* 101:4, in Henry Bettenson, *The Later Christian Fathers* (London: Oxford University Press, 1970), 107.

335 Hippolytus, *Refutation of All Heresies* 10:29, in ANF 5:152; cf. Irenaeus, *Against Heresies* 3:9:3, in ANF 1:423. "He also Himself was to offer in sacrifice for our sins the vessel of the Spirit. . . ." *Barnabas* 7, in ANF 1:141. "God the Word did dwell in a human body, being within it as the Word, even as the soul also is in the body. . . ." Ignatius, *Philadelphians* 6, in ANF 1:83.

336 Origen, *Against Celsus* 2:9, in ANF 4:434. Though perhaps Tertullian preceded him. See Tertullian, *On the Flesh of Christ* 11, in ANF 3:532. On the other hand, other passages make Tertullian's position somewhat ambiguous. See Tertullian, *Against Praxeas* 27, in ANF 3:624.

337 John Chrysostom, *An Address to Those Who Have Not Come to the Synaxis* 6, in Bettenson, *The Later Christian Fathers*, 171.

338 Ambrose, *An Exposition of the Gospel According to Luke* 4:16, in Bettenson, The *Later Christian Fathers*, 181.

339 Augustine, *On the Trinity* 1:12, in NPNF Series 1, 3:30. On the other hand, Athanasius, who believed Jesus' human nature consisted only of a body, taught that Jesus meant He was ignorant with respect to His flesh. Athanasius, *Discourses Against the Arians* 3:43, in NPNF Series 2, 4:417.

340 Hilary of Poitiers, *On the Trinity* 10:24, in NPNF Series 2, 9:188.

[341] ECD 281.

[342] ECD 343.

[343] Davies, *The Early Christian Church*, 257.

[344] ECD 142. Greek *dokein* = "to seem."

[345] Cyril of Alexandria, *Letter* 46:13, in *Letters* 1-50, translated by John I. McEnerney (Washington, D.C.: The Catholic University of America Press, 1987), FC 76:204.

[346] Harnack, *What is Christianity?*, 236.

[347] ECD 93; cf. Ignatius, *Smyrnaeans* 1, in ANF 1:86; Hippolytus, *Against Noetus* 15, in ANF 5:229; Tertullian, *On the Flesh of Christ* 23, in ANF 3:541.

[348] Irenaeus, *Against Heresies* 2:28:6, in ANF 1:401; cf. Eusebius, *The Proof of the Gospel* 5:1, vol. 1, 232-233.

[349] ECD 94; cf. *The Pastor of Hermas*, Similitude 5:5.

[350] Gregory of Nazianzus, *Oration* 31:5, in NPNF Series 2, 7:319; cf. Origen, *De Principiis* Preface 4, in ANF 4:240.

[351] Bettenson, *The Later Christian Fathers*, 11.

[352] Gregory of Nazianzus, *Oration* 31:8, in NPNF Series 2, 7:320.

[353] ECD 113.

[354] ECD 113-119.

[355] ECD 119-123.

[356] Latter-day Saints should definitely take note of this point because they often make the mistake of assuming the mainline Trinity consists of one person who reveals himself in three different modes. Thus arguments that show the early Church believed in a godhead of three separate persons completely miss the point! It is understandable, though, that many Latter-day Saints make this mistake, since a large proportion of mainline lay-Christians, unable to understand the highly philosophical Nicene doctrine, mistakenly believe in modalism. In fact, even many highly educated ministers misunderstand the Trinity. For example, a Presbyterian minister representing his faith in Leo Rosten's *Religions of America* (New York: Simon and Schuster, 1975), 203, says, "When God is spoken of as three Persons -- Father, Son, and Holy Spirit -- Presbyterians do not think of Him as three individuals. That is tritheism. One God reveals Himself in three manifestations."

[357] Tertullian, *Against Praxeas* 25 in ANF 3:621.

[358] Osborn, *The Emergence of Christian Theology*, 188-190.

[359] Hippolytus, *Refutation of All Heresies* 10:29, in ANF 5:151; cf. *The Apostolic Tradition* 21:11b, p. 35.

[360] Hippolytus, *Scholia on Daniel* 7, in ANF 5:189; cf. Davies, *The Early Christian Church*, 122.

[361] ECD 234-235. Christopher Stead calls this interpretation a "tempting approximation," (Stead, *Philosophy in Christian Antiquity*, 167) but in reality there were a bewildering variety of usages. For an excellent discussion, see Stead, *Divine Substance*, or for a shorter summary, see Stead, *Philosophy in Christian Antiquity*, 160-172.

[362] Stead, *Philosophy in Christian Antiquity*, 167.

[363] Bettenson, *The Early Christian Fathers*, 330. See also Urban, *A Short History of Christian Thought*, 54.

[364] Eusebius, *The Proof of the Gospel* 5:5, vol. 1, 250. Likewise, Origen could critisize those who " deny the divinity of the Son, giving Him a separate existence [Greek *ousia*] of His own, and making His sphere of essence fall outside that of the Father, so that they are separable from each other." Origen, *Commentary on John* 2:2, in ANF 10:323. But in the same section Origen declared the Father to be the "only true God," and Jesus to be an "image" of the prototype. Indeed, in another place Origen explained that "*every* intellectual nature is consubstantial with every other!" Stead, *Philosophy in Christian Antiquity,* 168; cf. Origen, *De Principiis* 4:4:9.

[365] Beisner, *God in Three Persons*, 107.

[366] ECD 228.

[367] ECD 231.

[368] Hansen, R., "The Achievement of Orthodoxy in the Fourth Century AD," in Williams, ed., *The Making of Orthodoxy*, 145.

[369] ECD 231.

[370] ECD 5, 237.

[371] Hansen, R., "The Achievement of Orthodoxy in the Fourth Century AD," in Williams, ed., *The Making of Orthodoxy*, 143-144.

[372] See ECD 240-251.

[373] ECD 247-248.

[374] Actually, Athanasius played only a minor role at Nicea, but was quite an important figure at many of the subsequent councils.

[375] ECD 247-248.

[376] Pelikan, *The Emergence of the Catholic Tradition (100-600,)* 197.

[377] See Pelikan, *The Emergence of the Catholic Tradition (100-600,)* 200-210; Harnack, *History of Dogma* 4:41.

[378] ECD 240-247. Some may be surprised that Athanasius is represented here as creating a break from tradition, since Athanasius vehemently denied this. However, Christopher Stead assures us, "Athanasius is commonly and rightly regarded as the pioneer of a new theology of the Trinity; but this judgment would certainly have surprised him. He regards himself as upholding the invariable tradition of the Church, and is far less open to suggestions from the philosophers." Stead, *Philosophy in Christian Antiquity*, 158.

[379] ECD 234.

[380] ECD 236, 250; cf. Hansen, R., "The Achievement of Orthodoxy in the Fourth Century AD," in Williams, ed., *The Making of Orthodoxy*, 146. "Indeed, until Athanasius began writing, every single theologian, East and West, had postulated some form of Subordinationism. It could, about the year 300, have been described as a fixed part of catholic theology." Hansen, R., "The Achievement of Orthodoxy in the Fourth Century AD," in Williams, ed., *The Making of Orthodoxy*, 153.

[381] ECD 235, 254; Stead, *Philosophy in Christian Antiquity*, 166.

[382] Hansen, R., "The Achievement of Orthodoxy in the Fourth Century AD," in Williams, ed., *The Making of Orthodoxy*, 146.

[383] ECD 238.

[384] Davies, *The Early Christian Church*, 194. As Davies points out, this solution was primarily brought about by the Cappadocian theologians, Gregory of Nazianzus, Gregory of Nyssa, and Basil of Caesarea. However, it is interesting to note that these theologians stressed the divine unity less than Athanasius. "Father, Son and Spirit were therefore compared to three individuals having the same nature or species, all equally divine. Of itself this formulation gave a comparatively weak expression of the divine unity. . . ." Stead, *Philosophy in Christian Antiquity*, 162.

[385] Basil of Caesarea, *On the Holy Spirit* 47, in NPNF Series 2, 8:30.

[386] Jantzen, *God's World, God's Body*, 14.

[387] Augustine, *On the Trinity* 5:9, in NPNF Series 1, 3:92, brackets in original. While I have been careful throughout this discussion to distinguish between the "orthodox" doctrine and Modalism, I tend to think that the only difference between the two is in the application of meaningless terms by "orthodox" theologians. So also Christopher Stead:

> In practice 'substance' takes on a sense which is suggested by 'numerical unity'; and if we stick to the 'Aristotelian' doctrine that there are just two possible senses, we are forced to conclude that the three Persons simply are the same individual. There may perhaps be a better exegesis, which takes account of the uniqueness of divine being; but if so, it has not come my way. Stead, *Philosophy in Christian Antiquity*, 163.

[388] Richard Cartwright, "On the Logical Problem of the Trinity," in *Philosophical Essays* (Cambridge, MA: The MIT Press), 193.

[389] Cyril of Jerusalem, *Catechetical Lectures* 16:24, in NPNF Series 2, 7:121.

[390] Wagner, *After the Apostles*, 79.

[391] Joseph Smith, in TPJS 353-354.

[392] According to what Oscar Cullman says, the Mormons are right, for the pre-existence of Christ in the new Testament does not "indicate unity in essence or nature between God and Christ, but rather a unity in the work of revelation, in the *function* of the pre-existent one." Oscar Cullman, *The Christology of the New Testament*, translated by Shirley C. Guthrie and Charles A.M. Hall (Philadelphia, 1959), 247.

[393] Mircea Eliade and Ioan P. Couliano, *The Eliade Guide to World Religions* (San Francisco: Harper Collins, 1991), 82.

[394] Origen, *De Principiis* Preface 5, in ANF 4:240.

[395] See Chapter Note 2.

[396] ECD 180.

[397] Origen, *De Principiis* 2:9:6, in ANF 4:292. Note, however, that Origen says "We may perhaps hazard a guess" that the soul had a premortal fall. Origen, *De Principiis* 2:8:3, in Bettenson, *The Early Christian Fathers*, 207. He emphatically *did not* teach this as part of the tradition he inherited. Furthermore, the *Clementine Recognitions* specifically rejected the idea of a pre-cosmic fall. *Clementine Recognitions* 2:60, in ANF 8:114. Note also that Origen speculated that John the Baptist may have been an angel before his mortal birth. (The Greek text of the Old Testament Origen referred to would have used the word *angellos* for "messenger.") "We have read this prophecy about him, 'Behold, I send My messenger (angel) before Thy face, who shall prepare Thy way before Thee;' and at this we ask if it can be one of the holy angels who is sent down on this ministry as forerunner of our Saviour." Origen, *Commentary on John* 2:25, in ANF 10:340.

[398] *Clementine Recognitions* 1:28, in ANF 8:85.

[399] Clement of Alexandria, *The Instructor* 1:7, in ANF 2:224.

[400] Henry Chadwick, *Early Christian Thought and the Classical Tradition* (New York: Oxford University Press, 1966), 48. Compare also two passages from another work of Clement. See *Excerpts of Theodotus* 17, 50, in ANF 8:45, 49.

[401] Moses 3:5.

[402] Justin Martyr, *First Apology* 10, in ANF 1:165.

[403] Justin Martyr, *Dialogue with Trypho* 5, in ANF 1:197.

[404] *Mathetes to Diognetus* 5-6, in Arnold, *The Early Christians After the Death of the Apostles*, 109-110. "For though some would have deceived me according to the flesh, yet my spirit is not deceived; for I have received it from God. For it knows both whence it comes and whither it goes, and detects the secrets [of the heart]." Ignatius, *Philadelphians* 7, in ANF 1:83, brackets in

original.

[405] *Epistle of Barnabas* 6, in ANF 1:141, with footnote 9, brackets in original.

[406] *The Pastor of Hermas*, Vis. 2:4, in ANF 2:12.

[407] *2 Clement* 14:2, in Grant, ed., *The Apostolic Fathers*, vol. 2, 126.

[408] Robert G. Hammerton-Kelly, *Pre-Existence, Wisdom, and the Son of Man* (Cambridge: Cambridge University Press, 1973), 193

[409] Hammerton-Kelly, *Pre-Existence, Wisdom, and the Son of Man*, 22, 224, 270.

[410] Hammerton-Kelly, *Pre-Existence, Wisdom, and the Son of Man*, , 154. See also Titus 1:2, "In hope of eternal life, which God, that cannot lie, promised before the world began."

[411] Hammerton-Kelly, *Pre-Existence, Wisdom, and the Son of Man*, , 156, 152.

[412] Albert Schweitzer, *The Mysticism of Paul the Apostle*, translated by William Montgomery (London, 1931), 116.

[413] *The Gospel of Thomas* 49, in Antoine Guillaumont, H.-Ch. Puech, G. Quispel, W. Till, and Y.A. Al Masih, *The Gospel According to Thomas* (New York: Harper and Brothers, 1959), 29.

[414] *Christian Sibyllines*, in NTA 2:741.

[415] NTA 1:289.

[416] *Pistis Sophia*, in TOB, 380.

[417] Note how Lactantius seems to have believed that Jesus and Satan were generated in the same manner, but "the disposition of the divine origin did not remain" in Satan:

> He produced a Spirit like to Himself, who might be endowed with the perfections of God the Father. . . . Then He made another being, in whom the disposition of the divine origin did not remain. Therefore he was infected with his own envy as with poison, and passed from good to evil; and at his own will, which had been given to him by God unfettered, he acquired for himself a contrary name. . . . Lactantius, *Divine Institutes* 2:9, in ANF 7:52.

[418] Davies, *The Early Christian Church*, 235.

[419] Jonas, *The Gnostic Religion*, 44.

[420] *Clementine Recognitions* 2:60, in ANF 8:114.

[421] Whittaker, J., "Plutarch, Platonism, and Christianity," in Blumenthal and Markus, *Neoplatonism and Early Christian Thought*, 60.

[422] *Clementine Recognitions* 1:1, in ANF 8:77.

[423] Robert J. O'Connell, *The Origin of the Soul in St. Augustine's Later Works* (New York: Fordham University Press, 1987), 16.

[424] O'Connell, *The Origin of the Soul in St. Augustine's Later Works*, 11.

[425] O'Connell, *The Origin of the Soul in St. Augustine's Later Works*, 228.

[426] Augustine, *Retractions* 1:1, 3, in Bettenson, *The Later Christian Fathers*, 232; cf. ECD 345-346.

[427] Whittaker, J., "Plutarch, Platonism, and Christianity," in Blumenthal and Markus, *Neoplatonism and Early Christian Thought*, 60-61.

[428] Steven E. Robinson, *Are Mormons Christians?* (Salt Lake City: Bookcraft, Inc.), 66.

[429] In this vein, an interesting note is made by *The Universal Jewish Encyclopedia* about the translation of Psalm 8:6:

> In passing it may be noted that the customary rendering of Ps. 8:6, "Thou has made him (man) but little lower than the angels," is inexact, and that a correct translation would be "but little lower than God (or gods,)" and that accordingly the verse makes no reference whatever to angels. *The Universal Jewish Encyclopedia*, 10 vols. (New York: Universal Jewish Encyclopedia Co., Inc., 1939-1943), 1:309.

[430] ECD 469-470.

[431] Irenaeus, *Against Heresies* 4:38:4, in ANF 1:522.

[432] Irenaeus, *Against Heresies* 5: Preface, in ANF 1:526.

[433] Justin Martyr, *Dialogue With Trypho* 124, in ANF 1:262.

[434] Jerome, *The Homilies of Saint Jerome*, vol. 1 (FC 48), translated by M.L. Ewald (Washington, D.C..: The Catholic University of America Press, 1964), 106.

[435] Clement of Alexandria, *Stromata* 7:10, in ANF 2:539.

[436] Origen, *Commentary on John* 2:3, in ANF 10:323.

[437] Prestige, *God in Patristic Thought* (London: Oxford University Press, 1956), 73.

[438] Robert M. Bowman, "'Ye Are Gods?' Orthodox and Heretical Views on the Deification of Man," *Christian Research Journal* (Winter/Spring 1987): 18ff.

[439] Bowman, "'Ye Are Gods?' Orthodox and Heretical Views on the Deification of Man," 18.

[440] Davies, *The Early Christian Church*, 192.

441 Athanasius, in ECD 352.

442 Le Guillou, *The Spirit of Eastern Orthodoxy*, 100.

443 Gregory of Nazianzus, *Oration* 29:19, in NPNF Series 2, 7:308.

444 Athanasius, *Discourses Against the Arians* 1:42, in NPNF Series 2, 4:330-331.

445 ECD 226.

446 Origen, *Against Celsus* 3:41, in ANF 4:480.

447 Origen, *Commentary on John* 2:2, in ANF 10:323.

448 Origen, *De Principiis* 3:6:3, in ANF 4:345.

449 Origen, *De Principiis* 4:1:36, in ANF 4:381.

450 Justin Martyr, *First Apology* 6, in William A. Jurgens, *The Faith of the Early Fathers* (Collegeville, MN: The Liturgical Press, 1970), 1:51.

451 Jurgens, *The Faith of the Early Fathers*, 1:56, n. 1.

452 Justin Martyr, *Dialogue With Trypho* 124, in ANF 1:262.

453 Likewise Hippolytus:

> Now in all these acts He offered up, as the first-fruits, His own manhood, in order that thou, when thou art in tribulation, mayest not be disheartened, but, confessing thyself to be a man (of like nature with the Redeemer,) mayest dwell in expectation of also receiving what the Father has granted unto this Son. Hippolytus, *Refutation of All Heresies* 10:29, in ANF 5:152.

454 Peter , in *Clementine Homilies* 16:16, in ANF 8:316.

455 Irenaeus, *Against Heresies* 5:36:3, in ANF 1:567.

456 Irenaeus, *Against Heresies* 4:20:5-6, in ANF 1:489.

457 Lactantius, *Divine Institutes* 6:23, quoted in Samuel Angus, *The Mystery-Religions*, (New York: Dover Publications, 1975), 106-107.

458 Clement of Alexandria, *The Instructor* 3:1, in ANF 2:271.

459 Benz, E.W., "Imago Dei: Man in the Image of God," in Madsen, ed., *Reflections on Mormonism*, 215-216.

460 Joseph Smith, in TPJS 345.

[461] Joseph Smith, in TPJS 345.

[462] I recognize that non-LDS readers might consider this approach a little too "convenient," but I see no way of getting around the fact that one must test Joseph Smith's claims as they stand. Each reader must decide whether the evidence for early Christian antecedents to Joseph Smith's teachings is sufficient to show that he truly participated in the restoration of primitive Christianity.

[463] Stead, *Philosophy in Christian Antiquity*, 102. Stead uses the example of Revelation 1:4: "'From Him who Is and who Was and who Is to Come' expresses God's perpetuity within and throughout all ages." However, he points out that when Christianity became Hellenized, "This doctrine came to be developed in an absolute sense which goes well beyond anything that we find in the Bible." Stead, *Philosophy in Christian Antiquity*, 128, emphasis in original. For an excellent discussion of the scriptural evidence for this point, see Hopkins, *How Greek Philosophy Corrupted the Christian Concept of God*, 345-370.

[464] James Strong, *The New Strong's Complete Dictionary of Bible Words* (Nashville: Thomas Nelson Publishers, 1996), 470.

[465] Irenaeus, *Against Heresies* 2:27:1-9, in ANF 1:399-402.

[466] Irenaeus, *Against Heresies* 4:38:1-4, in ANF 1:521-522.

[467] Stead, C., *Divine Substance*, 187-188.

[468] Irenaeus, *Against Heresies* 4:38:4, in ANF 1:522.

[469] Irenaeus, *Against Heresies* 5: Preface, in ANF 1:526.

[470] Irenaeus, *Against Heresies* 4:38:1-4, in ANF 1:521-522.

[471] Elmer Towns, *Theology for Today* (Dubuque, IA: Kendall Hunt Publishing Company, 1989), 3

[472] Barker, *The Great Angel*, 85-86.

[473] Segal, A.F., *Two Powers in Heaven: Early Rabbinic Reports About Christianity and Gnosticism*, (Leiden: E.J. Brill, 1977.)

[474] Daniélou, *The Theology of Jewish Christianity*, 134.

[475] Hammerton-Kelly, *Pre-Existence, Wisdom, and the Son of Man*, 15.

[476] Hammerton-Kelly, *Pre-Existence, Wisdom, and the Son of Man*, 28.

[477] E. Theodore Mullen, *The Assembly of the Gods: The Divine Council in Canaanite and Early Hebrew Literature* (Chicago: Scholars Press, 1980), 215-221.

[478] *The Apocalypse of Abraham* 22, in H.F.D. Sparks, ed., *The Apocryphal Old Testament* (Oxford: Clarendon Press, 1984), 384.

[479] David Winston, "The Iranian Component in the Bible, Apocrypha and Qumran," *History of Religions* 5 (1965): 212.

[480] *Wisdom of Solomon* 8:19-20 NEB

[481] *Sefer Haparshiyot, Midrash Kee Tov, "Alef" Machon Lehotzaat Sefarim*, 31, quoted in Nissim Wernick, "A Critical Analysis of the Book of Abraham in the Light of Extra-Canonical Jewish Writings" (Ph.D. diss., Brigham Young University, 1968), 22.

[482] Hammerton-Kelly, *Pre-Existence, Wisdom, and the Son of Man*, 138.

[483] Origen, *Commentary on John* 2:25, in ANF 10:341.

[484] *Secrets of Enoch* 23:2, in Rutherford H. Platt, Jr., ed., *The Forgotten Books of Eden* (New York: Random House, 1980), 89.

[485] *Secrets of Enoch* 30:12-13, in Platt, ed., *The Forgotten Books of Eden*, 92.

[486] *1 Enoch* 39:4-7, 40:5, 61:12. Quoted in Wernick, "A Critical Analysis of the Book of Abraham in the Light of Extra-Canonical Jewish Writings," 23.

[487] Hammerton-Kelly, *Pre-Existence, Wisdom, and the Son of Man*, 276.

[488] *The Universal Jewish Encyclopedia*, vol. 1, 304.

[489] Joseph Smith, in TPJS 68.

[490] NTA 2: 590-591.

[491] *Epistula Apostolorum* 14, in NTA 1:198.

[492] See also Chapter Note 1.

[493] "And also with Michael, or Adam, the father of all, the prince of all, the ancient of days. . . ." (D&C 27:11.)

[494] Joseph Smith, in TPJS 157.

[495] *The Mysteries of Saint John the Apostle and Holy Virgin*, in E.A.W. Budge, *Coptic Apocrypha* (London: Longmans and Co., 1910), 246.

[496] Segal, *Two Powers in Heaven*, 111, 113.

[497] Segal, *Two Powers in Heaven*, 253.

[498] Segal, *Two Powers in Heaven*, 137.

[499] Clement of Alexandria, *Exhortation to the Heathen* 11, in ANF 2:203, brackets in original.

[500] Irenaeus, *Against Heresies* 4:37, in ANF 1:521. Similarly, Origen taught that God is able to

use the presence of evil to our advantage:

> God does not create evil; still, he does not prevent it when it is displayed by others, although he could do so. But he uses evil, and those who exhibit it, for necessary purposes. For by means of those in whom there is evil, he bestows honour and approbation on those who strive for the glory of virtue. Virtue, if unopposed, would not shine out nor become more glorious by probation. Virtue is not virtue if it be untested and unexamined. Origen, *Homilies on Numbers* 14:2, in Bettenson, *The Early Christian Fathers*, 192.

[501] NTA 2:107.

[502] *Clementine Homilies* 3:28 in ANF 8:241.

[503] *Clementine Homilies* 2:52, in ANF 8:238.

[504] Introduction to *The Mystical Theology of Pseudo-Dionysius*, in TOB, 719.

[505] "As in Adam, or by nature, they fall, even so the blood of Christ atoneth for their sins." (Mosiah 3:16.)

[506] "Every spirit of man was innocent in the beginning; and God having redeemed man from the fall, men became again, in their infant state, innocent before God." (D&C 93:38)

[507] See also Polycarp, *Philippians* 5, in ANF 1:34.

[508] *Mathetes to Diognetus* 6, in ANF 1:27.

[509] Clement of Alexandria, *Stromata* 7:3, in ANF 2:528.

[510] Peter, in *Clementine Recognitions* 5:8, in ANF 8:145.

[511] *Barnabas* 6, in ANF 1:140.

[512] Papias, Fragment 2, in ANF 1:153, brackets in original.

[513] *The Pastor of Hermas*, Sim. 9:29, in ANF 2:53. Hermas also speaks of a class of people who had been "born good": "When the Lord, therefore, saw the mind of these persons, that they were born good, and could be good. . . ." *The Pastor of Hermas,* Sim. 9:30, in ANF 2:53.

[514] Wagner, *After the Apostles,* 194. Since Jesus' Father was God, Tertullian argued that Jesus' soul was not tainted by original sin because he (Tertullian) considered women to merely be channels for the male sperm, which developed into a human being.

[515] Tertullian, *On the Soul* 40, in ANF 3:220. Certainly modern genetic studies have confirmed the fact that the body has much more influence on human behavior than Tertullian was willing to give it credit for.

[516] Tertullian, *On the Soul* 39, in ANF 3:219.

[517] Origen, *Commentary on Romans* 5:1, in Bettenson, *The Early Christian Fathers*, 204.

[518] Urban, *A Short History of Christian Thought*, 139; cf. Bammel, C.P., "Adam in Origen," in Williams, ed., *The Making of Orthodoxy*, 81.

[519] Clark, *The Origenist Controversy*, 219.

[520] Augustine, *Letter* 163:7 (addressed to Jerome,) in NPNF Series 1, 1:525.

[521] ECD 345.

[522] John Calvin, in Dillenberger, ed., *John Calvin: Selections from His Writings*, 159. It is less well-known that Martin Luther also taught this doctrine. See Martin Luther, *The Bondage of the Will*, translated by Henry Cole (Grand Rapids: Baker Book House, 1976), especially 43-44, 70.

[523] *Mathetes to Diognetus* 7, in ANF 1:27

[524] Justin Martyr, *First Apology* 43, in ANF 1:177.

[525] Irenaeus, *Against Heresies* 4:37:1-2, in ANF 1:518-519, brackets in original.

> God therefore has given that which is good, as the apostle tells us in this Epistle, and they who work it shall receive glory and honour, because they have done that which is good when they had it in their power not to do it; but those who do it not shall receive the just judgment of God, because they did not work good when they had it in their power so to do. Irenaeus, *Against Heresies* 4:37:1, in ANF 1:519.

[526] Clement of Alexandria, *Stromata* 7:3, in ANF 2:527.

> And neither praises nor censures, neither rewards nor punishments, are right, when the soul has not the power of inclination and disinclination, but evil is involuntary. Whence he who prevents is a cause; while he who prevents not judges justly the soul's choice. So in no respect is God the author of evil. But since free choice and inclination originate sins, and a mistaken judgment sometimes prevails, from which, since it is ignorance and stupidity, we do not take pains to recede, punishments are rightly inflicted. Clement of Alexandria, *Stromata* 1:17, in ANF 2:319.

[527] Peter, in *Clementine Recognitions* 5:6, in ANF 8:144.

[528] Lactantius, *Divine Institutes* 7:5, in ANF 7:200. So also Origen:

> We, however, who know of only one nature in every rational soul, and who maintain that none has been created evil by the Author of all things, but that many have become wicked through education, and perverse example, and surrounding influences, so that wickedness has been naturalized in some individuals. . . . Origen, *Against Celsus* 3:69, in ANF 4:491.

And Methodius:

Now those who decide that man is not possessed of free-will, and affirm that he is governed by the unavoidable necessities of fate, and her unwritten commands, are guilty of impiety towards God Himself, making Him out to be the cause and author of human evils. Methodius, *Banquet of the Ten Virgins* 8:16, in ANF 6:342.

[529] Gregory of Nazianzus, *Oration* 37:13, in NPNF Series 2, 7:341-342.

[530] Cyril of Jerusalem, *Catechetical Lectures* 4:21, in NPNF Series 2, 7:24.

[531] Augustine, *On Grace and Free Will* 33, in NPNF Series 1, 5:458.

[532] Augustine, *On Rebuke and Grace* 13, in NPNF Series 1, 5:476-477.

[533] Augustine, *To Simplicianus* 1:16, in Bettenson, *The Later Christian Fathers,* 211-212. See also Christopher Stead's excellent discussion of Augustine's doctrine of original sin. Stead concludes, "Whatever merits there may be in recognizing that men are corrupted by inherited defects and a sinful environment, there can be no excuse for the theory of inherited guilt, which makes even new-born infants into detested sinners in the eyes of God; nor is there any coherent defence of the view that we ourselves somehow participated in a sin committed by Adam many centuries before our birth." Stead, *Philosophy in Christian Antiquity*, 232.

[534] Augustine, *On Rebuke and Grace* 44, in NPNF Series 1, 5:489.

[535] Augustine, *On Rebuke and Grace* 14, in NPNF Series 1, 5:477.

[536] See Dillenberger, ed., *John Calvin: Selections From His Writings,* 31.

[537] E.g. the Roman Catholics. See Rosten, ed., *Religions of America*, 48-49.

[538] See Moroni 8. "Those who are without the law" *do not* include mentally capable unbelievers because "good and evil have come before all men; he that knoweth not good from evil is blameless; but he that knoweth good and evil, to him it is given according to his desires, whether he desireth good or evil, life or death, joy or remorse of conscience." (Alma 29:5)

[539] *The Pastor of Hermas*, Sim. 9:29, in ANF 2:53.

[540] See Aristides, *Apology* 15, in ANF 10:278; Justin Martyr, *Dialogue With Trypho* 88, in ANF 1:243; ECD 168. As for Irenaeus, he "nowhere formulates a specific account of the connexion between Adam's guilty act and the rest of mankind." ECD 172.

[541] Clement of Alexandria, *Stromata* 4:25, in ANF 2:439. See also the following: "What is involuntary is not matter for judgment. But this is twofold,--what is done in ignorance, and what is done through necessity. For how will you judge concerning those who are said to sin in involuntary modes?" Clement of Alexandria, *Stromata* 2:14, in ANF 2:361.

[542] ECD 179-180.

[543] Clement of Alexandria, *Stromateis* 3:16, translated by J. Ferguson (Washington, D.C.: The Catholic University of America Press, 1991), FC 85:319.

[544] Tertullian, *Against Marcion* 2:15, in ANF 3:309; cf. ECD 176.

[545] Bammel, C.P., "Adam in Origen," in Williams, ed., *The Making of Orthodoxy*, 81. Unfortunately, there is no English translation of Origen's *Commentary on Romans* currently available.

[546] Bammel, C.P., "Adam in Origen," in Williams, ed., *The Making of Orthodoxy*, 83. Compare the following:

> We find in the prophet Isaiah, that the fire with which each one is punished is described as his own; for he says, "Walk in the light of your own fire, and in the flame which ye have kindled." By these words it seems to be indicated that every sinner kindles for himself the flame of his own fire, and is not plunged into some fire which has been already kindled by another, or was in existence before himself. Origen, *De Principiis* 2:10:4, in ANF 4:295.

[547] Cyprian, *Epistle* 58, in ANF 5:354.

[548] Cyril of Jerusalem, *Catechetical Lectures* 4:19, in NPNF Series 2, 7:23-24.

[549] O'Connell, *The Origin of the Soul in St. Augustine's Later Works*, 233. See also the following: "Now, inasmuch as infants are not held bound by any sins of their own actual life, it is the guilt of original sin which is healed in them by the grace of Him who saves them by the laver [baptism) of regeneration." Augustine, *A Treatise on the Merits and Forgiveness of Sins* 1:24, in NPNF Series 1, 5:24.

[550] E.g. see Rosten, ed., *Religions of America*, 203 for the example of the Presbyterians. See 29 for the example of the Baptists.

[551] E.g. in Semi-Pelagianism and Arminianism -- see Charles P. Krauth, *The Conservative Reformation and Its Theology* (Minneapolis: Augsburg Publishing House, 1963), 418.

[552] Joseph Smith, in TPJS 375.

[553] Joseph Smith, in TPJS 193.

[554] Haroldson, E., "Good and Evil Spoken of," *Ensign* 25 (August 1995): 10, translation from Raisanen, "Joseph Smith und die Bibel: Die Leistung des mormonischen Propheten in neuer Beleuchtung," *Theologische Literaturzeitung* (Feb. 1984): 83-92.

[555] Ignatius, *Magnesians* 8, in ANF 1:62.

[556] Tatian, *Address to the Greeks* 31, in ANF 2:77.

[557] Theophilus, *Theophilus to Autolycus* 3:29, in ANF 2:120.

[558] Eusebius, *Ecclesiastical History* 1:4:6-10, in NPNF Series 2, 1:87-88. Compare also the following:

> The law and life of our Saviour Jesus Christ shows itself to be such, being

a renewal of the ancient pre-Mosaic religion, in which Abraham, the friend of God, and his forefathers are shown to have lived. . . . Yes, and equally with us they knew and bore witness to the Word of God, Whom we love to call Christ. They were thought worthy in very remarkable ways of beholding His actual presence and theophany. Eusebius, *The Proof of the Gospel*, 1:5, vol. 1, 25-26.

[559] Daniélou, J., *The Lord of History: Reflections on the Inner Meaning of History*, tr. Abercrombie, N., (Chicago: Henry Regnery, 1958,) 2. Curiously, the Cardinal ascribes this doctrine to the "Greek idea of perfection as something which has always been the same." However, the fact that Jewish Christian writings like *Barnabas* and the Jewish Pseudepigrapha teach it refutes this interpretation.

[560] Clement of Alexandria, *Stromata* 7:2, in ANF 2:524.

[561] Eusebius, *The Proof of the Gospel* 4:8, vol. 1, 177.

[562] see Joseph Smith, in TPJS 60.

[563] *Barnabas* 14, in ANF 1:146, brackets in original; cf. *Barnabas* 4, in ANF 1:138-139.

[564] Paul did say that "we are sanctified through the offering of the body of Jesus Christ once for all" (Hebrews 10:10,) but that does not mean the world can't reject His message, as it has done so many times before.

[565] Clement of Rome, *1 Clement* 32, in ANF 1:13.

[566] Clement of Rome, *1 Clement* 30, in ANF 1:13.

[567] Henry H. Halley, *Halley's Bible Handbook* (Grand Rapids: Zondervan, 1965), 659.

[568] *1 Clement* 21, in ANF 1:11, brackets in original.

[569] *1 Clement* 31, in ANF 1:13.

[570] Ignatius, *Magnesians* 10, in ANF 1:63.

[571] Polycarp, *Philippians* 11, in ANF 1:35.

[572] *Barnabas* 21, in ANF 1:152.

[573] *Barnabas* 19, in ANF 1:148.

[574] *2 Clement* 3-4, in ANF 7:518.

[575] *Pastor of Hermas*, Vision 3:1, in ANF 2:13.

[576] *The Acts of Paul*, in ANT, 273.

[577] Irenaeus, quoting the Elders who knew the apostles in Grant, *Second-Century Christianity*, 80.

See also *Against Heresies* 4:27:2

[578] *Epistle of the Apostles*, in ANT, 494.

[579] David W. Bercot, *Will the Real Heretics Please Stand Up: A New Look at Today's Evangelical Church in the Light of Early Christianity* (Henderson, TX: Scroll Publishing Co., 1989), 73-74. While Latter-day Saints can legitimately point to some Gnostic doctrines as possible remnants of the truth, it is ludicrous for the Protestants to do so. Protestants often loudly protest against the LDS that there never was a *total* apostasy. But if they want to provide evidence for this assertion, they must be able to point to an unbroken line of teachers who taught their doctrines. We put forward the challenge: "Where are they?" Perhaps the historical record is too spotty to expect this challenge to be met, but it serves to show how ridiculous it is for Protestant critics of Mormonism to denounce us as outside "historic Christianity."

[580] Article of Faith 3.

[581] Bonnel, J.S., in Rosten, *Religions of America*, 203.

[582] Justin Martyr, *First Apology* 61, in ANF 1:183.

[583] A fragment attributed to Irenaeus, in ANF 1:574, brackets in original.

[584] *Clementine Homilies* 11:25-26, in ANF 8:289-290.

[585] *Apostolic Constitutions* 6:15, in ANF 7:456-457.

[586] *Didache* 7, in ANF 7:379.

[587] Clement of Alexandria, in Eusebius, *Ecclesiastical History* 3:23, in NPNF Series 2, 1:150-151.

[588] Everett Fergusen, ed., *Encyclopedia of Early Christianity* (New York: Garland Publishing, 1990), 133.

[589] Tertullian, *On Baptism* 18, in ANF 3:677.

[590] Gregory of Nazianzus, *Oration* 40:28, in NPNF Series 2, 7:370. However, it should also be said that Gregory believed that unbaptized infants, and presumably even baptized infants, would receive neither reward nor punishment in the afterlife. See Gregory of Nazianzus, *Oration* 40:23, in NPNF Series 2, 7:367.

[591] Ferguson, *Encyclopedia of Early Christianity*, 133. Perhaps Greek religious influence had some effect, also, since H.J. Rose reports that in Greek cults "a baby was put through a ceremonial corresponding in some measure to baptism." H. J. Rose, *Ancient Greek Religion* (New York: Barnes and Noble, 1995), 11.

[592] John Chrysostom, *To the Neophytes*, in Bettenson, *The Later Christian Fathers*, 169.

[593] Augustine, *Enchiridion* 93, in NPNF Series 1, 3:266; cf. ECD 485.

[594] Joseph Smith, in TPJS 314.

[595] Tertullian, *On Baptism* 12, 6, 8, in ANF 3:674-675, 672; cf. ECD 209.

[596] Cyprian, *Epistle* 72:9, in ANF 5:381.

[597] Cyprian, *Epistle* 71:1, in ANF 5:378.

[598] Cornelius of Rome, in Eusebius, *Ecclesiastical History* 6:43, in NPNF Series 2, 1:288-289.

[599] Joseph Smith, in TPJS 310.

[600] Joseph Fielding Smith, *Doctrines of Salvation*, 3 vols. (Salt Lake City: Bookcraft, 1955), 2:18.

[601] McConkie, *Mormon Doctrine*, 762.

[602] Justin Martyr, *Dialogue with Trypho* 5, in ANF 1:197; cf. Davies, *The Early Christian Church*, 100.

[603] Irenaeus, *Against Heresies* 5:31, in ANF 1:560-561, brackets in original.

[604] Tertullian, *On the Soul* 55, in ANF 3:231.

[605] Tertullian, *On the Soul* 7, in ANF 3:187.

[606] Tertullian, *On the Soul* 58, in ANF 3:234-235.

[607] Origen, *De Principiis* 4:1:23, in ANF 4:372.

[608] Origen, *De Principiis* 2:11:6, in ANF 4:299.

[609] Origen, *Against Celsus* 6:25, in ANF 4:584.

[610] Jerome (quoting Origen,) *Letter* 124:7, in NPNF 2, 6:240-241.

[611] Clement of Alexandria, *Stromata* 6:14, in ANF 2:505.

[612] ECD 483.

[613] ECD 484.

[614] ECD 484. Augustine's main objection was as follows:

> Then what a fond fancy is it to suppose that eternal punishment means long continued punishment, while eternal life means life without end, since Christ in the very same passage spoke of both in similar terms in one and the same sentence, "These shall go away into eternal punishment, but the righteous into life eternal!" If both destinies are "eternal," then we must either understand both as long-continued but at last terminating, or both as endless. For they are correlative,--on the one hand, punishment eternal, on the other hand, life eternal. And to say in one and the same sense, life

eternal shall be endless, punishment eternal shall come to an end, is the
height of absurdity. Wherefore, as the eternal life of the saints shall be
endless, so too the eternal punishment of those who are doomed to it shall
have no end. Augustine, *The City of God* 21:23, in NPNF Series 1, 2:469.

This seems to be flawless logic, but the Lord gave another option in a revelation to Joseph Smith:
"Eternal punishment is God's punishment. Endless punishment is God's punishment." (D&C
19:11-12) It is called this because "Endless is my name." (D&C 19:10) Therefore it could also
be said that "Eternal life" is God's life, and hence the term "eternal" has no reference to the
duration of "Eternal punishment" or "Eternal life," but rather to the eternity of the God who
bestows punishment and life.

[615] Ignatius, *Trallians* 9, in ANF 1:70.

[616] *Discourse of Apa Athanasius Concerning the Soul and the Body*, in Budge, *Coptic Homilies*,
271-272.

[617] *Book of the Resurrection of Christ by Bartholomew the Apostle*, in Budge, *Coptic Apocrypha*,
184, brackets in original.

[618] *The Gospel of Bartholomew*, in ANT, 169, brackets in original.

[619] From a Syriac appendage to a letter from Jesus to King Abgar, in Eusebius, *Ecclesiastical
History* 1:13, in NPNF Series 2, 1:102.

[620] *The Gospel of Nicodemus*, in ANF 8:438.

[621] *The NIV Study Bible* (Grand Rapids: Zondervan, 1985), 1893. John Calvin gave the
following strange explanation. "He descended to hell. That signifies that he was afflicted by
God, and felt the horror and severity of the divine judgment, so that he might stand between the
wrath of God and satisfy his justice in our name." John Calvin, in Dillenberger, ed., *John Calvin:
Selections From His Writings*, 291.

[622] 1 Peter 3:19, in James Moffatt, *The Moffatt New Testament: Parallel Edition* (New York:
Harper & Brothers Publishers, 1922).

[623] Text note to 1 Peter 3:19, in Moffatt, *The Moffatt New Testament*.

[624] *The NIV Study Bible*, 1894.

[625] Justin Martyr, *Dialogue with Trypho* 45, in ANF 1:217.

[626] Clement of Alexandria, *Stromata* 6:6, in ANF 2:491.

[627]*Clementine Recognitions* 1:58 in ANF 8:113.

[628] Irenaeus, *Against Heresies* 4:27:2, in ANF 1:499, brackets in original.

[629] Clement of Alexandria, *Stromata* 6:6, in ANF 2:490.

[630] Origen, *Against Celsus* 2:43, in ANF 4:448.

[631] *The Pastor of Hermas*, Sim. 9:16, in ANF 2:49.

[632] Justin Martyr, *Dialogue with Trypho* 71-72, in ANF 1:234-235.

[633] *The Odes of Solomon* 42:15-26 in Platt, ed., *The Forgotten Books of Eden*, 140.

[634] Halley, *Halley's Bible Handbook*, 600. In the fourth century John Chrysostom also offered this interpretation of the passage. See John Chrysostom, *Homilies on 1 Corinthians* 40:1-2, in NPNF Series 1, 12:244-245.

[635] *The NIV Study Bible*, 1757.

[636] *The NIV Study Bible*, 1757.

[637] For instance, Jehovah's Witnesses are even so bold as to change the wording of the passage in their Bible: "Otherwise, what will they do who are being baptized for the purpose of [being] dead ones?" 1 Corinthians 15:29, *The New World Translation*, brackets in original. This is *not* justified by the Greek text.

[638] R.E. DeMaris, "Corinthian Religion and Baptism for the Dead (1 Corinthians 15:29): Insights from Archaeology and Anthropology," *Journal of Biblical Literature* 114 (1995): 661.

[639] Lake, tr., *The Apostolic Fathers*, 2:263.

[640] *The Pastor of Hermas*, Sim. 9:16, in ANF 2:49.

[641] *Epistle of the Apostles*, in ANT, 494, brackets in original.

[642] Clement of Alexandria, *Stromata* 6:6, in ANF 2:491-492.

[643] Heber Q. Hale, in Duane S. Crowther, *Life Everlasting* (Salt Lake City: Bookcraft, 1967), 221.

[644] Porter, J.R., "Oil in the Old Testament," in Martin Dudley and Geoffrey Rowell, eds., *The Oil of Gladness: Anointing in the Christian Tradition* (London: SPCK, 1993), 40.

[645] *The Gospel of Nicodemus*, in ANF 8:438-439.

[646] Fillion, *La Sainte Bible commentee d'apres la Vulgate*, translated in Barker, *The Divine Church*, vol. 1, 68.

[647] Epiphanius, *Panarion* 28, in Philip R. Amidon, tr., *The Panarion of St. Epiphanius, Bishop of Salamis*, (New York: Oxford University Press, 1990).

[648] John Chrysostom, *Homilies on 1 Corinthians* 40:1, in NPNF Series 1, 12:244.

[649] I have been unable to ascertain when, exactly, baptism for the dead was lost to the Catholic Church. Hermas at least hinted at the practice in the second century, and by the fourth century Epiphanius and Chrysostom made it clear that they no longer believed in it. However, the writings from the late second and third centuries are conspicuously silent about the issue. The

index of texts for ANF lists only two instances in the entire pre-Nicene period where 1 Corinthians 15:29 was even mentioned, and both of these were by Tertullian. Indeed, Tertullian's comments are quite puzzling. In a treatise on the resurrection he seems to have simply assumed that the passage referred to vicarious baptism.

> But inasmuch as "some are also baptized for the dead," we will see whether there be a good reason for this. Now it is certain that they adopted this (practice) with such a presumption as made them suppose that the vicarious baptism (in question) would be beneficial to the flesh of another in anticipation of the resurrection; for unless it were a bodily resurrection, there would be no pledge secured by this process of a corporeal baptism. Tertullian, *On the Resurrection of the Flesh* 48, in ANF 3:581-582.

In his treatise against Marcion, however, he mentioned his recent treatise on the resurrection, and then put forward two contradictory means of explaining away the passage:

> Let us now return to the resurrection, to the defence of which against heretics of all sorts we have given indeed sufficient attention in another work of ours. But we will not be wanting (in some defence of the doctrine) even here, in consideration of such persons as are ignorant of that little treatise. "What," asks he, "shall they do who are baptized for the dead, if the dead rise not?" Now, never mind that practice, (whatever it may have been.) The Februarian lustrations will perhaps answer him (quite as well,) by praying for the dead. Do not then suppose that the apostle here indicates some new god as the author and advocate of this (baptism for the dead. His only aim in alluding to it was) that he might all the more firmly insist upon the resurrection of the body, in proportion as they who were vainly baptized for the dead resorted to the practice from their belief of such a resurrection. We have the apostle in another passage defining "but one baptism." To be "baptized for the dead" therefore means, in fact, to be baptized for the body; for, as we have shown, it is the body which becomes dead. What, then, shall they do who are baptized for the body, if the body rises not again? Tertullian, *Against Marcion* 5:10, in ANF 3:449-450.

Perhaps the Catholics dropped the practice in reaction to its public acceptance by such heretical groups as the Marcionites, and this might explain Tertullian's apparent struggle to explain it away.

[650] *Clementine Recognitions* 1:52 in ANF 8:91. In another passage Peter assured Clement's brother that even if his father died before receiving baptism, he would still be saved if he were one of the elect:

> "My lord Peter, I say nothing against your right and good counsels; but I wish to say one thing, that thereby I may learn something that I do not know. What if my father should die within the year during which you recommend that he should be put off [from baptism]? He will go down to hell helpless, and so be tormented forever." Then said Peter: "I embrace your kindly purpose towards your father, and I forgive you in respect of things of which you are ignorant. . . . For those who have lived righteously, for the sake of God alone and His righteousness, they shall come to eternal rest, and shall receive the perpetuity of the heavenly kingdom. For salvation is not attained by force, but by liberty; and not through the favour of men, but by the faith of God. Then, besides, you ought to consider that God is prescient, and knows whether this man is one

of His. But if He knows that he is not, what shall we do with respect to those things which have been determined by Him from the beginning?" *Clementine Recognitions* 10:2, in ANF 8:192-193.

[651] And the apostles, near the end of Jesus' discourse in the *Epistle of the Apostles*, which included mention of the doctrine of salvation for the dead, said: "And we will preach it to those to whom it is fitting." *Epistula Apostolorum* 40, in NTA 1:219. Note also that even though Chrysostom was contemptuous of the practice of baptism for the dead, he refused to discuss the subject openly:

> But first I wish to remind you who are initiated of the response, which on that evening they who introduce you to the mysteries bid you make; and then I will also explain the saying of Paul: so this likewise will be clearer to you; we after all the other things adding this which Paul now saith. And I desire indeed expressly to utter it, but I dare not on account of the uninitiated; for these add a difficulty to our exposition, compelling us either not to speak clearly or to declare unto them the ineffable mysteries. Nevertheless, as I may be able, I will speak as through a veil. John Chrysostom, *Homilies on 1 Corinthians* 40:2, in NPNF Series 1, 12:244.

[652] Peter, in *Clementine Recognitions* 7:38, in ANF 8:165.

[653] Davies, *The Early Christian Church*, 102.

[654] Davies, *The Early Christian Church*, 121.

[655] Nibley, "Baptism for the Dead in Ancient Times," in *Mormonism and Early Christianity*, 100-167.

[656] Bernard M. Foschini, "'Those who are Baptized for the Dead' 1 Cor. 15:29," *Catholic Biblical Quarterly* 13 (1951): 71.

[657] Foschini, "Those who are Baptized for the Dead," 71. It is ironic that a Catholic should raise this particular argument against baptism for the dead. Linwood Urban writes that Martin Luther had a similar objection to medieval Catholic practice:

> Luther soon realized, however, that his objections to the sale of indulgences applied with equal force to Masses offered on behalf of the dead. Like indulgences, Masses were bought and sold in the belief that remission of penalty would be granted to individuals in purgatory without regard to the state of their souls. Urban, *A Short History of Christian Thought*, 283.

[658] Foschini, "Those who are Baptized for the Dead," 71.

[659] Foschini, "Those who are Baptized for the Dead," 71.

[660] Rosten, *Religions of America*, 205.

[661] Joseph Smith, in TPJS 199.

[662] Joseph Smith, in TPJS 200.

[663] Ignatius, *Smyrnaeans* 3, in ANF 1:87.

[664] Ignatius, *Trallians* 9, in ANF 1:70.

[665] Justin Martyr, *First Apology* 18, in ANF 1:169. Justin admitted elsewhere that he knew of some Christians who denied the resurrection, but he did not consider them real Christians:

> For I choose to follow not men or men's doctrines, but God and the doctrines [delivered] by Him. For if you have fallen in with some who are called Christians, but who do not admit this [truth], and venture to blaspheme the God of Abraham, and the God of Isaac, and the God of Jacob; who say there is no resurrection of the dead, and that their souls, when they die, are taken to heaven; do not imagine that they are Christians, even as one, if he would rightly consider it, would not admit that the Sadducees, or similar sects of Genistae, Meristae, Galilaeans, Hellenists, Pharisees, Baptists, are Jews (do not hear me impatiently when I tell you what I think,) but are[only] called Jews and children of Abraham, worshipping God with the lips, as God Himself declared, but the heart was far from Him. Justin, *Dialogue With Trypho* 80, in ANF 1:239, brackets in original; cf. Wagner, *After the Apostles*, 167.

[666] Irenaeus, *Against Heresies* 4:18:5, in ANF 1:486. Consider also the following statement:

> For He who in the beginning caused him to have being who as yet was not, just when He pleased, shall much more reinstate again those who had a former existence, when it is His will [that they should inherit] the life granted by Him. And that flesh shall also be found fit for and capable of receiving the power of God, which at the beginning received the skillful touches of God. . . . Irenaeus, *Against Heresies* 5:3:2, in ANF 1:529, brackets in original.

[667] Tatian, *Address to the Greeks* 6, in ANF 2:67; cf. Davies, *The Early Christian Church,* 100-101.

[668] Tertullian, *On the Soul* 56, in ANF 3:232.

[669] *Epistle of the Apostles*, in ANT, 493.

[670] *2 Clement* 9, in ANF 7:519.

[671] Justin Martyr, *On the Resurrection* 4, in ANF 1:295.

[672] Papias, in Grant, *Second-Century Christianity*, 66.

[673] Athenagoras, *The Resurrection of the Dead*, in ANF 2:152.

[674] Davies, *The Early Christian Church*, 30.

[675] Davies, *The Early Christian Church*, 58.

[676] "All beings who have bodies have power over those who have not." Joseph Smith, in TPJS

181.

677 *Apocalypse of Abraham* 19, in Sparks, *The Apocryphal Old Testament*, 382. Notice also the following passage from the *Clementine Homilies*, which speaks of the desire of demons to obtain bodies:

> But the reason why the demons delight in entering into men's bodies is this. [Demons] Being spirits, and having desires after meats and drinks, and sexual pleasures, but not being able to partake of these by reason of their being spirits, and wanting organs fitted for their enjoyment, they enter into the bodies of men, in order that, getting organs to minister to them, they may obtain the things that they wish, whether it be meat, by means of men's teeth, or sexual pleasure, by means of men's members. Peter in *Clementine Homilies* 9:10, in ANF 8:277, brackets in original.

678 *Epistle of the Apostles* 19, in ANT, 491-492. It should be noted that this passage not only supports the LDS belief that one must be resurrected to be perfected, but also the doctrine of the subordination of the Son to the Father and the corporeality of the Father.

679 John Whittaker explains:

> The almost universal Hellenistic rejection of the body and the identification of mind and man served to render the idea of the resurrection of the body thoroughly objectionable to the average Hellenistic mind. And indeed the idea of the resurrection was to cause considerable embarrassment to Christian Platonists. Whittaker, "Plutarch, Platonism, and Christianity," in Blumenthal and Markus, eds., *Neoplatonism and Early Christian Thought*, 56; cf. Daniélou, J., *Gospel Message and Hellenistic Culture*, 24.

680 Origen, *Against Celsus* 5:14, in ANF 4:549, brackets in original; cf. Davies, *The Early Christian Church*, 145.

681 Eusebius, *Ecclesiastical History* 3:39, in ANF 1:154.

682 Eusebius, *The History of the Church from Christ to Constantine*, 3.39, 151-152. Even Jerome, who was strongly anti-millenarian, had to admit that such beliefs could not be condemned because so many of the earlier fathers and martyrs had held them. Bonner, G., "Augustine and Millenarianism," in Williams, ed., *The Making of Orthodoxy*, 239.

683 Norman Cohn, *Cosmos, Chaos and the World to Come* (New Haven: Yale University Press, 1993), 199.

684 Justin Martyr, *Dialogue with Trypho* 80, in ANF 1:239, first set of brackets in original.

685 Davies, *The Early Christian Church*, 133.

686 ANF 1:561.

687 Note also that the paradise of Adam and Eve was in a Terrestrial state, and translated beings dwell in this sphere awaiting the resurrection, as well. See Chapter Note 2.

[688] Origen, *De Principiis* 2:10:2, in ANF 4:294.

[689] Origen, *Commentary on John* 2:3, in ANF 10:324-325.

[690] John Chrysostom, *Homilies on 1 Corinthians* 41:4, in NPNF Series 1, 12:251.

[691] Irenaeus, *Against Heresies* 5:36:1-2, in ANF 1:567, brackets in original.

[692] Clement of Alexandria, *Stromata* 6:14, in ANF 2:506.

[693] ANF 2:506.

[694] Daniélou, *The Theology of Jewish Christianity*, 179.

[695] *The Lost Books of the Bible* (New York: Bell Publishing Company, 1979), 240.

[696] *Epistula Apostolorum*, in NTA 1:210.

[697] Daniélou, *The Theology of Jewish Christianity*, 174; However, it is clear from the passages which mention two heavens in the *Recognitions* that the two heavens spoken of are the visible heaven, which men can see, and the invisible, where the angels, etc., dwell. See *Clementine Recognitions* 9:3, in ANF 8:183; *Clementine Recognitions* 3:27, in ANF 8:121; *Clementine Recognitions* 2:68, in ANF 8:116. There is no mention of any division in the invisible heaven, but the following passage may be an oblique reference to the three degrees: "Be this therefore the first step to you of three; which step brings forth thirty commands, and the second sixty, and the third a hundred, as we shall expound more fully to you at another time." Peter, in *Clementine Recognitions* 4:36, in ANF 8:143. The footnote to this passage makes clear that whatever it referred to was most likely part of the esoteric tradition.

[698] Daniélou, *The Theology of Jewish Christianity*, 174.

[699] Irenaeus, *Proof of the Apostolic Preaching* 9, in ACW 16:53.

[700] Daniélou, *The Theology of Jewish Christianity*, 176.

[701] *The Gospel of Philip*, in , James M. Robinson, ed., *The Nag Hammadi Library in English* (San Francisco: Harper & Row, 1977), 140, brackets in original.

[702] *The Pastor of Hermas*, Sim. 9:19, in ANF 2:50.

[703] Origen, *De Principiis* 2:10:8, in ANF 4:296.

[704] *The Gospel of Bartholomew*, in ANT, 173.

[705] Clark, *The Origenist Controversy*, 131.

[706] See also Chapter Note 3.

[707] *Jewish Creation Legend (Haggadah,)* in TOB, 29.

[708] It is also interesting to note that Hippolytus recorded a tradition that seems to support the LDS teaching that the apostle John was translated: "John, again, in Asia, was banished by Domitian the king to the isle of Patmos, in which also he wrote his Gospel and saw the apocalyptic vision; and in Trajan's time he fell asleep at Ephesus, where his remains were sought for, but could not be found." Hippolytus, *On the Twelve Apostles*, in ANF 5:254-255.

[709] Joseph Smith, in TPJS 170.

[710] Irenaeus, *Against Heresies* 5:5:1, in ANF 1:531, brackets in original.

[711] Peter in *Clementine Recognitions* 1:52, in ANF 8:91.

[712] Origen, *De Principiis* 3:5:3, in ANF 4:341-342.

[713] Clement of Rome, *1 Clement* 35, in ANF 1:14.

[714] *Jewish Creation Legend (Haggadah,)* in TOB, 17.

[715] Joseph Smith, in TPJS 157.

[716] Davies, *The Early Christian Church*, 60-61.

[717] *1 Clement* 42, ANF 1:16, brackets in original.

[718] Clement of Alexandria, in Eusebius, *Ecclesiastical History* 3:23, in NPNF Series 2, 1:150.

[719] Hippolytus, *The Apostolic Tradition* 2, 8-9, pp. 2-3, 13-17.

[720] Bettenson, *The Early Christian Fathers*, 43.

[721] *1 Clement* 40, in ANF 1:16.

[722] *Apostolic Constitutions* 3:10, in ANF 7:429.

[723] ECD 35.

[724] E.g. Ignatius insisted that "apart from [the bishops and elders] there is no elect Church, no congregation of holy ones, no assembly of saints." Ignatius, *Trallians* 3, in ANF 1:67.

[725] *2 Clement* 17, in ANF 7:522.

[726] Wand, *A History of the Early Church to A.D. 500*, 26-27.

[727] Wand, *A History of the Early Church to A.D. 500*, 3.

[728] Ignatius, *Trallians* 3, in ANF 1:67.]

[729] Irenaeus, *Against Heresies* 4:8:3, in ANF 1:471. In fact, laymen in the patristic period did have an active role in the Church.

> History shows that *laymen* took an active part in all of the internal
> workings of the Church. They had an important role to play in the liturgy,
> which was still, at that time, a "popular" liturgy, that is, a liturgy for the
> people. They had their word to say in the election of bishops, and the
> nomination of priests. They contributed to the drawing up of church laws
> and customs; prepared some of the matter for discussion at the councils,
> and even took part in them. They administered church properties, and it
> was an accepted thing that they should be allowed to preach. . . ; the
> records show that they often did so. LeClerq, J., "The Priesthood in the
> Patristic and Medieval Church," in Nicholas Lash and Joseph Rhymer,
> eds., *The Christian Priesthood* (London: Darton, Longman & Todd,
> 1970), 55.

However, in the Middle ages this all changed so that there developed a vast chasm between the clergy and the laity. See LeClerq, 56-62.

[730] Sinclair B. Fergusen, David F. Wright, and J.I. Packer, eds., *New Dictionary of Theology* (Downers Grove, Illinois: InterVarsity Press, 1988), 531.

[731] Noll, *Christian Ministerial Priesthood*, 43; cf. J.H. Elliot, *The Elect and the Holy: An Exegetical Examination of I Peter 2:4-10 and the Phrase "Basileioun hierateuma"* (Leiden: E.J. Brill, 1966), 223.

[732] Origen, *Homilies on Leviticus* 9:1:3, translated by Gary W. Barkley (Washington D.C.: The Catholic University of America Press, 1990), FC 83:177.

[733] Irenaeus, *Against Heresies* 4:33:7, in ANF 1:508, brackets in original; cf. Ignatius, *Ephesians* 5, in ANF 1:51.

[734] Irenaeus, *Against Heresies* 4:26:2, in ANF 1:497, brackets in original.

[735] Cyprian, *Epistle* 39:5, in ANF 5:318.

[736] Cyprian, *Epistle* 26:1, in ANF 5:305.

[737] Tertullian, *Prescription Against Heretics* 32, in ANF 3:258, brackets in original.

[738] Tertullian, *Prescription Against Heretics* 41, in ANF 3:263.

[739] Tertullian, *Exhortation to Chastity* 7, in ANF 4:54.

[740] Clement of Alexandria, quoted in Eusebius, *Ecclesiastical History* 2:1, in NPNF Series 2, 1:104.

[741] *The Community Rule* 8, in Vermes, *The Dead Sea Scrolls in English*, 85.

[742] *Didache* 11, in ANF 7:380-381.

[743] *1 Clement* 44, in ANF 1:17. Jean Daniélou claims that these men were clearly the "heirs of the Twelve," and were different from any of the priesthood officers normally discussed. He also asserts that this institution must have been created by Christ Himself. Daniélou, *The Theology of*

Jewish Christianity, 355.

[744] From a Syriac appendage to a letter from Jesus to King Abgar, in Eusebius, *Ecclesiastical History* 1:13, in NPNF Series 2, 1:101.

[745] Joseph Smith, in TPJS 151.

[746] Davies, *The Early Christian Church*, 90.

[747] Bettenson, *The Early Christian Fathers*, 90, n. 1.

[748] Ignatius, *Smyrnaeans* 8, in ANF 1:89-90, brackets in original.

[749] Davies, *The Early Christian Church*, 131.

[750] Davies, *The Early Christian Church*, 131-132.

[751] Davies, *The Early Christian Church*, 132.

[752] Origen, *Homilies on Leviticus* 6:3:1, FC 83:120.

[753] Bettenson, *The Early Christian Fathers*, p.267.

[754] Theophilus, *To Autolycus* 2:31, in ANF 2:107.

[755] Ignatius, *Smyrnaeans* 9, in ANF 1:90.

[756] Hippolytus, *The Apostolic Tradition* 3:4, p. 5.

[757] Clement of Alexandria, *Stromata* 7:7, in ANF 2:533.

[758] *Didache* 13, in ANF 7:381.

[759] Origen, *On Prayer* 28:9, translated by John J. O'Meara (New York: Newman Press, 1954), ACW 19:112.

[760] Origen, *Commentary on John* 1:3, in ANF 10:298. However, Ignatius wrote that Christ was the only High Priest "by nature." Ignatius, *Smyrnaeans* 9, in ANF 1:90. Perhaps others can become "High Priests" by grace.

[761] *Epistle of Barnabas* 15, in ANF 1:147, brackets in original.

[762] *Didache* 14, in ANF 7:381.

[763] Ignatius, *Magnesians* 9, in ANF 1:62.

[764] Davies, *The Early Christian Church*, 63-64.

[765] Justin Martyr, *First Apology* 67, in ANF 1:185-186.

[766] Eusebius, *Ecclesiastical History*, 6:19, in NPNF Series 2, 1:268.

[767] Decker and Hunt, *The God Makers*, 136.

[768] *Odes of Solomon* 6, in Platt, ed., *The Forgotten Books of Eden*, 122.

[769] Jung, C. G., "Transformation Symbolism in the Mass," in Joseph Campbell, ed., *The Mysteries* (Princeton, NJ: Princeton University Press, 1955), 280-281.

[770] One rationale for continuing the LDS practice of using water in the sacrament is that the Word of Wisdom, the LDS health code, forbids the drinking of alcoholic beverages. However, I am *not* suggesting that the early Christian Church had any such health code. The Word of Wisdom explicitly states that it was designed "in consequence of evils and designs which do and will exist in the hearts of conspiring men in the last days. . . ." (D&C 89:4.) Therefore, there is no need to suppose that this revelation was a restoration of anything from a former dispensation, especially in light of the fact that the New Testament shows Jesus drinking wine.

[771] Hegesippus, quoted in Eusebius, *Ecclesiastical History* 2:23, in NPNF Series 2, 1:125.

[772] *Acts of Thomas*, in ANF 8:539.

[773] *Acts of Thomas* 121, quoted in Daniélou, *The Theology of Jewish Christianity*, 371.

[774] Irenaeus, *Against Heresies* 5:1:3, in ANF 1:527; cf. Daniélou, *The Theology of Jewish Christianity*, 371.

[775] Clement of Alexandria, *Stromata* 1:19, in ANF 2:322.

[776] Cyprian, *Epistle 62*, 13, in ANF 5:362.

[777] Davies, *The Early Christian Church*, 54.

[778] Hatch, *The Influence of Greek Ideas and Usages Upon the Christian Church*, 308.

[779] *Apostolic Constitutions* 8:29, in ANF 7:493. Apparently by this time they also used water (holy water?) for anointing.

[780] Halliburton, J., "Anointing in the Early Church," in Dudley and Rowell, eds., *The Oil of Gladness*, 86.

[781] Halliburton, J., "Anointing in the Early Church," in Dudley and Rowell, eds., *The Oil of Gladness*, 89.

[782] Jehovah's Witnesses have recently made this criticism. See "The Mormon Church: A Restoration of All Things?," *Awake!* (November 8, 1995): 24.

[783] *Apostolic Constitutions* 2:25, in ANF 7:471.

[784] Pope Urban I, *Epistle to All Christians* 1, in ANF 8:619.

[785] Cyprian, *On the Unity of the Church* 26, in ANF 5:429.

[786] Davies, *The Early Christian Church*, 108-109.

[787] *Barnabas* 3, in ANF 1:138, brackets in original.

[788] *The Pastor of Hermas*, Sim. 5:1, 3, in ANF 2:33-34.

[789] Joseph Smith, in TPJS 91.

[790] E.g. see Decker and Hunt, *The God Makers*, 209.

[791] Young, Brigham, in JD 3:318.

[792] It is interesting to note that Brigham Young explicitly stated this was the case for his notorious "Adam-God" teachings.:

> I may say things this afternoon that do not belong to the world. What if I do? I know the Lord is able to close up every person's mind who have eyes but see not, hearts but do not understand; so I may say what I please with regard to the Kingdom of God on the earth, for there is a veil over the wicked that they cannot understand the things which are for their peace. Brigham Young, "For this is Life Eternal," discourse given in General Conference, October 8, 1854, Ms. Brigham Young Papers, d 1234ff marked: Addresses—1854, July - Oct. Editing spelling, punctuation, grammatical corrections and scriptural references by Elden J. Watson, April 1974.

[793] Hugh W. Nibley, *Temple and Cosmos* (Salt Lake City: Deseret Book and F.A.R.M.S., 1992), 64.

[794] John A. Widtsoe, "Temple Worship," *The Utah Genealogical and Historical Magazine* 12 (1921): 58.

[795] Boyd K. Packer, *The Holy Temple* (Salt Lake City: Bookcraft, 1980), 154.

[796] Packer, *The Holy Temple*, 155.

[797] Packer, *The Holy Temple*, 71-79.

[798] James E. Talmage, *The House of the Lord* (Salt Lake City: Bookcraft, 1962), 99-100.

[799] Packer, *The Holy Temple*, 38.

[800] Talmage, *The House of the Lord*, p.100.

[801] John A. Widtsoe, ed., *Discourses of Brigham Young* (Salt Lake City: Deseret Book Company, 1954), 416.

[802] "Temple Ordinances," and "Symbolism," in Daniel H. Ludlow, ed., *Encyclopedia of*

Mormonism, 4 vols. (New York: Macmillan, 1992), 4:1444, 3:1430.

[803] Joachim Jeremias, *The Eucharistic Words of Jesus* (Philadelphia: Fortress Press), 125-130.

[804] Morton Smith, *The Secret Gospel* (New York: Harper and Row, 1973), 84; cf. Ernst Müeller, *A History of Jewish Mysticism* (New York: Barnes and Noble, 1995), 44.

[805] Jeremias, *The Eucharistic Words of Jesus*, 130-132.

[806] Guy G. Stroumsa, *Hidden Wisdom: Esoteric Traditions and the Roots of Christian Mysticism* (New York: E.J. Brill, 1996), 41; cf. 56.

[807] *Clementine Homilies* 19:20, in ANF 8:336. "For the most sublime truths are best honoured by means of silence." Peter, in *Clementine Recognitions* 1:23, in ANF 8:83.

> But if he remains wrapped up and polluted in those sins which are
> manifestly such, it does not become me to speak to him at all of the more
> secret and sacred things of divine knowledge, but rather to protest and
> confront him, that he cease from sin, and cleanse his actions from vice.
> Peter, in *Clementine Recognitions* 2:4, in ANF 8:98.

[808] *Clementine Recognitions* 2:4, in ANF 8:98.

[809] *Clementine Recognitions* 3:1, in ANF 8:117.

[810] Ignatius, *Romans* 9, in ANF 1:104, brackets in original.

[811] ECD 43.

[812] Origen, *Against Celsus* 1:7, in ANF 4:399.

[813] Origen, *Against Celsus* 3:60, in ANF 4:488.

[814] Tertullian, *Prescription Against Heretics* 41, in ANF 3:263.

[815] Lactantius, *Divine Institutes* 7:26, in ANF 7:221.

[816] Basil of Caesarea, *Treatise De Spiritu Sancto* 27, in NPNF Series 2, 8:40-41.

[817] Basil of Caesarea, *Treatise De Spiritu Sancto* 27, in NPNF Series 2, 8:42.

[818] Stroumsa, *Hidden Wisdom*, 31, n. 13.

[819] Clement of Alexandria, *Stromata* 4:1, in ANF 2:409; cf. Stroumsa, *Hidden Wisdom*, 42; Wagner, *After the Apostles*, 178. Daniélou asserts that the Jewish Christian "Gnosis" was the knowledge of the eschatological secrets, emphasizing the "Cosmic mysteries" written in the first chapters of Genesis, as well as their fulfillment in Christ. Daniélou, *The Theology of Jewish Christianity*, 366.

[820] Stroumsa, *Hidden Wisdom*, 43; cf. 156.

821 Daniélou, *The Theology of Jewish Christianity*, 365.

822 Davies, *The Early Christian Church*, 102.

823 Ignatius, *Trallians* 2, in ANF 1:67, brackets in original.

824 *Mathetes to Diognetus* 4, in ANF 1:26.

825 Tertullian, *Apology* 7, in ANF 3:23.

826 Athanasius, *Defense Against the Arians* 1:11, in NPNF Series 2, 4:106.

827 ECD 193.

828 See Chapter Note 3.

829 Stroumsa, *Hidden Wisdom*, 133.

830 John J. Gunther, *St. Paul's Opponents and Their Background* (Leiden: E.J. Brill, 1973), 294.

831 See Stroumsa, *Hidden Wisdom*, 69.

832 Stroumsa, *Hidden Wisdom*, 33.

833 Hippolytus, *The Apostolic* Tradition 23:14, in R.P.C. Hanson, *Tradition in the Early Church* (London: SCM Press, 1962), 32.

834 Hanson, *Tradition in the Early Church*, 32.

835 Johann L. Mosheim, *Historical Commentaries on the State of Christianity*, 2 vols. (New York: S. Converse, 1854), 1:375-376.

836 Clement of Alexandria, *Stromata* 1:12, in ANF 2:312.

837 Clement of Alexandria, *Stromata* 7:2, in ANF 2:524.

838 Clement of Alexandria, *Stromata* 5:4, in ANF 2:449.

839 Clement of Alexandria, *Stromata* 5:4, in ANF 2:450.

840 Clement of Alexandria, *Exhortation to the Heathen*, 12, in ANF 2:205.

841 E. Louis Backman, *Religious Dances in the Christian Church and in Popular Medicine*, (Westport, CT: Greenwood Press, 1977), 19; see also Nibley, H., "The Early Christian Prayer Circle," in *Mormonism and Early Christianity*, 45-99.

842 *Epistle of the Apostles* 13-14, in ANT, 489.

843 NTA 1:191.

[844] Backman, *Religious Dances in the Christian Church and in Popular Medicine*, 22.

[845] Clement of Alexandria, *Stromata* 7:7, in ANF 2:534.

[846] Backman, *Religious Dances in the Christian Church and in Popular Medicine*, 22.

[847] Backman, *Religious Dances in the Christian Church and in Popular Medicine*, 24-25.

[848] Davies, *The Early Christian Church*, 64

[849] *Odes of Solomon* 27, in Platt, ed., *The Forgotten Books of Eden*, 133, brackets in original; cf. Justin Martyr, *Dialogue With Trypho* 90, in ANF 1:244.

[850] *First Book of Adam and Eve* 58, in Platt, ed., *The Forgotten Books of Eden*, 39.

[851] *The Secret Gospel of Mark*, in Smith, *The Secret Gospel*, 15, third set of brackets in original.

[852] *The Secret Gospel of Mark*, in Smith, *The Secret Gospel*, 17, brackets in original.

[853] For a review of the use of sacred vestments in antiquity, see Nibley, H., "Sacred Vestments," in *Temple and Cosmos,* 91-138.

[854] Backman, *Religious Dances in the Christian Church and in Popular Medicine*, 18. See also *The Pastor of Hermas*, Simile 9.

[855] Origen, *Homilies on Leviticus* 9:1:3, FC 83:177.

[856] Origen, *Homilies on Leviticus* 6:2:7, FC 83:120.

[857] Wagner, *After the Apostles*, 265, n. 19.

[858] Anointing rites were certainly part of the secret tradition. Clement gives us this clue in his *Stromata*: "It was not possible to send you by letter, openly, these instructions about charisms [anointings]." Clement of Alexandria, *Stromata* 5:26:5, quoted in Stroumsa, *Hidden Wisdom*, 113. Margaret Barker speculates that the white linen garments the High Priest wore into the Holy of Holies on the Day of Atonement also represented the heavenly garment. Barker, *The Great Angel*, 125.

[859] Ignatius may give us a clue about these "passwords." Max Pulver summarizes Ignatius of Antioch's teaching:

> For Ignatius, the believer must repeat the destiny of his God, he must become an imitator of God. . . . For this he must also have knowledge of the secret name of God and of certain formulas, such as the recurrent though much varied "Thou art I and I am thou." Pulver, M., "Jesus' Round Dance and Crucifixion According to the Acts of St. John," in Campbell, ed., *The Mysteries*, 176-177.

[860] *The Ascension of Isaiah*, in TOB, 527, 529.

[861] *Secrets of Enoch* 22:7-8, in Platt, ed., *The Forgotten Books of Eden*, 89; cf. Porter, J.R., "Oil in the Old Testament," in Dudley and Rowell, eds., *The Oil of Gladness*, 40.

[862] See Chapter Notes 2-3.

[863] *The Gospel of Nicodemus* 8-9, in ANF 8:437. Cf. Compton, T.M., "The Handclasp and Embrace as Tokens of Recognition," in Lundquist and Ricks, eds., By *Study and Also by Faith*, vol. 1, 620-621.

[864] *1 Enoch* 71:3, in James H. Charlesworth, ed., *The Old Testament Pseudepigrapha*, 2 vols. (New York: Doubleday, 1983), 1:49.

[865] Porter, J.R., "Oil in the Old Testament," in Dudley and Rowell, eds., *The Oil of Gladness*, 40. Origen claimed the Jewish festivals were shadows of their heavenly equivalents. Origen, *Commentary on John* 10:12, in ANF 10:389.

[866] For a more complete treatment of the correspondence between the Catholic Liturgy and the Endowment, see Marcus von Wellnitz, "The Catholic Liturgy and the Mormon Temple," *BYU Studies* 21-22 (Winter 1981 - Fall 1982): 3-35. For a discussion of how the ritual elements of the Endowment could have been confused with those of baptism and the eucharist, see Chapter Note 5.

[867] Mosheim, *Historical Commentaries on the State of Christianity*, vol. 1, 390-391.

[868] John H. Miller, *Fundamentals of the Liturgy* (Notre Dame, Ind.: Fides Publishers Association, 1959), 83.

[869] Joseph Rykwert, *Church Building* (New York: Hawthorn Books, 1966), 14.

[870] See Cyril of Jerusalem, *Catechetical Lecture* 19, in NPNF Series 2, 7:144-146.

[871] Cyril of Jerusalem, *Catechetical Lecture* 20, in NPNF Series 2, 7:146-148.

[872] Cyril of Jerusalem, *The Works of Saint Cyril of Jerusalem*, vol. 2 (FC 64), translated by Leo P. McCauley and Anthony A. Stephenson (Washington, D.C.: The Catholic University of America Press, 1970), 161.

[873] Cyril of Jerusalem, *The Works of Saint Cyril of Jerusalem*, vol. 2, 163.

[874] Cyril of Jerusalem, *Catechetical Lecture* 21, in NPNF Series 2, 7:148-151.

[875] "Why they who come forth from the laver of baptism are anointed on the head; why, too, after baptism, their feet are washed, and what sins are remitted in each case." Ambrose, *On the Mysteries* 7, in NPNF Series 2, 10:321. The Latter-day Saints also have an ordinance of the washing of feet (see D&C 88:139-140) which is used in a different context, but it is still interesting to note that the fourth-century church used this rite in their cult practice, as well.

[876] Cyril of Jerusalem, *Catechetical Lecture* 22:8, in NPNF Series 2, 7:153; Davies, *The Early Christian Church*, 59. The editors of the Catholic translation of Cyril confirm this fact, as well. See Cyril of Jerusalem, *The Works of Saint Cyril of Jerusalem*, vol. 2, 162, 184.

[877] Arthur McCormack, *Christian Initiation* (New York: Hawthorn Books, 1969), 65.

[878] Wharton B. Marriott, *Vestiarum Christianum, the Origin and Gradual Development of the Dress of Holy Ministry in the Church* (London: Rivingtons, 1868), xxxiii-xxxiv.

[879] Marriott, *Vestiarum Christianum*, p. 188; cf. Exodus 28:4.

[880] Jerome, *Letter to Fabiola*, quoted in Marriott, *Vestiarum Christianum*, 13-14.

[881] Wellnitz, "The Catholic Liturgy and the Mormon Temple," 20, and references therein.

[882] Cyril of Jerusalem, *Catechetical Lecture* 23:2, in NPNF Series 2, 7:153.

[883] Cyril of Jerusalem, *Catechetical Lecture* 23:3, in NPNF Series 2, 7:153.

[884] Cyril of Jerusalem, *Catechetical Lecture* 23:4-8, in NPNF Series 2, 7:153-154.

[885] Cyril of Jerusalem, *Catechetical Lecture* 23:9-10, in NPNF Series 2, 7:154-155.

[886] Charles Walker, *The Ritual "Reason Why"* (Oxford: A.R. Mowbray & Co., 1901), 127.

[887] Cyril of Jerusalem, *The Works of Saint Cyril of Jerusalem*, vol. 2, 194. John Chrysostom may also have given reference to this practice in his discussion of Paul's mention of baptism for the dead:

> But first I wish to remind you who are initiated of the response, which on that evening they who introduce you to the mysteries bid you make; and then I will also explain the saying of Paul: so this likewise will be clearer to you; we after all the other things adding this which Paul now saith. And I desire indeed expressly to utter it, but I dare not on account of the uninitiated; for these add a difficulty to our exposition, compelling us either not to speak clearly or to declare unto them the ineffable mysteries. Nevertheless, as I may be able, I will speak as through a veil. John Chrysostom, *Homilies on 1 Corinthians* 40:2, in NPNF Series 1, 12:244.

[888] Cyril of Jerusalem, *Catechetical Lecture* 23:11-20, in NPNF Series 2, 7:155-156.

[889] Hatch, *The Influence of Greek Ideas and Usages Upon the Christian Church*, 298.

[890] Cyril of Jerusalem, *Catechetical Lecture* 23:21, in NPNF Series 2, 7:156.

[891] Cyril of Jerusalem, *Catechetical Lecture* 23:22, in NPNF Series 2, 7:156.

[892] Charles W. Heckethorn, *The Secret Societies of all Ages and Countries*, 2 vols. (New Hyde Park, New York: University Books, 1965), 1:107.

[893] ECD 27.

[894] Smith, *The Secret Gospel*, 137

[895] Mosheim, *Historical Commentaries on the State of Christianity*, vol. 1, 376.

[896] NTA 1:190.

[897] Rose, *Ancient Greek Religion*, 9.

[898] For a more complete review of much of this evidence, see Nibley, H., "Evangelium Quadraginta Dierum: The Forty-day Mission of Christ -- The Forgotten Heritage," in *Mormonism and Early Christianity*, 100-167.

[899] Hamblin, W.J., "Aspects of an Early Christian Initiation Ritual," in Lundquist and Ricks, eds., *By Study and Also by Faith*, vol. 1, 211-212.

[900] J.J. Buckley, "A Cult Mystery in the Gospel of Philip," *Journal of Biblical Literature* 99 (1980,): 569-581. Cf. Hamblin, W.J., "Aspects of an Early Christian Initiation Ritual," in Lundquist and Ricks, eds., *By Study and Also by Faith*, vol. 1, 212.

[901] *The Gospel of Philip*, in Robinson, ed., *The Nag Hammadi Library in English*, 140, brackets in original.

[902] *The Gospel of Philip*, in Robinson, ed., *The Nag Hammadi Library in English*, 142.

[903] NTA 1:273.

[904] Irenaeus, *Against Heresies* 1:21:3, in ANF 1:346.

[905] Irenaeus, *Against Heresies* 1:21:3, in ANF 1:346.

[906] Widengren, *Mani and Manichaeism*, 52. Cf. Compton, T.M., "The Handclasp and Embrace as Tokens of Recognition," in Lundquist and Ricks, eds., *By Study and Also by Faith,* vol. 1, 621-622.

[907] NTA 1:258-259.

[908] *The Sophia Jesu Christi*, in NTA 1:246. In one other Gnostic document, the *Apocalypse of Adam*, it is related that originally such mystical instruction was given by three heavenly messengers to Adam. Jesuit scholar George MacRae summarizes: "Father Adam explains how in the Fall he and Eve lost their glory and knowledge. . . . Through the revelation imparted to Adam by three heavenly visitors, however, this knowledge is passed on to Seth and his seed." MacRae, G.W., Introduction to the *Apocalypse of Adam*, in Robinson, ed., *The Nag Hammadi Library in English*, 256.

[909] NTA 1:263.

[910] Jean Doresse, *The Secret Books of the Egyptian Gnostics* (London: Hollis and Carter, 1960), 71.

[911] Pulver, M., "Jesus' Round Dance and Crucifixion According to the Acts of St. John," in Campbell, ed., *The Mysteries*, 176-177. "Thou art I and I am though" is also to be found in a fragment of a lost Gnostic *Gospel of Eve*. Stroumsa, *Hidden Wisdom*, 48; cf. Epiphanius, *Panarion* 26:2:3.

[912] *The Two Books of Jeu*, NTA 1:263.

[913] Pulver, "Jesus' Round Dance and Crucifixion According to the Acts of St. John," in Campbell, ed., *The Mysteries*, 173.

[914] Pulver, "Jesus' Round Dance and Crucifixion According to the Acts of St. John," in Campbell, ed., *The Mysteries*, 189.

[915] *The Acts of John*, in NTA 2:227, 230.

[916] Pulver, "Jesus' Round Dance and Crucifixion According to the Acts of St. John," in Campbell, ed., *The Mysteries*, 192-193.

[917] Stroumsa, *Hidden Wisdom*, 157.

[918] Stroumsa, *Hidden Wisdom*, 85.

[919] *Clementine Homilies* 2:17, in ANF 8:232.

[920] Stroumsa, *Hidden Wisdom*, 6.

[921] Stroumsa, *Hidden Wisdom*, 39. A first step in this reaction was Irenaeus's argument that if there *were* secret doctrines, they would have been given to the bishops who succeeded the apostles:

> For if the apostles had known hidden mysteries, which they were in the habit of imparting to "the perfect" apart and privily from the rest, they would have delivered them especially to those to whom they were also committing the Churches themselves. Irenaeus, *Against Heresies* 3:3, in ANF 1:415.

However, it should be pointed out that Irenaeus *was not* denying the *existence* of esoteric traditions, but rather their identification with the ridiculous doctrines propounded by the Gnostics. Stroumsa, *Hidden Wisdom*, 35.

[922] Stroumsa, *Hidden Wisdom*, 6, 180.

[923] Stroumsa, *Hidden Wisdom*, 129.

[924] Stroumsa, *Hidden Wisdom*, 167-168.

[925] Stroumsa, *Hidden Wisdom*, 160.

[926] Stroumsa, *Hidden Wisdom*, 146.

[927] Basil of Caesarea, *Treatise De Spiritu Sancto* 27, in NPNF Series 2, 8:41-42.

[928] Stroumsa, *Hidden Wisdom*, 36.

[929] Stroumsa, *Hidden Wisdom*, 70-71.

[930] Stroumsa, *Hidden Wisdom*, 157.

[931] Stroumsa, *Hidden Wisdom*, 45.

[932] Augustine, *Homilies on the Gospel of John* 96:2, in NPNF Series 1, 7:372.

[933] Augustine, *Homilies on the Gospel of John* 96:3, in NPNF Series 1, 7:372.

[934] Augustine, *Homilies on the Gospel of John* 96:4, in NPNF Series 1, 7:373.

[935] Augustine, *Homilies on the Gospel of John* 97:2, in NPNF Series 1, 7:374.

[936] Augustine, *Homilies on the Gospel of John* 98:8, in NPNF Series 1, 7:380.

[937] LDS scholar John Tvedtnes offers a novel explanation for Jesus' statement:

> In the Apocrypha. . . we read of a young woman, Sarah, who had been married to seven husbands (all brothers), each of whom was killed on the wedding night by a demon. But in the story (*Tobit* 6:10-8:9,) Sara ultimately marries an eighth husband, Tobias, son of Tobit, who, following instructions from the archangel Raphael, manages to chase the demon away and is therefore not slain. Of special interest is the fact that the archangel (who, according to *Tobit* 3:17, had been sent to arrange the marriage) tells the young man that his wife had been appointed to him "from the beginning" (*Tobit* 6:17.) This implies that she had not been sealed to any of her earlier husbands, which would explain why none of them would claim her in the resurrection, as Jesus explained. But if she were sealed to Tobias, the situation changes. Assuming that the Sadducees (whose real issue was one of resurrection, not of eternal marriage) were alluding to this story but left off part of it, this would explain why Jesus told them, "Ye do err, *not knowing the scriptures*, nor the power of God" John Tvedtnes, "A Much-Needed Book That Needs Much," review of *One Lord, One Faith*, by Michael T. Griffith, *FARMS Review of Books* 9 (1997): 41.

[938] Robert M. Grant, *After the New Testament* (Philadelphia: Fortress Press, 1967), 184.

[939] Origen, *De Principiis* 2:11:2, in ANF 4:297.

[940] *2 Clement* 12, in ANF 7:520.

[941] Irenaeus, *Against Heresies* 1:21:3, in ANF 1:346.

[942] *The Gospel of Philip*, in Robinson, ed., *The Nag Hammadi Library in English*, 142.

[943] *The Gospel of Philip*, in Robinson, ed., *The Nag Hammadi Library in English*, 139.

[944] *The Gospel of Philip*, in Robinson, ed., *The Nag Hammadi Library in English*, 151.

[945] *The Gospel of Philip*, in Robinson, ed., *The Nag Hammadi Library in English*, 135.

[946] Clement of Rome, *1 Clement* 38, in ANF 1: 15.

[947] Ignatius, *Polycarp* 5, in ANF 1:95.

[948] Wagner, *After the Apostles*, 180.

[949] David G. Hunter, *Marriage in the Early Church* (Minneapolis: Fortress Press, 1992), 15; cf. Clement of Alexandria, *Stromata* 7:12:70; *Instructor* 2:10:83. The *Clementine Homilies* also advance marriage as the ideal, but no hint of an eternal marriage doctrine is given. See *Clementine Homilies* 3:68, in ANF 8:250.

[950] Hunter, *Marriage in the Early Church*, 16.

[951] Tertullian, *Exhortation to Chastity* 6, in ANF 6:53-54.

[952] Augustine, *Reply to Faustus* 22:47, in NPNF Series 1, 4:288.

[953] Justin Martyr, *Dialogue With Trypho* 141, in ANF 1:270.

[954] *Didache* 11, in ANF 7:380-381.

[955] Daniélou, *The Theology of Jewish Christianity*, 351.

[956] Robinson, T., "Hebrew Myths," in Samuel H. Hooke, ed., *Myth and Ritual* (Oxford: Oxford University Press, 1933), 185. Some have seen the Hebrew Goddess as a foreign importation, but Margaret Barker notes that there is not complete correspondence between the goddess of Israel and those of other nations, and concludes that she was not a foreign goddess at all. Barker, *The Great Angel*, 52, 57.

[957] Widengren, G., "Early Hebrew Myths and Their Interpretation," in Samuel H. Hooke, ed., *Myth, Ritual, and Kingship* (Oxford: Clarendon Press, 1958), 183.

[958] Gordon B. Hinckley, in R. Clayton Brough, *Teachings of the Prophets* (Bountiful, UT: Horizon Publishers, 1993), 121.

[959] Barker, *The Great Angel*, 54.

[960] Philo, *On Flight and Finding* 109, in Colson and Whitaker, tr., Philo, 5:69.

[961] Origen, *Commentary on John* 2:6, in ANF 10:329-330. For a comprehensive listing of all known fragments of the *Gospel of the Hebrews*, see TOB 333-335.

[962] *The Apocryphon of John*, in Robinson, ed., *The Nag Hammadi Library in English*, 103.

[963] Edwin M. Yamauchi, *Pre-Christian Gnosticism* (London: Tyndale Press, 1973), 95-98.

[964] *The Hymn of the Pearl*, in Jonas, *The Gnostic Religion*, 114.

[965] *The Gospel of Philip*, in Robinson, ed., *The Nag Hammadi Library in English*, 138.

[966] NTA 1:245-246.

[967] *The Gospel of Philip*, in Robinson, ed., *The Nag Hammadi Library in English*, 139, brackets in original.

[968] Barker, *The Great Angel*, 185.

[969] Wagner, *After the Apostles*, 179. See also Clement of Alexandria, *Who is the Rich Man That Shall Be Saved?* 37, in ANF 2:601, where Clement discusses his belief that the Son also had a female aspect.

[970] Gunther, *St. Paul's Opponents and Their Background*, 289-290.

[971] Gunther, *St. Paul's Opponents and Their Background*, 296-297.

[972] Hippolytus, in Gunther, *St. Paul's Opponents and Their Background*, 296, brackets in original.

[973] Widengren, G., "Early Hebrew Myths and Their Interpretation," in Hooke, ed., *Myth, Ritual, and Kingship*, 175.

[974] See Smith, S., "The Practice of Kingship in Early Semitic Kingdoms," in Hooke, ed., *Myth, Ritual, and Kingship*, 40, and Gurney, O.R., "Hittite Kingship," in Hooke, ed., *Myth, Ritual, and Kingship*, 108. Cf. Nibley, *Temple and Cosmos*, 157-162.

[975] Robinson, T., "Hebrew Myths," in Hooke, ed., *Myth and Ritual*, 183.

[976] Backman, *Religious Dances in the Christian Church and in Popular Medicine*, 10.

[977] *The Testament of Job* 46-51, in Sparks, ed., *The Apocryphal Old Testament*, 644-646.

[978] Müeller, *A History of Jewish Mysticism*, 52.

[979] Müeller, *A History of Jewish Mysticism*, 54-55.

[980] Müeller, *A History of Jewish Mysticism*, 54.

[981] Origen, *Against Celsus* 5:44, in ANF 4:563; cf. Stroumsa, *Hidden Wisdom*, 122-123.

[982] TOB, 123-124.

[983] E.S. Drower, *The Secret Adam* (London: Oxford University Press, 1960), xvi.

[984] Doresse, *The Secret Books of the Egyptian Gnostics*, 105.

[985] Drower, *The Secret Adam*, ix.

[986] Drower, *The Secret Adam*, 66.

[987] Drower, *The Secret Adam*, 24.

[988] Hatch, *The Influence of Greek Ideas and Usages upon the Christian Church*, 283-290.

[989] Angus, *The Mystery-Religions*, 95-96, 137.

[990] Angus, *The Mystery-Religions*, 106-108.

[991] Angus, *The Mystery-Religions*, 92.

[992] Angus, *The Mystery-Religions*, 59-60, 142.

[993] Backman, *Religious Dances in the Christian Church and in Popular Medicine*, 3.

[994] Angus, *The Mystery-Religions*, 127.

[995] Erwin R. Goodenough, *Jewish Symbols in the Greco-Roman Period*, 13 vols., (New York: Bollingen/Pantheon, 1953-1958), vol. 3, figs. 839, 842; 2:45-50. See also Leclerq, "Sabazios," in *Dictionaire d'archéologie chretienne et de liturgie*, 15:213, cited in Compton, T.M., "The Handclasp and Embrace as Tokens of Recognition," in Lundquist and Ricks, eds., *By Study and Also by Faith*, 1:615.

[996] See M.J. Vermaseren, *Mithras: The Secret God,* translated by T. Megaw and V. Megaw (London: Chatto and Windus, 1963), 97-98, figs. 32-33; Compton, T.M. "The Handclasp and Embrace as Tokens of Recognition," in Lundquist and Ricks, eds., *By Study and Also by Faith*, 1:619.

[997] Angus, *The Mystery-Religions*, 123.

[998] Gilbert Murray, *Five Stages of Greek Religion* (Garden City, NY: Doubleday Anchor Books, 1955), 143.

[999] Angus, *The Mystery-Religions*, 78.

[1000] Bruce M. Metzger, *Historical and Literary Studies: Pagan, Jewish, and Christian* (Grand Rapids: Wm. B. Eerdmans, 1968), 4-5, brackets in original.

[1001] Rahner, H., "The Christian Mystery and the Pagan Mysteries," in Campbell, ed., *The Mysteries*, 343, 345-346.]

[1002] Rahner, "The Christian Mystery and the Pagan Mysteries," in Campbell, ed., *The Mysteries*, 346.

[1003] Angus, *The Mystery-Religions*, 49.

[1004] "Freemasonry and the Temple," in Ludlow, ed., *Encyclopedia of Mormonism*, 2:528-529.

[1005] This was evidently true even as late as Tertullian:

> There is absolutely nothing which makes men's minds more obdurate than the simplicity of the divine works which are visible in the act, when compared with the grandeur which is promised thereto in the effect; so that

from the very fact, that with so great simplicity, without pomp, without any considerable novelty of preparation, finally, without expense, a man is dipped in water, and amid the utterance of some few words, is sprinkled, and then rises again, not much (or not at all) the cleaner, the consequent attainment of eternity s is esteemed the more incredible. Tertullian, *On Baptism* 2, in ANF 3:668.

[1006] Hippolytus, *Refutation of All Heresies* 6:41, in ANF 5:92-93.

[1007] John, J., "Anointing in the New Testament," in Dudley and Rowell, eds., *The Oil of Gladness*, 68.

[1008] John, J., "Anointing in the New Testament," in Dudley and Rowell, eds., *The Oil of Gladness*, 64; cf. ECD 195.

[1009] Irenaeus, *Against Heresies* 1:21:3, in ANF 1:346.

[1010] John, J., "Anointing in the New Testament," in Dudley and Rowell, eds., *The Oil of Gladness*, 65, second set of brackets in original.

[1011] Patrick Madrid, "In Search of 'The Great Apostasy,'" Catholic Answers tract.

[1012] "The term 'apocalyptic literature' is taken to refer to a body of revelatory writing produced in Jewish circles between 250 BCE and 200 CE and subsequently taken up and perpetuated by Christianity. It includes not only the genre 'apocalypse' but may also include other related types of literature, such as testaments, hymns, and prayers, which share some of its more important characteristics and motifs; that is, it does not have a common literary form but is diverse and even hybrid in its literary expression. The apocalypse type of writing, which forms the core of this literature, is a record of divine disclosures made known through the agency of angels, dreams, and visions. These may take different forms: an otherworldly journey in which the 'secrets' of the cosmos are made known, or a survey of history often leading to an eschatological crisis in which the cosmic powers of evil are destroyed, the cosmos is restored, and Israel (or 'the righteous') is redeemed." Bruce M. Metzger and Michael D. Coogan, eds., *The Oxford Companion to the Bible* (Oxford: Oxford University Press, 1993), 34.

[1013] For a good summary of much of the evidence, see Jean Daniélou, *The Dead Sea Scrolls and Primitive Christianity*, translated by Salvator Attanasio (Westport, CT: Greenwood Press, 1979).

[1014] Jean Daniélou, *The Theology of Jewish Christianity*, translated by John A. Baker (Philadelphia: The Westminster Press, 1973), 10, emphasis in original; cf. Adolf von Harnack, *History of Dogma*, 7 vols., translated by Neil Buchanan (New York: Dover, 1961), 1:287.

[1015] J.N.D. Kelly, *Early Christian Doctrines*, Revised ed. (San Francisco: Harper Collins, 1978), 6.

[1016] Rodney Stark, *The Rise of Christianity: A Sociologist Reconsiders History* (Princeton, NJ: Princeton University Press, 1996), 49.

[1017] Daniélou, *The Theology of Jewish Christianity*, 55-85.

[1018] Some have suggested that these anti-Pauline, Judaizing sects represented the most primitive form of Christianity. E.g. Hans-Joachim Schoeps, *Jewish Christianity: Factional Disputes in the Early Church*, translated by Douglas R.A. Hare (Philadelphia: Fortress Press, 1969). However, this interpretation is based on the assertion that there was a major rift between the Hellenizing Christians, led by Paul, and the original Church, led by Peter and James the Lord's brother. While Latter-day Saints can recognize the tensions that must have existed within the Church as it moved beyond the borders of Palestine, we see no reason to discount the portrayal of the relationship between Paul and the rest of the Apostles in the New Testament, as we have received it.

[1019] Hermas was an early Christian prophet who lived in Rome during the early second century, and was the brother of bishop Pius. Daniélou u believes that Hermas was a converted Essene. Jean Daniélou, *The Dead Sea Scrolls and Primitive Christianity*, 125-128.

[1020] Daniélou, *The Theology of Jewish Christianity*, 8.

[1021] Kelly (*Early Christian Doctrines*, 26) points out that Gnosticism was not really a movement, as such, since although there were a multitude of Gnostic teachers, there was no single Gnostic organization or church.

[1022] Hans Jonas, *The Gnostic Religion* (Boston: Beacon Press, 1963), 32, 34.

[1023] Joseph Smith, in Joseph Fielding Smith, ed., *Teachings of the Prophet Joseph Smith* (Salt Lake City: Deseret Book, 1976), 217. Hereafter cited as TPJS.

[1024] Jonas, *The Gnostic Religion*, 49-51.

[1025] Jonas, *The Gnostic Religion*, 25.

[1026] Eusebius, *Ecclesiastical History* 3:32, in Philip Schaff and Henry Wace, eds. *The Nicene and Post-Nicene Fathers*, Series 2, 14 vols. (New York: The Christian Literature Publishing Company, 1890-1900), 1:164. Hereafter cited as NPNF Series 2.

[1027] Adolf von Harnack, *What is Christianity?*, tr. Thomas B. Saunders (Philadelphia: Fortress Press, 1957), 191-192.

[1028] In reality the interaction between Judaism and Hellenism was quite complex. Martin Hengel, *Judaism and Hellenism: Studies in their Encounter in Palestine during the Early Hellenistic Period*, 2 vols. (Philadelphia: Fortress Press, 1974). On the other hand, consider how classicist James Shiel describes the reaction of the student of Greek thought to the Greek New Testament. "Yet when he attempts to read this document of the ancient mind he is surprised. Its style of expression is not that of the Greek he knows. It feels rather like a veneer of Greek over a Semitic mode of expression." James Shiel, *Greek Thought and the Rise of Christianity* (New York: Barnes and Noble, 1968), 1.

[1029] Harry A. Wolfson, *The Philosophy of the Church Fathers*, vol. 1 (Cambridge, Mass.: Harvard University Press, 1964), 1:9-10.

[1030] Harnack, *What is Christianity?*, 200.

[1031] James Shiel, *Greek Thought and the Rise of Christianity*, 1.

[1032] Daniélou, J., *The Lord of History: Reflections on the Inner Meaning of History*, translated by

N. Abercrombie (Chicago: Henry Regnery, 1958), 1.

[1033] Shiel, *Greek Thought and the Rise of Christianity*, 1.

[1034] Harry Wolfson of Harvard University gives three reasons for the rise of this "philosophized Christianity."

First, it came about through the conversion to Christianity of pagans who had been trained in philosophy. Second, philosophy was used by Christians as a help in their defense against accusations brought against them [by the pagans]. Third, philosophy was found to be of still greater usefulness as an immunization or an antidote against the heresy of Gnosticism. The Gnostics happened to have done what Paul said he was not going to do: they adorned the faith of the New Testament with 'persuasive words of wisdom'. [Therefore, some of the Fathers] undertook to set up a new Christian philosophy in opposition to that of the Gnostics Wolfson, *The Philosophy of the Church Fathers*, 1:11-14.

[1035] J. Rebecca Lyman, *Christology and Cosmology: Models of Divine Activity in Origen, Eusebius, and Athanasius* (Oxford: Clarendon Press, 1993), 10.

[1036] Edwin Hatch, *The Influence of Greek Ideas and Usages upon the Christian Church* (London: Williams and Norgate, 1914), 350.

[1037] W.D. Davies, "Israel, the Mormons and the Land," in Truman G. Madsen, ed., *Reflections on Mormonism: Judaeo-Christian Parallels* (Provo, UT: Religious Studies Center, Brigham Young University, 1978), 91.

[1038] Joseph Smith, in TPJS 345.

[1039] George Brantl, *Catholicism* (New York: George Braziller, 1962), 41.

[1040] Plutarch, quoted in Eusebius, *Preparation for the Gospel* 14:16, translated by E.H. Gifford (Oxford: The Clarendon Press, 1903), 812.

[1041] Tertullian, *Against Marcion* 2:27, in Alexander Roberts and James Donaldson, eds. *The Ante-Nicene Fathers*, 10 vols. (Buffalo: The Christian Literature Publishing Company, 1885-1896), 3:319. Hereafter cited as ANF.

[1042] Origen, *Homilies on Genesis* 3:1, translated by Ronald E. Heine (Washington D.C.: The Catholic University of America Press, 1982), 89.

[1043] Origen, *De Principiis* Preface 9, in ANF 4:241.

[1044] *Clementine Homilies* 16:19, in ANF 8:316. *The Clementine Recognitions* also seem to imply that God is cognizable only through the senses:

Then said Peter: "Give us then, as I have often said, as being yourself a new God, or as having yourself come down from him, some new sense, by means of which we may know that new God of whom you speak; for those five senses, which God our Creator has given us, keep faith to their own Creator, and do not perceive that there is any other God, for so their nature necessitates them." Peter, in *Clementine Recognitions* 2:60, in ANF 8:114.

The so-called "Pseudo-Clementine" literature, including the *Homilies* and *Recognitions*, were likely put into their present form during the third and fourth centuries, but trace their roots to a common second-century source. R.M. Grant calls the *Recognitions* "a favourite piece of 'Sunday afternoon literature'" of the second century. Robert M. Grant, *Second-Century Christianity* (London: Society for Promoting Christian Knowledge, 1946), 10. Many scholars consider them to be a product of a widespread branch of Jewish-Christianity of which we have no other witness. Fergusen, ed., *Encyclopedia of Early Christianity* (New York: Garland Publishing, 1990), 768-769.

[1045] Cherbonnier, E. LaB., "In Defense of Anthropomorphism," in Madsen, ed., *Reflections on Mormonism: Judaeo-Christian Parallels*, 162; cf. G.E. Wright, *God Who Acts* (London: SCM Press, 1952), 49-50.

[1046] Christopher Stead, *Philosophy in Christian Antiquity* (Cambridge: Cambridge University Press, 1994), 120.

[1047] Stead, *Philosophy in Christian Antiquity*, 98.

[1048] *Clementine Homilies* 17:16, in ANF 8:322-323.

[1049] Kelly, *Early Christian Doctrines*, 247-248.

[1050] Hansen, R., "The Achievement of Orthodoxy in the Fourth Century AD," in Rowan Williams, ed., *The Making of Orthodoxy: Essays in honour of Henry Chadwick* (New York: Cambridge University Press, 1989), 153.

[1051] Henry Bettenson, *The Early Christian Fathers* (London: Oxford University Press, 1956), 330. See also Linwood Urban, *A Short History of Christian Thought* (Oxford: Oxford University Press, 1995), 54.

[1052] Daniélou, *The Theology of Jewish Christianity*, 146.

[1053] *The Ascension of Isaiah*, in Willis Barnstone, ed., *The Other Bible* (San Francisco: Harper and Row, 1984), 528.

[1054] *The Pastor of Hermas*, Commandment 11, in ANF 2:27-28.

[1055] Specifically, Hermas seems to have identified Jesus with Michael. Daniélou, *The Theology of Jewish Christianity*, 123-124. However, this may not be particularly significant, since other Jewish Christian texts speak of Jesus appearing to mortals disguised as one of the archangels. Daniélou, *The Theology of Jewish Christianity*, 131.

[1056] Robert M. Grant, *The Early Christian Doctrine of God* (Charlottesville, Virginia: University Press of Virginia, 1966), 81.

[1057] Hatch, *The Influence of Greek Ideas and Usages upon the Christian Church*, 268.

Then I replied, "I shall attempt to persuade you, since you have understood the Scriptures,[of the truth] of what I say, that there is, and that there is said to be, another God and Lord subject to the Maker of all things; who is also called an Angel, because He announces to men whatsoever the Maker of all things–above whom there is no other God–wishes to announce to them.... I shall endeavour to persuade you, that He who is said to have appeared to Abraham, and to Jacob, and to Moses, and who is called God, is distinct from Him who made all things,–numerically, I mean, not[distinct] in will." Justin Martyr, *Dialogue with Trypho* 56, in ANF 1:223, brackets in original.

[1058] Justin Martyr, *Dialogue With Trypho* 127, in ANF 1:263.

[1059] Justin Martyr, *First Apology* 6, in William A. Jurgens, *The Faith of the Early Fathers* (Collegeville, MN: The Liturgical Press, 1970), 1:51. Father Jurgens insists that this is the correct translation of Justin 's statement, and admits that here Justin "apparently [made] insufficient distinction between Christ and the created Angels." Father Jurgens continues, "There are theological difficulties in the above passage, no doubt. But we wonder if those who make a great deal of these difficulties do not demand of Justin a theological sophistication which a man of his time and background could not rightly be expected to have." Jurgens, *The Faith of the Early Fathers*, 1:56, n. 1. "This passage presents us with considerable difficulties. The word 'other,' used in relation to the angels, suggests that Jesus himself is an angel." Grant, *The Early Christian Doctrine of God*, 81.

[1060] Justin Martyr, *First Apology* 13, ANF 1:167.

[1061] Peter, in *Clementine Recognitions* 2:42, in ANF 8:109.

[1062] Metzger and Coogan, eds., *The Oxford Companion to the Bible*, 548-549.

[1063] "Let us plead the justice of our cause; trusting in the arm of Jehovah, the Eloheim, who sits enthroned in the heavens." Joseph Smith, *History of the Church of Jesus Christ of Latter-day Saints* (Salt Lake City, Utah: Deseret Book, 1980), 5:94. Likewise, Brigham Young spoke the following with reference to the Father, "We obey the Lord, Him who is called Jehovah, the Great I Am, I am a man of war, Elohim, etc." Brigham Young, in J. Watt, ed., *Journal of Discourses*, 26 vols. (Liverpool: 1854-1886), 12:99.

[1064] See "The Father and the Son: A Doctrinal Exposition by the First Presidency and the Twelve", in James E. Talmage, *The Articles of Faith* (Salt Lake City, Utah: Deseret Book, 1984), 420-426.

[1065] Otto Eissfeldt, "El and Yahweh," *Journal of Semitic Studies* 1 (1956): 25-30; Margaret Barker, *The Great Angel: A Study of Israel's Second God* (Louisville, KY: Westminster/John Knox Press, 1992). For a good summary of the current scholarly debate, see Larry W. Hurtado, "What Do We Mean by 'First-Century Jewish Monotheism'?," in E.H. Lovering, Jr., ed. *Society of Biblical Literature 1993 Seminar Papers* (Atlanta: Scholars Press, 1993), 348-368.

[1066] Eusebius, *The Proof of the Gospel* 4:7, tr. W.J. Ferrar (New York: The Macmillan Company, 1920), 1:176.

[1067] Barker, *The Great Angel*, 81.

[1068] See *Apocalypse of Abraham* 17:11 and 13:1 (footnoted alternate reading), in H.F.D. Sparks, ed., *The Apocryphal Old Testament* (Oxford: Clarendon Press, 1984), 381, 378.

[1069] Alan F. Segal, *Two Powers in Heaven: Early Rabbinic Reports About Christianity and Gnosticism* (Leiden: E.J. Brill, 1977), 262, 149.

[1070] Daniélou, *The Theology of Jewish Christianity*, 147-163.

[1071] Peter Hayman, "Monotheism – A Misused Word in Jewish Studies?", *Journal of Jewish Studies* 42 (1991), 1-15. See also Jonathan Goldstein, "The Origins of the Doctrine of Creation Ex Nihilo", *Journal of Jewish Studies* 35 (1984), 127-135; Jonathan Goldstein, "Creation Ex Nihilo: Recantations and Restatements", *Journal of Jewish Studies* f38 (1987), 187-194; David Winston, "Creation Ex Nihilo Revisited: A Reply to Jonathan Goldstein", *Journal of Jewish Studies* 37 (1986), 88-91.

[1072] Winston, "Creation Ex Nihilo Revisited: A Reply to Jonathan Goldstein",

[1073] *Sefer Yesira* 20, quoted in Hayman, "Monotheism – A misused Word in Jewish Studies?", 2.

[1074] *Bereshit Rabba*, quoted in Hayman, "Monotheism – A misused Word in Jewish Studies?", 2, emphasis in original.

[1075] *Pastor of Hermas*, Vision 1:1, in ANF 2:9, brackets in original.

[1076] *Pastor of Hermas,* Vision 1:3, in ANF 2:10.

[1077] Gerhard May, *Creatio Ex Nihilo: The Doctrine of 'Creation out of Nothing' in Early Christian Thought*, tr. A.S. Worrall, (Edinburgh: T&T Clark, 1994), 8.

[1078] Xenophon, quoted in May, *Creatio Ex Nihilo*, 8.

[1079] May, *Creatio Ex Nihilo*, 9-22.

[1080] Young, F., "'Creatio ex Nihilo': A Context for the Emergence of the Christian Doctrine of Creation," *Scottish Journal of Theology* 44 (1991), 141. The one text that might bear negatively on this view is from Rabban Gamaliel II (ca. 90/110 A.D.) A philosopher challenged him by stating that God was indeed a great artist, but he had also found pre-existent material to help him. To this Gamaliel responds that all this primitive material is created by God. May, *Creatio Ex Nihilo*, 23. However, David Winston has pointed out that Gamaliel likely reacted negatively to the philosopher's statement because he used the verb *sy'* to imply that God was "actively assisted" in the creation. Winston also provides prima facie evidence that the Rabbis did *not* hold to any doctrine of *creatio ex nihilo*. Winston, "Creation Ex Nihilo Revisited: A Reply to Jonathan Goldstein", 91.

Recently a graduate student at Marquette University, Paul Copan, has challenged the notion that *creatio ex nihilo* is a post-Biblical invention in an Evangelical scholarly forum. Paul Copan, "Is *Creatio Ex Nihilo* a Post-Biblical Invention? An Examination of Gerhard May's Proposal", *Trinity Journal* 17NS (1996), 77-93. However, Copan does not deal with May's primary evidence – the description by ancient authors of creation as "out of nothing" where pre-existent matter is clearly presupposed. And while he cites Jonathan Goldstein's views, he nowhere mentions the fact that Goldstein has conceded the weakness of his position in debate with David Winston.

[1081] Tertullian, *Against Marcion* 2:5, in ANF 3:301.

[1082] TPJS 350-352.

[1083] Robert G. Hammerton-Kelly, *Pre-Existence, Wisdom, and the Son of Man* (Cambridge: Cambridge University Press, 1973), 15.

[1084] Hammerton-Kelly, *Pre-Existence, Wisdom, and the Son of Man*, 28.

[1085] David Winston, "The Iranian Component in the Bible, Apocrypha and Qumran," *History of Religions* 5 (1965): 212.

[1086] *Sefer Haparshiyot, Midrash Kee Tov, "Alef" Machon Lehotzaat Sefarim*, 31, quoted in Nissim Wernick, "A Critical Analysis of the Book of Abraham in the Light of Extra-Canonical Jewish Writings" (Ph.D. diss., Brigham Young University, 1968), 22.

[1087] Hammerton-Kelly, *Pre-Existence, Wisdom, and the Son of Man*, 138.

[1088] Origen, *Commentary on John* 2:25, in ANF 10:341.

[1089] *Secrets of Enoch* 23:2, in Rutherford H. Platt, Jr. , ed., *The Forgotten Books of Eden* (New York: Random House, 1980), 89.

[1090] *Secrets of Enoch* 30:12-13, in Platt, ed., *The Forgotten Books of Eden*, 92.

[1091] *1 Enoch* 39:4-7, 40:5, 61:12. Quoted in Wernick, "A Critical Analysis of the Book of Abraham in the Light of Extra-Canonical Jewish Writings," 23.

[1092] Hammerton-Kelly, *Pre-Existence, Wisdom, and the Son of Man*, 22, 134, 224, 270.

[1093] *The Pastor of Hermas*, Vis. 2:4, in ANF 2:12.

[1094] *2 Clement* 14:2, in Robert M. Grant, ed., *The Apostolic Fathers*, (New York: Thomas Nelson & Sons, 1964-1968), 2:126.

[1095] Hammerton-Kelly, *Pre-Existence, Wisdom, and the Son of Man*, , 154.

[1096] *Clementine Recognitions* 1:28, in ANF 8:85.

[1097] *The Apocalypse of Abraham* 22, in H.F.D. Sparks, ed., *The Apocryphal Old Testament*, 384.

[1098] Justin Martyr, *Dialogue With Trypho* 124, in ANF 1:262.

[1099] Jonas, *The Gnostic Religion*, 35.

[1100] *The Poimandres of Hermes Trismegistus*, quoted in Jonas, *The Gnostic Religion*, 153.

[1101] 11Q13, in Michael Wise, Martin Abegg, Jr., and Edward Cook, *The Dead Sea Scrolls: A New Translation* (San Francisco: Harper San Francisco, 1996), 456.

[1102] *War Scroll* 17, in Wise, Abegg, and Cook, *The Dead Sea Scrolls: A New Translation*, 165.

[1103] Gregory of Nazianzus, *Oration* 29:19, in NPNF Series 2, 7:308.

[1104] Stead, *Philosophy in Christian Antiquity*, 188.

[1105] Peter , in *Clementine Homilies* 16:16, in ANF 8:316.

[1106] Kelly, *Early Christian Doctrines*, 234-235; Christopher Stead, *Divine Substance* (Oxford: Clarendon Press, 1977); Stead, *Philosophy in Christian Antiquity*, 160-172.

[1107] Jean Daniélou, *Gospel Message and Hellenistic Culture*, tr. John Austin Baker, (Philadelphia: The Westminster Press, 1973), 376-378.

[1108] Kelly, *Early Christian Doctrines*, 92-93.

[1109] Joachim Jeremias, *The Eucharistic Words of Jesus* (Philadelphia: Fortress Press), 125-130; Morton Smith, *The Secret Gospel* (New York: Harper and Row, 1973), 84; Ernst M.eller, *A History of Jewish Mysticism* (New York: Barnes and Noble, 1995), 44; Stroumsa, G. G., *Hidden Wisdom: Esoteric Traditions and the Roots of Christian Mysticism*, (New York: E.J. Brill, 1996); also Cardinal Daniélou's *The Theology of Jewish Christianity*.

[1110] *Clementine Homilies* 19:20, in ANF 8:336. "For the most sublime truths are best honoured by means of silence." Peter, in *Clementine Recognitions* 1:23, in ANF 8:83.

But if he remains wrapped up and polluted in those sins which are manifestly such, it does not become me to speak to him at all of the more secret and sacred things of divine knowledge, but rather to protest and confront him, that he cease from sin, and cleanse his actions from vice. Peter, in *Clementine Recognitions* 2:4, in ANF 8:98.

[1111] Robert M. Grant, *After the New Testament* (Philadelphia: Fortress Press, 1967), 184.

[1112] John Tvedtnes, "A Much-Needed Book That Needs Much", *FARMS Review of Books* 9 (1997): 33-42, see p. 41.

[1113] Origen, *De Principiis* 2:11:2, in ANF 4:297. Even where eternal marriage was not necessarily implied, many Jewish Christian groups regarded marriage as a requirement for those of marriageable age. A.F.J. Klijn and G.J. Reinink, *Patristic Evidence for Jewish-Christian Sects* (Leiden: Brill, 1973), 33, 79.

[1114] *Didache* 11, in ANF 7:380-381.

[1115] Daniélou, *The Theology of Jewish Christianity*, p. 351.

[1116] *The Gospel of Philip*, in James M. Robinson, ed., *The Nag Hammadi Library in English* (San Francisco: Harper and Row, 1977), 139.

[1117] *The Gospel of Philip*, in Robinson, ed., *The Nag Hammadi Library in English*, 142.

[1118] Stuart George Hall, ed., *Melito of Sardis On Pascha and Fragments* (Oxford: Clarendon Press, 1979), xxxviii.

[1119] Robinson, T., "Hebrew Myths," in Samuel H. Hooke, ed., *Myth and Ritual* (Oxford: Oxford University Press, 1933), 185. Some have seen the Hebrew Goddess as a foreign importation, but Margaret Barker notes that there is not complete correspondence between the goddess of Israel and those of other nations, and concludes that she was not a foreign goddess at all. Barker, *The Great Angel*, 52, 57.

[1120] Widengren, G., "Early Hebrew Myths and Their Interpretation," in Samuel H. Hooke, ed., *Myth, Ritual, and Kingship* (Oxford: Clarendon Press, 1958), 183.

[1121] Gordon B. Hinckley, in R. Clayton Brough, *Teachings of the Prophets* (Bountiful, UT: Horizon Publishers, 1993), 121.

[1122] Origen, *Commentary on John* 2:6, in ANF 10:329-330.

[1123] Melito, Fragment 17, in Hall, ed., *Melito of Sardis On Pascha and Fragments*, 85.

[1124] *The Apocryphon of John*, in Robinson, ed., *The Nag Hammadi Library in English*, 103.

[1125] Joseph Smith, in TPJS 345.

[1126] Stead, *Philosophy in Christian Antiquity*, 102. Stead uses the example of Revelation 1:4: "'From Him who Is and who Was and who Is to Come' expresses God's perpetuity within and throughout all ages." However, he points out that when Christianity became Hellenized, "This doctrine came to be developed in an absolute sense which goes well beyond anything that we find in the Bible." Stead, *Philosophy in Christian Antiquity*, 128, emphasis in original. For an excellent discussion of the scriptural evidence for this point, see Richard R. Hopkins, *How Greek Philosophy Corrupted the Christian Concept of God* (Bountiful, UT: Horizon Publishers & Distributors, Inc., 1998), 345-370.

[1127] James Strong, *The New Strong's Complete Dictionary of Bible Words* (Nashville: Thomas Nelson Publishers, 1996), 470.

[1128] Irenaeus, *Against Heresies* 2:27:1-9, in ANF 1:399-402.

[1129] Grant, *The Early Christian Doctrine of God*, 124.

[1130] Harnack, A., *What is Christianity?*, 13-14.

[1131] TOB, 445-447.

[1132] Sparks, ed., *The Apocryphal Old Testament*, 363-367.

[1133] Fergusen, ed., *Encyclopedia of Early Christianity*, 63.

[1134] ANF 7:387-388.

[1135] Fergusen, ed., *Encyclopedia of Early Christianity*, 90.

[1136] Fergusen, ed., *Encyclopedia of Early Christianity*, 92-93.

[1137] TOB, 517-519.

[1138] Fergusen, ed., *Encyclopedia of Early Christianity*, 110-111.

[1139] ANF 2:125-127.

[1140] Fergusen, ed., *Encyclopedia of Early Christianity*, 121-126.

[1141] Davies, *The Early Christian Church*, 80; Wand, *A History of the Early Church to A.D. 500*, 40.

[1142] Fergusen, ed., *Encyclopedia of Early Christianity*, 139-140.

[1143] Fergusen, ed., *Encyclopedia of Early Christianity*, 190.

[1144] TOB, 554.

[1145] Fergusen, ed., *Encyclopedia of Early Christianity*, 217.

[1146] Fergusen, ed., *Encyclopedia of Early Christianity*, 214-216.

[1147] Fergusen, ed., *Encyclopedia of Early Christianity*, 216-217.

[1148] Fergusen, ed., *Encyclopedia of Early Christianity*, 246-248.

[1149] Fergusen, ed., *Encyclopedia of Early Christianity*, 250-251.

[1150] Wand, *A History of the Early Church to A.D. 500*, 24-25; Fergusen, ed., *Encyclopedia of Early Christianity*, 262; Noll, *Christian Ministerial Priesthood*, 34.

[1151] Fergusen, ed., *Encyclopedia of Early Christianity*, 267.

[1152] Cohn, *Cosmos, Chaos, and the World to Come*, 176; TOB, 485, 495; Platt, ed., *The Forgotten Books of Eden*, 81.

[1153] Fergusen, ed., *Encyclopedia of Early Christianity*, 307-308.

[1154] Fergusen, ed., *Encyclopedia of Early Christianity*, 309.

[1155] Fergusen, ed., *Encyclopedia of Early Christianity*, 325-327.

[1156] TOB, 350-351.

[1157] TOB, 87-88.

[1158] TOB, 299-300.

[1159] Fergusen, ed., *Encyclopedia of Early Christianity*, 397-400.

[1160] Fergusen, ed., *Encyclopedia of Early Christianity*, 400-402.

[1161] Fergusen, ed., *Encyclopedia of Early Christianity*, 403-404.

[1162] Fergusen, ed., *Encyclopedia of Early Christianity*, 417.

[1163] Davies, *The Early Christian Church*, 81; Fergusen, ed., *Encyclopedia of Early Christianity*, 421.

[1164] Fergusen, ed., *Encyclopedia of Early Christianity*, 451-452.

[1165] Fergusen, ed., *Encyclopedia of Early Christianity*, 471-473.

[1166] NTA 1:259-261.

[1167] Fergusen, ed., *Encyclopedia of Early Christianity*, 495-497.

[1168] Wand, *A History of the Early Church to A.D. 500*, 54; Fergusen, ed., *Encyclopedia of Early Christianity*, 514-516.

[1169] Fergusen, ed., *Encyclopedia of Early Christianity*, 524-525.

[1170] Fergusen, ed., *Encyclopedia of Early Christianity*, 568-569.

[1171] Grant, *Second-Century Christianity*, 69.

[1172] Fergusen, ed., *Encyclopedia of Early Christianity*, 595.

[1173] Wand, *A History of the Early Church to A.D. 500*, 56-60.

[1174] Grant, *Second-Century Christianity*, 15.

[1175] Fergusen, ed., *Encyclopedia of Early Christianity*, 654.

[1176] Platt, *The Forgotten Books of Eden*, 120; Grant, *Second-Century Christianity*, 11.

[1177] Wand, *A History of the Early Church to A.D. 500*, 72-76; Fergusen, ed., *Encyclopedia of Early Christianity*, 667-669.

[1178] Hatch, *The Influence of Greek Ideas and Usages Upon the Christian Church*, 323.

[1179] Halley, *Halley's Bible Handbook*, 763; Fergusen, ed., *Encyclopedia of Early Christianity*, 686.

[1180] Fergusen, ed., *Encyclopedia of Early Christianity*, 742.

[1181] Grant, *Second-Century Christianity*, 10.

[1182] Fergusen, ed., *Encyclopedia of Early Christianity*, 768-769; ANF 8:69-76.

[1183] Fergusen, ed., *Encyclopedia of Early Christianity*, 803-804.

[1184] Wand, *A History of the Early Church to A.D. 500*, 79.

[1185] Sparks, ed., *Old Testament Apocrypha*, 617-621.

[1186] Wand, *A History of the Early Church to A.D. 500*, 62; Fergusen, ed., *Encyclopedia of Early Christianity*, 895.